D1542036

IMPERIALISM

AND THE

ANTI-IMPERIALIST

MIND

IMPERIALISM
AND THE
ANTI-IMPERIALIST
MIND

LEWIS
FEUER

PROMETHEUS BOOKS

Buffalo, New York

To Sidney Hook

Whose wisdom, indomitable spirit, and readiness
to reason with those with whom he disagrees
have inspired three generations

91 90 89 88 87 86   5 4 3 2 1

Library of Congress Catalog Card No. 86-42575
ISBN 0-87975-339-0

CONTENTS

PREFACE

Whether Western civilization has entered upon a declining phase, whether a mood of anti-civilization is spreading, such as that which marked the decay of the Roman Empire, is the question that most haunts political philosophers today. If the American ethic and its power fail to direct the world's social evolution during the coming years, that controlling role will in all likelihood fall into the hands of the Soviet Union. It is now generally recognized that Soviet Marxism has evolved into the ideology of an expanding Soviet imperialism. Although a new Age of Imperialism thus seems a foreseeable alternative, most Western intellectuals and peoples would repudiate the idea that only an American imperialism can halt and reverse the Soviet expansion; they would deny that any "logic of events," insofar as such logic is discernible, suggests that the only practicable alternative might be the rise of an American imperialism. Indeed, several generations of idealistic and sincere anti-imperialist literatures, pamphlets, exposés, and propaganda have transformed the adjective "imperialist" into a word that virtually ignites an impulse to self-denunciaton.

This essay therefore tries to reopen the question of the basic character of imperialism. Is imperialism indeed a universal theme of history? Were Lenin and Hobson mistaken in thinking it probably the last stage of a predatory order? If so, does the distinction between the modes of imperialism—the progressive mode as opposed to the regressive—become more central in our judgment of American policy? Anti-imperialist literature has perhaps beclouded the great fact that the world's advances have been associated with the eras of progressive imperialism. The experience of the Nazi species of imperialism, with its intellectual and emotional trauma, has perhaps misdirected many thinkers into supposing that anti-Semitism and racism arise from an inherent dynamic of imperialism. Therefore, it becomes important to inquire how the Jews, as a persecutable minority, have fared in the setting of a progressive imperialism from the time of Alexander the Great to the British in the nineteenth century.

A progressive imperialism is one in which energies are liberated for the advancement of civilization and creative activity. The psychological portrait of the imperialist character by anti-imperialist writers has perhaps been largely a projection of the underlying psychology of the anti-imperialists themselves. To what extent, therefore, can the political confusion, mood of defeat, and retreat of Western society after World War II be attributed to the reluctance of the United States to take up the world's leadership in a straightforwardly progressive imperialist spirit?

1

Has its own self-doubt at critical periods allowed the Soviet Union to strengthen itself as the agency of an irreversible, regressive imperialism? To help fashion an American political philosophy that may define the American role without obeisance to self-lacerative ideology is the ultimate aim of this book.

I

IMPERIALISM

A. Introduction: Progressive Imperialism and Regressive Imperialism

Our age is said to be one in which imperialism is finally ending and in which, consequently, new vistas for humanity are opening. Certain simple facts, however, contravene this verdict of the end of imperialism. When civilization has moved forward in the past, it has invariably been propelled by a strong imperialist movement on the part of the most advancing society. Athenian civilization was at its height when Athenian imperialism flourished most; Roman civilization was most developing and highest when it felt an imperialist mission; French civilization and science were the highest in Europe when Napoleonic imperialism sought to extend their hegemony. British civilization was at its highest in the Victorian age when it took pride in its imperialist vocation to organize and guide large portions of the world. Such an imperialist role was latent in the events at the end of World War II for the United States. Yet America—the most altruistic society the world has ever seen, holding steadfast to its eighteenth-century vision of a world in which all peoples would establish their counterparts of the American republic, prizing liberty, safeguarding rights, and devoting themselves to the arts and sciences—rejected that role, for the word "imperialist" grated harshly on the American conscience.

If we examine the various theories of imperialism that have been propounded we find that a sociological invariant is exhibited by all those theories most favored by the intellectual class. They all affirm a condemnatory axiom—their "axiom of indictment," we might call it—that imperialism is evil, that it is the evil behavior of rapacious capitalists or atavistic warriors, or perhaps more generically, an evil that lurks in all human beings; presumably too, as historic evil, it carries ineluctably the fatality of its own self-punishment. The doctrines of the Marxists—Kautsky, Lenin, and Rosa Luxemburg—the theories of Schumpeter and Veblen, and the writings on dependency in underdevelopment have been variants on this theme, part of that scroll of self-inculpation with which intellectuals have enveloped the documents of our civilization. Have basic truths of the constructive character of imperialism been obscured?

At the outset, we must clearly distinguish between the two varieties of imperialism that have alternated and competed in the world's history—the progressive and the regressive. Like all social classifications, they are not absolute and sharply demarcated; rather, they define the poles for a continuum in which the various imperialist societies take their place, some more progressive in most respects, others more regressive. Nonetheless, in our own time the Nazi imperialism has approximated in people's experience an absolute regression, an approach to the absolute zero in the scale of human regression. The awesome experience of the Jews with the Nazi destruction has completed a repugnance toward the word "imperialism." The expression "Nazi Imperialism" is a by-word for human cruelty and degradation. Curiously, Marxists have most frequently used the expression. Nevertheless, from the Marxist standpoint it would be difficult to call the Nazis "imperialist", for in the Marxist sense the essence of imperialism is its extraction of a higher rate of surplus value from a more backward population; and if a population were exterminated, it would cease to be a source of surplus value. The Nazis did have plans for further exterminations or reductions of populations, apart from the Jews; they expected to depopulate the Slavic areas, resettling them with Germans. Such a conquest-state, aiming at depopulation, extermination, destruction, or retardation, shall, however, in our extended usage, obviating linguistic quibbles, be called a "regressive imperialism."[1]

Counterposed thus to the great cases of "progressive imperialism"— the Alexandrian, Roman, British, French, and Dutch—have been those of "regressive imperialism," such as the Nazi variety and, in several respects, the Mongolian and Spanish. A progressive imperialism like the Alexandrian or Roman was founded on a cosmopolitan view of man, a conception of human worth to be found among all men; it led to what we might characterize as a "participatory imperialism." A Spaniard, a Gaul, or a Greek might, under the Roman Empire, if he possessed the necessary talent, rise to the highest grades of the military or civil service, or even become Emperor. A progressive imperialism elevates living standards and cultural life; it brings education and the arts to its more backward areas. It establishes a universal rule of law and security of person. A regressive imperialism, on the other hand, aims at a perpetual exploitation or extermination of peoples whether less or more advanced; the echelons of its military and civil services and government are permanently closed to the conquered peoples; restraints are enforced against their cultural and technical development, and their social and even physical existence may be terminated by the imperialist force.

1. Regressive Imperialism: The Mongol Case

Naturally, in the continuum of imperialisms, even a regressive one may have some progressive features. The genocidal Mongol imperialists have been credited by some scholars with having contributed in some way to the advancement of civilization. The practice of genocide, however, is the most regressive activity in which an imperialist power can engage; not even a Nietzschean evolutionist would have approved the kind of selection that took place when the Mongol barbarians destroyed central Asian and Middle Eastern peoples far more advanced than themselves. Their "cold and deliberate genocide," writes J. J. Saunders, "has no parallel save that of the ancient Assyrians and the modern Nazis."[2] The populations of the cities and towns of eastern Iran were literally annihilated and the buildings reduced to rubble; the Mongols, as nomads, hated walled cities "with a kind of frenzy of destruction."[3] The townsfolk would be assembled outside the walls and divided into batches for massacre according to the quotas set by commanders for the individual soldiers, who then wielded their battle-axes; corpses were disemboweled to remove swallowed jewels. Regressive, blood-soaked cruelty reached an animal level. Withal, Genghis Khan never lost sight altogether of the material interest, that reason-rescuing motive in human history. Though they slew hundreds of thousands of unarmed civilians, the Mongols "always selected a number of useful craftsmen, artisans and engineers who were deported into the heart of the empire to work for their masters." Also, "they commonly permitted, after a decent interval, the rebuilding of the cities they had burnt and ruined, since they were satisfied that ruins produced no revenue and that a flourishing trade and manufacture was a source of wealth and prosperity to them."[4]

But Mongol imperialism itself brought no higher culture and technology to the conquered areas. As a "tributary imperialism," unlike the British and French varieties, it developed no new industries, exported no capital, and engaged in little trade: its practice was like that of gangsters, demanding payments for "protection," but on an intercontinental scale. Local gangsters, primarily parasites on the mercantile community, have indeed much in common spiritually with the legendary Genghis Khan. Even gangster imperialists, however, may recognize that genocides are no way to maintain a high rate of spoliation. When, after the Mongols had subjugated a Chinese province, one general proposed to exterminate the Chinese peasants and turn their farmlands into pastures for the Mongol horses, Genghis allowed himself to be persuaded otherwise by a Chinese scholar, Yeh-lii Ch'u-ts'ai; the latter eloquently emphasized that if the province were well-organized it would yield the Mongols every year in revenues 500,000 ounces of silver, 80,000 pieces of silk, and 400,000 sacks of grain. Sadism allowed itself to be delimited by economic calculation.[5]

Nonetheless, the impact of the Mongol imperialism was predominantly regressive. The civilizations of eastern Iran and central Asia never really regained their previous splendor. True, a *Pax Mongolica* guaranteed the security of the overland trade routes from Europe to China.[6] Costly, however, and time-consuming as modes of transport, they lacked the symbiotic presence of large, prosperous towns along the roads that might have made for interstitial economic connections. A fourteenth century

Italian merchant reported of the great caravan roads: "The road you travel from from Tana to Cathay is perfectly safe, whether by day or night, according to what the merchants say who have used it."[7] Genghis Khan, however, had exacted a disproportionate price from civilization for guaranteeing it protection against robber bands. He described his own resolute primitivism in 1219 in a letter to Ch'ang Ch'un, a Taoist philosopher. Much like the barbarians who gloated over the sacking of Rome, he took pride in the fallen Peking:

> Heaven has abandoned China, owing to its haughtiness and extravagant luxury. But I, living in the northern wilderness, have no inordinate passions. I hate luxury and exercise moderation. I have only one coat and one food. I eat the same food and am dressed in the same tatters as my humble herdsmen.[8]

The noted English historian, Eileen Power, cautioned that it would be unfair to remember only "the early onslaughts of the Tartars, the first period of destruction under the four great Khans (1206-57)." Granted that "the early invasions were orgies of the most barbarous slaughter," she pleaded that "the subsequent period of settled government" proved their true greatness.[9] The "Tartar Engine," she argues, "wrought one of the most startling revolutions in the history of the world up to that date by bringing into contact for the first time the two ends of the earth, Europe and the Far East."[10] Too easily does one forget, however, how sparse were the caravans of merchants and missionaries that traveled the overland route to China and that, in any case, the sea route to the Far East has been the favored one since Roman times. The extinction of cities is not easily undone, and the trade in slaves, furs, and silk that persisted remained peripheral to Western European societies and scarcely fostered the kind of commercial capitalism that would lead toward an industrial revolution.

2. The Spanish Case

Historical romance surrounds the coming of the Spanish *conquistadores* to the New World. Undoubtedly too, for all their cruelties, such a commander as Hernan Cortés brought an end to the human sacrifice that was practiced by the Indians of Mexico and an end to the powers of their sorcerers.[11] Nevertheless, the regressive component in Spanish imperialism manifested itself during several centuries.

The mark of regressive imperialism when it attempts to organize the economic life of a subjugated people is that the political relations of forcible domination are extended into the economic controls. What ensues is best called "an economy of spoliation." A spoliative regime is concerned with short-run profits and is indifferent to the reinvestment that might not only guarantee its own long-term gains but advance the welfare of the native laborers and their families. An economy of spoliation is invariably accompanied by a steady decline in the population of the native laborers, for by means of weaponry, torture, and threats of punishment and death, the wages of the laborers are forced arbitrarily below what they would have been in a competitive market. An economy of spoliation is thus not to be associated with or explained analytically by Marx's concept of surplus value, for according to Marx's scheme the capitalist rate of profit is determined through the processes of capitalist competition, as the workers themselves sell their labor-power for the maximum wages that their bargaining on the market can command. In an economy of spoliation, however, the labor assignments are controlled, for instance, by empowered magnates in mines or plantations. In New Spain and Mexico, for example, these *encomenderos,* as they were called, had the power of exacting labor from the Indians on their *encomiendas.* (An *encomienda* was a native village, part, or group "commended" to a Spanish soldier who managed it: though not a feudal lord, he could levy tribute and unpaid labor.)[12] What followed was a rapid decline of the Indian population through overwork, malnutrition, and disease. The measure of spoliation, the amount of exacted labor, increased as the number of laborers available diminished; more force was used to obviate the increased wages that would have been the consequence of a shortage of labor in the capitalist market.

As J. H. Parry writes: "This constant and strenuous endeavor to increase the revenue from the Indies ultimately depended for its success upon the labor of the native Indians. Throughout the sixteenth century, however, the Indian population declined; a slow, continuous decline, punctuated three or four times during the century by catastrophic plunges due to major epidemics which left the population permanently enfeebled and depleted. The story was much the same in all provinces where Indians were in regular contact with Europeans." In desperation, the public authorities in New Spain and Peru took the power of exacting forced labor into their own hands. But the *repartimiento* persisted; "Indian villages, half depopulated and deprived of their surviving labor supply by the *repartimiento,* could hardly feed themselves."[13] The *repartimiento* was a system according to which all Indian villages were required to provide a weekly quota of laborers for hire; when the public authority assumed this power, it signified an even more concentrated power and force than that of the many *encomenderos.*[14] The mines especially took a heavy toll of Indian lives. A kind of "crude mass production" in the "immensely productive silver veins" came into existence in New Spain and Potosi (Bolivia) beginning in the middle of the sixteenth century. A large body of officials supervised the industry as the Crown claimed a fifth of the metal produced. The work was done mainly by Indians recruited chiefly by coercion under the *repartimiento* system. "Over-work and under-feeding, but even more the epidemics which spread in crowded conditions" took their added tax in Indian lives. In New Spain, the steady drop in the Indian population, sometimes sharply so, continued until the middle of the next century.[15] The population of central Mexico, estimated at having been approximately eleven million in 1519, declined by 1597 to less than a fourth of that number—2.5 million.[16] The friars of the missionary orders, sometimes Erasmian in their sympathies, condemned the heartlessness of the *encomenderos* and the mining directors, though availing themselves of Indian labor to build the plentiful and large churches of Mexico. They also wrote treatises on the inhumanity of the "whole enterprise of the Indies," and in time, especially as the returns from the mines diminished, the Spanish imperialist system became more passively feudal.

Meanwhile, the continuous drainage of silver to Spain engendered problems that the rigid Spanish economy could not adequately resolve. A great increase in prices throughout Europe posed an opportunity that was met by English, French, and Dutch merchants. But Spanish towns and industries languished; the population declined drastically as enterprising young men sought their easy fortunes in such places as New Spain and Peru, while the more spiritual and sometimes intelligent congregated in monasteries. If many Spaniards prospered in the Indies, "the steady drift overseas of courage and ability was a serious loss to Spain."[17] Spain and even New Spain had their universities, but the fresh spirit of the new science found no welcome where the society itself rested on an enforced system of spoliation. Spanish regressive imperialism squandered human beings and their intellectual potentialities. By the middle of the seventeenth century the majority of *encomiendas* in Venezuela and northwest Argentina had fewer than twenty adult Indian males, and "many had shrunk to five or six—far too few to support a Spanish family."[18] The Caribbean Indians were mostly gone, and in Chile Negroes replaced the vanishing aborigines. In Mexico and Central America, in the middle of the seventeenth century, the "docilized" population finally stabilized and may even have begun to increase slightly. But they were isolated from the growing liberation taking place in Western bourgeois civilization.

The country that directs regressive colonial regimes is invariably itself affected by its own psychological penalties and regressive symptoms. By the end of the seventeenth century, Spanish life felt the anxieties of "decadence," "a great deterioration in conditions of private life and national strength" that were understood as chiefly "an outgrowth of policies followed in the sixteenth century." Throughout the seventeenth century, economic and social analysts (*los arbitristas*) "anatomized their country's malaise," but the energies of the nation seemed exhausted. Able men seemed scarce. The experienced French ambassador noted in 1671-

1673: "Fifteen years ago one still found Ministers of reputation in the Councils . . . But [in 1671-73] . . . I found few remains of the old Spain, either public or private";[19] the riches of the Indies had ceased to infuse their deceptive prosperity. "Poverty and degradation were widespread," write R. D. Hussey and J. S. Bromley, and skilled workingmen were so lacking that "many workers, like many of the controlling figures in trade, finance and the scanty luxury industries, were foreign: French, Genoese, and Flemings in large numbers," as well as some English and Dutch.[20] Spain's own trade with its American colonies had so much diminished that its ships to Vera Cruz, which had once borne eight thousand or more tons a year, now averaged about fifteen hundred tons.[21] And Spain's numbers had fallen by 1688 to between six and seven million persons, about two million less than in 1600.[22]

In the famed address of *Ruy Blas,* Victor Hugo defined the outcome of regressive imperialism—the inevitable material and spiritual impoverishment:

Spain, its virtue and greatness gone; the state impoverished; its troops and riches no more; its three hundred ships lost to God's anger; Spain become a sewer emanating impurity, and its great Spanish people, miserable and tired in every member, seeking sleep in the shadow.[23]

By contrast, the character of progressive imperialism was most clearly set forth by Britain's political philosopher, John Stuart Mill. The occasion for Mill's analysis came during the debate over British imperialism in India that followed the Sepoy Rebellion in 1857. The intellectual critics of imperialism were making their first major appearance. Karl Marx wavered uncertainly between affirming Britain's "civilizing mission" and adopting the congenial idiom of a protesting Jeremiah.[24] But John Stuart Mill went before the Parliamentary Commission to defend the work of the East India Company. Having spent most of his mature life in its service, he knew the workings of imperialism better than any intellectual of his time.[25] He did not blink at the cultural and political backwardness of the Indian people and felt that the British administration could be trusted to improve their cultural level far more than any native despot. And even despotism, if it affected British rule, would still, he felt, be moved by a more genuine spirit of service and justice that might lay the groundwork for the obsolescence of its own rule. As the East India Company's chief defender, Mill wrote four pamphlets to try to save its existence and to obviate a direct governmental rule through a secretary of state. Throughout he was the noble utilitarian, moved, as Abram L. Harris once wrote, by an "unflagging devotion to the welfare of the Indian ryot" that was part of his "liberal humanitarianism." Mill, the only modern philosopher who devotedly pursued the career of imperialist administrator, had entered the office of the East India Company in 1822, as a fledgling of seventeen years. Almost from the outset he became the "chief conductor of correspondence in its Political Department." He drafted more than seventeen hundred dispatches during thirty-five years, becoming in 1856 the company's chief examiner. His defense of the company has been called by its proponents "a magnificent and moving document."[26] A defender of capitalist imperialism, Mill feared the far greater evils of a state socialist, regressive imperialism.

B. The Latent Structure of Anti-Imperialist Theories

An ecological metaphor runs through the literature indicting imperialism: the imperialist country is depicted as a predator feeding upon its prey, or a parasite exploiting a subjugated, unwilling host. J. A. Hobson, whose book *Imperialism* had such a lasting impact on public opinion and largely formed Lenin's conception, envisaged a final stage in which imperialist countries finally had degenerated into parasitic, functionless aggregates. For Hobson the decline of every imperialist civilization was a theorem in the sociobiology of parasitism. "The stamp of 'parasitism' is upon every white settlement among these lower races . . . an alien body of sojourners, a 'parasite' upon the carcass of its host, destined to extract wealth from the country and retiring to consume it at home." "The direct cause of Rome's decay" was, in Hobson's view, the imperialist parasitism that corrupted its population. "The new Imperialism differs in no vital point from this old example . . . [N]ature is not mocked: the laws which, operative throughout nature, doom the parasite to atrophy, decay, and final extinction, are not evaded by nations any more than by individual organisms."[27]

To Rosa Luxemburg, the imperialist countries were like predators who finally destroy their prey so utterly that, no further fresh supply of prey being available, the predators themselves must perish. As she wrote: "Historically, the accumulation of capital is a kind of metabolism between capitalist economy and those pre-capitalist methods of production without which it cannot go on and which, in this light, it corrodes and assimilates. Only the continuous and progressive disintegration of non-capitalist organizations makes accumulation of capital possible."[28] But in so doing, imperialism "cuts the very ground from under the feet of capitalist accumulation."[29] Imperialism thus "takes forms which make the final phase of capitalism a period of catastrophe," a time of violence and aggression.[30] The accumulation of capital creates the "conditions for the decline of capitalism." Its militarism is a weapon for forcing natives to become a proletariat, to work for wages. Yet capitalism is "the first mode of economy which is unable to exist by itself, which needs other economic systems as a medium and soil." And in Kantian vocabulary, Rosa Luxemburg saw the capitalist predator mode of economy as the only one which could not universalize itself into a world social form; a world capitalism could no more exist than could a world society of robbers: "Although it strives to become universal . . . it must break down—because it is immanently incapable of becoming a universal form of production. In its living history it is a contradiction in itself."[31] Rosa Luxemburg believed that imperialism, if it persisted, would be the prelude to a decline in the world's civilization; only a socialist transformation, she declared, could prevent that decline. "The expansion of capital, which for four centuries had given the existence and civilization of all non-capitalist peoples in Asia, Africa, America, and Australia over to ceaseless convulsions and general and complete decline, is now plunging the civilized peoples of Europe itself into a series of catastrophes whose final result can only be the decline of civilization or the transition to the socialist mode of production."[32]

To Lenin, likewise, imperialism was a concluding chapter in the history of capitalism, the outcome of its desire to exploit cheap colonial labor and to export thereto its surplus capital. So bent was Lenin on casting capitalism as the arch-villain, the arch-evil of history, that he tried to brush aside the fact that imperialism has been a recurrent manifestation of every known political-economic system, especially during its growing, often progress-bearing stage: "Rome," Lenin observed in passing, "founded on slavery, pursued a colonial policy, and achieved imperialism." Nonetheless, Lenin felt it was only capitalist society that should truly be called imperialist: "General arguments about imperialism, which ignore, or put into the background the fundamental difference of social-economic systems, inevitably degenerate into absolutely empty banalities, or into grandiloquent comparisons like 'Greater Rome and Greater Britain.'"[33]

Clearly, however, the scientific standpoint is concerned with those general social and psychological laws that would help explain when, where, and why diverse societies have entered upon imperialist careers. And such laws that might enable one to comprehend the drive toward a Greater Rome or a Greater Britain would be no more "empty banalities" than are Newton's laws of motion and gravitation, or Darwin's theory of natural selection, with its universal application to all biological species. Scientific generality is "banal" only to the person who wishes to blind himself to the universals in human nature. Such general laws are neither trivial nor tautologous.

Lenin, like Rosa Luxemburg, wanted to see the end of imperialism coterminous with that of capitalism. The era of exploitation would expire, all that would be over, and socialism would follow on capitalist decline. "[T]he division of all territories of the globe among the great capitalist powers had been completed," wrote Lenin. "The dominance of monopolies and financial capital," that highest point in the internal development of capitalism, was proceeding simultaneously. Lenin coalesced the two phenomena with a kind of easy logic and wrote: "Imperialism is capitalism in that stage of development" characterized by the dominance of monopolies and finance capital. Imperialism, moreover, according to Lenin, is "parasitic or decaying capitalism," "parasitism raised to a high pitch:" "the exploitation of oppressed nations . . . transforms the 'civilized world' more and more into a parasite on the body of hundreds of millions of uncivilized nations." In the Roman Empire. Lenin observed, "the Roman proletarian lived at the expense of society. So, likewise, imperialism today corrupts an upper stratum of the Western proletariat." Such is the nature, Lenin argued, of "moribund capitalism."[34]

II
UNDERSTANDING PROGRESSIVE IMPERIALISM

A. Imperialism as a Universal Theme of History

1. Imperialism as Recurrent Among All Social Systems

The evidence of history is overwhelming that imperialism is indeed a universal theme of history and that its capitalist manifestation is not its last. A people with a sense of vigorous energies, with zest, adventure, and creativity, and endowed with a capacity for leadership, will experience an imperialist calling. There will be the merchant's pursuit of profit, the miner's quest for ores, the soldier's taste for glory, but there will also be the schoolmaster's mission to educate, the scientist's venture to find fresh wonders of fact, the doctor's desire to battle disease, the missionary's conviction that he brings a higher morality.

Such writers as Hobson maintained that imperialism abroad was necessarily incompatible with the survival of democracy at home. Yet Athenian imperialism was precisely most endorsed by the democratic party, while Alexander the Great, and the Macedonian imperialism that followed, were inspired by something like the dream that the Stoic, Zeno of Citium, later set down—to found a great republic of all the races, animated by Hellenic culture.[1] As W. W. Tarn has written: "Aristotle's State had still cared nothing for humanity outside its own borders . . . Alexander changed all that. When he declared that all men were alike sons of one Father, and when at Opes he prayed that Macedonians and Persians might be partners in the commonwealth . . . he proclaimed for the first time the unity and brotherhood of mankind. . . . [H]e was one of the supreme fertilizing forces of history," giving to "Greek science and Greek civilization a scope and an opportunity such as they had never yet possessed."[2] Of Alexander's troops, it was well said to the Persian Emperor Darius, "And do not suppose that they are led by a desire for gold and silver"; their discipline stemmed from a call to greatness.

Similarly, the great advances toward democracy in nineteenth century Britain took place precisely during the time when Britain's imperialism was rising to its height: Disraeli, who introduced into Parliament the bill that brought the franchise to the British working class, also acted a decade later to entitle his queen "Empress of India" and to secure Britain's control of the Suez Canal. Though intellectuals in the Labor Party, in subsequent years, tended to be moral critics of imperialism, the workingmen in the Trades Union Congress, on the other hand, were noticeably aloof to their indignation.[3]

More than two thousand years earlier, when the radical, socialistic brothers Gracchi were dramatically dominant in Roman politics, Gaius Gracchus "devised an extensive scheme of colonization proposing to send picked men to various locations in Italy and elsewhere, and to re-build such ruined areas as Carthage; it was the aristocratic Senate that opposed this enterprise of imperialism."[4]

The Gracchi, writes Tenney Frank, "while disclaiming a policy of aggression, desired to develop the state's possessions as far as possible and make them profitable. They desired the provincial funds with which to ameliorate domestic conditions; they wished to colonize neglected farm lands and harbors throughout the whole empire."[5] Disciples of Stoicism, they interpreted its philosophy of a "socialistic democracy" to coalesce with that of a society guided by Roman imperialism. Roman political parties usually joined together to enlarge Rome's empire; "the populace, of course, under normal conditions was always favorable to expansion if it did not cost too much."

The "socialism" of the Gracchi actually envisaged nothing more than a widespread individual ownership of land. Tiberius Gracchus defended such a reform as contributing to the triumph of Roman imperialism. The slave-worked plantations of Italy, he warned, were causing a dearth of free men that would finally weaken the army; on the other hand, "with a strong army," Romans might become the "masters of the rest of the habitable world." The appeal of "the nationalized form of imperialism stirred the Roman citizenry."[6]

Tiberius Gracchus, as Plutarch tells us, was inspired by a Stoic ideologist of the left, Blossius. More orthodox in his Stoicism than those who devised ways to accommodate their doctrine to the oligarchical Senatorial party,[7] Blossius had the consequentialism of the ideologist; interrogated by the consuls who were executing the Gracchan adherents, he declared that if Tiberius had commanded him to burn the Capitol, he would have done so, for Tiberius never would have commanded anything not for the public good.[8] With his life spared, Blossius fled to Asia to join in a rebellion that was widely supported by Asian slaves and peasants; they planned to found a "heliopolis," a "City of the Sun," in which all men would be free.[9] Such was the philosophy of Stoic imperialism.

What mode of socio-economic system indeed has not had its imperialist phase? Medieval Europe, beginning to break out of its centuries' constraints and to experience a sense of intellectual revival and adventure, embarked on the Crusades, a feudal imperialism.[10] The Arabs in their Moslem awakening had embarked on their nomadic imperialism.[11] The Tartars ranged across Asia and into Europe to found their imperial society. From the Egyptians, Babylonians, and Assyrians to the current

Soviet and Chinese Communist states, all have had their imperialist drives. Far from imperialism being the last stage of capitalism, as Lenin and Rosa Luxemburg projected in their ideological drama, it has been the third stage of communist society, that which follows on the communists' seizure of power and their subsequent consolidation.

2. Imperialism and the Language of Socialist Ideology

To Lenin and Rosa Luxemburg with their ideology that the end of imperialism signified the end of capitalism, it seemed a self-contradictory notion to conceive that an imperialist dynamic could animate the structures of socialist societies.[12] But not only does the Soviet Empire extend into central Europe with its armies garrisoned in Czechoslovakia, Poland, and Eastern Germany and into Afghanistan in South Asia, but its military advisers and Cuban auxiliaries are found in several African countries.[13] Rival Communist Empires compete for supremacy over the smaller communist satrapies. Each denounces the other as imperialist; each has been correct. In 1966 the Communist Premier of Cuba, Fidel Castro, denounced the Chinese Communists for their imperialist designs on Cuba. The Chinese Communist diplomats, he complained, were acting towards Cuba the same way that the United States representatives had. When it came to trade negotiations they took an "obvious extortionist" position, displaying moreover an "absolute contempt" toward Cuba. "It was not simply a matter of more or less tons of rice," said Castro, "but of a much more important and fundamental question for the peoples: whether in the world of tomorrow the powerful nations can assume the right to blackmail, extort, pressure, attack, and strangle small nations, whether in the world of tomorrow, which the revolutionaries are struggling to establish, there are to continue to prevail the worst methods of piracy, oppression, and filibusterism that have been established in the world since a class society . . . and, in the contemporary world, the imperialist states."[14] The cardinal proposition was thus demonstrated: communist imperialism is not only possible but it exists.

Marxist ideologists have always, of course, experienced a strong emotional resistance to the expression "communist imperialism," for it is a conjunction which seems to mock the grammar of their ideology. Leon Trotsky, toward the end of his life, finally dared ask, despite the ideological constraints: "Can the present expansion of the Kremlin be termed imperialism?" Embattled though he was with the "Moscow bureaucracy" which he excoriated as driven by "the tendency to expand its power, its prestige, its revenues," he still refused "to employ the term of 'imperialism' for the foreign policy of the Kremlin, except with qualifications," lest he be accused of identifying "the policy of the Bonapartist bureaucracy with the policy of monopolistic competition," an identification that "petty-bourgeois democrats" might make, but not Marxists.[15] Trotsky evidently did not differentiate the motives of Communist imperialism from the capitalist variety: the quest for power, prestige, and revenues was a social invariant which could take different special forms under the diverse initial conditions constituted by diverse societies. But Trotsky, in straits to preserve the Communist hope in its historic purity, tried to lay the blame for the Communist imperialist drive on a distorted, uncultured, mediocre bureaucracy. Probably, had fate brought him to power, he might well have lent to that drive all the passionate eloquence of his words.

3. Schumpeter's Theory of the Atavistic Character of Imperialism

If Lenin and Trotsky could never bring themselves to acknowledge the sociological possibility of a Communist imperialism, the economist Joseph A. Schumpeter felt that, strictly speaking, there was no society possible that was an example of a *capitalist* imperialism.

To Schumpeter, who wished to exculpate capitalism from any involvement with imperialism and to establish that any relationship between them was not an intrinsic one but extrinsic and inessential, imperialism was a phenomenon "atavistic in character." It was, he held, one of those many "surviving features from earlier ages that play such an important part in every concrete social situation. . . It is an atavism in the social structure, in individual, psychological habits of emotional reaction."[16] Like the Spencerian Victorian optimists, like Spencer himself and his socialistic disciple, Veblen, Schumpeter believed that imperialist atavism would dissolve under the impact of modern industrial life. "Since the vital needs that created it have passed away for good, it too must gradually disappear. . . . It tends to disappear as an element of habitual emotional reaction, because of the progressive rationalization of life and mind . . . in which heretofore military energies are functionally modified. If our theory is correct, cases of imperialism should decline in intensity, the later they occur in the history of a people and of a culture."[17] And what then of a possible socialist imperialism? Here Schumpeter responded categorically: "The type of industrial worker created by capitalism is always vigorously anti-imperialist," and the socialist movement, in its anti-imperialism, expresses the conscious will of the workers.[18]

Now, it does seem true that imperialism declines during a society's latter stage, not, however, because of the society's industrial and scientific advance but rather as the consequence of the general spread of a decadent spirit. British society in the nineteenth century was highly and frankly imperialist when its industry and parliamentary politics were rapidly developing. And the workingman is not rendered "anti-imperialist" by virtue of a capitalist, or industrial, "habituation." During the Vietnamese War, for instance, the American intellectual class became nearly unanimous in denouncing America's role as "imperialist." By contrast, it was the American working class, the "hard hats" as they came to be known, who both spontaneously and through their organization, the American Federation of Labor-Congress of Industrial Organizations, persisted in their overwhelming support for America's military activity. As far back as 1912, the Progressive movement, led by Theodore Roosevelt, won the support of many workers and "middle-class America" alike; the Progressives evoked "a new sense of delight in the rise of the United States as a world power." Dedicated, in Herbert Croly's words, to "the promise of *American* life," they "consequently saw nothing incongruous in supporting American investments abroad" to expand its markets, though they simultaneously condemned big business at home for exploiting labor with low wages.[19]

Was there a basic contradiction in the progressive ideology, as their critics charged, between their humanistic values and their nationalistic convictions? Not from the standpoint of a democratic imperialism, that, regarding its values and way of life as the best, believes honestly that its highest calling is to bring those values and that way of life to others.[20] Progressives generally, from Oscar Straus to Senator George W. Norris, supported President Theodore Roosevelt in the aggressive steps he took to create the republic of Panama and build the Panama Canal.[21] Beginning with the Spanish-American War, anti-imperialists averred that such a policy of expansion violated American political principles set forth in the Declaration of Independence. "The anti-imperialists made great efforts to attract labor support, but on the whole were unsuccessful."[22] "The people were stirred by the thought of . . . an empire second to none." When William Jennings Bryan ran for the presidency in 1900 as the anti-imperialist candidate, he was rejected by the popular vote in much the same fashion as the opponent of the Vietnam War in 1972, George McGovern. To the famed liberal editor Herbert Croly, progressivism and imperialism went hand in hand. The Spanish-American War, in his eyes, had shown that "far from hindering the process of domestic amelioration, [it] gave a tremendous impulse to the work of national reform."[23]

The first venture of the United States into an imperialist polity was noteworthy for the fact that economic inducements played so small a part.[24] Rather, the appeal was to the sense of adventure, leadership, and good works. Thus, when at the close of the Spanish-American War the United States Senate debated as to whether the Philippine Islands should be annexed, anti-annexationists did not charge the imperialists with a desire for pecuniary profits; rather, they assailed the imperialist drive as compounded of a "lust for power and greed for land, veneered with the tawdriness of false humanity." To which a spokesman for imperialism from Colorado rebutted with words that for all their naiveté probably expressed the prevalent current of feeling: the imperialist drive, in his view, had its source in "our virile strength . . . that Anglo-Saxon restlessness

. . . which will not be quenched until we have finally planted our standard in that far-off archipelago which inevitable destiny has intrusted to our hands."[25]

The president of the United States, William McKinley, was a fitting spokesman for an age in which popular philosophers from Emerson to Mary Baker Eddy affirmed the primacy of the mind and which William James portrayed as an age of rich varieties of personal religious experience. President McKinley experienced the kind of direct individual contact with his God's energy that James loved to describe. Walking the floor of the White House anxiously, night after night, praying for guidance, the answer was vouchsafed to President McKinley; "there was nothing left for us to do but to take them all, and to educate the Filipinos, and uplift and civilize and Christianize them."[26] Notwithstanding irreverent professors who naturally suggest that this purported religious intuition was the stale residue of clergymen's utterances and the religious press rather than a direct message from God, the evangelical theme was the dominant one in President McKinley's mind, not the sober considerations of economic calculation that probably would have counseled otherwise.

According to the atavistic theory of imperialism, moreover, the class of professional soldiers constitute the active proponents of both militarism and imperialism: militarists, because soldiers, it is argued, always wish to militarize their societies; that is, they wish to organize its social structure with a view to maximizing the society's armed strength and psychological readiness for war; and imperialists, because soldiers, it is further argued, see their egos enhanced when their country, through its armed force, conquers, dominates or rules others. As far as the United States is concerned, however, the evidence assembled by Richard Carl Brown, in his book, *Social Attitudes of American Generals 1898-1940,* invalidates this thesis of atavism. Until at least the summer of 1940, for instance, "those military leaders who spoke or wrote upon the subject at all, thought that the sending of the expeditionary force to Europe in 1917-1918 had been a great mistake. They recommended concentration on hemispheric defense, and some advocated giving up the Philippines and drawing our Pacific line of defense back to the Hawaiian Islands." Military leaders were influenced by a non-imperialist variety of economic consideration; that is, they wanted a defense that would be "easier and cheaper." Although liberal and socialist writers during this period reveled in depicting military chieftains as instigators of expansion and imperialism and as would-be oppressors of native races, the record shows a predominant absence of such drives or intentions. "Army leaders generally were against our policy of expansion, or at least neutral in the matter. To be sure, they did their duty when acting in an official capacity in Cuba or the Philippines." All of which helps explain what is an anomaly of American history from the standpoint of either the atavistic or Marxist theory of imperialism—the fact "that the Army languished and almost died during the 1920s when the so-called 'vested interests' were in control of the government."[27] The revival of the Army began only when the Democratic New Deal administration of Franklin D. Roosevelt came into power, supported by American labor, left liberals, the stricken farmers, the bankrupt, the jobless, and the lower middle class.

Then what of Schumpeter's theory that imperialism is an atavistic phenomenon, wholly at odds with capitalist, industrial, or socialist psychology? It was natural for Schumpeter, an intellectual son of the nineteenth-century belief in progress, to regard modern imperialism as a transient atavistic episode. He recalled the wonderful discussions with fellow students in Böhm-Bawerk's seminar in Vienna, with such Marxist foemen as Otto Bauer and Karl Renner.[28] In the writings of Eduard Bernstein, the wisest of the Marxists and the inaugurator of "revisionism," Schumpeter read about the concept of atavism in socialist theory,[29] for Bernstein courageously assailed Marx's advocacy of a "dictatorship of the proletariat" as "a reversion, as political atavism," as a formulation belonging to a "lower civilization"; indeed, Bernstein considered as atavistic all the talk of "writers in the *belles lettres* style" who aimed to discredit the middle class by studying it "'naturalistically' in the café."[30] Imperialist actions, in Schumpeter's eyes an irrational political behavior, stemmed accordingly from regressions, from presumably unconscious fixations and resurgences that Schumpeter expected would be clarified by the sociological students of Freud.[31]

Do the insights into aggressive, power-seeking behavior provided by Freud, James, and Adler validate Schumpeter's belief that imperialism is a transient atavism, being rendered obsolescent by the development of modern capitalism and industry? And if imperialism can take irrational, regressive, and destructive forms, is it also true that it can channel just as well rational, liberalizing, and creative energies? An atavistic phenomenon is a regressive form of behavior that manifests itself under conditions of great strain, especially those that ensue when problems are deemed insoluble or pressures intolerable. A frustrated child regresses to an infantile pattern, weeping, turning to its mother's caress for solace; a frustrated man may flail about, acting as he once did in his childhood rebellions. As far as its intellectual manifestation is concerned, regression involves a retreat from rational processes of thought to some mode of the irrational, to myth, superstition, credulity; from science to anti-science. Regression involves a propensity, moreover, to some form of sado-masochistic behavior, for its causative frustrations generate strong aggressive impulses, while the restraints of culture, conscience, and fellow-feeling are at least partially collapsed.

The great progressive imperialist movements, on the other hand, have taken place precisely at times characterized by intellectual progress rather than regress, when something like an intellectual or scientific renaissance was taking place, when a spirit of exuberance and adventure rather than defeat and timorousness prevailed. When England under Elizabeth, for example, was entering upon an imperialist vocation, its intellectual spirit was becoming more rational; it was the age of Francis Bacon and William Gilbert, of Shakespeare and Ben Jonson.

Indeed, Francis Bacon, most eloquent and persuasive advocate of the inductive method and the supreme spokesman for the future of science at the very outset of its modern rebirth, was also the first great spokesman for the British imperialism to be. Scientific rationality and the imperialist drive went hand in hand; as a leading student of Bacon's political thought has said, "in Bacon, imperialism is also (and chiefly) the imperialism of Baconian science."[32] Bacon felt that Britain had a call to "greatness," that it must stop the expansion of Spain, a country hostile, in his view, to all the liberties and scientific progress for which he stood. Britain, rather than trying to conquer European lands, must, he noted, establish its "plantations" in unsettled, undeveloped domains across distant seas: "I like a plantation in a pure soil; that is, where people are not displanted to the end to plant in others . . . The people wherewith you plant ought to be gardeners, ploughmen, laborers, smiths, carpenters, joiners, fishermen, fowlers, with some few apothecaries, surgeons, cooks, and bakers."[33] To withstand the rival French imperialism, Bacon put his trust in "the middle people of England" who, he said, "make good soldiers, which the peasants of France do not."[34] This was to be a commercial imperialism, maintained by English naval power "because the wealth of both Indies seems in great part but an accessary to the command of the seas."[35] The "merchants," wrote Bacon, were an empire's arterial passages: "if they flourish not, a kingdom may have good limbs, but will have empty veins, and nourish little."[36] And they must be sustained by the fortitude of a "stout" people, relying not on mercenaries but its "militia of natives . . . good and valiant soldiers . . . Neither is money the sinews of war (as is trivially said), where the sinews of men's arms, in base and effeminate people, are failing."[37] A rising, progressive people will be a correspondingly commercial, scientific, and imperialist people; such imperialism is not atavistic but creative. Decay comes when those energies have become effete.

All of Bacon's successors, moreover, the philosophers of the British empiricist school—John Locke, George Berkeley, David Hume—were advocates of the rising British imperialism, and a wiser, more rational group of philosophers has never adorned the intellect of any nation. A practising imperialist, Locke, as secretary of the Lords Proprietors of Carolina, wrote advertisements to attract settlers, and drafted in 1669 *The Fundamental Constitutions for the Government of Carolina*. Almost thirty years later in 1697, as Commissioner of the Board of Trade, Locke was drawing plans to develop Virginia, the "poorest, miserablest and worst country in America." To advance the spirit of a participatory imperialism he secured the ouster of the dictatorial governor, Sir Edmund Andros. Locke was the co-worker of Britain's proponent for imperialism, Anthony Ashley Cooper, who staunchly opposed religious persecutions on the grounds that persecutors drove from a country its most industrious citizens and retarded economic development. As Maurice Cranston writes: "He [Locke] was the complete progressive capitalist in politics; he might almost have been invented by Marx."[38]

Locke's successor, George Berkeley, the gentle, noble, and idealistically spirited Irish dean, author of the first philosophic masterpiece composed on the American continent, celebrated in 1726 the future of American imperialism in a "prophecy" in verse:

> There shall be sung another golden Age
> The rise of Empire and of Arts . . .
> Not such as Europe breeds in her decay,
> Such as she bred when fresh and young . . .
> Westward the Course of Empire takes its Way,
>   The four first Acts already past,
> A fifth shall close the Drama with the Day,
>   The world's great Effort is the last.[39]

Soon afterward, in 1728, Berkeley set out for the New World to found a college in Bermuda (or possibly Rhode Island) to educate the sons both of settlers and Indians in either the arts, agriculture, or trades. His project aroused the British imagination. When the scheme miscarried, however, Berkeley gave his support instead to the plan of James Oglethorpe for colonizing Georgia with distressed debtors, furnishing them with adequate tools and provisions.[40]

Even the skeptical David Hume, despite his personal antipathy to the English, welcomed the growing British power for maintaining "her station, as guardian of the general liberties of Europe, and patron of mankind." Hume's conception of Empire also was a participatory one; the colonies, he observed a few years before 1776, were "no longer in their infancy"; he had longed to see them in revolt in 1768. Hume himself served as a military officer in an ill-fated expedition on the coast of Brittany against the French East India Company; he remained an imperialist despite the official bungling and the needless bloodshed.[41]

The spirit of scientific inquiry is the most rational pursuit of man, the most free from atavistic regression. From its beginning it has been linked to progressive imperialism. As far back as Hellenistic times, Alexander's imperialism, with no sign of atavistic regression, was in fact the occasion for his organizing perhaps the world's first scientific expeditions, aimed at providing his former teacher Aristotle with botanical and zoological specimens. More than two thousand years later, Napoleon's 1798 Egyptian expedition conveyed in its ships a company of France's most illustrious scientists: Gaspard Monge, Saint-Hilaire, Claude Louis Berthollet (whom Napoleon deeply admired), and Joseph Fourier.[42] And British imperialism in the eighteenth and nineteenth centuries created the opportunity for its young scientists to voyage to distant oceans, islands, and subcontinents to study unknown species of plants and animals—as did Darwin, Wallace, Hooker, Huxley, and Bates; or to chart the stars in the Southern skies—as did Sir John Herschel; or to measure the characteristics of Sudanese tribesmen, as did Francis Galton.[43] As the botanist Joseph Hooker wrote Darwin in 1854: "From my earliest childhood I nourished the desire to make a creditable journey in a new country, and write such a respectable account of its natural features as should give me a niche amongst the scientific explorers of the globe."[44]

Imperialism thus is not necessarily associated with an atavistic regression. To be sure, when imperialism manifests itself under communistic societies, pro-communists say it's an atavistic survival from capitalism; when it takes place under capitalist systems,[45] pro-capitalists say it's a survival from feudalism; when it took place under feudal regimes, pro-feudalists no doubt reflected that it was a survival from nomadic, barbarian bands. The recurrence, however, suggests that in imperialist movements, some universal component of human nature has sought expression. The significant political issue is whether the imperialist drive of a given country is rational or irrational, progressive or regressive.

Of all the world's imperialisms, the French was the most self-consciously bourgeois and rationalistic. Far from indulging in atavistic, irrationalist metaphysics, it rejected from its inception in a Comtist spirit all the barbarian and metaphysical relics of the feudal militarist mentality. Jules Ferry, its most important leader, was utterly bourgeois in his philosophy. A lawyer and a lawyer's son, a loyal pupil of liberal Comtist positivism, Ferry, as a collaborator on a positivist review, wholly endorsed Comte's slogan, "Order and Progress," together with its program for the leadership of the scientist and industrialist. Here was no atavistic Schumpeterian reverting to barbarian beginnings, nor even a Marxist predator. On the contrary, Jules Ferry was a positivist imperialist, a believer in bringing organization and science to the backward. When his colleagues shouted at him their metaphysical slogan, "Rights of Man! 1789!" he, as a Comtist, having transcended the metaphysical stage to ascend to the scientific, replied that higher races had a duty to civilize the lower and that to do otherwise was to take "the road toward decadence."[46] As a bourgeois positivist, he worked to expel Catholic influences from the Republic by depriving religious orders of the right to teach and by making elementary education compulsory and secular. As part of that same secular mission he subscribed to "la mission civilisatrice." He directed an imperialist campaign in Indochina that contravened all sound principles of bourgeois profit-making. Though he talked of markets and investments, in 1885 the state of Tonkin had purchased only seven million francs worth of French goods. An avowed anti-clerical, he could nevertheless invoke the well-being of French missionaries to justify an expedition to Madagascar that was also economically a loss. Right-wing parliamentary leaders repudiated this bourgeois imperialism as wasteful of resources, forgetful that the real potential enemy was the Germans.[47]

Nonetheless, the overwhelming Republican majority rejoiced in their sense of France as the civilizing master. What if the Senegal was a domain of disease, entrapping French soldiers in its jungle of heat and lurking treachery? The tricolor was incommensurable with the ledgers of economic bookkeeping. In 1874, a book by Paul Leroy-Beaulieu advocating colonization was ridiculed as an "anachronism." Eight years later, however, the citizenry of the bourgeois republic were prepared to consider that in view of the fact that half the globe was in a "barbarous" stage it behooved the "persevering action of civilized peoples" to elevate them.[48]

The imperialist emotion has involved a cluster of vector-variants for all the basic human interests: the economic imperialism of the merchant and the manufacturer was matched with the philanthropic imperialism of anti-slavery and aboriginal protection societies; the political imperialism of self-asserting, ambitious, Platonic guardians was counterweighed with self-abnegating, would-be religious ministers to the backward. Such a cluster of motivational vectors, exemplified through the whole range of character-types, bespeaks an underlying common emotional wave that carries them to work congruently. That common attribute, the liberation of creative energies and leadership on the world stage, has been the defining characteristic of progressive imperialism.

All the political creeds thus partook of the imperialist experience, whether they were capitalist or Marxist, Comtist or Catholic. If British businessmen and missionaries spoke of the "white man's burden" to civilize backward peoples, Cecil Rhodes commented mockingly that British policy was "philanthropy plus five percent;" yet one senses that even if the five percent declined to zero, it would still be sustained by philanthropy and the will to empire.[49]

Karl Marx and Frederick Engels, accepting the same burden, assigned responsibility, for it however, to the proletariat. Marx was still alive when Engels, queried by Karl Kautsky as to the proper socialist policy toward the colonies, replied that the European working class might find itself compelled to wage "defensive wars" against the "semi-civilized countries." Though hoping that the colonial peoples would follow in the wake of the European "victorious proletariat," Engels acknowledged "all sorts of destruction" might erupt in the backward areas "while the European proletariat would be unable to intervene, not out of principle, but because having its hands full" at home, it might find itself unable to "conduct any colonial wars." And when proletarian power was consolidated and it was safely able to conduct colonial wars? Would a "proletarian America" have felt freer to conduct a "defensive war" against the Arabian oil monarchs? In any case, the European working class was assigned the task of guiding the "native" peoples.[50]

The foremost leader of French socialism, Jean Jaurès, adored by all for his ethical and generous spirit, from the sceptical Anatole France to the believing poet Charles Péguy, took the imperialist phenomenon as a historical universal: "The law of expansion and conquest to which all peoples yield seems as irresistible as a natural law; and even though we denounce eloquently all the villainies, all the corruptions, all the cruelties of the colonial movement, we shall not stop it." When a revolt against French rule broke out in 1903, Jaurès defended the "moral action" of France which, he declared, was bringing "security" and "well-being" and providing "means of development infinitely superior to those of this despoiling, anarchic, violent, evil Moroccan régime which aided by the outbreaks of a morbid and bestial fanaticism, absorbs and devours all the resources of this country."[51] A socialist France would, in Jaurès's view, inherit the civilizing mission of its bourgeois predecessor. A socialist England likewise, he expected, would retain its colonial empire, which indeed had increased the well-being of both the native peoples and the English workers.

Similarly, in the great debate in the Belgian parliament when Emile Vandervelde, the head of the Socialist party, took the lead in exposing the atrocities in King Leopold's Congo Free State, Vandervelde still acknowledged the recurrent pattern of imperialism as a universal theme. He told the Chamber: "Colonization is a fact in all time, and people will continue to colonize whatever the economic system."[52]

Does it follow then that imperialism is simply the recurrent social manifestation of a universal will-to-power? To such a conclusion David Landes has been led: "it is in the nature of the human beast to push other people around." Whenever there is a disparity of power, he argues, "people and groups have been ready to take advantage of it."[53] The weaker party tries, for its part, in an Alfred Adlerian way, to undo its position of inferiority: "In the long run, the weaker party will never accept his inferiority, first because of the material disadvantage it entails, but even more because of the humiliation it imposes. In return, the stronger party must ceaselessly concern itself with the security of its position. . . . each strong point requires outposts to defend it, and each outpost calls for new ones beyond it."[54]

The notion of "power" imports perhaps several psychological misconceptions concerning imperialism. First, we might note the language: "the nature of the human beast"—the animal-like, presumably predatory, exploitative, or bullying character of imperialism. Yet as the classical scholar Gilbert Murray once noted, in the great imperial organizations, such as the Roman Empire, "far greater expenditure of time and energy is devoted to the good of its members, to such ends as education, transport, industry, agriculture, government, and the administration of justice." Such a Roman official as Pliny, writing letters to Trajan, "seems to feel that the service of Rome was for him the nearest approach possible to the service of God." For, despite all its imperfections, "when all deductions were made, the Roman Empire meant peace throughout the known world; it meant decent and fairly disinterested government; it protected honest men from thieves and robbers, it punished wrongdoers; it gave effective help to towns wrecked by blizzards or earthquakes, or to provinces where the crops had failed. It spread education and civilized habits . . . If Pliny had been asked what was the greatest calamity that could befall the human race, he would probably have answered, 'The overthrow of the Roman Empire.'" If native cultures disintegrated and vanished, it was in large part, Pliny would have said, because their peoples preferred the superior attainments of Roman culture to their own. That was why the religion of *Roma Dea* became the common civic religion.[55]

Bergson once said: "Imperialism is, as it were, inherent in the vital urge. It is at the bottom of the soul of individuals as well as the soul of peoples."[56] This drive, impetus, or vector is not a matter of simple aggression, of "pushing people around." A creative motive to develop civilization, even a heroic conception of duty, is an essential ingredient. Nor is it a kind of neurotic insecurity that leads an imperialist people to a multiplication of lands, of annexations. Such great empires as the Roman and Chinese defined their borders and for hundreds of years then adopted what was a defensive strategy. The great empires, moreover, were pre-eminently those in which the "weaker parties" merged with the stronger, accepting the latter's culture as superior and prizing the new citizenship. If British and French and American imperialism could not take this route, it was in part because they were faced with a situation (as we shall see) that had never confronted the Romans. Yet when British imperialism was at its height, young Winston Churchill, as Under-Secretary of State for the Colonies, not only was a social reformer at home, advocating the "universal establishment of minimum standards of life and labor," "a net over the abyss," but also the imperialist, "determined to see that justice was done to humble individuals throughout the empire."[57] Romans granted citizenship and equality to other white peoples; but they never really had to consider the granting of citizenship to the subjects of a black or yellow province; Roman writers in fact generally reserved "a superior or contemptuous tone" toward Ethiopian characteristics.[58] Western imperialist nations, however, had mixed feelings as to whether their own civilization could withstand the strains of a multi-racial empire, the majority of whose members might be led by ideological egalitarians who indulged an animus towards the advanced culture.

B. The Neo-Marxist "Dependency" Theory of Imperialism

To the Communist International, convened in their Sixth Congress in 1928 at Moscow, the predatory-prey character of imperialism was an axiomatic tenet that they enacted formally as a thesis: "The parasitic nature of imperialism. . . . [T]he ruling imperialism in relation to the colonial country," they asserted, "acts primarily as a parasite sucking the blood from the economic organism of the latter. . . . The profits obtained. . . . are sucked out of the country . . . despoiling them [the colonies] . . . exhausting the reserves of human productive forces in the colonial countries."[59]

The predator-prey analogy has a rather obvious flaw when critics of imperialism try to use it as a heuristic principle for understanding. Nowhere among natural predators do we find that their chief effect is to raise the population of their prey manifold. Yet the impact of imperialism, in the greater proportion of cases, especially in the great centers of population such as Java and India, was precisely to augment the growth of population. In Java as long ago as 1860, the writer Multatuli charged in his celebrated anti-imperialist novel *Max Havelaar* that gross exploitation under Dutch rule had led to a decline in population.[60] If so, some highly exceptional provincial phenomenon was involved, for as the naturalist Alfred Russel Wallace, the co-discoverer of the theory of natural selection, pointed out, during that nineteenth-century era the population of Java had risen from about 3.5 million in 1800 to 5.5 million in 1826, to as much as over 9.5 million in 1850, "an increase of seventy-three percent in twenty-five years." The census of 1865 produced a figure of 14,168,416, an astonishing increase of nearly fifty percent in fifteen years, a rate of increase that promised to double the population in about twenty-six years. Wallace found the Javanese people "well-fed and decently clothed." "[T]his vast population is on the whole contented and happy," he wrote; such incidents of exploitation that took place, he judged, were the outcome principally of the heritage of the rule of native princes.[61] The same favorable trend in Java's population continued during the remaining years of Dutch rule. "By 1930 the native population of Java had grown to almost 40.9 million." As the Dutch extended their control from the coastal regions to the interior, they put an end to the sanguinary tribal wars. "Pacification" also meant the building of roads, irrigation works, sanitary measures, and a chance for Javanese to move from overpopulated areas to unoccupied ones, to reclaim lands from the jungle.[62]

Neo-Marxist theory, however, wishes to derive all the problems that beset Asia and Africa from the workings, presumably malevolent, of Western imperialism. As a Harvard-educated Marxist, for instance, has asserted: "The truth is—and this is the key to understanding the whole of modern history—that the underdevelopment of the Third World is the product of the very same historical process which resulted in the development of the advanced capitalist world."[63] A curious inversion of ideology too has taken place with respect to the over-population of the Asian people. Previously, the anti-imperialists charged that imperialism was responsible for the depopulation of colonial peoples; confronted, however, with the contrary evidence, their charge has been "dialectically" transmuted into its opposite. They now charge imperialism with having promoted the growth of population for its own exploitative purposes. Thus, the ecological leftist Barry Commoner, writes: "The Dutch apparently deliberately fostered the increase in the Indonesian population in order to increase the labor forces that they needed to exploit the natural resources." In such guise, Dutch imperialism has been alternately charged with decreasing *and* increasing the Javanese population, depending on the need to safeguard, whatever the facts, an emotional *a priori* Marxist postulate.[64]

Meanwhile, Indonesia, India, and China, now free from any imperialist presence, have for several decades been continuing their growth in population; Western medical science and sanitary practice, combined with the traditional Asian conceptions of family, have been a fruitful combination of conditions for this rise in numbers. The death rates, especially among children, have declined. Even Japan, which never allowed any Western imperialism to intrude, was affected by this fructifying conjunction of Western medical science and the traditionally large Asian family; hence its population, except during a few post-war years, also grew rapidly. There is no documentary evidence that any imperialist government ever schemed how to extract more "surplus value" in the next generation from an enlarged "agricultural or mining reserve army;" actually it would more likely have been worried by the knowledge that large families to come might cause social strains with their added demands for jobs and higher wages, and probable riots and revolts. A proclivity for guilt, however, among many Western critics that congealed in the words "colonialism" and "imperialism" still shapes a self-punitive perspective: "The advanced countries have an obligation to repay their debts to the former colonial countries," writes Commoner.[65]

Most characteristic of Neo-Marxism today, therefore, is its so-called "dependency" theory of imperialism according to which it is alleged that the various peoples of Latin America, Africa, and Asia are "underdeveloped" because it was to the economic interest of the imperialist nations to keep them so. When first adopted as a thesis on imperialism by the Sixth World Congress of the Communist International at Moscow in 1928, the theory conceded that though colonial exploitation involved "a certain encouragement" of production in the colonies, that production was confined "to such lines" as corresponded to the interests of "the imperialist monopoly," thus strengthening "the dependence" of the colony on "the imperialist metropolis." "Real industrialization," on the other hand, especially "a flourishing engineering industry," was, the Communists argued, not encouraged. The "essence . . . of colonial enslavement" was that "the colonial country is compelled to sacrifice the interests of its independent development and to play the part of an economic (agrarian-raw material) appendage to foreign capitalism."[66] Before World War II, the chief British communist theoretician, R. Palme Dutt, elaborated upon this doctrine, alleging that Indian native handicraft industries had been sacrificed to provide a market for British textiles;[67] such industries were presumably destroyed by compelling peasants to buy Lancashire goods instead. Furthermore, imperialist capital, the Marxists alleged, was concentrated in plantations and mines because imperialist rulers had no desire to embark on industrial investment that might compete with home manufactures. In similar fashion, Neo-Marxists today argue that the skewed, one-sided development of the recently colonial countries was inherent in the nature of imperialism. Colonial underdevelopment, they affirm, was inseparable from the exploitation essential to capitalist imperialism, and this economic relationship of dependency inevitably bore as its spiritual superstructure the colonial mentality of inferiority.[68] Thus responsibility for the retardation of economic development in the backward lands was laid at the door of the imperialist. Latin America "as well as Asia and Africa" are held to have been "subjected" by the world capitalist system "to an ever-increasing degree of colonial or neocolonial *economic* subordination," ruling through the instrumentalities of a domestic class structure. Not until the Latin American people "destroy the capitalist class structure through revolution and replace it with socialist development" can historical underdevelopment, it is argued, be turned into development.[69]

It cannot be denied that the "dependency" theory is effective for diverting blame from one's own nation for any of its backwardness and casting its pall upon the advanced nations. One thinks of a class of schoolboys in which the indifferent and least conscientious pupils blame the superior students for being left behind and try to make them feel guilty for their higher abilities or harder work. But what if an inferior class of schoolboys have had poorer teachers or poorer schools? Such a class might blame the central government for having neglected them. The ideology of dependency is congruent with a revolt of the undercivilized that absolves them of responsibility for their condition and evolves instead a sociological excuse that indicts the advanced peoples; according to the economic "logic" of the dependency ideology, a people is undercivilized in proportion to the extent that it has been exploited by the overcivilized.

Oddly enough, the "dependency theory" is entirely inconsistent with the Marxist premises from which it argues, for according to Marxist-Leninist doctrine, the aim of imperialism is to extract superprofits by exploiting colonial workers who can be hired at a rate of surplus value that much exceeds what is possible in the home country.[70] But if native labor was cheap in the mines of Malaysia, or the oil wells of Java, there was no reason, in that case, why that same abundant labor in these over-populous countries should not therefore have been employed next in smelters, in refining plants, and then in textile and steel factories, provided that their productivity were not so low as to offset their relative cheapness. The imperialist quest for profit should thus have led generally to the successive industrialization of every branch of a colony's economic activity. Indeed, something like such a sequence of events did take place in the case of the development of textile manufactures in India and China. The Sassoons, a Jewish family that had migrated to Bombay from Baghdad in 1833, first pioneered a large business in the importation of textiles. In the course of time, the company founded by David Sassoon acquired a monopoly of trade in Indian yarn and English textiles. Then Albert-Abdullah Sassoon realized the potential advantages that the available raw cotton and cheap labor made possible. With the help of machines imported from England he would be able to manufacture textiles more cheaply in India than the British could in Britain, whereupon "a vast manufacturing of cotton goods sprang up under their auspices and that of their associates."[71] Within a few years various members of the Sassoon family had launched several mills, and by the latter part of the century the Jacob Sassoon Mill, with its one-hundred thousand spindles and two thousand looms was the largest in the country. Another plant in Bombay that combined all operations from the processing of the raw cotton to the decoration of the textiles flourished as well. In 1909 the family founded the Eastern Bank, Ltd., to serve its banking needs, completing an evolution from trading capitalism to "finance capitalism."

"Dependency" ideologists forget the extent to which a hostile political climate, partially engendered, indeed, by ideologists perhaps not unlike themselves with their armory of slogans, has inhibited, and still inhibits, the free process of the circulation of capital. Anti-imperialist ideology is perhaps itself a force making for economic retardation. The Sassoon family, for instance, feeling that their family investments might be imperiled by the agitation for Indian independence and the anti-technological campaign of Mahatma Gandhi, began to transfer their interests to Chinese trade and manufactures. Sir Victor Sassoon (1881-1961), the great-grandson of the emigrant David, became known as "the man who made modern Shanghai."[72] Presumably his Chinese textile mill is now operated, perhaps less efficiently, under socialist auspices.

To all the variants of the "dependency" school of anti-imperialism, John Stuart Mill's defense of progressive imperialism, his memorandum on the East India Company, was an early prescient reply. Written (as we have seen) in 1858 on behalf of the East India Company when it was facing dissolution by parliamentary act, and entitled uninvitingly *Memo-*

*randum of the Improvements in the Administration of India during the
Last Thirty Years and the Petition of the East India Company to Parliament,* the title page omitted its author's name, yet all knew its authorship
(except for one line) and Earl Grey pronounced it to be "the ablest
state-paper he had ever read."[73] Mill had served the East India Company
for a quarter of a century from 1823 to 1858, rising to its highest executive
office. His father, James Mill, a predecessor in that position, also had
been "at the very centre of power and in a position to carry into practice
the principle of utility as he had expounded it in his *History of British
India.*"[74] The elder Mill, described by the philosopher Bain as "a born
leader of men," acquired an unprecedented influence in the making of
policy toward India, and his son won a similar regard.[75]

To critics who said that British capitalist advancement was inevitably
associated with Indian underdevelopment, Mill replied:

> It is often asserted that the country is covered with the remains of tanks
> and other works of irrigation which the native rulers constructed, and
> which the British Government has allowed to decay. The fact is over-
> looked, that most of these were already in a state of decay before the
> country came into our possession; long periods of disorder and military
> devastation having destroyed the funds which should have repaired
> them, and the security which would have admitted of their repair.
> Many works which are supposed to have fallen into decay, never were
> completed; many were allowed to decay by the native sovereigns.

By contrast, wrote Mill, the activity of the East India Company in the
construction of irrigation works "for many years past has been exemplary."[76] The Ganges Canal, begun in 1848, "the greatest work of irrigation ever constructed," with more than twelve hundred miles of main
channels of distribution completed or in active progress, was serving 1,134
villages.[77] British railroad construction in India, furthermore, had not
been a needless capital investment designed, as hostile critics later alleged,
to extract revenues from the people, but was rather an essential stimulus
to economic growth. "In every case the existing channels of trade have
been followed," wrote Mill.[78] The chief cotton-producing districts had
received essential railway transport to markets. Commercial, agricultural,
military, and political aims alike were served by the new railway lines.

To those who said British imperialism had inflicted on the peasants
an "enserfment" to the money-lenders, Mill replied that "the agricultural
populations of large districts are, for the first time in memory, out of debt
to money-lenders and to their landlords."[79] The security that Britain had
brought from "the ravages of war and fiscal rapacity" had given rise to "a
great and rapid growth of general prosperity," with a "remarkable increase
of cultivation and population."[80] A thriving export of rice and cotton had
been promoted; indeed, the government had taken the lead in 1840 in

agricultural experimentation, bringing to India "ten experienced cotton-planters from the United States" whose experiments had proved successful in Southwestern India.[81] The burden upon the Indian peasant of excessive taxation, moreover, had been much alleviated. Although "under the native Governments and in the earlier periods of our own," the demands of revenue often exceeded the limits of a fair rent, the British rule had reduced excessive assessments. "The history of our government in India has been a continued series of reductions in taxation."[82]

The policy of the East India Company, Mill declared, had been to promote individual peasant ownership of land as far as possible. But in so doing it ran up against the resistance of the village communities. Nevertheless, in the Punjab, the Northwestern Provinces, and parts of the west and south of India, "the ryotwar system, or that which recognizes the actual cultivator of the soil as its proprietor," became, in Mill's words, "the general system."[83] To be sure, critics of imperialism have inclined to regard benignly the institution of the village community as a kind of primitive communism. More painstaking students, however, of the actual workings of village communities, as in the Russian *mir* in the nineteenth century, have found that as far as enterprising persons were concerned, they were a mainstay of torpor, tedium, and antipathy to improvement.[84]

Moreover, far from transforming India into an area reserved for their monopolistic trade, the British rulers abolished the navigation laws in 1848, ending the discriminatory duties imposed on goods carried in foreign vessels. Duties were still imposed on many foreign imports and exports, but in 1846 the home authorities were planning to terminate these "admitted defects."[85] Meanwhile a greater free market in India had been promoted by the removal of local tariffs and taxes on trade. The last of them having been abolished in 1856, Mill could write: "There are now no internal customs in British India."[86]

Above all, the British government had labored honorably to introduce a new conception of human dignity through "the measures for raising and civilizing the oppressed races." There were, for instance, in parts of India, "numerous hill tribes," believed to have been the country's aborigines, driven off by the Hindu invasion. "These people," wrote Mill, "had been treated like wild beasts by the native Government, and, by a natural consequence, had become the scourges of the country." But now: "The robber tribes were induced to settle as peaceful cultivators. Lands were assigned to them, tools supplied, and money advanced for cultivation." They were made to understand "that they were not considered as wild animals to be hunted down . . . In no single instance has this policy failed."[87] The native courts of justice too were being rapidly extended in their jurisdiction; the practices of self-destruction, such as widows' burning themselves, were prohibited and being eradicated.[88] Government colleges had been founded; in the villages, circle schools for education were the most recent experiment.[89] Thus John Stuart Mill concluded that the British Company's government in India "has a right to take pride to itself for having accomplished so much; and most certainly cannot be justly reproached, by any existing Government or people, with not having effected more."[90]

Of course, debate concerning the record of the British in India never ends, as unrealized possibilities are considered that may perhaps have been remote from the practicable alternatives in the eighteenth and nineteenth centuries. In such problems of retrospective judgment, the wisest procedure is to consult the opinion of men who share our liberal values, have an unquestionable integrity, possess enough energy and intelligence to be well-informed of the facts, and have as well the courage to act upon their views. Such a man indeed was James Mill. In the last volume of his *History of British India,* "a survey of the government of India by the East India Company more completely through the whole field . . . than was ever taken before," and not sparing "the unfavorable" as well as the favorable points, he concluded: "That, in regard to *intention* I know no government, either in past or present times, that can be placed equally high with that of the East India Company"; the schemes and measures adopted were "considered as conducive to the welfare of the people whom they governed" and often sacrificed the company's important interests to those of the people; where it was "little successful," it was owing chiefly to the distance "of a voyage of several months from the scene of action"; and finally, "there is nothing in the world to be compared with the East India Company, whose servants, as a body . . . have, except in some remarkable instances . . . maintained a virtue which, under the temptations of their situation, is worthy of the highest applause."[91]

For all their philosophic and personal estrangements, John Stuart and James Mill, son and father, agreed with respect to their moral judgment of British imperialism.

Withal, the very success of capitalist imperialist measures in India reinstated the Malthusian problem of overpopulation. India, with about one-sixth of the world's population, had large cities and rural areas with a density of population about the highest in the world. When arid tracts were transformed through irrigation into flourishing canal colonies, their populations grew at once enormously. The consequence was that standards of living failed to keep pace with technical advancement. Death-rates in the cities remained exceptionally high and the general health poor.[92] These Malthusian and cultural phenomena were scarcely the epiphenomena, however, to the alleged predatory practices of a Western civilization, as the theoreticians of Third Worldism, dispensing globules of guilt, would have it.

More than a half-century after Mill's defence of the British East India Company, the founder of revisionist socialism, Eduard Bernstein, affirmed his recognition in 1911 that Britain's imperialism in India had brought the latter an increased population, based on flourishing trade, personal security, and orderly administration: "No nation has exercised in its colonies a sense of fairness, of live and let live, in such a degree as has the English," he wrote.[93]

C. The "Dependency" Theory and the United States

Lenin attacked modern imperialism as the last stage of capitalism, during which its imperialism had evolved from a commercial variety founded predominantly on the trade and exchange of consumers' goods to one based on the export of capital. The dependency theorists, on the contrary, assail capitalist imperialism on the opposite ground—that it never invested enough capital in the colonial countries, that it stopped short in its investment. John A. Hobson, the first to enunciate the predator conception and to forecast that the predator would degenerate in biological fashion into a parasite, felt it was sinful for capital to leave its home country, that it ought rather to be invested at home, thereby contributing to raise their own workingmen's level of consumption. The current vogue, however, in the theory of imperialism, blaming the advanced countries for the backwardness of "underdeveloped" countries, charges them with not exporting, or not having exported, their capital, the product of their advanced labor and technology, to backward countries. Thus, even when a communist country fails to achieve the economic progress that was supposedly, according to their doctrine, the foreseeable consequence of communism, it automatically castigates the United States for not according it grants of capital (on terms not specified). Thus, the foreign minister of the Yugoslav socialist republic, Eduard Kardelj, once reproached the United States:

> The export of capital from the developed countries to the rest of the world is low; [that] of course, hinders the growth[sic] the consumer capacity of the underdeveloped countries to absorb industrial commodities and, hence, holds down its productivity.

The classical critics of imperialism, such as Hobson, indicted it for its underconsumption at home; the Neo-Marxists, on the contrary, charge the imperialist countries with "overconsumption," with being "consumerist" societies. Thus, the Yugoslav communist theoretician declared that the "capital-glutted" countries are "raising their own consumption . . . [A] consumer society is the inevitable product of the present situation in international socio-economic relations."[94]

American critics similarly denounce the presumed American predators. Professing to speak for the "Third World" as the self-flagellating
Christian Apologists once did for the barbarians, an influential Neo-
Marxist writes: "During the past seven decades, the United States has
probably done more to impede the development of the Third World than
any other advanced country." Without impugning America's basic good-
will, its social system has nevertheless, according to this Neo-Marxist,
elevated it as the world's villain: "For at least eighty years, America has
worked against the poor of the planet in a spirit of sincere compassion."[95]

Once more, we seem in the presence of a compulsive *a priori* reasoning that blames American capitalism no matter what its policy. If it
exports capital, it is culpable; if it turns from the export of capital toward
raising its own living standards (as Hobson proposed), it is culpable. It is
a corollary of the new ethic of leveling that America must be defined as a
predator; only upon that axiom can the "Third World" attribute its
backwardness to America. Consequently, their revolt comes to bear the
imprint of those who, envious of achievement, resist an inquiry into
their own cultures and characters and fashion instead a "dialectical"
chain to derive their backwardness from the evil deeds of some putative
exploiter.

As a student of "dependency" theories has recently written: "Dependency theory in general substantially over-estimates the power of the international system—or imperialism—in southern affairs today."[96] At one
time, similarly, the poverty of the Chinese peasants was attributed in
great part to the exploitative activities of American imperialism. In 1931,
however, immediately prior to the commencement of the era of military
struggle with Japan and civil war, the entirety of American investment in
China was estimated at $196,606,400. To that profit-seeking segment
might have been counterbalanced the value of the property (in China's
service) of American missions and philanthropic, educational, and scientific institutions.[97] There were no American holdings whatsoever in the
securities of Chinese corporations, nor were there financial mechanisms
for concealed indirect exploitation. Sixty-five percent of the American
business investment was in Shanghai, and of that, almost a third was
embodied in two public utilities for the foreign settlement.[98] In short,
the American investment in China was minuscule. As far as the average
Chinese peasant was concerned, the impact of American economic imperialism was virtually zero. Missionaries and medical men, however,
were imparting techniques and information on public health, and a steady
output of Chinese intellectuals emanated from institutions subsidized by
American philanthropies. Sun Yat-sen, the father of the Chinese Republic,
learned his political doctrines from such Americans as Maurice William
and Henry George.[99] Chinese industrial backwardness was, however, a
heritage of the Chinese tradition and the Chinese philosophy of life,

scarcely an outcome of exploitative advances in Western civilization that reduced them to dependency by a "skewed development." Indeed, the only major Western theorist who had misgivings about China's embarking upon capitalistic industry was Karl Marx, who wondered whether that might postpone a socialist revolution in the West by reviving the world's capitalistic stage.[100]

There were sordid episodes, indeed, that accompanied the activities of imperialist powers in China. The British Opium War against China in 1840-1842 springs to mind, with the shameful insistence by the British government that the Chinese market remain open to Indian opium; and this war remains the most significant evidence for the claim that "the development of underdevelopment in China" was the outcome of the external pressures mainly of the Western imperialist nations on the Chinese society.[101] Nevertheless, the Chinese opium trade was scarcely a creation of the British merchants; it was embedded in Chinese life long before the entry of the English East India Company. Introduced into China in the seventh and eighth centuries by Turkish and Arab traders, opium was subsequently adapted to smoking during the seventeenth century, whereupon many Chinese became addicts. By 1729 the Chinese government was trying vainly to prohibit the drug's sale and use; the trade was mostly conducted by Portuguese. Meanwhile, under the Moghul Emperors, India had become the principal cultivator of opium, providing its rulers with much revenue. "When the Moghul Empire fell apart, the English salvaged and improved a system of state control to which they fell heir."[102] Though the English East India Company instituted a monopoly in the cultivation of opium in the Bengal province, in 1773 its actual distribution in China was in the hands of both British and Chinese smugglers.

The spread of opium use in China must finally be attributed more to endogenous social factors than to exogenous imperialist pressures. The English East India Company did derive profits from a demand that it already found widespread in the Chinese society. The British conscience itself had not yet awakened to all the evils of the opium addiction; literary intellectuals such as Coleridge and De Quincey experimented with and became addicted to the drug; at the nineteenth century's end Arthur Conan Doyle still depicted Sherlock Holmes as enthralled by morphia. To his credit, William Ewart Gladstone, then still a Tory, denounced the Opium War in Parliament as "unjust in its origin," and "calculated . . . to cover this country with permanent disgrace."[103] Justice, said Gladstone, was with the Chinese, though they were "pagans and semi-civilized barbarians," while "enlightened and civilized Christians" were acting at variance with their religion. He feared "the judgment of God upon England." He was as one with the Chinese emperor who, weeping, had asked how he could face the shades of his ancestors if he allowed his people to ruin themselves with this vile drug.[104] An extreme dogma of free trade, even if the commodity in question enslaved and enfeebled, still dominated British commercial capitalism.

But as British imperialism grew more advanced and industrial, it joined in efforts in 1907 to end the opium trade. Through the government of India it signed an agreement with China to diminish and terminate the export of Indian opium within ten years, while the Chinese, on their part, undertook to forbid its cultivation and consumption. If the aim of imperialist Britain had been to sap the manhood of Chinese and to make them psychologically "dependent," that was hardly what took place. Imperialism during that stage which Lenin called "monopoly capitalism" advanced in both political and economic morality. The Opium War was the kind of behavior that capitalist imperialism outgrew with its evolution.

It is, of course, a paradox that Neo-Marxists excoriate British capitalist imperialism for having allegedly inflicted a drug dependency on the Chinese, for Neo-Marxists are, or have been themselves in our time the advocates of the union of the "drug culture" with their political culture. One of their spokesmen, sentenced and imprisoned as a drug purveyor, has even declared that a drug dealer is most qualified to be the critic of society. Perhaps Neo-Marxism will one day re-interpret the Opium War as a constructive episode in the advancement of opium use that was regrettably repudiated by a latter monopoly capitalism which, seeking to exploit its workers more extensively, repressed the pleasures of addiction.

Today, however, "dependency theory" is most used to explain, or excuse, the relative backwardness of Latin America, its *dependencistas,* for whom it constitutes the chief ideological weapon against the presumably dollar-desirous "Uncle Sam."[105] The existence of authoritarian governments in Latin America and their frequent past hostility to industrial technology is attributed to the character of the "world system," dominated by the United States. Now there *have* been other authoritarian societies—Japan, with its Meiji Restoration, Czarist Russia beginning with Peter the Great, and Prussia, the dynastic state—that all committed themselves in various ways to industrialization. Wherefore, then, the retardation in the Latin American societies?

Oddly enough, American goodwill in one sense may have attenuated the motive for industrialization. Japan, Russia, and Prussia all realized that their national independence was precarious so long as they lacked the industrial base with which to maintain and equip large modern armies. The requirements of warfare have in certain periods been a most potent force for industrialization.[106] When America, however, promulgated the Monroe Doctrine, it placed the Western Hemisphere outside the bounds of European territorial imperialist expansion. The United

States Navy stood ready to intervene on behalf of any Latin American
state confronted with a European invader. The army of Napoleon III was
thus in 1866 compelled to withdraw from Mexico leaving the hapless,
artefactual Emperor Maximilian to his fate,[107] for with the American
Civil War ended, General Grant and his army became available as "the
very spearhead" for intervention against the foreign regime in Mexico.[108]

Curiously, the origin of the "dependencia" mentality lies in this fact of
the United States' anti-imperialist policy. Thus safeguarded from European imperialism, a "dependency mentality," an inferiority complex,
tended, to begin with, to develop on the part of Latin American countries
whose independence rested on the strength of the United States. Secondly,
since America could always be relied on to protect them militarily, there
was no urgency in having their own military-industrial base. Thus reasoned the Latin American rulers.[109] The Monroe Doctrine was resented
precisely because it underscored the ambiguous source of their own sovereignty. Even after its abrogation, the mentality of the *dependencista*
still persisted with the United States as the great object for blame, a
super-scapegoat. As one of Strindberg's characters observed, a benefactor
tends to be hated by his beneficiaries. Such was the psychological fate
that befell the well-meaning declaration of President James Monroe on
December 2, 1823: "The American continents . . . are henceforth not to
be considered as subject for future colonization by any European power,
[and] any interposition for the purpose of oppressing them . . . by any
European power" would be regarded as an unfriendly act towards the
United States.[110] If anything, as Dexter Perkins pointed out, "the Doctrine was more frequently cited to check, rather than to encourage,
American imperialism"; throughout later debates on policy in the Far
East, for instance, its imperative was invoked that America not allow
nations to annex or colonize parts of foreign continents.[111]

Metternich, the designer of the Holy Alliance, regarded the Monroe
Doctrine as an "audacious," "unprovoked" "act of revolt," that gave
strength to those "fostering revolutions wherever they show themselves,"
and reanimated "the courage of every conspirator."[112] If the guiding
mind of the conservative system felt that the Monroe Doctrine was a
radical, pro-revolutionary document, how then were the radicals and
revolutionists themselves able to perceive in the Monroe Doctrine precisely its opposite? How could they proclaim the Monroe Doctrine to be
the instrument of anti-democratic reaction and exploitation? Latin Americans of course have argued that the Doctrine was gradually elaborated
to confer upon the United States a police power over republics that could
be manipulated to its own advantage, as when it judged the public order
to have collapsed in Santo Domingo and Haiti. But such interventions in
the Caribbean, under the initiative notably of Franklin D. Roosevelt, as
Assistant Secretary of the Navy, were provoked by the spectacle of dis-

orders on islands close to the American mainland rather than by any promise of economic exploitation. As Dexter Perkins notes: "In countries such as Haiti, Santo Domingo, and Nicaragua, the cause of political stability was undeniably promoted by the coercive action of the United States." Throughout its career, furthermore, the Monroe Doctrine remained the principal political document that inhibited any European imperialist evolution on the continent of South America. The virtual ultimatum by President Theodore Roosevelt to the German government when it planned to intervene in Venezuela in 1902 was the most dramatic instance.

Despite such happy outcomes, or perhaps, on a deeper psychological level, because of them, Latin American nations came to regard North American "intermeddling" "with a general resentment," and cited with approbation the testimony of American critics that the Monroe Doctrine was the instrumentality of "dollar diplomacy."[113] With respect to the chief economic apprehension of the Latin American nations—that European governments might use military means to collect loans in Latin America—the United States and the Latin American nations, however, saw eye to eye.[114] The role of the United States as the key agent in preserving Latin American independence did not, however, rid it of the culpability that attaches to those who are prosperous, enjoy democratic government, preserve individual liberties, and act disinterestedly. To be innocent and guileless, and even generous, in one's action is the most exasperating offence in the minds of those embittered by a long co-existence with tyranny, repression, torpor and grandiosity, generalized ill-will, selfishness, and cynicism. Perhaps it was fanciful for the United States to have seen any threat to itself in Spain's longing to recover or retain its Latin American colonies; perhaps Jeffersonian revolutionary ideology deflected America's reasoning from the direction of sober, rational calculation and consideration.[115] Monroe's Secretary of State, John Quincy Adams, acknowledged in 1821 that the new Latin American countries, for all his pleasure in their revolutions, "have not the first elements of good or free government . . . Arbitrary power, military and ecclesiastical, was stamped upon their education, their habits, and upon all their institutions."[116] This awareness, even when partial, has more than anything else contributed to the counter-resentment of the politically and industrially undercivilized, the attitude of the *dependencistas* that the over-development of such as John Quincy Adams was at the expense of the underdevelopment of such as they.[117] Whatever the American contribution to Latin American independence, the phrase "Monroe Doctrine" conveyed to many resentment-prone intellectuals the suggestion of "hegemony."[118]

Britain was associated with the United States in supporting the Monroe Doctrine, and much also has been written to condemn the role of British imperialist investment in Argentina. The indictment, however, rests on little evidence. On the basis of his comprehensive *British Investments in Latin America, 1822-1949,* J. Fred Rippy concluded that foreign private capital was on the whole beneficial to Latin America; where poverty persisted, it seemed "to be the result mainly of scanty resource endowment, debilitating climate, disease, illiteracy, psychological attitudes, and hampering value systems."[119] Nonetheless, the springs of resentment are still fed by statistics of the large profits "siphoned out" by foreign companies, to which the author counters: "Limiting himself to British investments in Latin America, for example, the investigator will be compelled to conclude that for every highly profitable investment there were many others which yielded only moderate profits and not a few that resulted in losses."[120]

The United States too was once in a "dependency" relationship toward British and German capitalist interests (London and Frankfurt) that had, for instance, participated extensively in financing the construction of American railroads.[121] As late as 1910, eighty-five percent of British investment in the United States was still held in American railroads. Moreover, the total of all British investments in the United States constituted as much as forty-two percent of their investments outside the Empire; half of Britain's portfolio investment abroad was indeed outside the Empire's limits.[122] Before the Civil War, British investment was directed mainly in a cautious way toward the securities of the "well-situated trunk lines" along the Atlantic seaboard, though Illinois bonds too were a favorite with the London market. After the Civil War, however, British entrepreneurs were attracted to the American South and Southwest. "Almost every railway company of any importance had connections with London; as a result Southerners were able to obtain funds for expansion. Railway mileage in the South, which had increased little in the 1870s, almost doubled in the 1880s."[123] Meanwhile, too, British investments grew in the Chicago Great Western, in grain elevators and flour mills, in slaughtering and meat packing, and proceeded into enterprises concerned with the export of food to Europe. It should be borne in mind that the railroad itself was predominantly a British achievement: "Many of the major inventions connected with railways until late in the nineteenth century were British."[124] Imports of British rails sustained the expansion of the American railway system from the 1850s through the 1870s. German investors lent their hand especially during the 1880s, becoming much involved with the Northern Pacific, the Southern Pacific, the Central Pacific, and the Oregon Railway. Dutch investments were channelized toward their favorite St. Paul and Pacific, and the Kansas Pacific.[125] During the Civil War, itself, furthermore, a large quantity of American securities were sold to European investors.

Americans, however, from their earliest colonial days were free from the *dependencia* mentality. Venturesome, entrepreneurial, inventive, they appeared from the first in the pages of the enthralled travelers, de Crève-coeur and de Tocqueville, as filled with a free initiative and technical daring. "Self-reliance," the Emersonian theme, was the cardinal tenet of the American ethic. It was only a matter of time before they would be the full masters of their own industries and have settled all their international loans and borrowings.

"Dependency" is a state of mind that is based less on one's non-ownership of a technology than on the sense that one lives by a technology that one has neither helped fashion, nor mastered, nor improved, and toward which one therefore harbors a certain hostility. What is ominous in "dependency" theories of imperialism is that they "rationalize" this sense of resentment toward technology and achievement. The conflict between haves and have-nots becomes secondary to an equally basic animosity of the "know-nots" against the "know-hows," the hostility of the borrowers toward the originators. A mood of anti-scientism and anti-technologism comes naturally to the "dependency" anti-imperialists as they articulate the resentment and revolt especially of the undercivilized in backward regions, where people cling fanatically to doctrines of super-stition that Comtist sociologists once assigned to the transient first and second stages of pre-scientific society.

D. Consumers' Imperialism: Consumers' Desires as the Popular Basis for Imperialism

The rise of progressive imperialism brought to the European middle and working classes the chance to enjoy previously unknown goods and pleas-ures. Imperialism was founded on the new consumers' tastes and choices that were in turn made possible by the inventive genius of European (mainly British) and American experimenters. What has been called "peo-ple's imperialism" or "social imperialism" was not a phenomenon, as Engels and Lenin thought, of a kind of bribe given to the skilled labor aristocracy of the imperialist country from the heavy "super-profits" gar-nered through exploiting natives in a backward country.[126] Rather, it was the case that novel types of products could henceforth be manufactured cheaply for use by the people at large. The rubber of the Belgian Congo and Dutch Java, for instance, made possible the spread of the bicycle cul-ture that altered the lives of young British and American men and women in the late Victorian era. If we would appreciate what imperialism meant to the ordinary British person, it would be far more descriptive to speak of "bicycle imperialism" than "monopoly capitalist imperialism," for it was the new wave of young British and American bicycle enthusiasts, often the children of working class families, or young women workers aspiring to a freedom of movement, who helped enact the new imperialism. Raw materials like rubber that were relatively unimportant economically before 1880 answered to the new schedule of consumers' wishes.

The bicycle, for instance, became the vehicle of courtship for the young heroes and heroines of H. G. Wells's romances. In one later scientific fiction, his hero even became the partner in a bicycle business: "They were agents for several obscure makes of bicycle,—two samples constituted the stock,—and occasionally they made a sale; they also repaired punctures . . . The staple of their business was, however, the letting of bicycles on hire. It was a singular trade, obeying no known commercial or economic principles—indeed, no principles. There was a stock of ladies' and gentlemen's bicycles in a state of disrepair that passes description . . . and insistent boys could get bicycles and the thrill of danger for about an hour for so low a sum as threepence . . . Romantic possibilities of accident lurked in the worn thread of the screw that adjusted the saddle, in the precarious pedals." And on a bank holiday: "There were quantities of young men and women on bicycles and motor-bicycles."[127]

Even George Bernard Shaw, almost forty years old in 1895, while staying with his fellow socialists Sidney and Beatrice Webb, was moved to take leave from Fabian economics to learn to ride the bicycle: "My efforts set the coastguards laughing as no audience had ever laughed at my plays."[128] In France, young working people and intellectuals alike, from Lucien Herr, the apostolic socialist librarian to the physicists Pierre and Marie Curie, took to bicycles: in 1897, Frenchmen rode on 409,000 bicycles; automobiles, then in their infancy, numbered only 1200.[129] Even Sherlock Holmes in 1895 was stirred to a feat of chivalrous detection on behalf of the young music teacher, Violet Smith, "so ardent a bicyclist," who elicited the evil-minded intentions of a rogue returned from the South African mines.[130]

It was in the nineteenth century that for the first time in history those unable to afford horses or carriages sought a mode of individual transport within their means. In 1818 a German baron had adapted a hobby-horse so that it could be propelled by one's long strides on the ground; the wheels were wooden and the feet touched the earth. Then in 1839, a Scot, Kirkpatrick Macmillan, contrived to raise the feet from the ground and to move the rear wheel through treadles, connecting rods, and cranks. Further improvements then followed, with bicycle patents in France and America as well. A great international bicycle race from Paris to Bowen in 1869 lent the drama of competitive sport to cycling, and the manufacture of bicycles began in England in the same year. In 1874 came the landmark of the patent, in Coventry, of the first ladies' bicycle, and by 1884 two hundred varieties of bicycles competed on the consumers' market.[131]

An American book in 1889 on *The Cycling Art* especially hailed the ladies' bicycle: "Probably the most daring innovation the ladies have made in the domain of sports and pastime within the past decade consists in their riding the bicycle." Some persons, it noted, felt that the two-wheeler was inappropriate for a lady, who should confine herself to the more proper tricycle, to which the author responded: "It would be a shame to deny her the right to the less cumbersome and much neater mount. The ladies' bicycle certainly is the more modest appearing, if we were used to both, and it takes much less work to run it . . . Common prejudice cannot long sustain such a senseless discrimination to keep her on the 'trike'." The inventor of the first ladies' bicycle, James Starley, was ridiculed as he rode in Coventry's streets with the "jeers and contemptuous sneers of the lusty silk weavers and cynical watchmakers." Goaded into indignation, he finally rose and declared: "the time will come when *ladies* will ride these things through your streets." The author commented philosophically that indeed, "the noble city of its birth had become the centre of modern cycledom." In Washington, D.C., "apparently timid girls" won admiration by the dexterity and grace with which they mounted their machines, though even the author ackowledged that his masculine sense of superiority suffered "a tremendous blow within me." One woman wrote eloquently in the journal *Bicycling World* how it was such sport to leave far behind both trotting-horses and streetcars: "Even after riding ten miles I do not feel tired . . . My husband is very much pleased . . . my bicycle is keeping me too young in actions." No, she was not demanding votes for women. "Oh, no, indeed!" But she wanted the freedom of her bicycle.[132]

The efflorescence of the bicycle in Western civilization was made possible by the use of rubber tires. It took great labors by tireless inventors to make rubber thus usable. Surgeons in the early nineteenth century were availing themselves of its elasticity in their surgical tubes, and Charles Macintosh in 1823 was using it to make his leather waterproof. The wearer, however, of a macintosh or of Brazilian rubber shoes might find that on a hot summer's day his clothing's rubber oozed away. Consequently, the rubber shoe industry virtually collapsed. Even the government mail bags decayed as their rubber melted away. Beside, the melting rubber was odoriferous.

Then came Charles Goodyear, an unflagging, determined investigator who set himself to solve this problem and sacrificed family and fortune to do so, even enduring debtor's prison. In 1839, in the course of a lively argument with several men, Goodyear dropped a quantity of rubber mixed with sulphur on a red-hot stove.[133] To his surprise, it neither melted nor decomposed and was free from stickiness. Thus the discovery of the process of vulcanizing rubber originated; though ostracized by friends and relatives, Goodyear, after much further work, secured in 1844 his celebrated patent that brought a renaissance to America's rubber industry.

Though Goodyear himself never tried to construct rubber tires for bicycles, the solid rubber tires that were invented were so heavy that they made riding slow. It occurred to a Scottish veterinarian, John Boyd Dunlop, who used rubber gloves when he ministered to horses, that he might increase the speed of rubber tires by distending them with compressed air. He tried it out in 1887 on his ten-year-old son's tricycle; the child pedaled through the streets of Belfast triumphantly. And in 1889, a victory for the pneumatic tire on the race course vindicated the new invention. Thus the bicycle liberated children, women, and men—clerks, artisans, intellectuals, and miners alike.[134] And the consequence for the Belgian Congo, Java, and Brazil? A huge, growing demand for wild rubber (caoutchouc) and later for plantation rubber. Rubber became the object of joy, the "India rubber ball," in the *Child's Garden of Verses;* and it also made possible the spread of baseball throughout the countless sandlots of the United States; the newly manufactured balls made American boys into generations of ballplayers.

The author of *The Adventures of Tom Sawyer* was not comforted, however: Mark Twain wrote a bitter pamphlet, *King Leopold's Soliloquy,* that justly indicted the ruler of the Belgian Congo for his exploitation, mutilation, and depopulation of the African tribesmen who were virtually enslaved to provide quotas of raw rubber and ivory. King Leopold, to be sure, from his accumulated profits, built palaces and public structures in Belgian cities. But the most prolific fruit of his imperialism was the bicycle tire for millions of Europeans and Americans rather than his state monopolistic "surplus value."

Meanwhile the demand for ivory in Western Europe and America also had grown immensely. Largely the outcome of the rising intellectual culture of the middle class, it even reached in New York into the homes of the working class, as workingmen and businessmen sought to imbue their families with musical culture; their daughters were regarded with awe as votaries of the highest when they played the piano.

The piano evidently was invented around 1709 in Florence by Bartolomeo Cristofori, an instrument maker from Padua, then "in the service of the most serene Prince of Tuscany.[135] Cristofori had been dissatisfied with the limitations in volume and variation of the sounds produced by the harpsichord. At first a curiosity for Italian noblemen and their courts, the use of the pianoforte spread to central and western Europe. American inventors, especially Alpheus Babcock in 1825 and Jonas Chickering in 1843, both Bostonians, made structural improvements in the frames that enabled the tension of the strings to be increased sevenfold, while French inventors developed the pedal. The piano, once confined to the dimensions of the salon, was now capable of creating music loud enough for concert halls. A maker of pianos in Philadelphia, John Isaac Hawkins, fashioned the first successful low upright piano in 1800. The upright piano, by the mid-nineteenth century, "had become firmly established as the home instrument throughout Europe"; then American manufacturers began to make vast improvements.[136] It could now adorn theaters, play-houses, restaurants, and school assemblies, as well as simple homes. Therefore in the latter years of the nineteenth century the demand for ivory grew exponentially; it was the best material for the manufacture of the piano keys.[137] The growing pleasure of the European and American peoples in music, the "revolution" in popular culture, was the prime mover of the augmented quest for ivory in the Belgian Congo.

The piano, produced cheaply enough for the families in Manhattan tenement houses, was both a stimulus to and a product of imperialism; thus many American, British, French, and German workers enjoyed the fruits of imperialism, not measured in "super-profits" or a high rate of capitalistic "surplus value" but simply in the cheapness of the new cul-tural commodities.[138]

If "people's imperialism" could manifest itself in bicycles and pianos, it was generally a phenomenon which underlay the unparalleled achieve-ment in "consumers' satisfactions" that was the social essence of Western civilization. Every aspect of its higher standard of life, from novel foods to new, pleasurable activities was linked to imperialism; the consumer, not the capitalist, provided the approving market.

The ordinary Western European for the first time in history became well-washed. "The growing demand for soap, first among the middle, then the working classes, had called into being a prosperous and wide-spread industry."[139] Nigeria became a growing source for the palm oil of British cleanliness, which replaced the use of beef tallow;[140] in 1806 British merchants began by importing 150 tons of palm oil from the Nigerian "Oil Rivers"; by 1839, the figure was 13,600 tons, and in 1938, just prior to World War II, the figure had increased more than eightfold to 110,243.[141] Soaps became gentler and milder, and the lathers more ebul-lient; with the help of the safety razor, Britons became an agreeably beardless people.[142] The firm of James Lever took pride in the fact that the rising wages of the working classes "had brought soap within their means." To the working class housewife especially, "soap was not a luxury . . . but an indispensable necessity for her home." The rate of profit for Lever was low, but the large-scale enterprise and market brought it prosperity. With a certain poetic truth, the firm's new adver-tising could assure its users that their soap would eradicate the lines of grief: "'Twill make your brow as snowy white/As free from grief and care/As when with youth your eyes were bright."[143]

Perhaps those children who rebelled against the new discipline of washing brought about by "soap imperialism" were reconciled, however, to the "chocolate imperialism" that gave them one of their greatest de-lights. Chocolate was at first a drink available only to kings and their guests. The warrior Cortés had written to the Emperor Charles V at Seville in 1528 of this marvelous "chocolatl"—"the divine drink that builds up resistance and fights fatigue." He enclosed several sample packets.[144] For many years the secrets of chocolatl, reputed to be the food of the gods, "were closely held by the padres of the Spanish court." But in 1623 the Dutch West India Company and its seamen brought the chocolate bean and beverage into international trade.

More than a century had elapsed before an enterprising Frenchman opened a shop in London in 1657 that sold chocolate for beverages. In the eighteenth century chocolate clubs became fashionable, assisted by recipes that improved chocolate with milk. Sweet solid chocolate for eating was first developed in 1847 by an English firm. Chocolate became cheaper and more popular when the import duty on raw cocoa leaves was lowered, and Daniel Peter in Switzerland helped with a better milk chocolate recipe. The cultivation of cocoa beans brought unprecedented prosperity to farmers in the Gold Coast.[145] America, however, came to lead the world in the manufacture of cocoa and chocolate products, and its children, in this sense, have been among the world's foremost consumers' imperialists.

In England, the Quaker, John Cadbury, of Birmingham, a strong temperance man, was drawn in the pursuit of a pleasure in keeping with his creed to the making of chocolate. In 1813 he began the actual manufacture of cocoa and chocolate. His firm waxed mightily. By 1842, his price list offered fifteen kinds of eating or drinking chocolate and about ten forms of cocoa; among the former were "Churchman's Chocolate" and "French Eating Chocolate." The firm became renowned for its exemplary labor relations, the camp schools it encouraged, and the vocational and general education it provided with courses from gardening to Esperanto.[146] Millions of children and adults sang their praises of Cadbury's Chocolate. Has any socialist imperialism produced a single new commodity that can rival this achievement of capitalist imperialism?

E. "Dependency" Theory Falsified: Capitalist Development in India Under British Imperialism

There is little evidence to sustain the claim that Western imperialist powers sought and were able to impede, dismantle, or hamper the growth of native industries, making it impossible for local, self-supporting industrialization to get underway. In the anti-imperialist epistemology the proposition that underdevelopment is generated by the same forces that develop capitalism itself is an *a priori* rather than an empirical one.[147] As Morris D. Morris has written: "The British did not take over a society that was 'ripe' for an industrial revolution and then frustrate that development.

They imposed themselves on a society for which every index of performance suggests the level of technical, economic and administrative performance of Europe five hundred years earlier.[148]

Western capitalist competition, for instance, has often been charged with having forcibly terminated the Turkish, Middle Eastern, and Indian crafted textiles. Overlooked is the fact that Western cotton factories clothed the average Indian peasant far better than had the high-cost native handicraftsmen. If Asian and African areas had no part in the great waves of invention, of science and technological innovation, during the Industrial Revolution, it was because their societies and cultures had not nurtured the spirit of inquiry; the creative spirit of Arabic science had declined into the "Levantine" mentality,[149] a byword for an attitude of laziness, or aimlessness, long before the advent of Western capital.

Moreover, as Vera Anstey noted, the imported dyes in India were not only cheaper but suited "the taste of the people better. A redipping of cloth frequently takes the place of new clothes in India for the sake of variety, as fashions in material and style of clothing do not change."[150] But though the Indian hand production of cotton goods declined, by 1853 the first successful mechanized mill was started in Bombay, and such innovation became rapid in the last quarter of the nineteenth century. At times, the government, under the direction of such Liberals as Lord Morley, seeking to stimulate Indian development, tried in accordance with the theory of free trade to allow market forces to allocate investment; the state lent its helping hand by encouraging the establishment of technical schools. That the basic resistance to innovation and development arose from the Hindu psychology and culture itself is suggested by the fact that Parsees, such as J. N. Tata, rather than Hindus, were preeminent in the rise of the cotton manufacturing industry.[151]

The Parsees indeed were uniquely placed intellectually to lead an industrial awakening in India. Emigrants from Persia in the eighth century, they had brought with them technical and commercial skills. Ship builders in the eighteenth century, they were in the next century foremost among the inhabitants of Bombay, their favorite city, in literacy: forty percent of the Parsees in 1872 were literate as compared to fifteen percent of the Hindus. The Parsees, "unencumbered by religious and caste restrictions," mastered "English models set before them much more ardently than the Hindus."[152] But among the Hindus and Moslems, a philosophy of resignation was prevalent—not a spirit of enterprise and innovation, but one of withdrawal and passivity.[153] Nonetheless, Indian merchant capital kept growing throughout the nineteenth century, especially in Bombay. Foreign capital investment was slow in coming for "British investors hardly considered India as an investment-outlet for their surplus capital until railway-building started"; hence foreign capital was scarce until the eighteen-seventies.[154] Meanwhile, the Bombay merchants, led by the Parsees, learning zealously from the British the techniques of commercial capitalism, constituted by 1836 two-fifths of the firms in the Chamber of Commerce.

The life of Jamsetji Nusserwanja Tata, the famed Parsee industrialist, belies all the rhetoric of "dependency" theories. It is the story of a man who had the courage and vision to choose independent and original paths of economic development, from commercial capitalism to textile manufacturing capitalism, to iron and steel production, to developing hydro-electric power, and finally to the founding of a scientific research institute.[155]

Tata's firm made its first high profits during the American Civil War when it shipped large quantities of cotton and textiles to Britain.[156] A crash followed, though with recovery by 1877 Tata had founded the Empress Mills, into which he introduced the most modern machines for producing yarn. "There were only 13 mills in the Bombay Presidency in 1865, the number rose to 51 in 1877 . . . When India built her cotton industry, the hour of Lancashire tolled."[157] At times governmental policy annoyed him with such nuisances as its imposing, in 1896, of a three and one-half percent excise tax on cloth produced in Indian mills, a tax not repealed until 1926. Tata censured such actions as those of a "false imperialism," but he did not repudiate imperialism as such. Indeed, his own small community, the Parsees, he said, "have benefited more than any other class by English rule, and I am sure their gratitude is, as it ought to be, in due proportion to the advantage derived from it."[158] By 1914, India had become the fourth largest among the world's cotton manufacturing countries.[159] World War I brought it an unprecedented prosperity because the normal imports from Lancashire ceased to be available.

Seeking its own profit, British capital was led into a symbiotic development with Indian industry. Thus, Tata's interests did not remain confined to consumers' textile goods. If the Bombay mills had sounded the knell of Lancashire, the Tata Iron and Steel Company in the next generation tolled that of Birmingham. The need for an Indian steel industry was first posed by the boom in railway construction; the first contracts for building railways in India were signed in 1849, twenty-five years after Britain had seen its first railroads constructed. The contracts provided, in effect, for railway construction by private companies with a rate of return of about five percent guaranteed by the government. This mixed public-private imperialism evoked inefficient management that led to more direct governmental operation from 1870 to 1880. But in 1880 private companies returned to the field.[160] The government, wanting to cheapen the costs of such construction, decided in 1882 that the best way would be to encourage the manufacture of iron and steel in India itself.[161] The demand for steel came to be so great that by 1897-1898 large imports were required from America; one-half the steel imported into India came from countries other than Britain. Under such conditions, Lord Curzon could affirm as policy in 1902 "the great importance of developing Indian industries in general and the iron and steel industries in particular."[162] When the Tata Iron and Steel company was registered in Bombay in August, 1907, it was like a national holiday as people flocked to buy shares, rich and "ordinary folk" alike, "inspired by the dream of an India economically independent of other nations . . . The Tata office was besieged and the scene has been compared to that of a first night outside a London theatre: 'the people lined up in front . . . like Londoners, waiting for first night seats in the pit, some of them with stools and lunch boxes'. Altogether some 8,000 people subscribed within three weeks."[163] Tata's vision was the progenitor of the Indian Institute of Science at Bangalore and the hydro-electric schemes for utilizing the monsoon rainfall to drive the turbo-generators in the valleys. Mahatma Gandhi, the ascetic spokesman for Indian independence, conceded: "The Tatas represent the spirit of adventure."[164] In 1923, Sir Thomas Holland, director of India's Geological Survey, declared: "Without the Tata Steel Company, there can be no national India, and all political reforms must be non-productive."[165] The fashioning of the economic basis for independence out of the materials provided by British imperialism was best exemplified in Tata's work.

"Dependency" theorists, one must recognize, have tended to overlook a basic pattern in the history of imperialism: an expanding capitalist imperialism, by creating a demand for its products such as iron and steel that far exceeds the ability of the home country to meet, calls into existence the counterpart of its industries in its colony. Again what has misled the theorists of anti-imperialism is the predator-prey analogy that pervades their thinking. For what predator ever allowed his prey to develop those very organs of production on which the predator's power was based?

Furthermore, the British imperialist education that was imparted to "natives" was scarcely a curriculum for inculcation of inferiority complexes. Especially among the Parsees, it filled the younger generation with a sense of potentialities awaiting them that would challenge their will. A publication in 1862 reported: "The English education has worked a great change during the last twenty years . . . Among the young class there is almost a social revolution in manners and ways of life. Most of the Hindoo and expensive ceremonies and customs are in a fair way of being swept away."[166] Jamsetji Tata himself was a scholarship student, a "Green Scholar," at Elphinstone College, where he received an English liberal education.[167]

The higher learning reinforced the phenomenon of generational revolt in the House of Tata. After World War I, a favorite nephew of Tata's, Shapurji Saklatvala, became the only Communist member in the British

Parliament.[168] Saklatvala, having served the Tata Iron and Steel Company well as a geologist-prospector searching for iron ores in the Indian jungles, was appointed to its Manchester office. Becoming a member of the National Liberal Club, he had one day a "furious argument" with Lord John Morley, the Secretary of State for India; thereupon convincing himself that Liberalism was a hypocrisy, Saklatvala soon afterward, in 1910, joined the Independent Labor Party. Responsive to the call of the Communist International after the First World War for world revolution, Saklatvala in 1920 joined the Communist Party of Great Britain. He won election to Parliament as a labor member in 1922 from a London constituency, and in 1924 a seat as a communist candidate, despite the opposition of the official Labor Party.[169] In the British Parliament this Parsee Indian moved resolutions on behalf of human rights and Indian independence. Did he ever wonder whether such liberties would exist in the Communist world that he was helping to fashion?

No matter what the defects, however, in the logic and evidence of its indictment, the ideological emotion of anti-imperialism was contagious among the successive generations of the educated in the "backward" countries. Not unlike the Roman Christian Apologists who found a common platform with barbarian invaders, their anti-imperial successors, though Marxist in idiom, found in the Third World leaders a group of allies who regarded Western civilization with the same feelings of envy, admiration, and destructiveness that the barbarian chiefs had had for the Roman Empire. Later chiefs of new anti-Western states have directed an intense animus against Western civilization that fed disproportionately upon the growing sense of guilt, defeat, and impotence among Western intellectuals. They were themselves frequently the marginal offshoots of Western universities. Abdullah Tariki, the co-founder of OPEC (the Organization of Petroleum Exporting Countries), learned how to be "an effective radical" at the University of Texas; a prime minister of Libya, Suleiman Maghrabi, took his Ph.D. degree at George Washington University, and evidently earned a post-graduate sentence to jail for organizing an oil workers' strike;[170] and the Sheik Zaki Yamani, oil minister of Saudi Arabia since 1962, spent four years at Harvard, and subsequently enjoyed six residences—at Jidda, Riyadh, Taif, Beirut, Lausanne, and London, thereby having several stages upon which to alternate the characters he played—the native Moslem in Jidda kneeling before an Allah and his prophet, or the sophisticated diplomat in London taking pleasure in threatening to make Western industrial civilization stand on its head.[171] Middle Eastern potentates newly enriched by European and American oil revenues, and Arab terrorists subsidized by oil profits from Libya to Iran who bought their weapons from eager Soviet representatives, relished the predicament of Western nations unable, as in the days of the Barbary pirates, to enforce civilized standards in the Mediterranean.

The animus against civilization, as Freud pointed out, can take strange political forms, and perhaps even issue in the guise of anti-imperialist ideology. Colonel Muammar-el-Qaddafi, the ruler of Libya, who had long depicted himself as a fundamentalist disciple of Moslem doctrine, threatened to turn Libya "into a Communist nation," allied firmly with the Soviet Union.[172] It might seem paradoxical for Moslem theology and Leninist dialectic to merge, until one remembers that both can share a common resentment of Western civilization.

F. The Altruistic Ingredient in Progressive Imperialism

The tenacity of the imperialist theme in history is grounded in the fact that it is not solely a matter of money-seeking or even power-seeking; joining not only the aggressive and accumulational drives in human nature, it also expresses the agapic, possibly in some ultimate sense, as well as the "erotic" in man. A duality of drives characterizes those themes of history that are persistent, repetitive, and invariant. Around these themes alternating sets of motives can cluster. If imperialism has satisfied impulses for glory and accumulation, it has also satisfied the altruistic, the selfless, and the identificational loyalties of men. The young Oxonians and parsons' sons who, toward the end of the nineteenth century sought careers in the African colonial service, were doubtless much influenced by the philosophy of social idealism that Thomas Hill Green had earlier expounded with a moral force that continued to transmit itself through the revered Master of Balliol College, Benjamin Jowett. "At the close of the Victorian Age, one-sixth of the Indian Civil Service were drawn from Balliol men, as were three consecutive Governors-General."[173]

The desire for glory itself is a complex of latticed emotions: to the satisfaction of self-love and pride is united a longing for the approbation of those whom one most honors, reveres, or loves, or whose love one would have—a pleasure in one's demonstration of mastery combined with a wish for the sanction of tradition. And the agapic, altruistic component in imperialism can rise above the aggressive and accumulational. The enactment of educational opportunities in India, for instance, in 1833, was a step Britain took that contravened its economic interest. By granting an education to an Indian elite, Lord Macaulay noted in the course of the debate, Britain was making it probable that India would some day become independent. "The sceptre may pass away from us," he said in 1833.[174] With their English learning the Indian students would imbibe rationalist and liberal ideas, the directional landmarks of Magna Carta and the Petition of Right, Milton's *Areopagitica* and Bentham's utilitarianism, and later Harold J. Laski's liberal Marxism at the London School of Economics.[175] Thus it was that in 1941, Jawaharlal Nehru, later

India's first prime minister, wrote: "In India today, the middle-class intellectual is the most revolutionary force."[176] A Marxist might rebut that since the maintenance itself of the imperialist, exploitative system required the education of a native clerical, administrative class, the existence of the latter was no evidence for selfless, altruistic motives in the imperialist psyche. But if that were so then the supply of those educated could have been matched to the bureaucratic demand. Instead, however, an ethical decision was made to increase greatly the student population. The consequent growth of an intellectual class, largely unemployed or misemployed, made the social soil fertile for the spread of nationalist and socialist ideas. A backward economic culture and society failed to satisfy the intellectuals' ambition. Underlying this whole development, however, had been the initial English decision, based on an ethical, contra-economic altruistic conception of one's duty to humanity to bring education to Indian youth; ethical vocation prevailed over economic calculation.

What was true in the case of India was true of the British Empire generally. A duality of motive characterized the history of the major imperialist decisions of policy. Britain, for example, after 1807 began a campaign for the universal abolition of the slave trade by all nations. Its aim was in part to assist its own West Indian planters in their plight, occasioned when their own importation of slaves had been abolished; the government was undoubtedly concerned they would be at a disadvantage in competing with Spanish Cuba and Portuguese Brazil, which still allowed the slave trade. Nonetheless, the original British reform was still primarily the outcome of an ethic of human freedom, which continued to exert its imperative on political policy. John Locke, Britain's most representative philosopher, had written: "Slavery is so vile and miserable an estate of man, and so directly opposite to the generous temper and courage of our nation, that 'tis hardly to be conceived that an Englishman, much less a gentleman, should plead for't."[177] The same John Locke, however, as an administrator of slave-owning colonies in America and principal author of the *Fundamental Constitutions of Carolina*, stipulated that every freeman "shall have absolute power and authority over his negro slaves." He regarded slaves as captives taken in a just war; he was satisfied, as Peter Laslett writes, "that the forays of the Royal Africa Company were just wars of this sort."[178] Thus acquisitive and altruistic motives could co-exist and alternate in their dominance.

The religious, humanitarian ingredient in British imperialism is now denigrated, but to Britons of the nineteenth century, members during the Victorian age of such associations as the London Missionary Society, it was real enough. David Livingstone became a household word because, as Margery Perham wrote, he rekindled "the British humanitarian sentiment towards the coloured man," by concentrating it "upon the interior of tropical Africa." Traveling alone but for his African aides, he seemed like

a wandering knight, seeking holiness through noble works. It was Livingstone who revealed "the terrible fact that an Arab slave trade was even
then piercing deeply into the continent from the east and . . . draining it
of its life-blood." He awoke the Western conscience. Arabs, penetrating
into the Great Lakes regions and arming warlike tribesmen to serve as
their auxiliaries, raided villages, massacred the fighting men, and enslaved
the survivors: "The rough castrating, with heavy mortality, of youths,
destined as eunuchs for Eastern havens; the callous casual killing; the
indignities of the slave market," the sale to Arabia, to the Persian Gulf, or
even India, then ensued. It was estimated "that as early as 1840, 40,000 to
45,000 slaves passed through the Zanzibar market annually, of whom half
were exported, and with the slavers' improving weapons and wider pene-
tration the number must have risen steadily." According to Livingstone
and other observers, "for each one of the slaves who reached the markets
alive, some five or six others . . . must have died."[179]

For all his dedication to the Christian mission, Livingstone was a
man of Scottish common sense. He frankly conjoined "commerce and
Christianity," free trade and the free church, one might say, as the inseparable instruments for the salvation of the Africans. He enunciated his
imperialist creed in a famous lecture at Cambridge University in 1857
that was greeted with a reception "so enthusiastic that literally there were
volley after volley of cheers":

> The natives of Central Africa are very desirous of trading, but their
> only traffic is at present in slaves, of which the poorer people have an
> unmitigated horror; it is therefore most desirable to . . . open a way for
> the consumption of free productions, and the introduction of Chris-
> tianity and Commerce . . . These two processes of civilization—Chris-
> tianity and Commerce—should ever be inseparable. . . . By trading with
> Africa, also, we should at length be independent of slave labour.[180]

The horror that Livingstone had experienced at the ravages caused by the
Arab slave raids, the dead and mutilated among the smoking ruins,[181]
aroused all his conviction that the Christian higher ethic, with its concept
of the worth of the human soul, was a timelessly significant message.
Livingstone believed that African misery would be alleviated only when
their souls and bodies alike were saved.

Neither a theologian nor a mystic, Livingstone was likewise no primitivist adulator of native cultures. He found no "noble savage" in central
Africa.[182] "The more intimately I become acquainted with barbarians, the
more disgusting does heathenism become," he wrote in his journal.[183] But
he felt an evangelist's responsibility for the misery of these abject human
beings. When the unconverted native youth, Sehamy, who had marched
with him on journeys—four hundred miles on foot—and, praying together, had died of fever, Livingstone poured forth his grief: "Poor

Sehamy? Where art thou now? Where lodges thy soul tonight? . . . I could now do anything for thee. I could weep for thy soul . . . Oh, am I guilty of the blood of thy soul, my poor dear Sehamy? . . . Help me, O Lord Jesus, to be faithful to everyone."[184]

Without complacency or self-satisfaction, and avoiding the pitfall of martyrdom, he fulfilled what he took to be his task. He had a discoverer's ambition, and he achieved renown for his geographical discoveries, but that ambition was not what drove him to Africa.[185] Put to work as a boy in a cotton factory at the age of ten, buying a Latin grammar out of his first week's wages, becoming a spinner at eighteen, and always delighting in scientific works and books of travel, Livingstone was stirred by a conception of work that would advance a redeeming love. In this mood, he chanced to read an "Appeal to the Churches for qualified medical missionaries." The young workingman sought out the London Mission and found his vocation. He was indeed a Jude the Obscure turned religious imperialist, except that no Arabella seduced him, and his enemies were barbarian ignorance, slave traders' cruelty, and the jungle's heat and disease.[186] His character evoked the admiration and goodwill of whomever he encountered—Portuguese soldiers, Arab slave traders, and cannibal chiefs. He endured betrayals and desertions; when a porter absconded with his medicine chest on an expedition in 1867 he wrote sadly: "Feel as if I had received my death sentence." Livingston could never become hardened to the horrors of massacres, slave-raiding, and cannibalism that he witnessed; they always depressed him. Clawed by a lion so that his left arm was always impaired,[187] ambushed by swarms of mosquitoes, and running the gauntlet of spears, spiders, and stinging ants, his stores stolen or sold by unscrupulous Arabs and Africans, stumbling with paralysis, dysentery, and hemorrhoids, he never faltered in his mission, and died on an expedition. To his Cambridge audience, he spoke of African women as he would of Englishwomen: "They would be much handsomer if only they would let themselves alone—though unfortunately this is a failing by no means peculiar to African ladies."[188] The president of the Royal Geographical Society could write with little hyperbole that no man had fulfilled more completely his idea of "a perfect Christian gentleman" and that he would be a model "of singular nobleness of design and of unflinching energy and self-sacrifice."

In conjoining commerce and Christianity, Livingstone, like Lord Hailey later, enunciated the dual source of the great accomplishment of capitalist imperialism. It availed itself of the duality of men's motivation, of their self-concern as well as their altruism, to build higher standards of living and civilization for native people. African traders trying to sell goods brought new wares and new comforts to backward peoples. And, as one writer states, "demand for European consumer goods was in reality the only positive force directing the African away from the traditional values of the tribe."[189] Capitalist diffusion brought the world's greatest rise of consumers' needs among primitive peoples; it also, however, brought ideology to the new intellectuals.

Curiously, an unforeseen consequence of Livingstone's work was that a century later the leaders of the African independence movements were "mission boys," that is, youngsters who had gotten their education at schools conducted by missionaries.[190] Religious culture has always had its strains and incompatibilities with business culture. Whoever has lived in an imperialist colony has observed the tension that exists between the governmental functionaries and businessmen, on the one hand, and the clerical missionaries on the other; the former suspect the latter as incipient troublemakers, and they are not altogether wrong,[191] for the precepts of conduct that the churches impart, their moral advocacy of the poor, their prophetic denunciations of the rich, always are ill-matched with the prerogatives of the ruler. The native who is taught to read his catechism will also then be able to read a strike leaflet. Thus, Kwame Nkrumah, later the first prime minister of the Gold Coast, was both pupil and teacher in Catholic elementary schools before he went to America to study in 1935. Studying philosophy avidly—a subject generally quickening to revolutionary intellectuals—he then traveled to London in 1945, to sit at the feet, among others, of Britain's Marxist political scientist, Harold Laski. Campaigning later among his pre-literate countrymen to win votes for his Convention People's Party, he used the degrees and honors of imperialist education as a passport to power. Nkrumah made short shrift of his opponent Dr. Busia, Head of the Sociology Department at the University College: "People talk a lot about Dr. Busia, Dr. Busia. Who is Busia? He is not even good enough to undo my shoes. They say Busia is a learned man. Am I not an M.A.?" The crowd responded: "You are." "Am I not an M.Sc.?" The crowd responded in still louder tones. Then followed a dramatic pause, and Nkrumah spoke again: "People talk about Dr. Busia: Am I not an LL.D.?" The crowd was now beside itself, and shouted back, "You are."[192]

If ideas were weapons, then degrees could make dictators. The African anti-imperialist leaders were on occasion doctors of medicine or philosophy. Jomo Kenyatta, for instance, tactician of the terrorist Mau Mau movement and later president of Kenya, journeyed to England in 1931 and studied anthropology with Bronislaw Malinowski, the father of functionalism, at the London School of Economics; Kenyatta later published a doctoral dissertation, "Facing Mount Kenya." His anthropological thesis was a political manifesto as well, a call upon the Kikuyu to take pride in their culture as superior to the white man's civilization. His teacher Malinowski had once recommended the functionalist method in anthropology for its potential contribution to a well-managed imperialism.[193] Ideas, however, are multi-potential and mischievous in their application; left-wing functionalism could provide postulates for the revolutionary, anti-imperialist algebra.[194]

Thus Nkrumah, a child of Western education, learned from teachers who, like Laski, felt in large part that a decline of capitalist civilization was taking place. The African students tended, as African Marxists, to generalize this theory into the thesis that all white civilization was in decline. Nkrumah indicted the West for its alleged all-consuming purpose, the exploitation of his continent. "Thus all the imperialists without exception evolved the means, their colonial policies, to satisfy the ends, the exploitation of the subject territories . . . They were all rapacious . . . They took our lands, our lives, our resources and our dignity. Without exception, they left us nothing but our resentment, and later, our determination to be free."[195] It transpired, however, that Ghana under his rule (and that of his successors) for the next twenty years far exceeded in its indignities and cruelties anything that had been known under British imperialistic rule. "The long night of Nkrumaist rule left Ghanaian youth with little more than an impression that politics was a fraud and a sham."[196] Intellectuals especially suffered under that rule, for as with almost all Marxist rulers, Nkrumah had a suspicion of and aversion to "more intelligent and free-ranging minds."[197] The latter were humiliated under Nkrumah's dictatorship, imprisoned and exiled in ways never imagined when the imperialist governor, Sir Frederick Gordon Guggisberg, scion of a Polish Jewish peddler, had been responsible for the colony's rule.

As in the Gold Coast, so in Nigeria the efforts of British missionaries largely educated the generations of young Nigerians who led their movement for independence. Mainly financed by Calvinist Presbyterian Scots of modest economic means, by 1920 there were already 1602 mission schools in Eastern Nigeria, as compared to 160 government schools.[198] It is doubtful that those sincere supporters of the Lord's predestined will expected that their scholars would become Marxist determinists rather than Calvinist predestinarians, but even if they had, they would still probably have acted according to their religious vocation.

The republics of French Africa that achieved virtual independence under President Charles de Gaulle followed a route somewhat different from that taken by their fellow Africans in British colonies. The French black African colonies were generally lacking the oil or other natural resources of the British colonies—they had nothing like the oil of Nigeria or the cocoa of Ghana. Hence, they were inclined to maintain far closer ties with what was still, culturally, the French *métropole*. Their leaders, moreover, were unlike those of the British Africans in one notable respect: "Whereas the leaders of British West Africa—Nkrumah, Azikwe, and others—pursued their political studies in the United States [and England], the French African political chiefs pursued them in Paris."[199] With this cultural divergence went a philosophical one. British-trained Africans tended to be Marxist and positivist, like Nkrumah and Kenyatta; French-educated Africans tended to be, like Léopold Senghor, existentialists in philosophy. Even their Marxism was flavored with existentialism, and they were far more attracted to such a concept as "négritude" that expressed their voluntarist choice, rather than directly and "inevitably" enrolling themselves with the world "proletariat." More often, too, they were literary intellectuals in the tradition of the French governing élite, "la république des professeurs."[200]

III

A CASE STUDY
The Jews Under the Varieties of Imperialism

A. The Jews in Imperial Civilization: Ancient, Moslem, Dutch, English, and Napoleonic

Regressive imperialism is characterized by an animus against the rational culture of civilization. It is, as such, a form of rebellion, an anti-civilizational movement, an uprising energized by aggressive drives against cultural constraints. Genocidal behavior appears to be specifically characteristic of the imperialism of regressive societies, and has been so in our own time.

The Nazi imperialism of Adolf Hitler was a regressive imperialism driven by hatred, bestiality, and fanaticism, with none of those constructive, cosmopolitan, and creative emotions that have animated the world's classical imperialist movements, the Alexandrian and the Roman. Though Marxists denounced the Nazis ("Hitlerites" was the term they preferred to avoid the acronym for National Socialism), still in strict Marxist theory the Nazis did not merit the appellation of "imperialist," for from the Marxist standpoint, as I have noted, the essence of imperialism is its extraction of surplus value from a more backward population; a people that is exterminated, however, ceases to be a source of surplus value. Regressive imperialism, moreover, from the Tartar to the Nazi, is not confined to the destruction of backward peoples; it can be directed toward the extermination of societies and peoples either equally or more advanced than their own.

1. The Jews under the Alexandrian and Roman Imperialisms

The Jews' experience of imperialism throughout history has, however, mostly been a happy one; from the progressive imperialisms of Alexander and Julius Caesar down to the construction of new cities and new industries in New Zealand and South Africa in the nineteenth century, the Jews have felt their own creative social energies awakened by the imperialist opportunity.

Alexander the Great, as *The Jewish Encyclopedia* long ago observed, "had probably more influence on the development of Judaism than any one individual not a Jew by race."[1] His name became embellished with all sorts of legends. It was said that Alexander's benevolence to the Jews was founded on a dream he had had in which their high priest advised him to seek dominion over Asia. It was also said that he excused the Jews

from placing his statue in their temple; instead the priests that year named
their newborn sons after him. Alexander accepted Jewish recruits into
his army, but he generously allowed them to adhere to their own laws
and rituals; indeed, he is said to have allowed the Jews to be exempt
from their annual tribute every seventh (sabbatical) year. In Alexander's
imperialism the Jewish commercial class found the basis for extending
their trade; special privileges were accorded them in the newly-founded
city of Alexandria. As the British scholar Norman Bentwich wrote: "the
Jews on political and economic grounds, were a valuable element in his
[Alexander's] civilizing enterprise . . . [T]he effect of Alexander's action
in transplanting the Jews from Palestine to different points of the Empire
was to mark a new stage in the extent of the Jewish dispersion and a new
epoch in the history of civilization." Not only did they bring crafts and
trade but, as Josephus noted, to every city of the Greeks and barbarians
alike they introduced "our habit of resting on the seventh day."[2] And
under the Roman Empire as well the Jews found the social basis for an
important commercial role; according to Josephus, trade with Mesopotamia was controlled by Jews, as was the corn trade in Alexandria. The
Roman Empire made possible the great emigration of Jews from Palestine. Mostly voluntary in character, it was so extensive that as the philosopher Philo Judaeus of Alexandria noted: "No one country can contain the whole Jewish nation, by reason of its populousness; on which
account they frequent all the most prosperous and fertile countries of
Europe and Asia, whether islands or continents."[3] "[A] Jewish element
has penetrated into every city," wrote Strabo, the Roman-Greek geographer.[4] A whole section of Rome, noted Philo, "was occupied and inhabited by the Jews . . . And they were mostly Roman citizens, having
been emancipated; for, having been brought as captives into Italy, they
were manumitted by those who had bought them for slaves, without ever
having been compelled to alter any of their hereditary or national observances."[5] Philo Judaeus indeed recognized the achievement of the Roman
Empire as much as did any Roman writer. The assassination of Julius
Caesar affected the Jews "above all," noted the Roman historian Suetonius; they "flocked" to Caesar's bier "for several successive nights."
Then as Augustus became the first emperor, Philo observed, "all the
affairs of the state were in disorder and confusion; for the islands were in
a state of war against the continents, and the continents were contending
against the islands for the pre-eminence in honor . . . And then again,
great sections of Asia were contending against Europe, and Europe
against Asia, for the chief power and dominion; the European and Asiatic
nations rising up from the extremities of the earth . . . so that very nearly
the whole race of mankind would have been destroyed by mutual slaughter and made utterly to disappear, if it had not been for one man and one
leader, Augustus . . . who calmed the storms . . . healed the common

diseases which were afflicting both Greeks and barbarians . . . rendered the sea free from the vessels of pirates, and filled it with merchantmen . . . gave freedom to every city . . . increased Greece by many Greeces, and who Greecised the regions of the barbarians."[6]

From the time of Julius Caesar, under whose standard a Jewish contingent served in Egypt, the subsequent policy of the Roman emperors was mainly one of tolerance toward the Jews and their laws and customs. Apart from such a rare exception as during the reign of the virtually insane Caligula, the Jews were not required to worship the emperor.[7] Their communities maintained their autonomy, and Jewish soldiers were excused from service on their Sabbath.[8] "The Roman administration," notes A. N. Sherwin White, was "the consistent champion of Jewish privileges." Despite the rebellions in Judaea, "it is remarkable how the Roman government maintained its policy of protecting the privileges of the Diaspora."[9] The harsh measures that Hadrian decreed against the practices of Judaism were promulgated evidently only after the revolt of Bar Kochba in 132 A.D.

A large part of the Roman intellectual class, however, from the time of Cicero onward, was affected with a certain anti-Semitism, with a resentment for the Jews' intellectual pride and such institutions as their Sabbath and food observances.[10] Curiously, the Stoics, whose own cosmopolitan philosophy had Semitic roots, were especially hostile to the Jews; the enmity probably stemmed from the rivalry between two intellectual elites—the one deriving from the Greek philosophical culture, the other standing outside it and cultivating the values of the independent entrepreneur. Moreover, in the cities of Asia Minor and Syria, the Jews were regarded as being favored by the Roman administrators over their Greek neighbors because the latter were reputed to be "somewhat disloyal and anti-Roman."[11] And this anti-Semitism became an ingredient too in the doctrine of the late Christian emperors and the dominant Church Fathers. Precisely during the latter period of the decline of the Roman Empire, when its vulnerability to barbarian disvalues was augmented, anti-Semitism grew virulent; the Jewish population diminished rapidly in large part probably as a consequence of such external pressures.[12]

For all its heroism, the Jewish uprising of 66 A.D. against Roman rule must be regarded as having been essentially a Fundamentalist movement much like those in Middle Eastern Moslem countries today. Led by the Zealots, its program was on the affirmative side, to reinstate the absolute rule of God and the freedom of Israel, and on the negative side, to abolish the Roman census, tribute, and taxes. What the absolute rule of God would have meant when translated into specific institutions seemed vague and sometimes equivalent to a near anarchy, or more likely a religious or military dictatorship. The Zealot doctrine, from its first appearance in the agitation of Judas the Galilean, had nothing of the outlook of the rising Jewish merchant class with its far-flung connections throughout the Roman Empire. The Zealots' will to martyrdom, to their last stand at Masada in 70 A.D., would have hurtled the Jewish people into an extinction sanctified, in their eyes, by a pure theology.[13]

Pagan Roman emperors granted Roman citizenship to the Jews; Septimius Severus and Caracalla had opened all public offices to them without asking that they abandon their traditional religion. As late as the last decade of the fourth century the emperors, still defending the religious freedom of the Jews, protected their synagogues. The Jews' political rights were partially abrogated early in the fifth century under Christian emperors when they were excluded from the army, imperial high office, and the secret service. The Jews kept the right, however, to hold municipal offices (the decurionates), but then in 438 A.D. were deprived of that prerogative.[14] Anti-Semitism grew as the Roman Empire declined.

2. The Jews under Turkish Imperialism

During the period of feudal retrogression in early medieval Europe, when Roman imperial unity became a vague memory in people's minds, the Jewish population almost reached the vanishing point. According to the estimate of Irving Agus, "in the year 800 . . . the Jews of Northern Italy, Germany and France, must have numbered no more than eight to ten thousand souls." Thus, "the ancestors of Ashkenazic Jewry, in the year 800 C.E., numbered but about ten thousand." As late as 1159 to 1173, Benjamin of Tudela, journeying through most of the European Jewish settlements, added up a total of only 11,574 adult men.

The Asian and North African Jews, on the other hand, found a renewed vigor and prosperity under the aegis of the expanding, aggressive Moslem imperialism. The condition of the central community of Jews, the Babylonian, had deteriorated under the pre-Islamic Sassanid dynasty, but when that crumbled under the Arab attack and Mohammedan conquest in 637 A.D., writes Professor L. Rabinowitz, "the Jews entered upon a new era of prosperity. Jews and Nestorian Christians formed the bulk of the population between the Euphrates and the Tigris."[15] Having been persecuted by the last Persian kings, the Jews "rendered valuable assistance to the Mohammedans by whom their services were recognized and rewarded." The Moslem conquest of Egypt brought similar good tidings to the Jews: "In Egypt, too, Jewry regained its former glory . . . The Jewish people once more grew so populous and affluent that for centuries to come Egypt as well as the neighboring Kairouan became centers of science and Jewish learning."[16] Palestinian Jewry likewise, which under Byzantine rule had been oppressed and decimated, recuperated its powers.

Across the Mediterranean in Spain, "two centuries of ruthless persecution" on the part of the Visigothic kingdom also ended in 711 A.D.

with the successful invasion of the Moslem Arabs.[17] There was a respite from the forcible Christian baptisms, the forced sale or confiscation of possessions, the prohibition of commercial activity, the seizure of children, and the enslavement of elders. The Jews of Toledo in desperation had wanted in 693 A.D. to promote an Arab invasion; apprehended in their plot, they were obliterated as a community by the Visigothic King Egica.[18] When the Arab assault came in 711 A.D. with full force, the Jews, organizing themselves into military units, fought with the Arabs against the Christian princelings.[19] "In this way," as Rabinowitz writes, "there began for the Jews of Spain a period of unexampled prosperity and influence which was to develop into what is known in Jewish history as the Golden Age of Spain."[20]

As the trade routes between Christian Europe, the Moslem domains, Confucian China, and Hindu India were severed or decayed with desuetude during the early Middle Ages, the last links of international trade were maintained by Jewish merchants, especially that strange group of Jewish cosmopolitan caravaneers known as the Radamites, whose identity survived in the notation of an Arab manuscript. The Jews, as Henri Pirenne, the learned Belgian scholar, concluded, were "the only persons who were still engaged in commerce."[21] The Radamite Jews, according to a ninth century Arab geographer, knew the diverse languages of men: "These merchants speak Arabic, Persian, Roman, the language of the Franks, Andalusians and Slavs. They journey from west to east, from east to west, partly on land, partly by sea."[22] They followed torturous alternative routes across the Mediterranean to southern Arabia, then by sea to the Far East, or through Asia Minor and Mesopotamia to the Persian Gulf, or across northern Africa to Syria and Babylonia, or across Bohemia, to Southern Russia and central Asia to China. They exchanged furs, swords, and slaves, for spices—musk, aloes, cinnamon, camphor. These Jewish merchants expressed in an embryonic fashion the human yearning for a transnational sovereignty; in that era, as a small, politically powerless community, less pariahs than detachees, they could provide the agencies for an international trade otherwise impeded by religious animosities. "Christians could not trade in Mohammedan countries or could Moslems in Christian countries; consequently an opening was left for Jews, who were tolerated in both spheres as commercial intermediaries."[23] Such commercial activities were the seed-bed of a later commercial imperialism, contributing to the common bond of trading interests that would prove more powerful than the mutually repelling force of religious doctrines, and thus acting as the primary social force for human rationality.

Turkish imperialism later served likewise as a liberating force among the Mediterranean peoples—European, Middle Eastern and African— reaching its zenith during the reign of Suleiman the Magnificent (1520-

1566). Like the Roman and the Alexandrian imperialism, his too was to a considerable extent what we have called a "participatory imperialism," one in which all peoples brought into the empire have opened to them all careers—commercial, industrial, and professional; only "believers," however, were eligible for official posts in the military or the government. Despite that restriction, many persons not Turks by origin, but Bosnians, Dalmatians, Bulgarians, Hungarians, Sicilians, and Jews, could aspire to the highest places in the Moslem empire and were among its most powerful personages.[24] The Imperial ambassador at Constantinople, de Busbecq, wrote in 1555 a description of the Sultan's court:

> There was not in all that grave assembly a single man who owed his position to aught save his valor and his merit. No distinction is attached to birth among the Turks; the deference to be paid to a man is measured by the position he holds in the public service . . . It is by merit that men rise in the service, a system which insures that posts should only be assigned to the competent. Each man in Turkey carries in his own hand his ancestry and his position in life, which he may make or mar as he will. Those who receive the highest offices from the Sultan are for the most part the sons of shepherds or herdsmen, and so far from being ashamed of their parentage, they actually glory in it, and consider it a matter of boasting that they owe nothing to the accident of birth; for they do not believe that high qualities are either natural or hereditary . . . Among the Turks, therefore, honors, high posts, and judgeships are the rewards of great ability and good service. If a man be dishonest, or lazy, or careless, he remains at the bottom of the ladder, an object of contempt.[25]

When Spanish Jews were finally expelled from their country in 1492 by Ferdinand and Isabella, they found a warm welcome from the Turkish rulers.[26] Embattled with Catholic Spain for supremacy in the Mediterranean, the Turks regarded the Jews as the most trustworthy of allies. "The Christian world, true to its record rather than its name, was with rare exceptions closed to the refugees. Only the Moslem world was open." To Turkey the Jews brought handicrafts that the Turks lacked and commercial abilities that could compete with those of Venetian merchants. Every ship brought Jewish immigrants to the Turkish domain: "They introduced the technical processes of the manufacture of firearms, gunpowder and cannon" soon to be used in battle against Spanish warships; the sound of blacksmithies and iron foundries echoed in the Jewish quarters; Jewish glassmakers, textile and dye manufacturers, metalworkers, gold and silver miners brought an industrial renaissance to the Turkish domain.[27] The Geographer to the King of France, Nicolas de Nicolay, reported from Turkey that "they [the Jews] have in their hands the most and greatest traffic of merchandise and ready money that is in the Levant

. . . Likewise, they have amongst them workmen of all sorts and handicrafts, most excellent, and especially of the Maranes, of late banished and driven out of Spain and Portugal, who, to the great detriment and damage of Christianity, have taught the Turks diverse inventions, crafts and engines of war, to make artillery, harquebuses, gunpowder, shot and other ammunition; they have also there set up printing, not before seen in those countries."[28] The Turks' conquest of Egypt in 1517 added further to the commercial sea routes; on the island of Rhodes, linked to Alexandria, Jewish craftsmen, manufacturers, and merchants were exceptionally active, especially in the textile industry.[29] Despite discriminatory taxes, the Jews attained their highest prosperity under the liberal and constructive reign of Suleiman. Turkish military power rose, perhaps equal to that of Christian Europe, and Turkish cities, with resplendent architecture, overlooked the Mediterranean. Jewish merchants in Italian, Serbian, and French ports enjoyed the diplomatic protection of the Turkish government.[30] And when in 1556, under papal prodding, more than fifty Jews were executed as heretics in the Italian seaport of Ancona, in retaliation a boycott was proclaimed under Jewish auspices from Constantinople against the town of Ancona, the first instance in modern times of a trading boycott used in defense of liberties.[31] The singular career of Don Joseph Nasi (1524-1579), Duke of Naxos, "without question the most prominent and most powerful Jew in the world" in his generation, and evidently the prototype for Christopher Marlowe's vindictive portraiture in *The Jew of Malta,* was only possible in the relatively liberal precincts of the Ottoman Empire.[31]

3. Jewish Freedom under Seventeenth Century Dutch and English Imperialism

The burgeoning of the commercial imperialism of the Dutch towns in the seventeenth century opened a new era of freedom for the Jews, to be followed shortly by a similar liberation under the contemporaneous English imperialism. The story of the way "bourgeois" trade helped advance the rationality of the human mind is one of the most astonishing in history. The French philosopher, René Descartes, fleeing from the "servile restrictions" of his native France to work for many years in the calm of Amsterdam, described to a friend on May 15, 1631 the efflorescence of freedom in a bourgeois, imperialist town:

> You may pardon my zeal if I advise you to choose Amsterdam for your retreat. . . . [I]n this great town where I now am, there being not a soul but myself who is not in business, every one is so engrossed with his profits that I could live in it all my life without ever being seen by any one. I go to walk every day amid the Babel of a great thoroughfare with as much liberty and repose as you would find in your garden-

alleys. . . . If there be pleasure in seeing the fruit growing in your or-
chards . . . think you there is not as much in seeing the vessels arrive
which bring us in abundance all the produce of the Indies and all that
is rare in Europe? What other place could you choose in all the world
where all the comforts of life and all the curiosities which can be
desired are so easy to find as here? What other country where you can
enjoy such perfect liberty, where you can sleep with more security,
where there are always armies on foot for the purpose of protecting us,
where poisoning, treacheries, calumnies are less known, and where there
has survived more of the innocence of our ancestors?[33]

The Spanish and the Portuguese Jews who found a haven in the Netherlands beginning around 1593 experienced a similar joy in their new-found
freedom. The forces of the Spanish Empire having been finally defeated
in 1581, the United Provinces of the Netherlands, wishing to hold onto the
fruits of their war of independence, enacted a proclamation of religious
freedom. Thus Marrano refugees later began to emigrate to the Netherlands, and in those Dutch towns that accorded the most religious liberty
to their citizens, the Jews prospered.

Then in 1655 a curious diplomatic mission was undertaken: Rabbi
Menasseh ben Israel proceeded as a self-authorized envoy to Oliver Cromwell's government in England to negotiate the admission of Jews into that
realm.[34] Rabbi Menasseh's pamphlet *Humble Addresses* narrated how
much the Jews had contributed to Dutch imperialism: "In this most
renowned City of Amsterdam, where there are no lesse than 400 families . . . how great a Trading and Negotiation they draw to that City,
experience doth sufficiently witness. They have no lesse than three hundred houses of their own, enjoy a good part of the West and East-Indian
Compagnies."[35]

Rabbi Menasseh even dedicated a metaphysical essay of his to the
materially beneficent Dutch West India Company, for Amsterdam Jews
had joined with the Company to set up a colony in distant Pernambuco,
Brazil; they fought hard, as soldiers and officers, to defeat the Portuguese
in Brazil. The Jewish population of Dutch Brazil actually numbered 1,450
persons, almost as much as Amsterdam Jewry and more than half the
colony. Rabbi Isaac da Fonseca Aboab was deputized to serve as their
spiritual leader from 1642 to 1654. Twice he guided them through the
ordeals of Portuguese invasion; many Jews had already starved to death
during the first siege, when, as by a miracle, a Dutch fleet brought rescue.
Unfortunately, however, their numbers having been reduced by half
through war and famine, they were unable to withstand a second invasion
abetted by Negro insurrectionists. The Jews abandoned their colonial
enterprise. Most returned sadly to Amsterdam, where Rabbi Aboab recalled the Portuguese as "an abomination of Amalek."[36]

A handful of the Jewish colonists, meanwhile, found their way that year, 1654, to New Amsterdam (later New York), also a colony of the Dutch West India Company. Its governor, Peter Stuyvesant, not desirous of receiving them, asked permission of his Company home directors to expel them. The directors, however, denied his request in 1655 "especially," in their words, "because of the considerable loss sustained by this nation, with others, in the taking of Brazil, as also because of the large amount of capital which they still have invested in the shares of this company."[37] Thus a handful of Dutch-Brazilian Jews became the first Jewish immigrants in the history of New York, and a tradition of religious freedom was inaugurated under the auspices of the republican imperialism of the Dutch West India Company. Though the Amsterdam Jews excommunicated Baruch Spinoza in 1656, they would nonetheless have endorsed the philosopher's paean to Amsterdam: "The city of Amsterdam reaps the fruit of this freedom in its own great prosperity and in the admiration of all other people. For in this most flourishing state, and most splendid city, men of every nation and religion live together in the greatest harmony, and ask no questions before trusting their goods to a fellow-citizen, save whether he be rich or poor, and whether he generally acts honestly, or the reverse. His religion and sect is considered of no importance."[38]

The economist of the Netherlands, Pieter de la Court, thus rightly associated the freedom of trade in Holland with its religious and intellectual liberty: "Freedom or toleration in and about the service or worship of God, is a powerful means to preserve many inhabitants in Holland, and allure foreigners to dwell among us."[39] Thus contemporary liberalism was born in the setting of the Dutch imperialist towns.

Meanwhile, the mission of Menasseh ben Israel to England had succeeded, though indirectly, in securing the readmission of Jews to England. Menasseh made a strong personal impression on the Lord Protector, Oliver Cromwell. In Cromwell's eyes the Jews were potential allies for bringing more foreign trade and foreign experience to Britain's shores. They were, moreover, trustworthy co-fighters in the pending war against Spain, for having endured the Inquisition, they bore no more love for Spain than a Jew liberated from the Gulag Archipelago would have felt toward the Soviet Union.[40] Cromwell resolutely brought the matter before the Council of State, but serious opposition developed; an Advisory Conference, though agreeing that the law barring the Jews was invalid, was largely hostile toward them. Popular opinion, moreover, was stirred by pamphlets and rumors against the Jews. It was said, for instance, that they wished to transform St. Paul's Cathedral into a synagogue, and acquire the Bodleian Library at Oxford.[41] A fourth meeting saw merchants appearing to express their fears of Jewish competition and a consequent decline of English trade. A variety of restrictions were proposed on the residence, religious worship, personal, and legal rights of Jews in case they were admitted. Finally, late in the night, Cromwell rose and said he had been listening to speeches that were a babel of discordances. To the fearful merchants he said: "You say they are the meanest and most despised of all people. So be it. But in that case what becomes of your fears? Can you really be afraid that this contemptible and despised people should be able to prevail in trade and credit over the merchants of England, the noblest and most esteemed merchants of the whole world?" Yet even Cromwell did not think it prudent to call the question for a vote. The Whitehall Conference was not reconvened. "Cromwell had decided that public opinion was too strong for him."[42]

Meanwhile, however, Spain had declared war on England. A crucial legal case presented itself. The small circle of London Maranos, refugees from Spain though several were, risked being adjudged Spaniards by nationality and having their ships and property sequestrated. Joined by Menasseh ben Israel, they petitioned Cromwell directly, signing their names in their Hebraic form and dropping the Spanish surnames. One Portuguese Jew, explaining that he was not a Spaniard but "of the Hebrew Nation," told how his family had been hounded by the Inquisition, his mother maimed, his kindred burnt at the stake, while he was saved by the sanctuary provided by England's soil. Whereupon the Council of State after deliberation restored to him his sequestrated property.[43] Thus it was that by a concrete decision in a specific case, with the catalytic contrast posed by war with the Spanish empire, Britain's imperialism chose the liberal, progressive direction.

As unflinching enemies of Spanish hegemony, the Jews became allies of both the British and Dutch imperialisms. British imperialism in the West Indies followed the Dutch model. "In peace and in war, Dutch competition, Dutch influence, and Dutch example largely determined the nature of English colonial policy, as it came to be formulated in the second half of the seventeenth century."[44] In December, 1654, Cromwell launched the first naval and military expedition designed to conquer Spanish possessions in the West Indies. It became known as the "Western Design," and its conquest of Jamaica, after much fighting and losses for the English forces, marked the first addition to Britain's domain through an imperialist war.[45] It followed an ultimatum in which Cromwell, through the Spanish ambassador, demanded both freedom of religion and trade for English subjects in the Spanish colonies, to which the ambassador replied that this was equivalent to demanding "of his Master his two eyes." When the English captured Jamaica in 1655, they found Jews already there, principally persons who had fled from Brazil when it was re-conquered by the Portuguese from the Dutch .[46] According to an old document, because of those Brazilian wars, there were "swarms of Jews, formerly found in the West Indies."[47]

Jewish participation in British imperialism thus began early. Sir

Thomas Lynch, governor of Jamaica in the West Indies, was instructed by the British government to encourage Jewish immigration. Some Jamaican merchants, fearing the competition, opposed the step and asked instead for expelling all Jews beyond a restricted quota. Jamaican planters, on the other hand, wanted Jews' enterprise to break the merchants' oligopoly. The governor took his stand for the Jews; though they have, he explained, "great stocks and correspondence," they "are not numerous enough to supplant us, nor is it to their interest to betray us to the Spaniards. Furthermore, ye cannot find any but Jews that will adventure their good and person (against buccaneering) to get trade."[48] Governor Lynch, in accordance with the new treaty with Spain, had been ordered to end the buccaneering that flourished in that celebrated era of Henry Morgan, whose pirates, under the guise of privateering, pillaged ships and towns, and tortured inhabitants, soldiers, and sailors.[49] The Jews, reputedly the most courageous in the campaign, evidently made the best commercial imperialists for Britain.

As Gedalia Yogev has shown, many Jewish firms traded with the West Indies, especially in Jamaica and Barbados. To the London Jewish merchants, however, trade with Spain and Portugal and the importation of gold and silver to Britain were more significant; also the trade with Portuguese Goa brought access to coral diamonds.[50] The monopoly held by the English East India Company precluded direct Jewish participation in British imperialism in India until between 1680 and 1690, when the Company, with misgivings, agreed to allow Jewish merchants to settle in Madras. Two Jews during the next century became influential in the Company's affairs, though none was ever elected a Director.[51] But until 1786, "there were only very short periods without at least one Anglo-Jewish diamond merchant at Madras."[52] If London became the center for the purchase of uncut diamonds, Amsterdam Jewry became and remained the unchallenged center for their actual industrial cutting and polishing. The Jewish role in British imperialist trade had a curious social consequence: when several ships of the English East India Company arrived home in 1679, the Company announced the adjournment of sales "because the Jews were engaged in their feast of Tabernacles."[53]

4. Jewish Liberation under Napoleonic Imperialism

Modern history is often said to have begun with the French Revolution and Napoleon's advent to power. The rise of revolutionary and Napoleonic imperialism finally afforded to European Jewry the chance to break the ghetto walls and partake of equality and justice. In May 1800, General Napoleon Bonaparte, First Consul of France, leading his armies into Italy, won a great victory at Marengo and virtually incorporated most of the Italian mainland into the French empire; for the first time since

Rome fell, an Italian unity was restored. Under French imperial rule or guidance, writes Cecil Roth: "The equality of the Jews before the law was solidly established once more. Everywhere, they took advantage of the opportunities which opened up before them in this exciting new world. They expressed hyperpatriotic devotion to the emperor in prose and verse, both Hebrew and Italian. They were enrolled in the army, and laid down their lives in every campaign. The legend survives of how on the retreat from Moscow the Italian Jewish soldiers sang the Hebrew psalms round the campfire to the tune of the Marseillaise. They joined the National Guard, many becoming officers. For the first time, they were admitted to take a part in civic life."[54]

Under the new republic in Venice an Italian Jew, the president of the Chamber of Commerce, was ennobled for the first time; all discriminatory legislation was abrogated so that Jews could again own land and till the soil. The public schools were opened to Jewish children. The Jewish community at Trieste, still under Austrian rule, envied their brethren living under the liberties of the French empire. When Napoleon was defeated in 1814, "after a generation that had seen what freedom meant, conditions of the deepest degradation were re-established over the greater part of the Peninsula. Everywhere the Jews lost, not only the political rights which they had enjoyed with their neighbors under Napoleonic rule, but also the social rights."[55]

Napoleon's imperial project, consciously modeled on the Roman, followed its example likewise in dealings with the religions of foreign lands. General Bonaparte reminded the Army of the Orient as it embarked for the invasion of Egypt that "the Roman legions used to protect all religions," and that they should be as tolerant toward the mosques as they had shown themselves toward convents and synagogues.[56] The recollection of this liberalizing imperialism led the customarily skeptical and sardonic Heinrich Heine to reserve the language of reverence in his poetry and prose for the figure of Napoleon the Emancipator. He wrote *The Grenadiers* in 1814 as a lad of fifteen, and afterward said, "I have never swerved from my faith in the Emperor. I have never ceased to doubt his advent—My Emperor—the ruler of the People for the People."[57]

B. Under the Spanish Regressive Imperialism

The Jews, by contrast, fared badly and tragically during the centuries of Spanish imperialism. It is incumbent upon us, therefore, to inquire in what significant respects Spanish imperialism differed from the British, the Roman, the Athenian, or the Dutch.

Spanish imperialism, in the first place, was pre-eminently an example of state imperialism, rather than capitalist. "The decisive factor," writes the historian Antonio Dominguez Ortiz, "was that the undertaking was conceived from the outset as a state enterprise, and the Spanish state was strong." The state controlled the men and merchandise crossing the Atlantic, and the succession of Spanish monarchs "yielded not an inch of their political and economic monopoly of the overseas possessions."[58] The corps of the Spanish state imperialists consisted chiefly of men from the intermediate class of the *hidalgos,* the Spanish feudal nobility—second sons, soldiers, and officials, a large proportion of whom, such as Cortés and Pizarro, derived from the impoverished sheep-rearing region of Estremadura. They had a thirst for command, power, renown, and titles of nobility, but their imperialist conception was confined to feudal categories; they could only extract tribute and reproduce feudal plantations and their counterpart, a feudal mining system.[59] But the analogue of the venturous businessmen, Roman, Athenian, or British, and of their commercial imperialisms, was relatively lacking. Spain, living on the exhausted heritage of chivalry and crusades, failed, as Roger B. Merriman notes, "to grasp any of the principles of sound economics, which were just beginning to emerge in the end of the sixteenth century, and were subsequently to become one of the chief controlling forces of the modern world."[60]

Moreover, the first empire builders seemed to lack successors. Spain's best soldiers and sailors of the sixteenth century found no comparable continuators in the seventeenth. In Britain and Holland captains of war were followed by captains of industry, but Spain, though flowering in literature and art, failed to achieve the maturation of military energies into industrial ones.[61] The expulsion of the Spanish Jews, followed by an Inquisition directed against the *conversos,* represented the opening victory of a regressive elite—supported by a mass hatred—against a progressive one. As Henry Kamen, the most recent historian of the Inquisition, writes: "The expulsion of the Jews represented the victory of the feudalistic nobility over the class most identified with commercial capitalism. And the discovery of America meant the opening of new frontiers to the ruling classes of Castile."[62] The feudal nobility had felt its pre-eminent role challenged by an urban, capitalist, bourgeois Jewry. Moreover, as Ortiz states, the Inquisition had "the support of the great mass of the Spanish people, who were old Christian and instinctively hostile to the middle class of Hebraic descent, its love of innovation."[63] The Portuguese section of the Iberian peninsula saw the very same story unfold: "Businessmen, almost all of them crypto-Jews, were being driven into emigrating with their capital to Spain, the Indies, and ultimately Holland."[64] Portuguese Marranos who left their country and tried to engage in banking in Spain, soon found themselves harried by the Inquisition. For the first time in history the requirement of *limpieza de sangre* (purity of blood) appeared, automatically excluding those of Jewish descent from Spanish state and economic organizations. The extirpation of capitalistic potential in Spain meant that its imperialist ventures would remain fixated at a near-feudal level for lack of the ability and entrepreneurial skill to go on to new enterprises, and it meant that the Spanish would recede into somnolence as their silver and gold mines were depleted. The Inquisition had cowed intellectual zest in the sciences, mathematics, and trade alike: "The inhabitants had been drilled into unimpeachable orthodoxy."[65] Sudden arrests depressed the economic markets with forebodings and uncertainty: "Thus, when in 1647 the Marrano merchant-prince, Duarte da Silva, was arrested, the exchange on Lisbon slumped by 5 percent on the Amsterdam house."[66] A "profound night of mystery and silence was perhaps the most terrifying weapon of the Spanish Inquisition."[67] The Spanish mind retrogressed: the great empires—Athens, Rome, Britain, France, Holland— had been animated by liberal ideas of reason, law, and the dignity of man. The Spanish rulers ousted such ideas, even suppressing the writings of the liberal Erasmus, the most popular author in Spain.[68]

For all its inflow of gold and silver, the Spanish state empire could not adapt itself to socio-technological change and proved unable to defeat decisively the smaller, capitalist English and Dutch nations. During the reign of Philip II, as the Spanish historian Jaime Vives, writes: "We find no capital invested in the country either to increase the productivity of the agricultural soil or to form commercial companies to exploit the oceanic world . . . Castile's failure to comprehend the capitalist world made it impossible for her to compete with Europe."[69] During the period 1557-1560, Philip II was obliged to announce the financial bankruptcy of Spain, the first of a series. At the end of his reign, half of the budget was required to service his debts. He persisted in looking at economic questions theologically. Advised that the Philippines were an unprofitable holding, he replied that to maintain the Catholic religion he would devote all the revenues of his kingdom. A Spanish economist observed in 1600 that Spain's middle class, "the middling sort" (los medianos), was gone; there were "only rich and poor," but "no harmonious mean"—"there are none of the middling sort." This was both the economic cause and consequence of a regressive imperialism, constrained and constricted, and the repression of the Jews was a significant aspect of it.[70]

The expulsion of the Jews, as Salvador de Madariaga has written, subsequently led them to play "an important part in the disruption of the Spanish Empire."[71] Enrolling themselves under the banner of the Turks, the English, and the Dutch, the Jews gave their arms and wealth to those nations that were embattled with the Spaniards. Don Joseph Nasi, ennobled by the Sultan Selim II as Duke of Naxos, fought the Spanish power in the Mediterranean. Jewish merchants managed to find their way in such numbers to Puerto Rico that in 1606 its Bishop warned of the inflow of heretical books that accompanied these Hebrew "scouts who come to find out all about the land and its strength." Jews in Spain lent a helping hand to Francis Drake on his raid that "singed" the Spanish emperor's beard, while Simon de Caceres, serving in the next century in the English expedition to Jamaica, proposed raising a Jewish force under the English flag to wrest Chile from the Spaniards. The Jews could take service in the bourgeois trading, competitive, capitalist imperialisms of the English, the Dutch, and the Turks. Their experience with Spanish state socialist imperialism, with its totalistic ideology, had a profound lesson for them.

Spain's colonial empire in the Americas mirrored the regressive aspects of the imperialistic center. From the first, the Spaniards of the "Hapsburg Imperialism" sought primarily to make their fortunes in New Granada and New Spain by the direct exploitation of native Indian labor, dragooned into mining compounds. At first, "Hapsburg Imperialism" was monarchial imperialism, for Columbus's first voyage of discovery "was authorized and financed as a venture of Queen Isabella," with its profits to accrue to her heirs. "[T]he Indies were treated as the direct and exclusive possession of the crown."[72] For a while in the early part of the sixteenth century the incomes, profits, and privileges were shared with proprietors, the adventurous *adelantados,* who were virtual satraps with a limited sovereignty. The monarchy, however, soon replaced them with more pliable royal governors. The kind of system whereby, for instance, Columbus's family was guaranteed a tenth of the profits of the West Indies, which indeed they received until 1536, was terminated;[73] instead, though the richest mines would be kept by the crown, they might be rented or leased or sometimes sold to private individuals.[74] But the Spanish colonial bureaucracy remained dominant, and a highly centralized regime controlled the economies of what were accurately called New Spain, or New Castile, or New Granada. As C. H. Haring, the historian of *The Spanish Empire in America,* wrote: A "petrifaction of institutional life, which may already be observed in the second half of the sixteenth century, is the characteristic feature of Spanish policy in the Indies throughout the rest of the Hapsburg era. The creative vigor of earlier times seems to have been wholly exhausted. . . . The town councils in the Indies . . . entered upon a period of frank decadence. . . . The tendencies to centralization and uniformity were accentuated. A mistaken policy in Spain was matched by a colonial bureaucracy marked by extreme complexity and routine."[75]

The Spanish monarchy, above all, exercised a strict supervision in selecting those who were allowed to emigrate to the colonies. The British, whether in their colonies in the North American eastern seaboard or South Africa, allowed dissenters, both political and religious, and every variety of economic adventurer to emigrate. "Spanish emigration," on the contrary, "was put through a fine-meshed sieve."[76] Religious dissenters, Protestants, foreigners, Jews, were all excluded; no Cecil Rhodes, Barney Barnato, Alfred Beit, or John Winthrop or Roger Williams could legally enter the Spanish domain.[77] Even reconciled heretics as well as recent converts from Islam and, later, their sons and grandsons, were excluded from Hispaniola. And if some eluded the administrative decrees, they still would have to scheme how to remain unnoticed by the Inquisition, which in Spanish America as in Spain, invigilated the purity of the Faith.[78] For not only in Spain but in its American empire, the Inquisition remained active, albeit to a lesser extent.

Jews, though *conversos,* still aroused enmity for their entrepreneurial activity, and mass outbreaks took place against persons of Jewish descent.[79] The statute, indeed, prohibiting Jews and *conversos* from migrating to the Spanish Empire was frequently a permeable membrane. "Many Jews came as members of the crew and then 'jumped ship' in Vera Cruz (where a Jewish community was established soon after the conquest of Mexico)."[80] Licenses for entry were not required of members of a ship's crew, and Jewish shipowners and ship captains joined in helping the illegal Jewish immigrants. Sometimes Jews, availing themselves of Christian names on tombstones, secured licenses in the names of the departed and took their families along as servants. All the devices and more that Franz Werfel's play *Jacobowsky and the Colonel* has made well known were used by Jewish imperialists. But all their lives, nonetheless, they remained apprehensive of the Inquisition's scrutiny.

The merchant class among the "Judaizers" fell most afoul of the Inquisition in Spanish America. In the viceroyalty of Peru during the years from 1580 to 1640, twenty-two merchants and thirteen commercial travelers were tried for the offence of "Judaizing." The *converso* merchants, "instinctively" practitioners of competitive capitalism, built up and controlled "much of the trade of South America," buying and selling in the international and intercolonial markets despite the mercantilist prohibitions of the shortsighted home country. The interventions of the Inquisition could thus provoke crisis and panic on the financial market. In August 1635, the Inquisition in Peru struck mightily at Jewish "capitalist" enterprise; it arrested eighty-one persons, of whom sixty-four were accused as "Judaizers." The exposure of this "grand conspiracy," as it was denominated, "caused a financial panic as creditors rushed to recover their debts before the Inquisition confiscated the property of those arrested."[81] *Conversos* still at large fled, and Peru became a land of uncertainty, confusion, and near economic ruin. Torture, imprisonment, the galleys, modes of penance, and the stake followed for the "Judaizers," among them "the wealthiest and most powerful merchant in Lima," Manuel Bautista Perez, owner of an extensive library, and benefactor of the University of San Marcos; after trying to commit suicide, he faced his death with "great severity and majesty."

Spanish Jews and "Judaizers" had from the first been drawn by the challenge of imperialist enterprise, the hope for deeds and designs that were beset with obstacles in cleric-ridden Spain. Two "New Christian" financiers had provided Queen Isabella with the funds that made possible Columbus's voyage—Luis de Santangel and Gabriel Sanchez; de Santangel's cousin had been burned at the stake, although Luis himself survived thanks to the uncertain bounty of Ferdinand of Aragon. The first governor of Nuevo Leon in Mexico, the conquistador Luis de Carvajal, believed himself a faithful Catholic; but among the more than a hundred relatives whom he enlisted as settlers were "Judaizers"; most of them, including a nephew and namesake, were tortured and executed, while the governor himself, disgraced and impoverished, died in jail.[82]

The universities that were early founded in Spanish America could never flourish in an ether of intellectual repression; despite an ample leisured middle class, theological curricula and disputation for several centuries provided the only intellectual provender. Moreover, notwithstanding the presumed Roman Catholic racial universalism, universities in Mexico and Peru refused by statute to admit Negroes and persons of mixed blood.[83] Not until the nineteenth century was the racial bar repealed in Peru.

Most distinctively, the Spanish imperialist regime decimated and even rendered extinct entire populations of Indian laborers. Early in the sixteenth century, the Indians in the Antilles were assigned by groups of fifty, a hundred, or more to work on farms, ranches, and mines: "The results were disastrous. Men and women were worked beyond their strength, the infant mortality was high, the birth rate declined. . . . And the consequence was the rapid disappearance of the 41,257 aborigines from the American islands."[84] The lot of the Indians in Peru became "completely disastrous," especially in the silver mines of Potosi and the Andean highlands; despite an effort begun in 1657 to alleviate conditions, several generations later matters remained "as bad as ever." From such a background sprang the sanguinary Indian revolt in 1780. As the Indian population diminished or vanished, Negro slaves were imported to replenish the ranks of forced labor. Very soon, by the end of the sixteenth century, the Negro population in such islands as Cuba, Puerto Rico, and Hispaniola, and along the coastal mainland from Vera Cruz to Venezuela, far exceeded the number of white Spaniards.[85] And in Spain, depopulation ensued because young men left to seek their imperial fortune, while others, young priests and monks, took the vow of celibacy; in the Spanish Empire, depopulation was the consequence of regressive cruelty.

Spanish imperialism thus was hardly akin to the commercial variety of that of the British merchants who bought and sold goods in India. The imperialism of the free-trading merchants, the pursuers of profits in the exchange of commodities, raised standards of living and levels of population in the home country and colony alike. Imperialism for Spain, on the contrary, was regressive for home country and colony together. British industry grew stronger and pioneered the inventions of the Industrial Revolution, whereas "the industry of Castile . . . was destroyed by the sixteenth and seventeenth centuries," corrupted by an influx of gold and silver that induced sloth, and then bankruptcy.[86] The Spanish Empire became one of vast, manorial estates, lacking "the promise of private ownership which promotes immigration and assures the most profitable use of the soil."[87] Manufacturing industries altogether languished in its colonies.[88] Spain, buying the goods it needed from France, England, Italy, Germany, and the Netherlands, and even its grain from foreign nations, met its trade deficit with payments in the gold and silver from its American mines; its own merchants, manufacturers, workingmen, and towns were a deteriorating asset. As the mines of precious metals gradually became depleted, "Spain fell back exhausted by an imperial effort too vast for her moral and material resources."[89] Its regressive imperialism bankrupted both the colony and home country, even as a progressive imperialism might have advanced both.

C. As Imperialist Pioneers: South Africa and New Zealand

The modern assault on the Jews as malefactors of imperialism began with the twentieth century when the journalist John A. Hobson published his book *The War in South Africa: Its Causes and Consequences* in 1900. From this work evolved his later book, *Imperialism,* that became Lenin's principal intellectual source for his theory of imperialism. Hobson had wandered the streets of Johannesburg in 1899. This town, he reported, "is essentially a Jewish town."[90] (Lord Bryce a little more delicately described Johannesburg at that time as an "Anglo-Semitic town.") The official census with its figure of less than seven thousand Jews was, Hobson felt, misleading; the shop fronts, the business houses, the streets, convinced one "of the large presence of the chosen people," many of whom were indeed not British, but German and Russian Jews. He thought "the rich, vigorous and energetic financial and commercial families" were chiefly German Jews. The town directory showed sixty-eight Cohens and only twenty-four Joneses. The Jews, taking little part in the British agitation, "let others do that sort of work," in Hobson's opinion, but they would emerge as the "chief gainers" in the event of a British political advance. Impressed though he was by "the intellect of the Beits and Barnatos and other great capitalists" and their town, bristling and throbbing "with industrial and commercial energy," Hobson had nonetheless a marked antipathy to the Jews as imperialists; it was obviously one reason why he so strongly opposed any British military effort against the Boer Republics. A disciple of John Ruskin, disliking those who reasoned presumably according to economic terms rather than "humanistic values," Hobson found the boom-town atmosphere of Johannesburg repulsive. The ideas he had imbibed at Oxford were utterly different from those that stirred his fellow Oxonian, Cecil Rhodes.[91]

The Jews were indeed among the greatest, the most enterprising, and the most constructive of the South African imperialists. The discovery of diamond reserves in the Orange Free State and the Transvaal in 1867-70 was followed by a "stream of emigrants," notes *The Cambridge History of the British Empire,* "men vigorous, alien, enterprising, eager for wealth, heirs of an industrial civilization, and some of them imbued with liberal ideas of self-government and progressive administration. Diggers and shopkeepers were followed by capitalists, with large ideas of progress and ambition, personal and national, and with powers of organisation to carry them out. To a great extent these capitalists were cosmopolitan Jews. Their industry brought wealth to an impoverished land and emplanted there a new form of civilisation, with all its vices and virtues."[92] Indeed, Jewish countenances were so frequently visible in Kimberley that "in this cosmopolitan hotbed being English" was for Rhodes, evidently, "more than an advantage" as a "rare and lovely virtue."[93]

From the diamond fields Jewish capitalists migrated to the gold mines in the Rand. Such men as Alfred Beit, George Albu, Lionel Phillips, the Joels, and Barney Barnato (a man of astonishing "speculative daring"), became known as "Randlords,"[94] directing the development of the gold mines. With the founding of Johannesburg in 1886, the names of the Jewish pioneers became household words in South Africa: T. B. Kisch, a discoverer of the Kimberley mine; the Lilienfeld brothers, who bought the first big diamond; Harry Mosenthal, who first inspired the effort to consolidate the diamond workings.[95] There had been even earlier Jewish pioneers in South African imperialism, their "pioneering spirit thrusting forward into unknown and untried fields in the new lands." As early as the 1820s, Nathaniel Isaacs in Natal was noting the possibilities for the planting of sugar.[96] Isaac Baumann, in the 1840s, was among the first to introduce sheep-farming for wool and meat in Bloemfontein. The brothers de Pass in the mid-nineteenth century helped create the whaling, sealing, guano, and fishing industries in Natal.[97] In 1882, Sigmund Hammerschlag was among the area's first prospectors.[98]

But the Jewish entrepreneurs were hampered by the fact that they belonged "to a generation which had no opportunity . . . to acquire the techniques needed for engineering and other basic industries." And, of course, they had little capital. They tended, therefore, apart from the bold individuals in the diamond and gold fields, to develop secondary industries and to become the organizers of marketing. They set up cheese and sweets factories, brick works, glass factories, jam and tanning factories, and installed modern methods of flour milling in Johannesburg. Men such as Solly Wolf, Jack Joel, Morris Marcus, Alfred Mosely and Sigmund

Neumann wended their ways to the diamond camps to market the stones.[99] Over in the Eastern Transvaal, Ezrael Lazarus, a pioneer in scientific farming, became known as the "maize king," while in the Orange Free State J. B. Lurie bore the sobriquet of the "potato king." In Natal, Daniel de Pass introduced the Uba cane in 1887, thereby saving its sugar industry from extinction, while fifteen years later Samuel Baranow began his work proving, contrary to the pessimists, that cattle could be raised in Natal.[100]

Of the "big ten" companies that controlled the Rand mines in the middle of the 1890s, five were principally owned by Jews.[101] They were mostly averse however, to Cecil Rhodes's politically adventurist methods for extending British hegemony, preferring instead gradualist political procedures as the ground for economic development. Barney Barnato said of the Jameson Raid: "The conspiracy was a crime." He had, indeed, evinced no interest in the agitation to secure the vote for the Uitlanders. Many of the Russian Jewish immigrants actually supported the Boer cause; though "pro-Kruger" they were still economic tradesmen and developers, that is, micro-imperialists. The Boers therefore blamed the rich British Jews, the macro-imperialists, not their poor Russian co-religionists, for the advent of political crisis and war. And indeed, one Jew, Lionel Phillips, was among the four leaders of the Jameson Raid, and five Jews served with the sixty men in the ranks.[102]

The South African mines were developed not by personalities molded in the Calvinist, Protestant ethic, but by men such as Rhodes and Barnato, both moved by an indomitable ambition to prove the supremacy of their own sheer power and creativity.

Barney Barnato founded the diamond mining company that was for years the outstanding competitor to Cecil Rhodes' De Beers Company. Eventually the two companies were amalgamated, but Barnato's imperialism had a homespun, unpretentious character compared to that of Rhodes. The imperialism of Cecil Rhodes overflowed in romantic projections. His will, for instance, provided for a Secret Society, "the true arm and object whereof shall be the extension of British rule throughout the world."[103] The imperialism of Barney Barnato was more a matter of sheer exuberance of spirit; on the frontier a man could prove his mettle, and an East End cockney Jew could create a mining empire.

The Jewish imperialists were neither always dignified nor imposing characters. They led lives of extraordinary tension that took its toll on their bodies and nervous stability. The effervescent Barney Barnato could finally no longer endure the strain; forty-five years old, he jumped overboard on a voyage home to England. And Alfred Beit, the financial organizer of Cecil Rhodes' enterprises, suffered nervous collapse.

Barnato, a child of London's East End and never educated beyond the Jews' Free School, snorted enviously at Rhodes: "Rhodes looks down on me because I've never been to college like 'im. If I'd had his education, there would have been no Cecil Rhodes." As much at home with the lowly characters in his vice-ridden neighborhood as he was among the "young *momzers*" at Kimberley, Barnato was not only endowed with an unrivaled business acumen and aplomb, but joined to the arts of the negotiator the talents of the entertainer. He sang, he boxed, he declaimed. He was a "kopje-walloper," an itinerant buyer in the diamond diggings, doing business with miners who were "the scourings of the world's ghettoes." His Jewish-cockney accent and wit were tempered, as a boy, by the tutelage of an actress, but remained so stamped upon his speech that when he gave Hamlet's soliloquy it was unintentionally comical. In the diamond fields too, he would, as an impresario, present himself as "Signor Barnato, the Great Wizard from London." Even when his fortune had grown huge Barnato still indulged his craving for the stage. Indeed, he once played Dickens' scoundrel Fagin, but his interpretation was so naturally realistic that elders of the synagogue objected that he might arouse anti-Semitic feeling; Barnato never acted that part again.[104] To help collect money for the Kimberley Hospital, however, he undertook to present *Othello,* promising to match the box office receipts from his own resources. Moreover, to add to the attraction, he proposed to play the part of the noble Moor himself. This was more than the audience could assimilate. When Barney declaimed, "Unhappy that I am black," someone shouted back, "Then go and wash your face, Barney." Whereupon the Shakespearean actor turned pugilist and descended into the pit to joust with his chief heckler. He was indeed, as his biographer writes, "one of them, free alike with his fists and his drinks; rough-tongued undoubtedly." For all that, he remained within the Judaic fold, celebrating the holidays from the joyous Chanukah to the sombre Yom Kippur. In triumph he returned to England and, elegantly dressed, walked to the Great Synagogue with his mother. In defeat, toward his life's end, he "spent the whole of Yom Kippur at the synagogue and fasted the full twenty-four hours."[105]

The Jameson Raid, playacting the revolutionary overthrow of the Boer government, seemed to Barnato to be one of Rhodes's arrogances. Nevertheless, Barnato was unable to restrain himself when he heard the judge pronounce death sentences upon its leaders. He rushed to the front of the courtroom, hurling curses at the judge. Then he went personally to call upon the president of the Republic, that agrarian patriarch, the anticapitalist Calvinist, Paul Kruger. First he pleaded for mercy toward the prisoners, but when the president defended the trial and the sentences, Barnato threatened to bring down economic catastrophe upon the minuscule republic; he would close his mines, he threatened, and twenty thousand whites and a hundred thousand blacks would be out of work; Kruger's government would be ruined. Probably Barnato's stand contributed to the president's decision to commute the death sentences.[106]

Though recognized as the "unofficial champion of the diggings," and nicknamed "Pug" for his achievements in fisticuffs, Barney Barnato never took part in armed, military actions.[107] Not so his cousin, David Harris, who rcse to military leadership and was later knighted. In 1872 at the age of nineteen Harris also had migrated from London to South Africa. Hiking the six hundred miles to Kimberley's diamond fields, in due course he became associated with Rhodes and eventually became a director of the De Beers Consolidated Mines Ltd. that Rhodes and Barnato founded. Harris, in addition, fulfilled a military penchant. Having taken part in several "frontier wars" of the Cape Colony, in 1896, as lieutenant-colonel, he commanded the Griqualand West Brigade against the uprising of the native tribes in Bechuanaland. During the Boer War, he commanded the town guard when Kimberley was besieged for 125 days in 1899-1900. Withal, he was a founder and president of the Griqualand West Hebrew Congregation and was known in later years as the "grand old man" of Kimberley.[108]

Although three men are cited as the founders of Rhodesia—Cecil Rhodes, Dr. Jameson, and Alfred Beit[109]—"without Beit," according to Jan Smuts, marshal and prime minister of South Africa, "Rhodes might have been a mere political visionary, bereft of power of practical creation."[110] Beit, South Africa's pre-eminent builder of bridges, roads, and railways, was the man who engraved Rhodes's dreams upon the substance of financial realities. Their twenty years' friendship and understanding was "so absolutely complete and so perfect as to be almost without parallel amongst those whose names are known to history."[111]

Son of a Hamburg merchant, Alfred Beit showed no distinction in intelligence as a boy; he seemed an amiable, average lad. The family sent him to Amsterdam as an apprentice to a diamond firm. Then, at the age of twenty-two he found his way to Kimberley. The character of Alfred Beit was transformed: "The effect of his new environment was to create within him an entirely different business spirit, and to stimulate into action entirely new sources of brain power and ability. Within two years after his arrival this environment had converted the boy of mediocre talents, the lethargic undistinguished young apprentice, into a man of impetuous, unremitting energy and enterprise, whose solutions of financial problems and of business intricacies" seemed to bear the stamp of genius."[112] Beit became a British citizen and "an ardent imperialist."[113] Together with Rhodes he strove to circumvent the designs of other states and to enlarge British supremacy. He made his first fortune by building corrugated iron houses for the shelterless Kimberley miners, then a second one buying diamonds and diamond fields, and finally a third when the discovery of gold in 1885 drew him to the Witwatersrand. Working harder than most men, he became acknowledged as "the mastermind in making a success of the gold-mining industry on the Rand."[114] He gave away virtually all of the great wealth he acquired, as did his fellow bachelor Rhodes, in charitable bequests and philanthropies. Rhodes remarked that as far as Beit was personally concerned, "all that Beit wanted was to be rich enough to give his mother £1000 a year."[115] The "fiasco" of the Jameson Raid brought about a temporary collapse in Beit's health. He died in 1906 perturbed by rumors of the manufacture of synthetic diamonds.

The lure of economic adventure and the excitement of equal, open opportunities brought other young Jews to South Africa. On the mining frontier all men lived under virtual equality of condition. Equality of opportunity is most realized under such an initial natural equality of condition; the inequalities that then define themselves are commensurate with corresponding achievement. The elite of creative imperialism consisted of those whose creative powers were actualized on the mining frontier. Thus, Lionel Phillips, born in 1885 to a prosperous London Jewish family, acquired a smattering of engineering knowledge and, not yet twenty years old, was off to the diamond fields. Many years later, Sir Lionel Phillips, first chairman of Rand Mines, Ltd., became founder of the Johannesburg Art Gallery, the Kirstenbosch Botanical Gardens, and the restorer of the historic Vergelegen house.[116] In 1875, too, the brothers George and Leopold Albu, sons of a Berlin coach builder, left for Cape Town. Beginning as department store clerks, they soon became magnates of precious stones and then founders on the Rand of the General Mining and Finance Corporation, while Samuel Marks, born in a Lithuanian town under czarist despotism, and emigrating to the Cape as an itinerant peddler, later helped finance Rhodes's schemes. From Denmark came a Jewish geologist, Dr. Emil Cohen, whose report urged the possibilities for mining gold in the South African Republic.[117]

The new veins of gold stimulated the tremendous flow of industrial investment that began at the end of the nineteenth century.[118] Indeed, the Witwatersrand produced more gold than has ever reposed in the strongholds of Fort Knox.[119] When an American gold miner, Mark Twain, America's beloved writer, again an innocent abroad, had come to South Africa in 1896, he found himself thoroughly at home in the Witwatersrand. "I had been a gold miner myself, and knew substantially everything that these people knew about it except how to make money." He was entranced with the gold fields, "wonderful in every way. In seven or eight years, they have built up, in a desert, a city of 100,000 inhabitants . . . a city made of lasting material."[120] Indeed, Mark Twain had a more natural, empathetic understanding of the imperialist spirit than either of his contemporaries, Hobson or Lenin.

The dividing line between trader and prospector was a thin one on the mining frontier. Both shared the entrepreneurial venturesomeness. A group of German-Jewish traders, Sigmund Hammerschlag and three others, for instance, banded themselves into a syndicate for prospecting;

from it originated the Tweefontein Company.[121] "Half of Kimberley seemed to be prowling around the Eastern Transvaal"; the diamond men —Beit, Rhodes, Wernher, Barnato, Marcks, George and Leopold Albu— were moving to the gold regions, coming up to see things for themselves.[122] Isaac Sonnenberg, a California forty-niner and a veteran of the Union Army in the American Civil War, was drawn to the diamond diggings and then to the Witwatersrand.[123] The surplus "energies of men," as William James would have called it, were the reservoir for the social thermodynamics of imperialism.

Of the pioneers of mining organization in South Africa, the economic historian, Theodor Gregory, writes: "There probably has never been a dynamic group of business leaders in any part of the world which had, in the space of twenty odd years, done so much: there certainly has never been a similar group more subject to political malice and to religious and racial and social prejudice."[124] They wanted to make money, but they also expended lavishly for public purposes. Neither Marxist accumulators nor Prosperonian neurotics,[125] they were the bearers of civilization not as a burden but as creative adventure, and the vanishing of their kind is a signal of a civilization's decline.

While many Jews trekked to the mines and veld of South Africa, others sailed as imperialist seekers into the Pacific lands of the Antipodes, New Zealand and Australia. Indeed, the outstanding political figure in modern Jewish imperialism was the relatively unknown Julius Vogel, prime minister of the colony of New Zealand in 1873. During the decade of the seventies, Vogel's policies helped to double his colony's population from a quarter of a million to a half million; he brought a hundred thousand immigrants, built twelve hundred miles of railway, and trebled the value of the Colony's exports.

Born in London in 1835, "a Jew of the Ashkenazi rite," as *The Dictionary of National Biography*[126] described him, Julius Vogel listened as a boy to the tales of his grandfather, a merchant whose interests ranged the West Indies and South America. Excited by the news of the Australian gold fields, Vogel prepared himself for an imperialist career by studying at the Royal School of Mines. Then, seventeen years old, he set off in 1852 for Australia.[127] He experienced successive failures into early manhood but, his spirit unflagging, moved to Otago, New Zealand, where gold had been discovered. The young assayer next metamorphosed into a journalist, founding New Zealand's first daily newspaper, the *Otago Daily Times*.

Thus began the course which made Vogel "the most important political figure in the Colony."[128] He has not been depicted kindly by his critics; some of them have called him "Machiavellian." A noted historian of New Zealand, while admiring Vogel's public policies, characterized them as "extensions of a greedy and sanguine nature . . . revealed in his inveterate gluttony and gambling." Withal, this same historian acknowledges that Vogel was the first New Zealand politician with remarkable talents.[129]

Vogel believed in his country's future. As colonial treasurer, he borrowed boldly to construct railways and canals, encouraged immigration, and resolved relations amicably with the Maoris. He vigorously promoted afforestation and conservation measures. A developmental economist by nature, Vogel carried through the financing of the transport networks of roads and railroads that his country needed, and when the obsolete provincial governments began to stand in the way of development, he abolished them. The provincial authorities had also failed miserably to provide New Zealand's children with adequate education; more than two-fifths of the latter were not even on the school rolls. Vogel, described by a Colonial Office staffer as "the most audacious adventurer that perhaps . . . ever held power in a British colony," guided New Zealand's economy so that it "thrived as never before."[130] "In England's colonies of the new world," notes Vogel's biographer, "the spirit of racial intolerance, having no roots in tradition, was never a force to be reckoned with." Instead, "reserves of creative energy" were stirred and made manifest in these new communities.

Vogel retained a childish naiveté, a romanticism of the kind Disraeli had that tinctured his practical talents. He imagined a United Britain, a federated Empire, a reconquered United States, and equal rights for women. He ran "a lonely course . . . fascinated by the unattainable."[131] What prospectors called "gold fever" moved him, but the "fever" was more than an economic phenomenon. He was affected by nervous disorders; he felt his Jewishness keenly but with a dramatic pride that made him boast, as Disraeli did, of Jewish achievements; indeed, when his government supported the Women's Property Act and women's suffrage, Vogel in his parliamentary speech (1887) explicitly linked women's emancipation with that of the Jews:

"The emancipation which women have so far received reminds me forcibly of the great emancipation of a religious sect—the Jews. A time will be remembered when the Jews were shut out from almost every occupation . . . now I think I am hardly exaggerating the case when I say that half the power of Europe is in their hands, and that in the professions and as public men and statesmen in all parts of the world, they have eminently distinguished themselves."[132]

Vogel indeed expected something similar from the advent of women's emancipation. Audacious enough, moreover, to write a visionary novel, *2000 A.D. or Woman's Destiny,* Vogel returned home to Britain in 1880 to become possibly the only Jew in history to contest a parliamentary seat as an imperialist; he was unsuccessful.

Membership in the British Empire seemed as essential for New Zealand in Vogel's eyes as membership in the Roman Empire had seemed to Britons fourteen hundred years before. In 1870, indeed, fear had spread in

New Zealand that Britain would invite them to leave the empire; it was only allayed by Disraeli's return to power. Then, for a brief period, imperialism became an honored, self-conscious policy. Vogel grew as romantic about the Pacific Islands as Jack London and James Michener did in later generations. He embellished his vision of a beautiful Empire of Pacific Islands with the phraseology of a company promoter, blending the islands' poetry with calculations of trade returns and percentages of profit. But the romance was the reality, "the matured fancies of childhood" that could be nurtured to intersect in all its lines with reality.[133] Vogel, knighted, returned to New Zealand in February 1876 to be greeted by a torch-parade of seven thousand supporters, and their address: "We, the working men and citizens of Wellington . . . recognize in you a friend and patron of the working classes. . . We believe implicitly, not only in your genius, but in your earnestness and sincerity of purpose."[134]

To his novels of imperialism, *Alroy* and *Endymion,* Disraeli might have added one on democratic imperialism in the setting of the Pacific Islands: the bearers of his calling—the Jewish adventurers restless with a sense of the new worlds who, having ceased awaiting a Messiah in the fashion of their fathers, climbed instead their own Sinais and traversed their own deserts and seas.

If Jews from London's ghetto found in the imperialist world an opening for their talents, there was the unusual case already noted of the exotic family in Baghdad of David Sassoon, whose immense talents flowered under British imperialism. When the English East India Company was constituted, it had, unlike the Dutch, no Jewish participants because Jews could not then legally reside in England. Nonetheless, British rule in India made possible the unique career of David Sassoon. Virtually the hereditary leader of the Jewish community in Baghdad, Sassoon felt compelled to leave the city in 1829 when an anti-Jewish pasha came to power. In 1833 he emigrated to Bombay. Twenty years later David Sassoon signed his oath of loyalty as a British subject in Hebrew, thereby symbolizing the linkage between Jewish enterprise and an international free imperialist order.

The abilities of the strange Sassoon family of Baghdad then unfolded themselves. "Greatness is achieved by a country," wrote Cecil Roth, "which has the faculty (like the old Roman Empire) to welcome and absorb ability, whatever its source."[135] The history of the Sassoon family is indeed an Arabian Nights' tale of adventurous entrepreneurs and capitalists. The turbaned, bearded, gowned David Sassoon, creator of the first mechanical textile factories in India, was followed by a line of energetic sons and grandsons in novel industries from Bombay to Shanghai. Was its end foreshadowed in the elegant, sensitive great-grandson, Siegfried Sassoon? Poet in austere lines of war's sacrifice of its brave, he journeyed from pacific socialism to an Augustinian Catholicism, the lyricist and chronicler of a society grasped by the mood of decline.[136] Decorated for bravery, he sat at the feet of Bertrand Russell and imbibed Russell's anti-Americanism. The imperialist spirit of the turbaned great-grandfather, the builder of Bombay's Magen David Synagogue, metamorphosed with his fox-hunting descendant into the poetry of protest and self-reproach.

In the Middle East meanwhile, Britain's "oil imperialism," central to the maintenance of its naval superiority, had arisen. Among its originators and financiers was Marcus Samuel, whose part in developing the oil tanker had helped make possible the shipment of large-scale cargoes of oil through the Suez Canal. He had also in 1898 worked energetically to develop the oil resources of Borneo. When Samuel took the leadership in organizing the Shell oil combine, however, he aroused the concerns of the young Colonial Under-Secretary, Winston Churchill. Actually, Marcus Samuel had earlier offered the British government the control of the Shell Company, but the government had preferred organizing its own. When war came in 1914, Samuel ordered that the Shell Company make no profits out of the war and placed the entire Shell fleet, the largest among the oil carriers in the world, at the service of the British Admiralty. Although lampooned in 1913 by a British publication as a "typical Jew . . . stout, swarthy . . . thick-nosed, thick-lipped, bulge-eyed," Samuel's services to Britain during World War I were estimated by Lord Birkenhead as among the three most decisive for British victories; he referred especially to Marcus Samuel's role as a pioneer in the manufacture of much-needed toluol, a compound essential for making T.N.T. Samuel became Lord Bearsted in 1921.[137]

The participation of Jewish pioneers in the rise of British imperialism has, of course, elicited the ire of anti-imperialist critics. As the British historian, P. F. Clarke, observes: "Attitudes towards Jews in general became more controversial around the turn of the century. There was a distinct anti-semitic flavor to the denunciations by opponents of the Boer War, like Hyndman, of 'the Jews' War in the Transvaal.'" On the other hand, the imperialist Winston Churchill found a bastion of support in the Manchester Jewish community, becoming for his part as early as 1908 a supporter of the Zionist cause.[138] In later years, Marxist critics railed and hyphenated Zionism with imperialism; in time many espoused an un-hyphenated, though perhaps regressive Soviet imperialism.

Withal, the narratives of the Jewish imperialists illustrate the truth that imperialism is above all a phenomenon not of "surplus value" but, as we have noted, of *surplus energies*. Barnato, Harris, Beit, Vogel—none of them came from families with surplus capital to invest. They felt as very young men the attractions of a new, unknown, dangerous land many thousands of miles away. They felt vaguely that they might be creators of a novel domain and a novel industry. Without the imperialist vocation and opportunity, Barnato might perhaps have ended as a theater operator in London's East End, while Alfred Beit would have been a meticulous head clerk in an Amsterdam counting house. Such a restless, often creative drive has been a psychological source for imperialism in every historical age—among the Macedonians, the Romans, and the British. It manifested itself in Czarist Russia, which had no surplus capital, along the Siberian and central Asian frontiers, as well as among the British in the nineteenth century who had accumulated an investable surplus. But "surplus capital" was not a necessary condition for the imperialist drive as much as a reserve that was called into use.

D. Eduard Schnitzer, Scientist-Governor, as Emin Pasha of Equatoria

Strangest of all the Jewish imperialists and their most heroic personality was the scientist-physician Eduard Schnitzer. Under his adopted name "Emin" he achieved renown throughout the world when, in the aftermath of the triumph of the Mahdi uprising and Gordon's destruction at Khartoum, he continued despite his complete isolation from the civilized world to rule his province as governor of Equatoria; there, through years of devoted work, he laid the "first foundations of a well-ordered state."[139]

Eduard Schnitzer had turned to a career in distant lands when he found his practice of his medical profession frustrated in his native country. Born in 1840 in Prussian Silesia, Schnitzer was baptized at the age of six, shortly after his father died. Evincing unusual scientific talents early in his student years, especially in zoology and ornithology, he published several papers while still at the University. Having obtained his medical degree at Berlin, he found himself, however, denied the opportunity by the minister of education to take his qualifying examination. At first he tried to volunteer for service with the emperor Maximilian's army in Mexico, but events took him to Turkey as a government medical officer, and in 1870 to the staff of its Governor of Northern Albania. He merged his personality into a new identity as a Turk; though never formally converted to the Moslem religion, Schnitzer would be seen going to the mosque every Friday. He wrote his mother in 1872: "I am now completely naturalized, and have even adopted the disguise of a Turkish name . . . I have adopted a Turkish name in order to avoid being continually pestered with all sorts of questions as to my origin, etc."[140] Like a modern Joseph he found favor with his Potiphar's wife (and later widow), a young Transylvanian woman, and found a transient contentment in the household of slaves and Circassian girls. He reached Khartoum in the Sudan in December 1875, and for a while he served the legendary Governor-General Gordon as physician. Gordon was struck by the man's immense abilities; he knew languages, modern and ancient, speaking besides his "native" Turkish, English, German, French, Arabic, Albanian, and Italian; also he played Chopin and Mendelssohn at the pianoforte and never stopped making botanical, zoological, and anthropological investigations wherever he was. His political talents, furthermore, proved invaluable to Gordon on a diplomatic mission to the king of Uganda.[141] Then in 1878 Emin was appointed by Gordon as Emin Bey, Governor of Equatoria.

For the next eight years Emin ruled his vast primitive province as a benevolent scientific governor. He acted as medical officer and industrial educator; he taught the people new methods for tanning, reaping, and sowing; he taught them how to make soap, alcohol, and lubricating oil; he instructed in the art of weaving cloth. Not long after Emin took power, he wrote in his diary: "The curse of the slave traffic rests like a blight upon the land; no one thinks of improving his condition by any means but robbery, plunder, and slave-dealing."[142] Emin labored zealously and with much success both to emancipate the slaves and to eliminate the slave trade in his domain. By 1882, "he had entirely banished the slave-dealers from his borders."[143] That was why, when the Mahdist revolt spread through the upper Sudan, the people of his province remained loyal to Emin Pasha, supporting him in "resisting the Mahdists, whose success would be synonymous with a revival of slave-raiding. And this cooperation alone explains how Emin has hitherto defied the vastly superior power of the Mahdi," reported a German journal.[144] Though cut off from the means of replenishing his stores and ammunition by the fall of Khartoum, Emin Pasha refused to abandon his post. His province, wrote Emin, though "the most distant possession of Egypt . . . is at this very moment the only part of her entire dominions which is perfectly tranquil . . . The thousands of Negroes who reside in the neighborhood . . . have learned to feel like men since I . . . put an end to the slave trade here."[145]

News reached the European world in 1886 that Emin Pasha was still standing his ground three years after the Mahdist victory at Khartoum and had not ceased hoping that England, "true to her traditions of humanity and civilization, will come to our assistance." Since the anti-imperialist prime minister, Gladstone, refused to make any such move, an Emin Relief Committee was founded; shortly a relief force organized by Henry Morton Stanley, famous for a similar mission to Livingstone, departed from Zanzibar to rescue Emin. When, with less than one-fourth of his force, shattered by ambushes, diseases, and the jungle, he reached Emin, it was Stanley's expedition that had to be relieved far more than Emin, who provided his rescuers with clothes, boots, tobacco, and grain. Stanley discovered to his consternation that Emin Pasha did not want to desert his post and province: "The ten years of Emin's rule had left the remarkable man unchanged, save that they had taught him the secrets of African ornithology . . . During all that time, without relief or holiday, he had governed by conciliation a country equal to Ireland in extent and turbulence."[146] Rather than take flight, Emin was moved by the vision of ruling a self-sustaining Sudanese empire in the manner of the legendary Rajah Brooke in Sarawak, a rule based on liberal, scientific ideas, and allied to Britain.[147] As Emin told his British friend Felkin in 1887: "I have passed twelve years of my life here, and would it be right of me to desert my post as soon as the opportunity to escape presented itself?"[148] When Stanley insisted that it was imperative that Emin leave, Emin's own forces became restive and divided. The presence of Stanley's expedition itself provoked discord and disaffection among Emin's troops; they feared Emin would leave and that they might be forced likewise to go. Emin later charged Stanley's intervention with having provoked revolt, "nor can he dispute that I held and administered the province without his aid from 1882 to 1889."[149] Stanley himself acknowledged in the best-selling book he wrote, *In Darkest Africa, or The Quest, Rescue and Retreat of Emin Pasha,* that "this mild-mannered man, this student of science, governed for several years all alone" a people "practiced in dissimulation, adepts in deceit, and pastured in vice . . . During this portion of his career as Governor of Equatoria only unqualified praise can be given."[150] Emin Pasha, his position weakened, finally consented with great reluctance to depart. "All my collections, all my books, all my instruments must be left behind,"[151] he wrote sadly. For a brief period he tried to work under the German flag, but found that experience unpleasant. Determined to remain in Equatoria, he was working near its border, pursuing his zoological research and discovering new species, when he was murdered on October 23, 1892, at the orders of Arab chiefs seeking vengeance against him for his anti-slavery actions.[152]

To some extent the career of Emin Pasha suggests the pattern of a "Prospero complex": a man who sought to shed his past identity, who turned Turk, who had been frustrated in professional ambition in his home country. Later he obviously enjoyed the role of governor of cannibal Negro tribes whose very smell was offensive to him. He married an "Abyssinian woman" who bore him a daughter, Ferida, "a pretty little girl, not darker in complexion than her father, and greatly resembling him." Much attached to her, Emin said: "The little Ferida is all that is left to me in the world now." When his wife died in 1887, Emin's sorrow was profound; he wrote to a trusted friend, the Scottish missionary Alexander Mackay asking for a Bible. He begged his sister to look after his child and to see that she was educated in "many languages."[153]

Yet on further analysis, rather than a Prospero complex, one sees an overwhelming rationality that pervades Emin's lifetime, a working out of his life's basic scientific interests and human calling. Even hostile observers were impressed that he always reasoned with people, analyzed, gathered facts. "His ultra-conservative nature shrank from destroying anything but rather desired events to take their natural course, under gentle guidance."[154] He rejected Germany as did many a born Jew; doubtless he

inferred from his experience that a man with scientific aims would en-
counter persistent anti-Semitism. His scientific interests were those best
advanced by research in an equatorial area, for Emin's concerns were
similar to those of such men as Alfred Russel Wallace, Henry Walter
Bates, Joseph Hooker, and Charles Darwin, who also devoted many years
of their lives to voyages through Pacific Islands and explorations into the
Brazilian and African jungles, the Malay Archipelago, and the Andes
mountains; his scientific mission was precisely that which they had experienced. "None of the letters we had brought him gave him such pleasure as
those relating to his scientific researches," said Jephson, an officer of
Stanley's expedition.[155] It was "Emin's lasting and most prominent merit,"
said the German authorities in this field, to have provided the ornitho-
logical facts "upon a great tract of Equatorial Africa that so far as science
was concerned had hitherto been enshrouded in darkness." He had accumulated "a mass of valuable notes" especially concerning the birds,
devoting "the greatest attention to the very difficult problems of changes
of color, gradations and modifications of colorings, etc., induced by sex,
age, food, and time of year. Unwearied and untiring, he searched till he
arrived at unexceptionable results. . . . He was always active, with all the
extraordinary energy inherent in him, with enthusiastic, absolutely unselfish love of nature, and inspired by an irresistible impulse to contribute
to a knowledge of her treasures."[156] This Emin did despite the fact that he
was almost blind in later years.[157] The work he did "in making zoological
collections, observations, and notes," wrote the scientist Gustav Hartlaub,
"is astonishing in the highest degree. It could only have been performed by
a man whose heart was aglow with the pure fire of scientific instinct."[158]
Moreover, Emin remained a gentle, kindly spirit in his governmental
dealings, quite devoid of the sadism, repressed or expressed, that is the
central trait of imperialists, according to the theorists of the Prospero
complex doctrine. Stanley never liked Emin, yet he wrote of him: "Let me
say in plain Anglo-Saxon, that I think his good nature was too prone to
forgive, whenever his inordinate self-esteem was gratified. The cunning
people 'the crafty Egyptians' knew that they had but to express sorrow
and grief to make him relent . . . There was therefore too little punishing
and too much forgiving. This amiability was extremely susceptible and
tender, and the Egyptians made the most of it."[159] Emin's "spirit of
self-sacrifice more than once came dangerously near to being fatal to
him,"[160] observed R. W. Felkin.

Emin's overriding goals remained to the last scientific knowledge and
the advancement of the primitive people who had been entrusted to his
care. He was not known for or accused of using the Negro women to
constitute a harem as is the wont of the sultans. To his little half-black
daughter, whom he was careful to legitimize, he left all he owned in his
will, always showing her the greatest solicitude.[161] He did not think well of

the German Social Democrats, the party of August Bebel and Wilhelm Liebknecht that denounced imperialism in Marxist terms. "The social democrats have no sympathy for our endeavors and our labors," he wrote his sister in 1890, deploring the electoral success of the Marxist party.[162] Yet, after his many years' experience, Emin refused to sentimentalize about the Negroes: "I have really no hopes at all for a regeneration of Negroes by Negroes—I know my own men too well for that," nor did he see their redemption through conversion to the New Testament.[163]

Emin had left Prussia as a young man rejected by his friends and society; "At the University he experienced bitter disappointments, and many of his friends turned their backs on him."[164] His relatives "considered it desirable that Schnitzer should seek elsewhere that livelihood for which Germany, at any rate, seemed then to present no opportunity."[165] It is doubtful that he ever became reconciled to Germany even in his last years when it poured honors upon him and he briefly entered its service. "Though the Germans are my countrymen, I can never think of them in the same friendly way," he told Jephson, as he thought of the British expedition. As a Jew, he evidently regarded the Germans as Einstein did.[166] His hope had been to join and contribute to the British Empire which would civilize the African lands,[167] and it was only because of what seemed to be British recalcitrance that he tried the German service. But Emin persisted in disobeying German orders and a rupture soon followed. Meanwhile, an honorary degree came from Königsberg, and his old student fraternity, the "Armenia," that had ostracized him, restored him to their fold. Much moved, Emin inquired "what has become of all those who constituted the 'Armenia' in our time. I know absolutely nothing of any of them"; he also indicated doubts that he would ever survive his next journey into the African hinterland: "But no matter, my sphere of action now lies on African soil, and I suppose I shall leave my bones here,"[168] he wrote on March 30, 1890. A few months later, he told his sister sadly that when he looked through "the list of old members" that his fraternity sent him, his former fellow students "now officiating as pastors, professors, Government councillors, and other bigwigs," and thought of himself still roaming "through the world like a regular gypsy, without hearth or home," he felt "quite ashamed." Yet rallying himself, he refused to complain: "Every man must run the race prescribed for him."[169] "[A]s long as there are any woods and fields to be explored, as long as there is anything left to collect, although Stanley makes fun of it, no adverse comments shall mar the interest I take in Africa," he wrote to a friend's daughter. Emin's disparagers meanwhile were bruiting it about that Emin was a Jew.[170] Soon, however, Emin was dead.

Emin was not the first German physician to feel a calling to the study of nature in distant, primitive, and unknown lands. Within a few years after Vasco da Gama's voyage to the East Indies at the end of the fifteenth century, Jewish medical pioneers were journeying to those lands seeking both freedom and science. Most notably, Garcia da Orto, formerly professor at Lisbon, sailed for the East Indies in 1534 and became the chief contributor to the knowledge of its plants and the first European writer on tropical medicine. He said that in Spain "he would never have dared to affirm anything contrary to the Greek theorists . . . but in the heart of India, free from the fetters of convention in the midst of a free and luxurious vegetation, it mattered little what Dioscorides had said, or Pliny, Avicenna or Galen . . . Do not frighten me with them, I have seen."[171] Emin Pasha, scientist-imperialist, was of the same mind.

E. Jews as Imperial Officers in the Twentieth Century

The mantle of Jewish contribution to the British Empire passed during the twentieth century to men who served it in official capacities. Perhaps the most varied career on several continents was that of Major (later Sir) Matthew Nathan (1862-1939), whose work took him from Sierra Leone to the Gold Coast to Hong Kong and Natal, and who was the "valued friend" of the dauntless explorer and writer Mary Kingsley. Born of a Jewish family, Nathan graduated from the Royal Military Academy and served in 1884 in the Sudan expedition. When conditions in Sierra Leone became critical in 1899, the imperial-minded colonial secretary, Joseph Chamberlain, dispatched him there as interim governor. What Nathan accomplished aroused the enthusiasm of the reform-minded Mary Kingsley. He pursued an "energetic reform which was both prudent and popular." He followed similar policies both as governor of Hong Kong and, from 1907 to 1909, as governor of Natal.[172] Nathan's contribution above all was to guide his administration by the kind of ethic that persons such as Mary Kingsley represented—to try to understand native institutions and to guide educational and social measures according to the native's own evolving needs, values, and wishes.

This conception of the imperialist aim was shared by a successor of Nathan's of tremendous initiative. The forbears of Sir Frederick Gordon Guggisberg "were Jews of a quite different name, who lived in Russian Poland."[173] As a youth his great-great-grandfather had escaped across the Russian frontier rather than be conscripted into the czar's army. He wended his way to the village of Guggisberg in Switzerland where he worked as a glazier. When he married his employer's daughter he yielded to the father's demand that he become a Protestant and change his name. The sons of their marriage emigrated to Canada. Guggisberg's grandfather was the local butcher of Preston, Ontario, while his father was a drygoods merchant.

The future governor of Nigeria was born in 1869. After his father

died, Guggisberg's mother moved to Toronto where she later remarried a
British naval officer; thus young Guggisberg, with his strange heritage of
the ghetto ancestor who sought freedom from czarist tyranny, and the
sons and grandsons who labored as carpenters and storekeepers in Canadian towns, found himself at the age of ten in England.

After graduating from the Royal Military Academy in 1887, Guggisberg, like Nathan, was commissioned in the Royal Engineers and later
became an instructor in fortification at his alma mater. His vocation as an
imperialist was that of an engineer, a builder of works for human happiness. In 1919, he said with an engineer's rhetoric: "Whatever decisions I
may be called upon to make I promise the people of the Gold Coast that I
will always be guided by the fact that I am an Engineer, sent out here to
superintend the construction of a broad Highway of Progress along which
the races of the Gold Coast may advance, by gentle gradients over the
Ridges of Difficulty, and by easy curves around the Swamps of Doubt
and Superstition, to those far-off Cities of Promise—the Cities of Final
Development, Wealth and Happiness."[174] Guggisberg had considerable
experience behind him as a developmental engineer, director of surveys in
Southern Nigeria, surveyor-general of Nigeria, and director of public
works in the Gold Coast. *The Handbook of the Southern Nigerian Survey*
that he compiled came to be regarded as "model instructions," and the
rules laid down prevented the exploitation of natives by his staff: "unpaid
labor was forbidden; all goods bought were to be paid for at the recognized rate, and great care was to be exercised not to damage the crops."[175]

A builder akin to the old Roman imperialists, Guggisberg constructed
a new system of roads, a new harbor, and the first college in the Gold
Coast. He also brought to completion the magnificent African hospital at
Korle Bu. He could truthfully claim that "thanks to the new roads, I have
been the first Governor to enter many important towns in the Colony and
Ashanti," but more important, because of the new transport, "the prices
for cocoa paid to the farmer rose between 50 and 100 percent after the
arrival of the motor road."[176]

Before the roads and railways were constructed an endless line of
men, women, and children carried cocoa on their heads to the trading
center. The new motor roads liberated the burden-bearers.[177] Guggisberg
was the driving force too in the planning and construction of the deep-sea
port of Taboradi; though completed in 1928, a year after his departure, he
created the conditions in which the country's overseas trade could prosper
for another vital decade.[178] Above all, against the intense hostility of "a
large part of the European community and some Negro intellectuals as
well,"[179] Guggisberg conceived and directed the construction of a college
at Achimota that he hoped would grow into a university. This was part of
what has been called overwarmly "the Guggisberg revolution"—to provide
a school where the Gold Coast itself would educate its future teachers,

government officials, and practitioners of the scientific professions. "I should like to see fifty percent of the present European staff in technical departments replaced by natives," said Guggisberg in November 1919 to the Legislative Council.[180] In his farewell to Achimota on January 27, 1927, with two thousand people crowded into the Main Hall, and as many outside, the retiring governor said: "I am fully aware that in uttering these views I am adopting a revolutionary attitude that would terrify the majority of Governments, but nevertheless it is my firm conviction that, if Achimota is to be a complete success here . . . if it is to be a pride to the African, it must develop a free, inspired and natural life. This will be its greatest possible contribution to the education of the Empire."[181] The bells of the College Tower rang out for the first time. The next morning a long line of incoming students approached the Training College, every man with a bundle on his head and "a certain Nkrumah among them."[182]

Although Guggisberg held to no ideology of equality he had a "passion for equal rights and opportunities for the black man" and "an obsessional belief in the potentialities of the people whom he governed." In his book *The Future of the Negro,* he rejected the idea that the Negro race was inherently less intelligent or capable than the white, and he pointed to their attainments within "such a brief span of time."[183] But he felt no sympathy for notions of racial amalgamation or for "Europeanizing" the African, and he maintained that a considerable time for education must elapse before the Africans could completely govern themselves. He had no reverential *mystique* for popular institutions. To his critics this trait constituted a limitation of Guggisberg's philosophy. But the history of Ghana, from the era of Nkrumah's personal dictatorship, embellished with Marxist slogans, to that of the successive military rulers, does not falsify Guggisberg's standpoint.

Like Matthew Nathan and John Monash, Guggisberg chose the "discipline" of engineering as providing the best training for making an abiding contribution; each of them was relatively impervious to the allure of ideology that besets so many Jewish intellectuals.

Possibly the single-mindedness with which Frederick Gordon Guggisberg gave himself to his imperialist work was in part, as R. E. Wraith has suggested, the "sublimation" of the frustration he experienced in his marriage. Guggisberg's first wife, after a few unhappy years, ran away with a clergyman, leaving him with their two daughters. His second wife, an actress in the operettas of Gilbert and Sullivan, was a highly ambitious woman; she interceded with her friend, Elinor Glyn, the famed novelist of passionate romance,[184] to exert her personal influence for Guggisberg's advancement. Elinor Glyn evidently persuaded her admirer, the statesman Lord Milner, then colonial secretary, to examine Guggisberg's qualifications. Thus the engineer and director of the Department of Public Works was appointed governor of the Gold Coast. But his second marriage foundered in quarrels that were ugly. Guggisberg was even publicly humiliated. Arthur Conan Doyle, a close friend and a witness to their wedding, had a sense of the internal resources that would sustain Guggisberg in his personal defeat. Guggisberg did surmount his ordeals to become "the greatest Governor of West Africa."[185]

To locate, finally, the impelling emotion that kept this lonely, aloof man to his labors on behalf of the primitive, ignorant, and illiterate natives of the Gold Coast, perhaps one must penetrate to his unspoken, almost repressed Jewish origin. His second wife wrote long after his death: "No, Gordon Guggisberg was not a Jew, but of German extraction from Stuttgart—all his people came from Germany."[186] But one day his warm friend and co-worker, Lieutenant Colonel J. H. Levey, was afforded a brief glimpse of Guggisberg's deepest selfhood. He had watched Guggisberg taking to task a tribal chief who had accepted bribes; the chief was terrified in his guilt. Suddenly, Guggisberg "put his arms round the miscreant" and forgave and re-assured him; the chief left devoted and happy. Levey asked Guggisberg why could he never allow the sun to set on his wrath with any African. "'Levey,' was the reply . . . 'remember that the blood of an oppressed people runs in my veins. I never forgot it. I understood the people of the Gold Coast.'"[187]

Guggisberg "died obscurely and alone" in an English seaside boarding house.[182] His Gold Coast friends erected a tombstone over his untended grave.

There will be those who will hold that Guggisberg, afflicted by inadequacies in his sexual life, repressing his Jewish ancestry, and concerned about fulfilling the niceties of his role as an English gentleman, sought the psychological mantle of a proconsul. The thesis of the Prospero complex, however, would have its ideal-typical imperialist seeking in his career the opportunities for sadistic behavior, both sexual and economic, while regarding the colonial natives as less than human beings, their ignorance and poverty rendering them proper objects for exploitation. In this sense the thesis fails for governor, surveyor, and engineer Guggisberg. He gave himself to the Gold Coast people, delighted in work and took pleasure in building the roads, harbor, university, hospital, and all the works which bettered the lives of his people. He never became cynical towards the natives but regarded them as fellow-humans. All human beings bear within them the marks of repressed rejection, defeat, or deprivation; the great difference lies between those who resolve these vulnerabilities in constructive work that mitigates the world's future occasions of pain and those who cannot. In this sense, the forgotten Guggisberg was among the world's foremost creative imperialists.

Marxist and Prosperonian critics will insist, perhaps in an *a priori* fashion, as R. E. Wraith points out, that Guggisberg's purpose was to increase the profits of cocoa companies and merchants and that even a hospital contributes to a more efficient exploitation of labor power, while an educational system assists the recruitment of supervisory personnel—that Guggisberg, in short, was a "stooge of British monopoly capitalism." An older generation of Ghanaians, however, remember Guggisberg as the man "who first started to lead the Gold Coast out of colonial insignificance,"[189] who helped the peasant proprietors to cultivate almost all the cocoa beans, and who brought education to their ambitious young, even those who nurtured revolutionary plans. It was not British "monopoly capitalism" that extracted an inordinate profit; rather, the millions of British children eating chocolate bars that were tasty and cheap were the real beneficiaries. Guggisberg helped complete the chocolate revolution by extending its goods to working-class children, for British imperialism, as we have seen, was less a "monopoly capitalism" than a "consumers' imperialism."

World War I also saw the emergence for the first time since Bar Kochba in the second century A.D. of an outstanding Jewish military leader, Sir John Monash (1865-1931), truly a general of the British Empire. The noted military historian Liddell Hart wrote of him: "He had probably the greatest capacity for command in modern war among all who held command . . . If that war had lasted another year he would almost certainly have risen from commander of the Australian corps . . . he might even have risen to be Commander-in-Chief."[190]

The wartime prime minister of Great Britain, the indomitable David Lloyd George, thought likewise that "the only soldier . . . who possessed necessary qualifications for commander-in-chief" was this dominion general. And Earl Montgomery of Alamein, Britain's commander in World War II, wrote similarly from his background of experience: "I would name Sir John Monash as the best general on the western front in Europe; he possessed real creative originality, and the war might well have been over sooner, and certainly with fewer casualties, had Haig been relieved of his command and Monash appointed to command the British Armies in his place."[191] It was Monash's analysis of trench warfare that finally led the Allied governments "to go in for tank production in a big way." Monash, as Australian Corps commander, wrote: "The true role of the infantry was not to expend itself upon heroic physical effort, nor to wither away under merciless machine-gun fire . . . but on the contrary, to advance under the maximum possible protection . . . of mechanical resources . . . tanks, mortars and aeroplanes."[192]

Born in Melbourne to an immigrant family from Vienna that had been printers of Hebrew books and kinsfolk of the Jewish historian Heinrich Graetz, Monash took a doctorate in engineering and was a pioneer in introducing into Australia the techniques of reinforced concrete construction. He became president of the Victorian Institute of Engineers. Perhaps in part to assuage his domestic unhappiness, he cultivated an interest in military service. Commissioned in the Victoria militia in 1887, he read deeply into the history of the American Civil War and the writings of Colonel G. F. R. Henderson. He won a gold medal for an article on military history in the *Commonwealth Journal.*

Apart from the experience that an industrialist acquired in conducting large-scale enterprises, Monash was more fitted to cope with innovations in aircraft, weaponry, and technology generally. Warfare, Monash held, was essentially a problem of engineering akin to directing a large industrial undertaking. Moreover, as a lover of music he was probably the only one in the history of military science to regard military art as analogous to musical art: "A perfected modern battle plan is like nothing so much as a score for an orchestral composition, where the various arms and units are the instruments, and the tasks they perform are their respective musical phrases."[193]

Monash, the Jewish intellectual, found an opportunity for military leadership in a setting that only a far-flung empire with its challenge to vigor and originality could provide. As lieutenant general and commander of the entire Australian and New Zealand Army Corps in May 1918 he led his troops in breaking the German lines. When he returned to civilian life in Australia he re-planned the systems for generating and distributing electricity in Victoria. A year before he died in 1931 Monash was elevated to the rank of full general, the first Jew to hold this rank in any army.

The last, in a sense, of the Jewish imperialists was the picaresque Sir Roy Welensky; for several years he was a favorite character for newspaper sketches, for his career combined the most unusual and disparate elements.[194] He was evidently the only prime minister in history to have also been the heavyweight boxing champion of his country. From his father Michael, a Russian-Polish Jew from Vilna, Roy Welensky heard harrowing stories of life under czarist rule. At the age of sixteen, Welensky's father had severed his own trigger-finger in order to avoid serving as a conscript in the czarist Russian army. Then he emigrated to the United States and built up a fur-trading business in the Midwest. The diamond rush to Kimberley drew Michael Welensky to South Africa, however, where, after making and losing a small fortune, he went to Rhodesia seeking gold. He married a "hardy Afrikaner woman" and had thirteen children, of whom the last was Roy, born in 1907.

Though only half Jewish, Roy Welensky preserved his Jewish affiliation.[195] He was ambitious, enterprising, and endowed with a powerful and tall physical stature. His mother died when he was eleven, and his father, aged and defeated, could not help him. Welensky left school at the age of fourteen and moved from one occupation to another, much as young Americans once did on the frontier. He worked as a clerk, bartender, storekeeper, butcher, baker, and miner; his habits remained abstemious, for he was a teetotaler and loyal only to hot Russian tea. When he was seventeen years old he became a railway worker, serving as a locomotive fireman and then engineer. Meanwhile, however, he added to his income by pugilism, fighting his way in 1926 to the heavyweight championship and holding the title for two years. At the age of twenty-one he married an eighteen-year-old girl, a waitress in a Bulawayo café, who became the mother of his two children.

Self-educated and a voracious reader of history, Welensky became active in the Railway Workers' Union, a member of its national council, and a founder of the Northern Rhodesian Labour Party. "People paid their union dues when he asked for them and avoided anti-Semitic jokes in his presence."[196] His leadership in the railway union, "that most exclusive of white artisan elites,"[197] made him a natural appointee as director of manpower during World War II, and as such he had the chief responsibility for selecting workers to be released for military service.[198] Welensky became the advocate of a multi-racial partnership in the Rhodesias and an advocate of the latter's federation. He joined Sir Godfrey Huggins (later Lord Malvern) in working for this objective; Huggins became the first prime minister of the Federation of Rhodesia and Nyasaland, and in 1956 he endorsed Welensky as his successor.

Welensky called himself a "Socialist Conservative," holding that no "hard and fast philosophy" would solve the problems facing central Africa. He had a vision of African potentialities that others found unrealistic. Perhaps the ex-heavyweight champion retained too much of his Jewish political idealism. In 1945, after a strike of the African railway workers, Welensky stated his philosophy to the Northern Rhodesian Legislative Council: "We should face up to the position and guide it along proper lines . . . What I have in mind is some form of central organization consisting of experienced trade unionists and elected representatives of the African workers."[199] Critics on one side charged him with trying to move too rapidly to advance the black population; others said he was "a middle of the road white paternalist who often finds himself caught between racial extremes."[200]

British Laborites like Welensky and Sir Andrew Cohen, the assistant under-secretary of colonies in London, believed a strong multi-racial central African state "would act as a barrier to the advance of apartheid" and perhaps influence liberal opinion in South Africa itself.[201] But Welensky's policies were finally repudiated by the white voters themselves as racial lines hardened,[202] while the Federation itself fell apart in 1963. The Suez crisis became acute during the first months of Welensky's ministry. The British withdrawal, "symbolic of Britain's decline as a major power," deeply affected central African opinion and marked "a turning point in the fortunes of the Federation. It was not so much the question of British power which had been put to the test as that of will power . . . [I]t was one thing to have the means, another to believe that it was right or expedient to use them."[203] And when Ghana and Nigeria in West Africa secured their independence, the black intellectuals of the central African protectorates heard what they took to be the intimations of history and launched their movements for political independence and black majority leadership. Zimbabwe and Zambia replaced Southern and Northern Rhodesia, and Malawi replaced Nyasaland.

As racial divisions congealed in British Africa and war-weary Britain renounced imperialism, the African states took the direction of one-party dictatorships, usually weighted through their armies and bureaucracies by the hegemony of some particular tribe. The one-party state became their political norm, and the propensity for one-party states to affiliate themselves with a totalitarian imperialism remains an outstanding phenomenon in the latter part of the twentieth century.

Perhaps there was a certain dramatic appropriateness that the Jewish colonial civil servant, Sir Andrew Cohen, had so large a part in the organized dismantling of the British Empire in Africa. A man large and powerful in physique (he was a tall and imposing figure when he came to lecture at Berkeley), educated at Trinity College, Cambridge, he was also reputed to hold left wing political views. Born in 1909, he entered the Colonial Office, and as assistant under-secretary from 1947 to 1951 helped Arthur Creech Jones, the Laborite colonial secretary, to ready the African colonies for self-rule and independence. Creech Jones, once a workingman, high trade union official, and a conscientious objector in World War I, had been much influenced as a boy by the agitation of Morel and Casement. He found in Andrew Cohen a comrade in anti-imperialism, one who would cooperate with him to bring native African intellectuals to political power. "Up to now," said Andrew Cohen, "Nigeria has been governed by a benevolent autocracy of officials . . . The day of such autocratic government is passing and more and more educated Africans have got to be brought into the administrative machine."[204] Cohen was later dispatched as governor-general in 1952 to Uganda, already a troubled area, where he served until 1957. He was characterized as "perhaps the most imperious anti-imperialist in the history of the empire, and where his writ ran one somehow had the feeling that Victoria was still on the throne."[205] He was involved in a sharp controversy with the ruler of Buganda who wanted to take his tribe out of Uganda; Cohen's arguments prevailed, though the horrible tribal animosities that were in later years to disfigure an independent Uganda were already in evidence. In 1957 Sir Andrew Cohen was appointed permanent British representative at the United Nations Trusteeship Council, and three years later, when the age of "dis-imperialism" was entering its bloom, and the British government created a Ministry for Overseas Development, Sir Andrew Cohen became its head. There was no religious faith left in him, and when he died in 1968 his memorial service was held at St. Paul's Cathedral; but to honor his Judaic antecedents, the lesson was read by Chaim Raphael, formerly Hebrew lecturer at Oxford. An "immense assembly of African leaders" were present.[206]

From Barney Barnato to Sir Andrew Cohen—that indeed summarized the evolving role of the Jew in British imperialism in Africa. Despite his role in dismantling the British Empire, Cohen summed up its chief accomplishment: "One final point about British officers. Perhaps the most striking characteristic about them as a class is their concern for the people they are working for and with. Most of them not only work very hard, but identify themselves very closely, often parochially, with the people of their area . . . They care tremendously about what they are doing. That is why so often when they leave an area they are remembered with deep affection by the people."[207] Would the successive independent regimes be able to say as much?

One cannot leave the subject of Jewish imperialists without mentioning that during the years before World War I, when Germany directed the welfare of colonies in Africa and the Pacific, its most creative, far-seeing *Kolonialdirektor* was a man generally known as a Jew, Bernhard Dernburg. Actually, Dernburg's father had been baptized as a child. His son, Bernhard, philosophic in temperament, seems to have had much in common with the philosophical Kantian and socialistic Jewish industrialist, Walther Rathenau; in fact, the two men, though not close friends, at the suggestion of Chancellor von Bülow undertook joint journeys of inspection into Africa in 1907 and 1908.[208] Like Rathenau, Dernburg was in many ways "an example of Germany's new managerial class."[209] Also, like most of the German-Jewish bankers among whom he had grown up, he was an Anglophile and a member of the German Peace Society. Moreover, he had stayed long in the United States studying the American business methods that he admired.[210] Appointed Kolonialdirektor by Chancellor von Bülow in 1906, his office was raised to the rank of a ministry the following year.

The esteemed Hannah Arendt has argued that a proto-totalitarian drive was already latent in German imperialism in Africa. Certainly, the "brutal beatings" of African natives that were a part of the German administrative system in East Africa and Togo, and the cruelties directed against the Herero tribes in 1904-1905 when they revolted in Southwest Africa are redolent with a proto-exterminative animus.[211] The German forces led by Lothar von Trotha left survivors among the rebellious Herero deprived of their kin, their cattle, and their land, and laden with a permanent, implacable hatred of German *kultur*.[212] But this *Vernichtungstrategie* (strategy of annihilation) shocked many German people, whose representatives spoke their minds freely.

Dernburg himself brought quite a different spirit to the German imperialist venture; he became known both as a "scientific" colonialist and as one who, in a Kantian spirit, refused to regard the Africans as means only, as solely "economic men," but rather as ends in themselves and therefore deserving fair wages, decent housing, and protection from unfair labor contracts. Consequently, Dernburg acquired the reputation of a "Negrophile." Dernburg felt that with fair wages, the Negroes would become reliable workingmen and then, in due time, entrepreneurs. He also felt that corporal punishments debased the human potential and worth of the Africans. With "courage, determination, and a sense of publicity,"[213] Dernburg advocated his philosophy and policies in the Reichstag.

To promote agricultural development, it was essential that an adequate system of cheap railway transport replace the costly porterage. Under Dernburg's leadership from 1906-1914, a railway system was constructed with about forty-five hundred kilometers of track.[214] Other lines were extended, and although almost all the railways were owned by the government, the ownership of land by individuals making their own decisions as to crops was Dernburg's aim; local administrators, however, retained a propensity for assigning quotas. Dernburg was pleased that standards of living rose; more clothes, tools, utensils, tea, matches, and salt were sold.[215]

Perhaps the pattern of regressive imperialism then was not altogether a necessary development from the character of the earlier German imperialism. The unbridled destructive impulse toward the Jews, the will to exterminate whole cities and communities of Polish and Russian Jews was not in 1914-1918 a trait of the German psyche. As Professor C. Abramsky has written: "The German army, on the other hand, conducted a reasonable policy in the occupied parts of Poland, Lithuania, and White Russia; the army high command allowed Hebrew and Yiddish publications; sanctioned the legal activities of the Zionists, as well as of the Socialist Bund, hoping to encourage a new pro-German mood in the population. At the same time, it supported the national aspirations of the Poles."[216] Even the German emperor was concerned about maintaining the reputation of his regime for fair dealings with minority peoples. Fearing that the Young Turks might unleash further massacres and try to do next with the Palestinian Jews as they had already done with the Armenians, he brought pressure for a policy of tolerance. It is mostly forgotten now that Germany was "the first European power to assist the Zionists and protect their enterprise in Palestine."[217] German authorities during World War I treated the millions of Polish and Russian Jews in the occupied areas fairly: "They abrogated the restrictions enforced under the Russian regime; elementary education was made compulsory . . . secondary schools and universities were thrown open to Jewish students . . . Jews were given fair representation in municipal councils."[218] Liberal German Jews cooperated with the German government in setting up a proper administration for the occupied Jewish areas in Eastern Europe.[219]

Though anti-Semitism was not a pronounced trait in Turkey and the

Jews were esteemed as enemies of the Russian Czar, influential Turkish officials nonetheless began to play with the idea of conducting large-scale deportations of Jews from Jerusalem and Jaffa and to connive at their massacre. The German Colonel Kress, attached to the Ottoman Army, warned against the "unimaginable consequences . . . The terrible incidents of the Armenian exodus would have been repeated . . . Thousands would have died of starvation . . . and we Germans would have again been made scapegoats for this senseless measure." When the German Embassy intervened, these deportations were countermanded by the Turkish government.[220] Mass arrests of Jews took place, however, as at Haifa where the governor "'meant to outlaw them and deliver them to the rage of the [Muslim] population as had been done in the case of the Armenians.'"[221] All the Jews in Palestine were being accused of espionage, and the noted Jewish Zionist sociologist, Arthur Ruppin, received an appeal: "Something must be done, a strong power must intervene . . . Otherwise . . . the whole population will be destroyed."[222] Once again, in October 1917, the Kaiser's foreign minister intervened, and the German commander in the Middle East, von Falkenhayn, was able to get an unequivocal promise that the Jews would remain secure.[223] Jews had felt sufficiently identified with German society that, when the war broke out in 1914, they greeted it, as Ernst Simon wrote, as an "unbelievable experience, an intoxicating happiness which enabled them to forget their complicated egos and to be able to participate in the fate of the fatherland with millions of others."[224] The philosopher Martin Buber was among the foremost in expressing this identification. In America many years later, in 1961, Hans Morgenthau, the realistic political scientist, explained that "German Jewry, being predominantly middle-class in social composition and liberal in political and philosophic outlook, shared to the full the optimistic mood of the liberal middle classes . . . Why should it not look to the future with optimistic anticipation?"[225]

F. As Pariahs During the Decline of British Imperialism

At the outset of the interwar era, between 1918 and 1939, British imperialism continued a symbiotic relationship with Jewish participation in its new Zionist form. Jewish settlers in Palestine, far from exploiting the labor of others, wished to become laborers and farmers themselves and to find a respite from pogroms and persecutions by restoring to fertility a dry, denuded, and largely depopulated land that remained sacred in their memories. The British Empire offered them their opportunity; it was an empire, said Chaim Weizmann, later Israel's first president, that was built on "moral principles." A chemist and lecturer at the University of Manchester and the chief of the World Zionist movement, Weizmann meant what he said in all sincerity.[226] To Weizmann, as Isaiah Berlin has written, "England, above all other lands, stood for settled democracy, humane and peaceful civilization, civil liberty, legal equality, stability, toleration, respect for individual rights, and a religious tradition founded as much on the Old Testament as the New. She embodied all those free middle-class virtues." Weizmann remained devoted to England almost to the end, to her "generosity, steadfastness, integrity of character, and especially nobility of style."[227] This was a fidelity that was long reciprocated, and its withdrawal broke Weizmann's spirit. By 1939, the British appeasement of Hitler and his Nazis, the British failure in imagination and enterprise, and British retreat from moral principles, seemed to him to signify "exhaustion and defeat," the "gloomy condition of decline." To Winston Churchill, who almost alone among British statesmen shared Weizmann's concerns, Weizmann could say: "Remember, sir, our enemies are also yours."[228] The Cambridge economist John Maynard Keynes, on the other hand, asserting that an impoverished Britain must retrench from its moral commitments, allegedly incompatible, to the Jews and Arabs, seemed to Weizmann to be articulating a policy "suicidal" for Britain's greatness.[229] Having based his lifework on the hope that the new Jewish country would be associated with the British Empire, Weizmann noted grimly what he regarded as the latter's repudiation of honor and humanity.

As Britain's imperial vocation declined, a mood of anti-Semitism grew among its governing circles, its military officers, and the population generally. When the British government in 1937 proposed to allow no more than twelve thousand Jewish immigrants to enter Palestine each year, thereby depriving most refugees from Naziism of a possible Jewish sanctuary, Weizmann spoke his bitterness: "But this trifling with a nation bleeding from a thousand wounds must not be done by the British whose Empire is built on moral principles—that mighty Empire must not commit this sin against the people of the Book."[230]

The abrogation of moral principles of imperialism, however, was part and parcel of Britain's decline. The home secretary of Britain's wartime Cabinet, the respected Laborite Herbert Morrison, refused to receive more than two thousand Jewish refugees despite the offered guarantee that they would not constitute an economic charge because, in his opinion, such arrivals might "stir up an unpleasant degree of anti-Semitism (of which there is a fair amount just below the surface)." As late as May 1945, Morrison felt that if Jewish refugees were allowed to remain in England, "they might be an explosive element in the country." Anti-Semitic rumors concerning, for instance, Jews' evading military service, were making their rounds in tense wartime England. Closest to Weizmann's heart was the plan for organizing a Jewish army in Palestine with its own identity that would fight on European fronts against the Nazis for the liberation of fellow Jews from the death camps. With virtually one exception, the commanding circles of the British government and army reacted with hostility to the idea. Was it that some feared that the Jewish achievement in arms and courage, as in science and the arts, might contravene their prejudices? Alone in supporting the proposal, especially when in 1942 it appeared likely that the Nazis might invade Palestine itself even as the British withdrew, was the prime minister, Winston Churchill. He admonished his colonial secretary: "Now that these people are in direct danger, we should certainly give them a chance to defend themselves. . . . It may be necessary to make an example of some of these anti-Semitic officers and others in high places. If three or four of them were recalled and dismissed, and the reason given, it would have a very salutary effect."[231] Churchill pungently rebuked his cabinet that "it might have been thought a matter for satisfaction that the Jews in Palestine should possess arms, and be capable of providing for their own defense. They were the only trustworthy friends we had in that country," but his views got no support from colleagues who wanted no truck with separate Jewish units.[232] When the Middle East Commander-in-Chief, General Wavell, strenuously resisted the idea of a Jewish Army, Churchill commented tellingly: "General Wavell, like most British army officers, is strongly pro-Arab." Churchill could not, however, overcome his cabinet's recalcitrance. In the midst of the Holocaust, his own colonial office was mostly concerned with expelling Jews who had managed to escape through Turkey and Rumania.[235] The scheme of Weizmann and Churchill was delayed until 1944 when a Jewish Brigade was created.

Weizmann later recalled the agony of impotence during the War's worst year: "Day after day the reports of death chambers in Auschwitz and Maidanek poured in; day after day frantic cables came through Geneva begging for certificates . . . Even the Nazis were ready not to deport if you could show proof that a certificate will be forthcoming. . . . The Swedish government promised to take in 20,000 Jewish children if the British government were to undertake their transfer to Palestine after the war. The offer was turned down, and these children, like hundreds of thousands of others, went to the gas chambers. . . . [T]he Home Government was adamant."[234]

Throughout this unhappy time, Winston Churchill remained the surviving embodiment of the creative power, philosophy, and resolve of those who had once forged the empire. He responded sympathetically to Jews who shared his own Disraelian sense. His spontaneous ethical perceptions of events had never been warped by ideology. As a young member of Parliament, he had denounced the pogroms in the Russia of the czars and campaigned in his Manchester constituency against the Aliens Act that was designed to restrict the immigration of Russian Jews. As a colonial secretary in 1921-1922, he voiced an enthusiasm for the Jewish national home that he later reiterated to an embarrassed Stalin and achieved an accord that both Chaim Weizmann and Colonel T. E. Lawrence ("of Arabia") could approve.[236] Out of office in the 1930s, Churchill alone among British statesmen spoke and wrote straightforwardly against Nazi anti-Semitism. "Every kind of persecution, grave or petty, upon the world-famous scientists, writers, and composers, at the top down to the wretched little Jewish children in the national schools, was practiced, was glorified," he wrote in 1935 as he repeatedly assailed "the irresistible power of the Totalitarian State."[237] Churchill shared Weizmann's dream of a Palestine of three or four million Jews, and when during the war he would have to transmit to Weizmann the British Cabinet's refusals, he would feel "a twist in his heart."[238] The cabinet of 1939 he characterized as "a lot of lily-livered rabbits" who would "chop off a piece here and there" from the Jewish state. Weizmann wrote him in 1941 that the British cabinet seemed to wish to repress the existence of the Jews from its consciousness: though thousands of Palestinian Jews fought for the Allied cause, "our people are never mentioned; our name is shunned; all contact or co-operation with us is kept dark as if it were compromising." The foreign secretary, Anthony Eden, reacted to this letter by saying it made him even "less inclined to help Dr. Weizmann."[239]

"It was a cardinal principle of British policy that the Jews should not gain state sovereignty" concludes Bernard Wasserstein, a judicious and thorough student of the subject.[240] What lay behind this policy? Despite its virtual refusal to allow Jewish immigrants into Britain during and after World War II, the British government was, however, not unwilling to accept the immigration of between one to two million blacks from the West Indies and Africa. Were the blacks more intelligent, abler, or more skilled than the Jews, or more assimilable into the British nation? That is doubtful. But Laborite internationalist and conservative Christian alike might perhaps experience a certain exhilaration as having been among God's messengers of righteousness in extending the hand of salvation to peoples more backward than their own, peoples who had perhaps, in their view, fallen behind the advance of civilization. It was a collectively self-punitive ethic that contravened the British national interest and set aside rational criteria for admittance into one's peoplehood, but it brought a diverting, self-congratulatory feeling of righteousness, for the internationalist ethic of British Socialists and Christians had a strong element of "under-doggism" that yielded a high psychic dividend for their investment in presumable self-sacrifice on behalf of the backward, underdeveloped, and sometimes undercivilized. The Jews, by contrast, though cosmopolitans, were not apparently submissive in spirit. Despite their vicissitudes, they evidently regarded themselves as intellectually inferior to no one and possibly, it was surmised, even intellectually superior. Without benefit of the Protestant ethic, they were frequently endowed with a capacity to outwork any other group. Readers of books, auditors at concerts, patrons of universities, they were aristocrats without a landed base. Feelings of righteousness are more easily indulged by helping one's inferiors than in assisting one's superiors. Sir Frederick Pollock, the dispassionate jurist, indicated his opinion to his friend, Justice Holmes, that the chief cause for anti-Semitism was that Jews, being smarter, made others jealous.[241] The British people, losing confidence in themselves, with a consciousness that they were being displaced by competing powers were, like the declining Romans, more prepared to receive undercivilized barbarians than over-civilized Jews.

Thus, with the ebb of its imperial calling, British attitudes became affected for a time with a certain animus against the Jews. Ernest Bevin, the Laborite foreign secretary during the post-war years, and a trade union leader of long standing, found the Jews (especially the New York variety) as much of a nuisance as had the conservative military figures in Churchill's War Office. Britain unselfishly would take the most extraordinary measures between 1942 and the war's end to supply the entire food needs of the civilian population of Greece, then occupied by the Nazi army; the relief of Jews in the Nazi camps, on the other hand, was absent from the agenda for good works. Extraordinary efforts were made to assist the Warsaw outbreak of the Polish Home Army in the late summer of 1944; not even a symbolic effort was made to answer the Jewish appeal less than a year and a half earlier during the uprising of the Warsaw Ghetto.[242]

THE IMPERIALIST SPIRIT
AND THE ANTI-IMPERIAL MIND

A. The Ideology of Imperialist Guilt

Western peoples, it has been noted, have been peculiarly susceptible to feelings of guilt concerning their imperialist role. The guilt, it has sometimes been suggested, derives from the Christian myth of guilt and sin, for the Moslems, despite their many centuries of maltreatment of Africans, seem utterly devoid of such self-reproach.[1] The horrors of the Arabs' traffic in African Negro slaves, though well-chronicled, are rarely recited today. The traffic long outlasted the American Civil War.[2] Between the years 1860 to 1876 at least four-hundred thousand natives, it has been estimated, were enslaved for use in the Middle East and North Africa. The researches of the scholar, explorer and adventurer Richard Burton in Cairo and Alexandria led him to conclude that three-fourths of the natives of Darfur were transported in the slave caravans for Egypt, Arabia and Turkey.[3] The annual number of "mutilations" were about eight thousand A fourth of the boys castrated under the age of five died and the death rate rose with the victim's age to seventy percent for ten-year-olds. Twenty to forty thousand slaves were being taken annually to Zanzibar, a third of them dying every year from disease and malnutrition.[4] Nonetheless, the writings of Arab and black ideologists alike evince no trace of an Arab-Moslem guilt. One has heard of no televised Arab counterpart to the popular and influential film *Roots.*[5]

The "white man's burden," on the other hand, has been transmuted into a "burden not of power but of guilt," and as such, "taken up enthusiastically in our time."[6] Obviously, an ingredient other than a Christian influence is involved in generating this guilt concerning imperialism. The Calvinist notion of original sin is highly flexible, with many potential directions and applications. Scottish Calvinists and South African Calvinists have shared a common theology, but the former have condemned the system of apartheid while the latter have defended it. The Scottish Calvinsts, it is said, used the theological doctrine of predestination to reinforce capitalist individualistic drives; the South African Calvinists, on the other hand, beheld their racial differences and inequalities with respect to the blacks and decided they were predestined. Imperialists from the seventeenth to the nineteenth centuries showed little signs of bearing a burden of guilt. Obviously, certain changes affected the psyche of the late nineteenth and twentieth centuries that made Western white civilization guilt-prone.

The predator-prey analogy, as we have seen, runs through the literature of anti-imperialism. There is no case, however, in the biological world of plants and animals where the predator's activities result in a huge multiplication of the prey's population.[7] As we have seen, however, such was precisely the impact of imperialism on the greater part of the backward peoples. Imperialism brought with it a tremendous rise in the populations of Africa and Asia. From West Africa to Java it put an end to the tribal wars that, periodically decimating populations, made genocide a recurrent phenomenon. The death toll of epidemics was reduced by health measures. Although most of the colonial areas remained backward in technology, and pre-feudal, feudal, or absolutist in their social systems, they received at the hands of the imperialist power a set of medical and political services that were the high achievements of the Western capitalist nations. A social imbalance was thus created by the development of imperialism: the impact of its social measures was to reduce the death rate and to introduce the first educational opportunities in societies that remained predominantly pre-industrial in life and outlook, but the Malthusian principle of circular causality that had resulted in a balance between population and technology was thus disrupted.[8] The imperialist intervention negated such equilibrating mechanisms as disease, famine, and war; it typically introduced more sanitation and education, thereby causing a huge growth in population. A corresponding growth in economic development, however, usually failed to take place, no matter whether the country retained its independence or was administered by an imperialist power. Evidently certain socio-psychological conditions are necessary for a spontaneous, autonomous economic advance. Therefore, the relinquishment of imperialism has been followed by efforts in the quondam colonial countries to reinstate an equilibrium which, however, now eludes the self-regulating powers of automatic, natural adjustment. The compulsory sterilization program in India, the "peasantization" of urban dwellers in Cambodia, the re-tribalization in parts of Africa, are aspects of the equilibration to a lower level of societies in post-imperialist domains. Wherever the Western industrial system was more than peripheral to traditional tribal economies, where it evoked, for instance, a large de-tribalization of natives, as in the South African diamond and gold mines or Rhodesian copper mines, a change in the traditional values has been partially catalyzed. In traditional centers, on the other hand, machine technology remained absent; apart from local tradesmen, furthermore, an entrepreneurial middle class was missing. In physico-chemical systems, disturbances to equilibrium are resolved in accordance with what is known as the Principle of Le Chatelier: the system responds to reinstate an equilibrium that has been disturbed by a change in one of its factors by a transformation in the opposite direction that minimizes that change.[9] In primitive social systems, however, the introduction of health measures and education by the imperialist power may engender disequilibria for which the social system may have no adequate re-equilibrating resources.[10]

Among the political economists of the left, a doctrine has been fashioned that "neo-Malthusianism" is false, that it is not a surplus population but the extraction of surplus value that has made it difficult for the large numbers of backward peoples to raise their living standards. "Neo-Malthusianism, through the so-called theory of population explosion," write two neo-Leftist economists, "plays an ever more important role in a false attempt to explain the causes of underdevelopment"; rather, they hold, it is "the form of social organization" which to an "ever greater degree" is incapable of guaranteeing the population their standard of living.[11] But Communist China's attempts to cope with its multiplying numbers through massive propaganda and political pressure discouraging early marriage and large families, widespread Indian malnutrition, and the calamitous Cambodian starvation, are all evidence, often stark, that the primary source of the problem of "overpopulation" is not "capitalist imperialism" but the combination of advanced medical technology with the relative persistence of pre-industrial mores.

The heart of the problem was that imperialism, rather than acting as a predator, had instead suspended the predatory processes, both biological and social, enabling the quondam "prey" to increase unprecedentedly. Thus Communist governments in Cambodia and Vietnam then undertook to act the part of the predator; in the West, nonetheless, leftist ideologists, obedient to a self-accusatory imperative have tried to deform their perceptions so as to have a terminal image of the West as predator.

From such a neo-Marxist standpoint all Western civilization bears the sinister taint of the exploiter. Marxist language is used as a "guilt-inculcating idiom" to impugn Western standards and instate instead the African and the Asian as the consciences, the "super-egos," of the Westerner. The West, far from being cheered for its achievements, for its science, literature, art, and technology, is called upon to feel shame for them. Hitler is depicted as the logical conclusion of Christian bourgeois society, as the latent embodied demon always inhabiting the bourgeois mind; the bourgeois, it is even alleged, was displeased with Hitler only because white men were the objects of his genocide.[12] Yet the plain fact is that far more representative of the "Christian bourgeois" ethic than the irrational Adolf Hitler were Franklin D. Roosevelt and Woodrow Wilson, both of whom, altogether unlike the Nazi leader, were imbued with bourgeois rationality, bourgeois ethics and calculation. Moreover, in African-Asian history, genocide, large-scale massacre, and tribal extirpation have been much more a continuous phenomenon than the aberrant episodes in

Western civilization. Long before the advent of imperialism, Africans "dehumanized" one another on a massive scale. The history of African tribes is not infrequently a history of tribal genocide. Among the South African Zulu, "it was the settled conviction of every Zulu that his manhood was not complete nor his tribal standing established until he had 'washed his spears' in the blood of a foe." Under the despot Shaka, the massacre of the enemy's children and women had the aspect of a "frenzied butchery."[13] Shaka was murdered, but his successor, Dingane, was "no less brutal."[14] Neo-Marxist primitivists often write of the African's wonderful unity with nature. But the narratives of the deeds of the apparition-haunted witch doctors, with their intermittent role in abetting collective self-destruction, bespeak rather the sense of a disunity with a demonic nature and a consequent anxiety that was ever-present. In 1857 the witch-doctors provoked a killing of cattle among the Xhosas; as a result, between twenty-five to fifty thousand people died of starvation.[15] The communism of African tribes has been similarly lauded for its overcoming the alienation of men from each other.[16] Yet tribal communism, as a historical reality, "alienated" the most intelligent and enterprising tribesmen from the collective, dictatorial tribal authority. Tribal communism, for instance, thus prevailed in Rhodesia prior to the advent of the South Africa Company. It endorsed, however, a repression of the individual, making dominant the backwardness of the lazy and mediocre. Tribal custom dictated the sharing of food. "There was consequently little incentive to grow more crops"; lazy relatives were always at hand to take their workless shares. Tribal life was so filled with frustration that inter-tribal wars provided a socially useful safety valve for accumulated aggressive, resentful energies. Among the pastoral Nzoni and the agricultural Bemba alike, the "attributes of warriorhood" were thus invested with the supreme value.[17] It was the British South Africa Company that first brought the message and enforcement of peace.

The notion of Western guilt for Third World poverty and mutual destruction persists, however. As P. T. Bauer has indicated, underlying it is the reinforcing influence of Marxist ideology. The notion that the poverty of their peoples is the consequence of their exploitation at the hands of foreign nations is emotively axiomatic for many Asians and Africans. Since all peoples are presumed equal in intelligence, initiative, motivations for work, and cultural opportunity for the inventor and innovator, it follows that a people can be backward only because it is exploited. Yet most of the world's backward peoples obviously have led lives mainly isolated from imperialist domains; moreover, those areas of such countries as India and Indonesia that experienced British and Dutch imperialism became far more developed than they could reasonably have expected to be under the continued rule of rajahs and sultans. At this juncture, the gravamen of the indictment of Western civilization shifts rather to its presumed "cultural imperialism" and away from the "economic imperialism." The Third World, it is alleged, has been and is being corrupted by a form of "cultural dependence" on the West, through the allure of Western goods, Western films, Western books.[18] Nevertheless, precisely this mode of "cultural diffusion"—the spread of the arts, literature, science, and writing—has been the greatest contribution of imperialism from Roman and Athenian times onward. A peasant family in Japan told me once to my surprise why they preferred American movies on television to Japanese traditional plays—so much happened so quickly, the hero and heroine were cheerful, and there was a happy ending. Western capitalist literature, beginning with Defoe and Fielding in the eighteenth century, it might be said, contributed the "happy ending" hitherto relatively infrequent in the world's writings. The American cowboy movies too gave a sense of possibility and hope that the No plays lacked; naïf Western stories refused to acquiesce to ineluctable tragedy in every department of life; they were naturally neither martyrologies, nor lachrymologies, nor suicidologies, and shared something of William James' optimistic pragmatism.

A self-excusing postulate has been promulgated for the Third World. Despite large-scale massacres in India and Pakistan, tribal genocide in African republics, the prevalence of blatant personal tyranny, and the expulsion of racial minorities such as the Hindus from Kenya, it is presumed that "Third World governments are not really guilty." Western ideologists acquiesce to a unilateral principle that condones or welcomes immoralities on the part of one race even as they are condemned in another. The white Western ideologist who not infrequently cultivates hostility toward his own civilization, wishes to weigh it in the scales and to find it wanting; at the same time, he may exonerate and even feel exhilarated by the cruelty of the Third World. Churchmen feel a strange elevation in fulfilling a self-punitive role; international organizations experience an exaltation of holiness as they enact resolutions against civilized countries; their draftsmen, people "disillusioned with their own society," in their "toleration and even support of the brutal politics of many Third World governments" seem to reflect a curious mixture of guilt feelings and condescension."[19] No doubt Cyril Connolly spoke for many fellow intellectuals: "It is a wonder that the white man is not more thoroughly detested than he is . . . In our dealings with every single country, greed, masked by hypocrisy, led to unscrupulous coercion of the native inhabitants . . . Cruelty, greed and arrogance . . . characterized what can be summed up in one word, exploitation."[20]

From its inception, the critique of Western imperialism, even in those instances where it was justified, has been permeated by the strain of self-hatred for civilization. Perhaps the most celebrated episode in the denunciation of Western imperialism was that generated by the horrors perpetrated by the regime of the Belgian king Leopold II through his so-called Congo Free State. Much scholarship has been devoted recently to this episode. Roger Casement and E. D. Morel are remembered for having brought the facts to the attention of the world, while Mark Twain's bitter pamphlet, *King Leopold's Soliloquy*, written at the urging of E. D. Morel, is still reprinted as an anti-imperialist tract.[21]

However, reform movements in Western imperialism were always founded on the fact that the motivation of Western imperialism has invariably included a moral component. Because Western imperialism has arisen in countries that were pluralistic, parliamentary, capitalistic, and liberal, there have always been agencies prepared to expose, discuss, and correct misdeeds, abuses, and crimes. Thus, the history of British imperialism is punctuated with famous cases of the trials of imperialist officials: Warren Hastings faced the eloquent indictment of Edmund Burke and long years of trial; through the efforts notably of John Stuart Mill, Edward Eyre, the governor of Jamaica, was arraigned in 1865 before the public and parliament for his allegedly overzealous executions;[22] and even Robert Clive, the military conqueror of India, was shadowed by parliamentary inquiry. And it was also the British government that directed the investigations into the atrocities of the Belgian Congo.

Secondly, the worst episodes of imperialist cruelty have occurred when the imperialist venture was conducted under state socialist auspices. As E. D. Morel himself pointed out, it was the replacement of competitive capitalism by a state socialist monopoly which made possible the Congo system of horrors: "The wrong done to the Congo peoples originates from the substitution of commerce . . . . with the consequent onus upon the European to purchase that produce which modern industrialism requires, by a system based upon the right of a European state to expropriate the Native of tropical Africa from his land . . . . [T]he destruction of commercial relationship between the European and the African in tropical Africa means the enslavement of the African."[23] Though Leopold II held a virtually absolute sovereignty, his personal imperialism constituted in fact a Belgian "state imperialism." The profits he extracted from his Congo state enterprises went, as Jean Stengers writes, "almost exclusively to enrich the national heritage by acquisitions of property, by monumental constructions, and by works of urbanization. His obsession was not with his own fortune but with the embellishment of his country."[24] From the compulsory labor of Congo natives in the collection and coagulation of India rubber there arose the magnificent National Palace in Brussels used for conferences of notables and public convocations. When a socialist "people's imperialism" operates, all those competitive, pluralistic groups that in a capitalist setting are ready to unmask abuses, to denounce unfair practice and profiteering, and to indict illegal acts done for personal enrichment, are disabled. Socialistic "exploitation" always, say its practitioners, in self-extenuation, is done neither for self nor for personal profit, but for the people; therefore, who would charge them with guilt? "To serve the people" has been the most effective formula for self-exculpation from responsibility for one's personal cruelty that has ever been invented.

Thirdly, the worst imperialist atrocities have taken place when the state's enforcement of its aims was a task assigned to forces drawn from primitive tribes with primitive traditions of cruelty. A large part of the Belgian forces in the Congo were, as E. D. Morel observed, "recruited from tribes which are still notably cannibalistic . . . Cannibalism clings, and if you stick a rifle into a cannibal's hand, and put a uniform on his back, you don't thereby convert him into a vegetarian." During "the carnival of massacre" designed to subjugate the tribes to deliver their tributes of ivory and rubber, "the bulk of the black mercenaries" were Hausa and Yoruba tribesmen, drawn from British Nigeria.[25]

Finally, as we have seen, the moral standards that have been justly invoked against Christian Europeans were curiously relaxed when it came to judging the simultaneous actions of Moslem Arabs in Africa. Throughout the latter part of the nineteenth century, from the Sudan to the Congo, Arab slave traders were still engaged in "cannibal levies" and finding "their commissariat in the bodies of the slain." Western European dominion, because it usually terminated the "incessant wars" waged either to secure wives or victims for feasts, consequently contributed to the growth of the population.[26] By contrast, the Arabs tended to depopulate their areas of control. Nevertheless, howsoever the Arab raiders enslaved Negroes, castrated them, or exterminated them, critical Western intellectuals have not expected Moslem Arabs to conform to the standard they may have mandated for Christian Westerners.

The denunciators and unmaskers of purported "imperialist hypocrisy" have been convinced that this was an evil endemic to and inherent in Western civilization. Morel warned Europe of the inevitable aftermath, "the Nemesis of Europe's action in Africa." Would an Asian counterimperialism arise, he wondered, "as ruthless as our own has been," or even more—a retribution that a stern History would exact? Europe, he urged, must acknowledge for the African problem "a consciousness of past sins," or be adjudged "a hypocrite."[27] One's own anti-imperialist "virtue" is usually presumed to be free from hypocrisy. Roger Casement, consul for the British government, whose reports convinced official eyes of the horrors that had taken place in the Belgian Congo, was a man with a marred character; he hated the British world as that world from which he had to hide his homosexual deviations. Knighted by the British Empire, he died on the gallows as a traitor to that Empire.[28] To what extent, we shall ask, was his anti-imperialism a projection of the perverse feelings that moved him? The Belgian king Leopold evidently loomed in his mind as a hated father figure.[29] The industrious Morel "thought that the Congo before the advent of the white man had been a paradise of sorts." His friend Sir Harry Johnston who knew Africa at first-hand for many years told him, however, in 1907, "Frankly, it [the Congo] was not much better than the state to which Leopold has now reduced it." And in Morel's mind too, Leopold fulfilled the role of "totem of demonology."[30] The crimes of the Congo state imperialists were real enough and required no exaggeration. But the numbers Morel calculated for the depopulation of the Congo have been characterized as "figments of the imagination." The desire to idealize in primitivist fashion the African black, "untouched, untainted," as Casement said, was the converse of the desire to denigrate the achievements of one's own advanced society. Mark Twain, America's most wonderful writer, had a recurrent strain in him of contempt for the human species and all its works. Oscillating in despair between determinism and solipsism, in empathetic protest, a town's ne'er-do-well seemed to him *a priori* more admirable than its men of substance. In his anti-imperialistic tract he found, similarly, a subject that confirmed an indignation he felt toward all humankind.

This partially masochist strain, pervading the anti-imperialist critique and providing a groundwork for the animus against civilization, is the emotional core of contemporary regressive ideology. That is why the historical model of the Congo agitation and the character of the personalities involved is so significant. E. D. Morel wrote discerningly: "Roger Casement succeeded throughout his Congo and Putumayo labors in inoculating the diplomacy of this country with a moral toxin."[31] Thus during the latter part of the nineteenth century the attitude of socialists toward imperialism shifted. The classical socialists usually had been imperialists as well. In England, for instance, John Ruskin, with his socialistic protest against industrialism and his call for the restoration of human values in work and art, deeply moved many men, including such diverse figures as Mahatma Gandhi, Tolstoy, Charles A. Beard, and J. A. Hobson. But in his lecture at Oxford in 1870, Ruskin, as we have seen, also had called for England to rule as "mistress of half the earth," and to found "motionless navies" everywhere. Most significantly he had stirred the undergraduate Cecil Rhodes, later the greatest of imperialists.[32] Hobson, although drawn by Ruskin toward socialism, repudiated Ruskin's imperialism at the end of the century, composing instead Britain's classical anti-imperialist book.[33] Karl Marx himself never demanded that Western imperialism withdraw from Asia; hence, a leading contemporary Marxist writer on imperialism acknowledges "there was an unresolved discord in Marx's thinking about empire, between the idea of a western 'mission', and hatred of conquest," and that "Marx did not overcome the contradiction in his thinking . . . on imperialism" which was why "in the end he and Engels bequeathed to the socialist parties only a puzzlingly uncertain guidance here."[34] Neither Marx nor Engels had much regard for the guerrilla actions against imperialism: Marx deprecated an uprising in India in 1856-1857 as an affair of "a half-savage tribe . . . . put down, after *seven months' guerrilla warfare*," while Engels dismissed the North African Arab revolt against the French imperialists as the work of tribes of thieves standing against civilization and progress.[35]

The later left wing of Marxism, however, guided by such persons as Lenin and Rosa Luxemburg, came increasingly to identify themselves with anti-imperialist struggle as the foremost factor making for socialism. For many years Lenin had used "Asian" as an epithet for uncouth, uncivilized behavior, and Rosa Luxemburg herself characterized Lenin and his faction as having "Tartar-Mongolian savagery." In his last years, however, filled with hatred for European civilization, Lenin veered to the view that the decisive factor in the triumph of the world would be the allegiance of the backward peoples of the world to communism.[36] The backward peoples could adopt Soviet communism directly without any intervening stage of bourgeois development, he asserted. In Lenin's eyes, the Western European working class had failed; the elect of historical advance would not be of one's own European society but the Asian, backward part of one's self. Rosa Luxemburg smothered any sympathetic concern on her part for fellow Jews who experienced pogroms at the hands of Russian proletarians, and wrote reprovingly from prison to a Jewish friend: "Why do you come with your special Jewish sorrows? I feel just as sorry for the wretched Indian victims in Putamayo, the negroes in Africa."[37] Jewish anti-imperialists especially repressed any affection for fellow-Jews or for their own Jewish background.

The ablest critics of the Hobson-Lenin thesis, while demolishing its economic arguments, nonetheless wish themselves to be regarded as basically among the opponents of imperialism. Such historical analysts as D. K. Fieldhouse thus regard imperialism as a "delusion," as "irrational."[38] Lenin, Hobson and Rosa Luxemburg, though they excoriated imperialism, nevertheless conceded it was usually "rational" from the standpoint of the capitalists involved who were operating to maximize their profits. Thus Fieldhouse and his fellow-scholars hold that even in this sense imperialism was economically irrational; in the latter part of the nineteenth century, they note, "the new colonies were white elephants . . . their attraction for investors, except in mines, etc., was negligible; they were unsuitable for large-scale emigration, and any economic development that had taken place was usually the result of determined efforts by the European state concerned to create an artificial asset. Moreover, in most cases, the cost of administration was a dead weight on the imperial power. By 1900 all these facts were apparent and undeniable."[39] But the capital exports of Britain to such independent countries as the United States,

Canada, Australia, New Zealand, and Argentina, had not, as Lenin and Hobson believed, lowered the standard of living of Britons but had raised it by making possible the provision of "cheap and plentiful raw materials and food." Cheap tea, sugar, beef, and butter, were mostly the consequence of British investments in independent countries in trade exchanges that raised the standards of living of all concerned. Foreign investment therefore did not eventuate in an "under-consumption" on the part of the home working class. Such foreign investment, however, regarded by Lenin as part of "imperialism," was laden with the moral connotation of "exploitation."

What then, according to such writers, was the source of the imperialist drive? Its dynamic, argues Fieldhouse, "can properly be understood only in terms of the same social hysteria that has since given birth to other and more disastrous forms of aggressive imperialism. . . . In the new quasi-democratic Europe, the popularity of the imperial idea marked a rejection of the same morality of the account-book," the adopting of an ideology with such "irrational concepts as racial superiority and the prestige of the nation." Public opinion made of imperialism "a psychological necessity."[40] Was it all then "social hysteria," "aggressive nationalism"? Or has there been a rationality in imperialism to which these critics do not altogether do justice? By their logic, the classical imperialisms—the Athenian, Macedonian, and Roman—all would have stood condemned. But the Roman did spread throughout the Mediterranean a cosmpolitan legal system; it elevated those cultures that were lower and did not undermine the higher; where the Roman encountered Greek culture he did not destroy it but actually enhanced its chance of flourishing. And the Greeks under Alexander and the Ptolemies brought a higher culture to the static lassitude of Egypt and founded its great scientific institution at Alexandria. Roman imperialism in large measure inherited Alexander's notion of the common citizenship of all peoples. Similarly, the French imperialists spread concepts everywhere of the rights of man. In America, the progressive Republican, Albert J. Beveridge, of Indiana, the senator who fought hardest for a law to abolish child labor, was also the most ardent voice on behalf of an American imperialism.[41] Without exception, every people with burgeoning creative energies and aspirations has felt the desire to exert its leadership and communicate something of its attainment in civilization; the American impulse at the turn of the century to bring education, sanitation, and democracy to the Philippine Islands was not economic hypocrisy.[42] Were the Romans, the Greeks, the Englishmen of the eighteenth century, the Elizabethans, then hysterics? Or does hysteria perhaps more often characterize the self-hatred of the anti-imperialist?

B. The Will to Empire: the Prospero and Caliban Complexes

In order to "masochize" the theory of imperialism, to transform it into a self-critique of Western civilization, its critics have recently availed themselves of psychoanalytical categories. In particular, the purported psychoanalytical critique of imperialism explores the motivations of imperialists, arguing that they were mainly neurotic and that the imperialist, typically moved by a disturbed sexuality, projected his repressed desires upon colonial subjects whom he thus rendered into external embodiments of his forbidden wishes. The imperialist, it is argued, has often been moved by a sense of personal inferiority or ineradicable guilt to immerse himself in a surrogate world that grants him both a facile authority and a defense mechanism against anxiety. In an influential book, for instance, by Dominique O. Mannoni, *Prospero and Caliban,* Europeans are depicted as internalizing the Negro savage within their id, thereby personalizing their sheer untrammeled instincts. Living in a perpetual terror that their Negroid id would rebel against their effete super-ego's controls, "the negro, then, is the white man's fear of himself."[43] The consequence of this type of psychoanalytical argument is to instill and enhance feelings of guilt within the white man. If the imperialist system were indeed an elaborate projection of an anxiety arising from the repression of the Negro savage within ourselves, a way of hiding from the Mr. Hyde or Neanderthal man within us, we would all feel a heightened guilt.

Two questions confront us. First, does the purported psychoanalytical theory of imperialism give a truthful account of the motivations of imperialists? Or is it an example of what Freud called "wild psychoanalysis," a projection of ideological resentment through psychological categories? Second, what have been, by contrast, the motivations of anti-imperialists themselves? To what extent have the very same neurotic drives contributed to the activities and ideology of anti-imperialists? Have anti-imperialists constructed a psychology of imperialists that is a mirror-image of their own? Curiously, in the whole literature of imperialism and political psychology, the psychology of anti-imperialists has escaped any scrutiny.

The theory of the Prospero complex, we must note, is not merely the notion that the ranks of the imperialists, particularly their rank and file, are recruited from among those who have failed in their homelands. Long ago in 1613 the great author of *Don Quixote,* Miguel de Cervantes, described Spanish America as being "the refuge and haven of all the poor devils of Spain, the sanctuary of the bankrupt, the safeguard of murderers, the way out for gamblers, the promised land for ladies of easy virtue, and a lure and a disillusionment for the many, and a personal remedy for the few.[44] The Prospero complex affirms something more than the mobility of labor and enterprise which is, after all, a rational process; it asserts, rather, the existence of an unconscious compulsion in the imperialist's psyche: he wishes to vent his cruelty and aggression, or inflict sexual humiliation upon a subject race; he is motivated by sadism, of which imperialism is the political manifestation.

Have the great proponents and practitioners of imperialism indeed feared the Negro within themselves as the symbol of their own bestial emotions? Scarcely any evidence lies at hand for such a claim. Rhodes took pride in his Anglo-Saxon race; Barnato and Beit had theirs as Jews; nothing indicates that in their unconscious they were struggling with passions that they regarded as Negro in character. In Joseph Conrad's novels, his heroes are often defeated, depressed men who, feeling rejected by their own societies, seek to merge themselves in forgetfulness into native society. The lure of this Eastern society is matched by the feeling that one has been repelled or repudiated by one's own European society.

The "id argument" is a shrewd device, using psychoanalytical terminology to level all men by obtruding barbarian identities into every unconscious. But, apart from the terminology, what evidence is adduced from the psychology of the imperialists themselves? The self-punitive feeling evoked in the literary exposition itself is relied on to make the interpretation plausible.[45] To confirm his theory of the imperialist masochistic complex, Mannoni would have us examine "the best description of them . . . in the works [of] great writers who projected them on to imaginary characters . . . which though imaginary, are typically colonial."[46] *Lord Jim* is the principal novel of modern imperialism that he cites.[47]

Lord Jim, as Conrad portrays him, did indeed capture "much honors and an Arcadian happiness . . . The natives proclaimed him Tuan—God—the Lord." He had taken refuge in Patusan: "Nobody had been there—no one desired to go there," which to the analyst Helene Deutsch seemed behavior in "a state of insanity with delusions of grandeur."[48] Jim, a romantically ambitious daydreamer, with a "highly narcissistic ego ideal," was driven by his guilt, his gnawing "broken-down self-regard." Withdrawing into his loneliness and self-sacrifice, a "restitution process" rapidly took place. In Patusan, the ugly, degrading part of his ego was put aside. Not one of us is safe from a weakness unknown, repressed, hidden, says Marlow, the representative of wisdom who has befriended Jim. "He is one of us." And presumably that psychological, repressed weakness is, according to Mannoni, the source of the imperialist drive; for the imperialist character, from Mannoni's standpoint, is a defense mechanism against corroding guilt.

Thus Conrad's depiction of Lord Jim is taken as confirming Mannoni's theory of the Prospero complex that "no one becomes a real colonial who is not impelled by infantile complexes which were not properly resolved in adolescence," and that "colonial life is simply a substitute to those who are still obscurely drawn to a world without men—to those, that is, who have failed to make the effort necessary to adapt infantile images to real identity."[49]

Literature is often, however, more of a guide to the psychology of the novelist than to the social reality of his place and time.[50] Conrad the novelist evidently projected upon the character of the imperialist something of that own personal guilt that tormented him and that led him to a seaman's career in the Pacific seas; there are some who have held that that guilt was derived from his desertion of the Polish revolutionary cause to which his father had consecrated his life.

The actual character, however, upon whom the fictional person of Lord Jim was based refused to allow himself to be overwhelmed by guilt. Augustine Podmore Williams, twenty-eight years old, chief officer of the S. S. *Jeddah,* was, it has been shown, the historic model for Lord Jim. His ship sailed from Singapore on July 17, 1880 to pick up pilgrim passengers bound for the Arabian port of Jeddah. Williams, like Lord Jim, was the son of a vicar and had good professional prospects. But when his ship became disabled in the Indian Ocean and was apparently foundering, Williams, in panic, persuaded the captain to abandon the ship, especially for his wife's sake; the European crew did likewise. All the facts were ascertained by a Court of Inquiry in Aden in 1880, and the chief officer was universally condemned for his disloyalty to British traditions of seamanship. But did Augustine Podmore Williams thenceforth seek to hide himself and his ignominy in some self-abnegating labor in an inaccessible land? Not at all. Returning to Singapore, he secured employment, became chief superintendent for a shipchandlery company, and was called respectfully in later years "the Governor of Johnston's Pier." Tall, commanding in presence, he was even elected an official in the merchant seamen's organization. He prospered during the Singapore land boom, enough to set up his own business, though, indeed, he later went bankrupt. Married to an English girl when he was thirty-one, two and one-half years after the Jeddah disaster, he had sixteen children, the youngest being born when he was sixty-three. Evidently the prototype of Lord Jim was not affected with sexual inadequacy, nor did he lust for the women of an exotic race. When he died in 1916, the Singapore newspaper wrote: "Many wreaths were sent to the funeral . . . Archdeacon Swindell conducted the service." Another paper said he was lovingly called "Daddy."[51] He shouldered the burden of his one great failure but refused to allow anyone to taunt him for it. He "won back Singapore's esteem quickly."[52] He worked for the same company for twenty-eight years, especially useful because he could speak Malay.

Another actual personage used by Conrad as a model, Jim Lingard, was a trader in Borneo who was called "Lord Jim" because of his courtly manner; he worked in the rubber business, but having been driven to bankruptcy when the rubber market collapsed, he journeyed inland. He used his money to educate the children that his Indochinese wife bore him; the sons served in the British Army and a daughter became a schoolteacher.[53]

"I am devoted to Borneo," wrote Conrad to a relative when he was thirty-six.[54] And in Borneo, Conrad found the third character who was an exemplar for Lord Jim, the white rajah James Brooke, who ruled his rain forest kingdom, Sarawak, from 1847 to 1868. Brooke made it his life task to bring to these jungles "prosperity, education and hygiene"; he suppressed piracy, the slave trade, and head-hunting, and lived simply in a thatched bungalow. He resented, he wrote, "the rapacious Europeans" who through the centuries had rendered the situation of the Malays so desperate "till there is every reason to fear the extinction of the Malay races." Conrad, deeply admiring him, wrote in *The Rescue* that he was "a true adventurer in his devotion to his impulse—a man of high mind and of pure heart" who "lay the foundation of a flourishing state on the ideas of pity and justice . . . he was a disinterested adventurer," rewarded "in the veneration with which a strange and faithful race cherish his memory."[55]

Was Rajah James Brooke, a white man who became the ruler of an independent Asian state, moved by unresolved infantile complexes, afflicted by a Prospero complex?[56] Certainly his father did not wish him to embark on a trading expedition in the East Indies. "Gentlemen did not go in for trade."[57] From his own government in London, Brooke, the first white rajah of Sarawak, had no more than "marginal support."[58] Life in Britain, however, had left Brooke restless; he could not content himself with the round of parties and flirtations, the "slow stupor of inactivity," as he wrote at the age of twenty-nine, and he longed for "the opportunity of exploring an unknown country, and making discoveries."[59] On the eve of his return to the Far East in 1838, Brooke declared his desire to carry his vessel "to places where the keel of a European ship never before plowed the waters," to "gaze upon scenes which educated eyes have never looked on" with "no object of personal ambition, no craving for personal reward; these things sometimes flow attendant on worthy deeds or bold enterprises, but they are at best consequences, not principal objectives."[60] He found the province of Sarawak filled with "corruption and extortion" and exploitation, with its tribesmen compelled to sell their children into slavery to pay their keepers.[61] About twenty-five thousand pirates infested the Borneo coast and rivers, their own ranks reinforced from tribes grown desperate; trade languished because of the hazards.[62] Brooke owed much of his popularity to the vigorous action he took to halt a hundred boatloads of Iban headhunters. On November 24, 1841 James Brooke, thirty-eight years old, was proclaimed by the sultan of Brunei as the rajah and governor of Sarawak. He published once, as a responsible Platonic guardian, a code of eight laws: murder and robbery would be punished; trade would be free, and roads and rivers open; there would be no forced labor and no extortion; there would be a fixed schedule of revenues and common weights and measures, and an enforced public peace.[63]

The co-discoverer of the theory of natural selection, the naturalist Alfred Russel Wallace, an Owenite communist in spirit all his life, was profoundly impressed by the beneficent rule of Rajah James Brooke and recorded his impressions in *Malay Archipelago,* a book that inspired Joseph Conrad. Wallace spent several months of 1855-1856 in Borneo, staying some days with the Rajah himself. Brooke, in his view, combined "the highest talents for government" with "in a high degree goodness of heart and gentleness of manner." This, he thought, "is a unique case in the history of the world," for a private English gentleman "to rule over two conflicting races—a superior and an inferior—with their own consent, without any means of coercion," while "at the same time he introduces some of the best customs of civilization, and checks all crimes and barbarous practices." Moreover, the random recourse to suicide and murder, the "running amuck" to which Malays have resorted in deserved protest against the conditions of their lives, had vanished under the rule of Rajah Brooke. "Under his government, 'running amuck,' so frequent in other Malay countries, has never taken place, and . . . murders only occur once in several years. The people are never taxed except with their own consent, while almost the whole of the rajah's private fortune has been spent in the improvement of the country or for its benefit."[64]

Though Richard Cobden and the Aborigines Protection Society denounced the Rajah Brooke for having destroyed the pirate fleet,[65] his administration was indeed just and constructive. "Unfortunately, with regard to Borneo, the British Liberal conscience showed itself at its worst," writes Runciman, a historian of Sarawak. Brooke's "temperament, though liberal in a broad sense, was not akin to that of most Victorian Liberals, with its pious Puritan background. He was an adventurer and, though generous and altruistic, an egoist. He had, moreover, a love for expressing himself in writing impetuously."[66]

Was there an inferiority complex in Brooke, a sense of defeat? Did he internalize the Malay or Dyak in his repressed id? Did he lust for sexual liberties with them? Brooke did sire an illegitimate son in England, but he seems to have been above reproach in Sarawak. He was always self-confident, a leader, imaginative, with an adventurer's spirit. Does one say that the man who adventures into the unknown as a scientist is irrational, moved by a complex? Or is it the person who has repressed his sense of the unknown and the lure of adventure or allowed it to atrophy who is the one whose unconscious is subordinated to some inhibiting complex? Is the scientist's search for new truths itself then irrational? Brooke had an exuberant sense of abilities burgeoning within himself. Born in India, he felt the East India Company had become bureaucratized into indifference to new opportunities. He had distinguished himself in battle; there was no guilt he was expiating. Under his rule, a new era began for Sarawak; the coastal peoples harvested their crops in peace and coastal trade revived.[67]

Most straightforwardly anti-imperialist was the novel *Burmese Days* by the rare George Orwell.[68] It expressed the mood of personal discontent that Orwell experienced in his early imperialist career and that he discounted in later years, especially during World War II when he became more appreciative of the British Empire.[69] Serving in the Imperial Police from 1922 to 1927, with his writer's calling frustrated, Orwell's protagonist, Flory, thought he "grasped the truth about the English and their Empire. The Indian Empire is a despotism with theft as its final object. And as to the English of the East . . . Flory had come so to hate them . . . that he was quite incapable of being fair to them. . . . They lead unenviable lives; it is a poor bargain to spend thirty years, ill-paid, in an alien country." It was a "delusion," he wrote, to think they are "able and hardworking. . . . Outside the scientific services—the Forest Department, the Public Works Department and the like—there is no need for a British official in India to do his job competently. . . . The real work of administration is done mainly by native subordinates. . . . It is a stifling, stultifying world. . . . Free speech is unthinkable. . . . In the end the secrecy of your revolt poisons you like a secret disease."[70]

Is this the Burma that provided the background for the lives of the students of the class of 1937 at the University of Rangoon, who then were studying, it was said, to become shortly the rulers of an independent nation? U Nu, for instance, later the prime minister of Burma, experimented under British rule with all sorts of ideas; upon being inaugurated as president of the Burmese Students' Union, he declared: "I dislike democracy, where much time is wasted in persuading the majority. . . . It cannot work in the period of dictatorship of Hitler and Mussolini." The "idealistic youth of Burma" had managed indeed, under the lax British rule, to hitch their stars to "the least idealistic of all men—Hitler."[71] "From my earliest days in college," recalled U Nu, "I had been keen on writing and, above all, on writing plays. . . . So when I took my degree in 1929 it was my firm intention to become an English playwright." Reproached while in jail in 1940 for spending his time on plays rather than Marxist literature, U Nu replied that he would rather be the Maxim Gorky of Burma than its Lenin; evidently the atmosphere had not been so censorship-laden as to deprive him of the knowledge of such alternatives. Nor had British imperialism affected his Buddhist beliefs: when he was prime minister he postponed the opening of an American health center because of the unfavorable horoscope reported by Buddhist astrologers.[72]

In 1940, less than ten years after *Burmese Days,* Orwell himself paid tribute to the imperialists as having had something that the Left lacked—"a sense of responsibility." He recognized that "the general weakening of imperialism, and to some extent of the whole British morale that took place during the nineteen-thirties, was partly the work of the left-wing intelligentsia." With Britain at war, however, Orwell refashioned his concept of its empire. He thought that it had gone through two stages. The first had been glorious, a stage of individualistic empire building, allowing to such men as Clive and Nelson, from the middle and lower classes, a chance to act on their own initiative throughout "all the waste places on the earth." But then came the bureaucratic stage: "By 1920 nearly every inch of the colonial empire was in the grip of Whitehall. Well-meaning, over-civilized men, in dark suits and black-felt hats . . . were imposing their constipated view of life on Malaya and Nigeria . . . The one-time empire builders were reduced to the status of clerks," and it became "next door to impossible to induce young men of spirit to take any part in imperial administration."[73] In other words, the underlying grievance of the novelist-anti-imperialist was, it transpired, that he would have preferred a more adventurous and daring imperialism on the eighteenth-century model, that it was the imperialist in him that upon being frustrated turned to writing a novel of resentment.

In 1946, even as anti-imperialist movements were coming to power, Orwell ruefully recalled that before the British came to Upper Burma, its king, Thibaw, indulged in "periodical massacres of his own subjects," and celebrated his accession to the throne by executing eighty or so of his brothers; even the British anti-imperialists had been shocked. Though Orwell still caviled against "the disgusting social behavior of the British" and the "economic milching" by the Burma Oil Company, he conceded, however, that his novel had been "unfair in some ways."[74] Evidently deeper fears and more realistic anxieties had become of more moment to Orwell—the recrudescence of intertribal and interethnic massacres, in contrast to which the exclusiveness of British clubs would constitute a petty triviality, and the spread, abetted by a disorganized post-colonial anarchy of incompetence and corruption, of a Soviet totalitarian empire. The British imperialist adventures, Orwell realized, had brought with them a higher sense of humanity, a higher well-being, a higher sense of equality before the law, and individual rights. The Soviet imperialists, on the other hand, portended 1984. Thus Orwell tried to comprehend anew the ingredients in imperialism that its critics, including himself, had expunged.

The spirit of imperialist adventurousness had been keen indeed among young Britons apprenticed to the India Civil Services. Warren Hastings once wrote that "the boys of the service are sovereigns of the country under the unmeaning titles of supervisors, collectors of the revenue, administrators of justice."[75] Brooke was of this group too. Their motive, however, was an altogether rational and healthy one, for it is the repression of the sense of creative energies in youth, the failure of society to allow genius at its most imaginative, vigorous age to manifest itself that tends to engender problems and neuroses. Prospero's personality shared little with that of the imperialists. Content to be a book reader at home, Prospero went to sea because he was cast adrift, not by his own choice.

The young imperialists, by contrast, longing usually for other lands and impatient for new activities, were hardly to be confined to a library. As Hans Kohn pointed out: "Inequality in the level of civilization and civilizing energy are of the very essence of imperialism."[76] In this sense the great imperialists in history have been positive egalitarians, that is, persons who raised the level of civilization of backward peoples. Mountstuart Elphinstone, regarded as the greatest of the Indian administrators in the days of the East India Company, noted the aim of British imperialism: "The most desirable death for us to die" would be one that "would render it impossible for a foreign nation to retain the government."[77] By contrast, the axiom of the modern anti-imperialist movement has been a belief in the superiority of the primitive, the pre-industrial, the untainted by civilization. Theoreticians of anti-imperialism are negative egalitarians, with a wish to subtract from civilization itself.

The doctrine of the Prospero complex has thus been part of a curious retrogression on the part of those themselves affected by what might be called a "Caliban complex," a generic name for all those feelings, shared by many, that a higher virtue inheres in intellectual backwardness. The bearer of the Caliban complex hates (or is hostile in some degree toward) that which philosophers from Aristotle on have regarded as man's highest attribute: his ability to think, his intellect. The Caliban complex is usually present in some form whenever the thinker finds civilization something to denigrate.[78] When Marx in his discussion of British imperialism ridicules, in one of his moods, the "civilization-mongers" and then justifies Asian atrocities on the grounds that they are exempt from the standards of civilization, he is allowing himself to indulge a Caliban complex. Similarly, when Engels writes: "And in a popular war the means used by the insurgent nation cannot be measured by the commonly recognized rules of popular warfare, nor by any other abstract standard, but by the degree of civilization only attained by that insurgent nation,"[79] he is using this bit of cultural relativism to excuse barbarian cruelties. Marx, always prone to manipulating the cosmic scales of historical retribution, added that the cruelties of the Sepoy Rebellion were a reaction to English cruelties: "However infamous the conduct of the sepoys, it is only the reflex, in concentrated form, of England's own conduct in India . . . There is something in human history like retribution; and it is a rule of historical retribution that its instrument be forged not by the offended but by the offender himself." Perhaps the Sepoy mutilations were "revolting to European feeling," but, said Marx: "Cruelty, like every other thing, has its fashion, changing according to time and place."[80] The apologists for the Nazis might endorse this Marxian "logic," saying in effect that the Nazi extermination of the European Jews was the retribution of the Jews for their excessive achievements in science and the arts, a new fashion in cruelty, not to be judged by an abstract standard.

According to the ideology of the Prospero complex, moreover, no rational person would experience an imperialist vocation. "A person free from complexes," writes Mannoni, "would not in the first place feel the urge to go to the colonies," but should he by chance find himself there, "he would not taste those emotional satisfactions which, whether consciously or unconsciously, so powerfully attract the predestined colonial."[81]

Quite to the contrary, however, is the testimony of the abundant documents on the "Lives of the Imperialists," as we might call them. It becomes clear that, under the given social and personal circumstances, the vocation of the imperialist was the most rational choice—as rational as, for instance, the decisions of emigrants to leave Europe for the New World. Having realized truthfully that their creative talents would be largely stifled in the relatively closed, established, and comfortable society at home, the imperialist leader, usually a young man, intellectual in disposition, was rarely propelled by a quest for more complacent native women; endowed with an unusually strong imagination and sense of construction, and aware that he had powers that might be more productive in a novel setting, he enjoyed money less to accumulate it than for its constructive power. Tremendously loyal to personal friends in the imperialist adventure, and in turn gaining abiding loyalties, he preferred mostly masculine society, though not affected with homosexuality; sometimes bachelors but mainly faithful husbands, imperialist leaders were unabashedly convinced that superior white organization, knowledge, and technology were bringing an awakening to bleak and barren lands. Of such elements was constituted what John Strachey, with post-Marxist insight, called "the will to empire"; it is "now leaving us," he wrote, but in the eighteenth century, when "a daemonic will to conquer and to rule" had seized the British spirit, his own forebear had joined in that great effort.[82] "The will to empire," truly written, but "daemonic"? We associate the demonic in its more customary sense with the forces of the netherworld, with destruction, whereas the imperialist era witnessed an unparalleled transfer of constructive, creative energies. The imperialist motive, Bertrand Russell once observed, was derived from the creative impulse: "Some few people are able to satisfy this desire; some happy men can create an Empire, a science, a poem, or a picture."[83] Even the dour anti-imperialist J. A. Hobson was stirred by "the energies of men" (in William James's phrase) that were liberated in Johannesburg in 1899: "Never have I been as struck with the intellect and the audacious enterprise and foresight of great business men as here. Nor are these qualities confined to the Beits and Barnatos and other great capitalists; the town bristles and throbs with industrial commercial energy . . . Everyone seems alert and tense, eager to grasp the skirts of some happy chance and raise himself."[84]

That sense of a constructive liberation of energies, especially among young, adventurous men, has been a chief constituent of the progressive imperialist personality. Both India and South Africa were secured for Britain chiefly by young men; imperialism was a generational movement. With respect to India, as the historian Keith Feiling notes: "We forget it too often that the Presidency [at Fort St. David] was ruled by young men. When Roger Drake, governor from 1752 to 1756, was appointed, he was thirty; William Watts, chief at Kasimbazaar, when Hastings went there, was thirty-four, while boys in their middle twenties were third or fourth in every factory, and coining fortunes."[85] During the nineteenth century, moreover, India was indeed a land where young imperialist guardians ruled: "Almost from the day he arrived in India, a member of the Guardian caste was given authority which anywhere else he could hardly have attained with less than twenty years' experience."[86] India was won and administered by men of the younger generation. In South Africa, when Cecil Rhodes, Alfred Beit, Woolf Joel, and Barney Barnato were constructing their plan for amalgamating the diamond fields, none of them had yet reached the age of thirty-six.[87] Their tactics had the improvisational brilliance of youth. Clive, only twenty-six years old when he won his great victory at Arcot, went into battle with a tattered force of two hundred Europeans, drawn from the "refuse of England" and led by officers, mostly "young civilian volunteers," and an equal number of Indians. Using a strategy like that of "a reckless young man," engaged in "a schoolboy prank," he defeated an army at least twenty-five times larger, and henceforth was the living legend of "English courage and invincibility."

Almost all the young imperialists felt their hopes and abilities were impeded at home. Robert Clive's family had fallen on sorry days; his father, an unsuccessful lawyer, sent him to live with an aunt and uncle and subsequently directed him, as an "impoverished young gentleman" into the English East India Company; no unresolved complex moved Clive to the Indian subcontinent.[88] Warren Hastings, the son of a vicar unable to pay his debts, also raised by an uncle, was described at school as a normal, gentle boy; he went to India, he said, "from a consideration of the destitute state in which I was left."[89] Cecil Rhodes at home could look forward only to a parsonage. Did Hastings lust for native Indian women in preference to his English wife? As Philip Woodruff (Philip Mason) noted: "Hastings was passionately devoted to his work, and deeply in love with one woman, his wife."[90]

Without exception the great imperialists during their careers ran afoul of the established governing home authorities: Rhodes, discredited and disowned by the British government after the debacle of the Jameson Raid; Clive, the "heaven-born general," as William Pitt called him, who quarreled bitterly in England with his directors, accusing them of an "ignorance and indolence" that could lose a "great Empire acquired by great abilities, perseverance and resolution," and then himself charged in

Parliament for alleged crimes in India; and Warren Hastings as his long years' trial began, listening to Edmund Burke reciting the indictment of alleged crimes and misdeeds.

All of them had the sense of a mission, not unlike the calling of the intellectual that, however, they then recast into the achievements and routines of everyday life. Rhodes, already a millionaire, hastened to return to his revered Oxford to sit among the callow undergraduates to earn a coveted degree. He may not have acquired much formal learning, but he heard John Ruskin, the Slade Professor of Art; grasping Ruskin's summons to an imperial mission, he remained indifferent to undergraduate schemes for socialist leveling. Rhodes' imagination later soared to the fantasy of a secret society of young men who would plan for the world's organized rule by the Anglo-Saxon (English speaking) race. It was much akin to the fantasies of other imaginative contemporaries; H. G. Wells, similarly, in various versions articulated what became a plan for an Open Conspiracy of a new Order of Samurai to bring scientific rule to the world. Rhodes' design, tangentially connected with reality, helped give birth to the Rhodes Scholars at Oxford who, with history's perversity, have perhaps vacuously fulfilled their assigned historic mission. Neither Rhodes, nor Beit, nor Jameson would ever have been chosen to be Rhodes Scholars, observed the novelist Sarah Gertrude Millin. "They had not been leaders or sportsmen at school . . . Students they never became." The ranks of the Rhodes Scholars were far more apt to breed ideological anti-imperialists than imperialists.[91] Rhodes himself enveloped that imperialist mission with an almost religious aura; the young men who worked with him were known as the "Twelve Apostles." Edward Gibbon's *Decline and Fall of the Roman Empire* was the book most frequently consulted by Rhodes as he struggled to learn from it how to preserve the British Empire. He spent eight thousand pounds to record and collect all of Gibbon's authorities, a major scholarly project, a scholarship, indeed, for the practicing imperialist, that would have much pleased the enlightened Gibbon.[92] Rhodes thought of himself as a Roman and quoted Marcus Aurelius: "Take care always to remember you are a Roman." His friend, the physician Dr. Leander Jameson, who turned free-booter, read and re-read Walter Scott's novels identifying himself with the bygone romantic swashbucklers.[93] Warren Hastings, the symbol for a century of imperialism, with its deeds and misdeeds, had likewise a "large outlook and intellectual curiosity" that "deepened his interest in the history of those he was called upon to rule." During his first two years in India, still less than twenty years old, he mastered the Urdu and Persian languages, beside studying Hume and Diderot. As time went on he tended to identify with India, but never felt obliged to make it the ruler in his repressed unconscious, the id of a Prospero complex. Rather, he became the collector of Sanskrit, Arabic, and Persian manuscripts, founded a Mohammedan college from which magistrates were to be chosen, and helped organize the Bengal Asiatic Society. When his career in India was nearing its end, he wrote the introduction to a friend's translation of the Sanskrit philosophical classic, the Bhagavad-Gita.[94] His devotion to his wife remained lifelong. Clive, on the other hand, with an "almost total lack of interest in Indian customs and culture," was likewise scarcely haunted by an Indian presence in his id. He spent long, wearisome, hot days as a clerk haggling, buying and reselling goods to merchants and peasants; he was apt to devote his nights to Indian women. Given to periods of depression followed by "almost superhuman" releases of energy, troubled in victory's aftermath with severe breakdowns and abdominal disorder, ambitious to rank as a great orator and parliamentary power in Britain, and finally killing himself, Robert Clive was evidently a man of complexes, though there is no sign that the Prospero complex was among them.[95]

The famed governor-general of India, Lord William Bentinck, though a disciple of Edmund Burke, bore the mantle of a utilitarian philosopher during his arduous years as its reformer. When he met James Mill, he said: "I am going to British India, but I shall not be Governor-General. It is you that will be Governor-General." And indeed, Bentinck, during the seven years after he arrived in Calcutta in July 1828 achieved great reforms: he carried through the abolition of suttee, the self-immolative burning of widows, a reform which aroused more Indian antipathy than the decades of alleged British economic exploitation; he formulated and directed the practice of the Resolution of 1835 that authorized the founding of an educational system in India devoted to "European literature and science" and thereby inaugurated the greatest single step for bringing the Indian intellect into modern times; and he stimulated the development of every kind of mechanical industry in India, even if it meant an "immediate cost to British exporters"; he wrote his brother proudly of the success of "the first cotton manufactory upon the English fashion, with machinery and steam engines" that he had helped into existence. He believed in free trade and free science and encouraged Indians to go to Europe to "study in the best schools of all the sciences" and redeem India from "darkness." He believed, not untruthfully, that "under every description of Asiatic misrule" customs that were "barbarous and cruel" had flourished. His aim, he wrote, was to bring "the blessings of the European condition, in knowledge . . . in security of person and property . . . in morals." When he abolished suttee he argued this would help dissociate "religious belief and practice from blood and murder." In action, he was the highest synthesis of the Burkean conservative and the Millite liberal, and could write as a progressive imperialist that "the first . . . object of my heart is the benefit of the Hindus."[96]

Throughout his Indian years, Bentinck's morality was that of an evangelical Christian, with Quaker overtones; he alarmed his staff by riding horseback alone in his "Pennsylvania dress." As a young soldier in the European War, he had shared his fellow-officers' concern for conquests in love and had even wooed an Italian ballet dancer, but after he married Mary Acheson in 1803 they both confirmed their evangelical convictions and no personal scandal was ever imputed to them in their long, later lives. To his biographer he seemed like the British mining manager in Conrad's *Nostromo* who saw his silver mine and its "material interests" as finally bringing to that tropical, backward "rift in the darkness" the achievements of "law, good faith, order, security."[97]

The theory of the Prospero complex, however, affirms that the imperialist personality is affected with guilt for a sinful desire to exploit sexually the women of a colored race. Did such a guilt characterize the imperialist character? Perhaps we should distinguish between the imperialist chiefs, the organizers and strategists of new ventures, and the anonymous men, "the wastrels of the world," the virtual out-class of European society, who drifted, for instance, into the South African mining camps. Like the single, unattached men whom Bret Harte described in his stories of the California gold rush, they behaved in a similar manner. White women, indeed, were rarer in the South African camps than they had been in California. As J. A. Hobson had reported: "Every form of private vice flourished unchecked" in Johannesburg;[98] "saloons, gambling halls, and other dens of vice abound," while "the prize-ring of Johannesburg was the most famous in the world." Black girls ("slightly off-color") were auctioned off for their nights in the lawless squalor of the mining camps.[99] On the other hand the imperialist chiefs, Rhodes, Jameson, and Beit—the Englishman, the Scot, the Jew—the "curious trio of bachelors" who fashioned Rhodesia, were uninvolved with women, though all of them loved beauty in the arts.[100] Evidently, Rhodes never in his life was intimate with a woman;[101] perhaps his tuberculosis and heart disease contributed to this celibacy, though there was clearly an element of active misogyny. "The majority of my friends," Rhodes moreover observed, "were men of a race other than English."[102] Indeed, they were Jews, a fact his Oxford associates had already noticed. And the Jews, a chosen or self-chosen people, were of all peoples of the world probably least likely to internalize the African or Asian as an alter ego. Preeminently devoted to their families, the Jewish imperialists rarely found allure in the native Delilahs.

Of the second generation of pioneers to organize South African mining, Ernest Oppenheimer was undoubtedly the most outstanding. His name appears for a brief tribute from Alan Paton in his novel *Cry the Beloved Country:* "And they [the native laborers] take heart too, for Sir Ernest Oppenheimer, one of the great men of the mines, has also said that it need not be so. For here is a chance, he says, to try out the experiment of settled mine labor, in villages, not compounds, where a man can live with his wife and children . . . They want to hear your voice again, Sir Ernest Oppenheimer. Some of them applaud you, and some of them say thank God for you, in their hearts, even at their bedsides."[103]

The formative mind of the Anglo-American Corporation and promoter of the cyanide process that saved the South African gold mining industry from extinction, Oppenheimer himself had experienced violence at the hands of a mob during World War I and felt the vulgarity of ethnic hatred. His "emotional nature," his Jewish sensitivity to racial issues can scarcely be equated, however, with the Prospero complex diagram of a purportedly bestial Negro presiding over an unruly id. Oppenheimer, the first great industrialist to speak in the South African Parliament against the color bar, which white labor still supported, did so without ideological exaggeration; he noted in 1954 that less than one percent of the African population "has yet learned the basic European gifts of self-discipline and social organization, or even begun to learn the technical skills which make possible such basic operations as the mining and extraction of metals." While advocating that every individual should be given his full chance of development, he still believed the African rate of progress in the Rhodesian mines would be "extremely slow."[105]

The young men of the East India Company naturally had all the sexual tensions of young, unmarried men. Added to those strains were those of the sheer struggle for survival—the harsh, unremitting heat, snakebite, cholera, typhoid. Bengal itself in the eighteenth century had more robberies, assaults, and murders in proportion to its population than had the rowdy, lawless England of that time; robber bands roved in the thousands and housebreaking and kidnapping were common. In this frenetic atmosphere, "the British performed all their various activities . . . never certain they would survive the climate to return to the British Isles. Not surprisingly, numerous British lived each day as if it was their last day on earth."[106] Especially was this the case in the ranks of the British regular soldiers, who were drawn chiefly from the lowest strata of society; indeed, one batch of recruits shipped out from Gravesend was composed of felons and deserters, all in fetters; often they were disabled by venereal disease.[107] And those recruited in India itself were largely drawn from the drifters of all nations.

Withal, the fact of the matter was that British morality in India was much the same as that at home. Concubinage and native mistresses flourished in India in the eighteenth century just as their counterparts did in Britain. For many years the East India Company itself was favorably disposed toward the marriage or permanent alliance of its employees with Indian women. It was felt that Englishmen married to Indian women would be more attached to permanent residence in India. The Court of Directors of the East India Company as early as 1687 stated: "The marriage of our soldiers to the native women. . . is a matter of such consequence to posterity that we shall be content to encourage it with some expense."[108] Later, the company tried bringing batches of young English-women to Bombay, but the voyage was six months long, uncomfortable, and costly.[109] Finally, only English girls from families that could afford it traveled to India, and their husbands, naturally, came from the ranks of civil service bachelors. As late as 1810, the entire number of European women did not exceed two hundred and fifty. Thus, in the first half of the nineteenth century, marriage between British men and mixed or pure Indians grew more frequent. The reign of George III and especially the governorship of Cornwallis (1786-1793), famed for his British command during the American Revolution, were turning points in the direction of a higher sexual morality; "the private life and public character of Lord Cornwallis set bounds to the vicious and gross practices that had been current in the time of his predecessor. Laxity of conduct fell into disrepute."[110]

Above all, the completion of the Suez Canal and the development of steamships had the effect of diminishing racial mixture, for the voyage to India, so much less expensive and boring, brought many Englishwomen in its passages.[111] Soon, the English official who married a native woman found himself "practically ostracized. Public opinion held that when the occasion for intermarriage with Indians had disappeared", those who had recourse to it committed a "wanton outrage against society."[112] With the arrival of Englishwomen every year in increasing numbers, "there was a general uplifting and refining of English society in the country."[113]

In any case, the lax sexual racial usages of the British in India were nothing on the scale that accompanied, for instance, the Spanish imperialism in the Americas or the Portuguese in Brazil. The numbers of the Anglo-Indian community in 1969 were estimated as about three hundred thousand persons.[114] Evidently, three centuries of the British presence, unlike the Spaniards and Portuguese, had produced but a small percentage in the population that was racially mixed. Moreover, the children of mixed racial unions were mostly born in honorable circumstances. English soldiers, for instance, often married the widows of Moslem soldiers killed in battle, and English fathers tried to provide their children with education and preparation for careers.[115] It is said that Elihu Yale (who endowed Yale College in Connecticut) was among those who married Anglo-Indian women. He served in India from 1687-1699 and was for five years the president of Madras. Similarly, Thomas Pitt, governor of Fort St. George and grandfather of the renowned prime minister William Pitt, was, it is said, also married to an Anglo-Indian lady.[116]

Among the men of the British armed forces, the pattern of sexual behavior was, not unexpectedly, more lax than that of the Company officials, for during the first part of the nineteenth century it was still true that elder officers of the army frequently consorted with Indian women, but "among the younger servants such practice was by no means a fashionable vice."[117] Even among army officers, however, in the latter part of the nineteenth century, as leaves from duty became more frequent, travel more rapid, and English women more accessible, the commingling of British and Indians greatly declined. The custom that had been prevalent in Bengal of keeping "a female servant," principally for sexual reasons, died out.[118]

By the mid-nineteenth century, an evangelical, Old Testament Christianity imposed a sterner morality on Victorian imperialists.[119] Rather than experiencing guilt and remorse, British imperialists could pride themselves instead on their abolition of such Indian customs as female infanticide, the self-immolation of widows, and capital punishment for crimes of thievery. The graduates of Haileybury College, the academy of the East India Company, where the penetrating Thomas Malthus taught, were mostly "on the side of the tiller of the soil." Such an alumnus as Charles Edward Trevelyan, posted to a remote province where he seldom saw a European, was endlessly "full of schemes of moral and political improvement," as Macaulay wrote; even in courtship Trevelyan's conversation was of "steam navigation, the education of the natives, the equalization of sugar duties, and the substitution of the Roman for the Arabic alphabet;" evidently he was not atypical among his fellow graduates.[120] Thus in the mid-nineteenth century a historian of the East India Company would conclude: "I believe that our Indian Empire is the admiration and envy of the European world. There is not a foreign state that does not wonder at the marvellous success which has attended . . . the progress of our administration."[121] British India was no totalitarian society; not only was its army small, it had no auxiliary secret police. In the 1850s forty-five thousand English soldiers in a force that altogether with Indian troops numbered less than three hundred thousand were enough to maintain order in the Indian domain of two hundred million.[122] Seventy-five years later, during Britain's critical period in World War I, the reduced British garrison "at one period" numbered "only 15,000 British soldiers," and even the higher ranks of the Civil Service were "Indianized."[123] The Empire evidently was not enslaved by an army of complex-driven sadists. Has so small a force ever ruled so vast and populous a sub-continent?

The colonial servants in Africa were no more moved by sexuality than their counterparts in India, as the two closest students, L. H. Gann and Peter Duignan, have observed. Rather than search for a sexuality that led to colonial service, "perhaps it is more correct to say that empire building was a sublimation or alternative to sex. This seems to partially explain a Gordon, a Kitchener, or a Rhodes, who remained lifelong bachelors, and governors like Milner, Baden-Powell, and Lugard, who married late in life."[124] On the other hand, as long as the company of white women was scarce in the West and East African colonies, cohabitation with native women was common on the part of district officers. Around 1909, however, such practices began to diminish markedly. The Colonial Office had made known its disapproval and above all, white wives became more customary; those officers who engaged in unions with native women were ostracized. Homosexual behavior was universally disapproved, and there was far less opportunity for its secret practice in the African setting than in a metropolitan city such as London.[125]

A sexual impulse may indeed lend its power to the imperialist dynamic. Re-channelized and transformed, however, it bears small resemblance to the crude animalities suggested by the notion of the Prospero complex. The only one of the original Fabian essayists who was also a practicing imperialist and colonial governor, Sydney Olivier, once wrote an unusual short story, "An Empire Builder," that depicted the fusion of sexual impulse into imperialist drive. To Olivier, the chief Fabian imperialist, it seemed the sexual drive contributed a romantic component with its sublimated creativity and dedication of self, so that the repressed Victorian sexuality made for devoted and imaginative makers of empire, from the lowliest junior officer upward.[126] The Fabian imperialist himself never failed to recognize too the power of economic motivation: as with many colonial officials, he frequently felt himself the "only power" that stood between black proletarians and white would-be exploiters.[127] (However, as a great colonial official, Lord Hailey, once indicated, it was the shopkeeper and tradesman who were the chief agents in awakening the sense of a way of life more varied, interesting, and even more secure in tribesmen far from towns and cities).[128]

Among British imperialists the mission of its most renowned official practitioner in tropical Africa, Frederick Lugard, seemed to have originated from a struggle to master the ordeals of a frustrated, passionate, sexual love. Toward the end of his life Lugard wrote that "the sexual instinct . . . recognized as the most potent for good or ill . . . has certainly been so in my life."[129] His military career ended, he was on his way to becoming an almost hopeless and penniless "adventurer" as the consequence of a misguided romance. In 1886, at Lucknow, the bachelor Lugard, son of two "evangelical Anglicans," his father an East India Company chaplain, his mother a missionary, had fallen in love with "a woman, a re-married divorcee . . . famous, not only for her great beauty . . . but for intelligence—she published articles and verses—and her fearless skill in breaking horses."[130] The kind of colonial intrigue with its drift toward self-destruction that was the favorite theme of the storywriter, W. Somerset Maugham, ensued. Summoned to her bedside in the aftermath of an accident, he found her gone to London, whither he followed, desperate with anxiety. There he found her, "quite recovered," however, and preoccupied with a successor in her affections. Lugard was overwhelmed with desire, shame, and anger. Distraught, he evidently contemplated suicide. Then the memory of his boyhood hero, David Livingstone, returned. Recalling the medical missionary who had combated the Arab slave trade, Lugard thought of joining the similar "great and good work such as that being carried on by Emin Pasha."[131] He took ship to Suez and Africa, fearing during those weeks he was going mad and feeling keenly his loss of religious faith. Finally, through a British consul, he secured employment with the African Lakes Company, then embattled with Arab traders who "by brutal and callous massacres . . . and by a wholesale slave-trade . . . had exterminated whole tribes of natives."[132]

Thus began Lugard's unusual career in Nyasaland, later in Uganda and northern Nigeria, and the command of the West African Frontier Force. Antislavery became Lugard's cause. Evidently he was not above exaggerating and sensationalizing the depredations of the slave-raiding bands.[133] And his hostility to the capitalist and educational advances that were taking place in southern Nigeria led in 1914 to governmental procedures so unrepresentative that "to the Southern Nigerian educated elements it appeared that Britain had abandoned the liberal and humanitarian ideals of the nineteenth century."[134]

As Lugard's name has become identified as the theorist and statesman of the philosophy of indirect rule in the British colonial world, two opposing views concerning him have been debated. His admirers have seen Lugard as the indefatigable commander of expeditions in several African colonies to eliminate the Arab slave traders and as the respector of native institutions and modes of life, as well as the author of *The Dual Mandate in British Tropical Africa,* that evoked the admiration of both practical officials in the League of Nations and idealistic socialists in the British Labor Party. His critics, on the other hand, have perceived him as "a superb self-propagandist," whose notion of indirect rule through native chiefs was hardly an original idea but was the practice among British colonial officials everywhere that emerged when they had to solve pragmatically the problem of how tiny numbers of British officials and soldiers could administer vast areas populated with primitive warring tribes periodically raided by kidnapping bands. George Padmore, an idealistic Marxist writer regarded as having been "the foremost black figure in the Communist International" and subsequently the "ideological father of many black African nationalist movements," called Lugard "a young military freebooter." Lugard, ex-officer of the Indian Army, seemed to his critics so consumed with political ambition that he was prepared needlessly to provoke war with France. A distinguished scholar, however, adds: "No other British colonial governor in Africa had a comparable impact on the shape and nature of colonial rule."[135]

Whatever one thinks of Lugard, however, his book, *The Dual Mandate in British Tropical Africa,* remains as a kind of monument to the philosophy of British imperialism at its best: the mandate, on the one hand, to develop the resources of underdeveloped areas for the sake of the world as a whole, while on the other hand protecting the persons of the native peoples against exploitation and enabling them to preserve or modify their culture and institutions as they wished. Its philosophy, suffused with the idealism that Woodrow Wilson had imparted in principle to the League of Nations, is now regarded by many in this age of a hundred Third World sovereignties as the historical relic of a colonialism that had "an almost Satanic quality." Yet the worst of the modern European colonial governors, it is acknowledged, "never stooped to the crimes committed by post-colonial regimes as diverse as Burundi, Uganda, Equatorial Guinea, and the Central African Empire. Governor Binger compares favorably with Emperor Bokassa; Sir Andrew Cohen shines by comparison with Field Marshal Idi Amin."[136]

Does one find in Lugard the traits of the Prospero complex, the compulsion of a frustrated man to vent aggressions, resentments, and cruelties on defenseless native men and women—compulsions for attaining power in utter disregard of human friendship and dignity? Lugard's motivation toward an imperialist career was indeed catalyzed by the strains of blocked passion and sexual betrayal.[137] As Margery Perham writes: "He was exceptional in his great capacity for suffering and his inability to find relief from it either in hatred or in forgetfulness." The "therapy," however, that Lugard chose was a classical one: resolve your own misery by going among people far more miserable than yourself; your own personal sorrow is attenuated when you bring aid to people whose sorrows are more bluntly elemental and destructive of their human status; then, you may have the reward of hearing your name uttered by those who knew that you were selfless in danger and loyal to an ideal that transcended self. Lugard, like Rhodes, retained a loyalty to personal friends and a readiness to make sacrifices for a friend even if that person, in Lugard's case, had proved himself unworthy. He gave "friendship and material help until the day of her death," writes Margery Perham, "and this at great cost to himself in every sense."[138] If his greatness as an imperialist derived from such an emotional source, it was because he chose to lighten suffering rather than heighten it. He believed in the discipline of work, that restorer, as Freud said, of the sense of reality; "his industry was indomitable, and his abnormal hours of work became a legend in Africa."[139] He wrote a two-volumed work and essays and articles against the slave traders, in between his campaigns in diverse states. No one ever ventured to suggest that he used Negro women sexually; wherever he went, practices such as cannibalism ended; furthermore, "he absolutely forbade any white man to take the law into his own hands." He felt Britain was best suited to guide backward peoples to self-rule and "was distressed and ashamed" when he heard of any instance, such as the suppression of the Matabele rebellion, in which his own countrymen seemed to him to have fallen below "the British standard of justice and humanity."[140] He was, to be sure, impatient with the ponderous, bureaucratic machinery of companies and the Colonial Office, of both politicians and military officers; he himself tired of soldiering and wanted the chance at building an empire without having to be at another's order. In self-scrutiny he recognized "with much misgiving" that he was "not suited to work under any man."[141] His creative imagination, guided by ethical claims and impelled by boundless energies, called for expression. The woman whom he eventually married, Flora Shaw, was the colonial editor of *The Times,* and in such close secret contact with Cecil Rhodes at the time of the Jameson Raid that she was summoned for interrogation by the parliamentary Committee of Enquiry.[142] Lugard accepted their differences in judgment on more than one occasion, most notably when she reproved him for his hostility to Cecil Rhodes whom she admired, on the basis of her personal knowledge, for "the absolutely unsordid and unselfish nature of the devotion which he gives to the Imperial cause." Rhodes, she said, had "an unselfishness of aim greater and more complete than I have ever recognized before."[143] Few men would marry a woman after she had rendered such a tribute to another, a rival in the public esteem, least of all one affected by a Prospero complex.

In later years Lugard, himself born to a missionary mother, became the virtual chief authority cited on colonial questions by the "missionary lobby" in Britain, as a critic called it.[144] From the outset Lugard had admired the Scottish missionaries in Nyasaland highly: "There was not a single one whom I did not esteem. I have nothing but praise both of their methods and their work," he wrote. We tend nowadays in a more disenchanted age to see a Tartuffesque hypocrisy, a Prospero complex, or an underlying economic unconscious motivation behind humanitarian impulses. Ideologists especially find the sincerity of such motives questionable among all groups and parties except their own. But the missionary impulse was strong among the religious believers of Britain in church, chapel, and free church, and it could affect policy with its ethical mandate. As Sir Andrew Cohen, the last governor of Uganda, and the democratizer of its administration, wrote: "The main element in the decision to stay in Uganda was the determination of the missionaries to be able to continue their work of spreading Christianity and civilization, and the support which they were able to secure in Britain from very large numbers of ordinary religious people. . . . the interests of trade were a secondary motive only . . . In West and East Africa, the economic interests of European companies and countries, although they entered into the picture, were not the major motive or even the first in the field; not all the arguments of British historians can make me believe that they were."[145]

Most regnant in the psyche of the great imperialists was the impetus of creative power. Not the kind of aggression that Freud or Adler might hold to be innate, nor the destructive drive that is provoked by baffled impulse, nor the indulgence in violence for its own sake, nor even the re-direction of the energies of self-aggressive guilt to an outward task. Nor was the nisus to creative power reducible to the compulsive accumulation of surplus value that Marx held to be characteristic of the capitalist. (Rhodes, for example, was careless about money. "You don't seem to care for money," said someone to him. "I never tried to make it for its own sake," he replied. "It's a power. I like power." He was indifferent to fine houses, horses, yachts, servants. But he was drawn by what he called "my great idea . . . the pleasantest companion I have."[146] Clive marveled that he had taken so little when he could have enriched himself so much.) For the creative drive involved the same kind of obsession with an idea that the artist or scientist has.[147] Einstein trying to fathom for himself the mathematical equations which God might have chosen for His cosmology, the poet seeking the words in which pure creation might have spoken with no borrowed echo—their imperialism of the mind shared a mainspring with the power the imperialist sought; as rational as great art and science, it might transfigure any irrationality that affected its practitioners.

This underlying drive of a will to creative power is what has given continuity to the history of imperialism from India to Africa. Historians of imperialism have recently richly documented the fortuitous local series of regional crises and the individual responses they elicited that burgeoned into an almost continuous wave of expansion.

When such a wave phenomenon occurs, however, one can be sure (as a physicist would be) that there is a steadily impinging source. What, in other words, tended to determine how the given European power was going to respond to a series of diverse local crises? That underlying determining invariant was precisely an evolving imperialist psychology, its will toward imaginative power, responsibility, direction. An alternative choice was always available—withdrawal, but during the imperialist phase, that choice was spontaneously least attractive. Several scholars have argued that local crises in central Africa were followed by annexations because the controlling imperative was to safeguard the routes to economically valuable India. But military rationalizations, in terms of strategic requirements, can function much like economic rationalizations; they are used to thrust out of sight the underlying unconscious impulsion, the psychological longing for leadership's creative power that manifested itself through the series of discrete decisions. Such an exuberance of energies was common to economic, political, religious, and educational imperialists alike. Karl Marx himself once skirted (dangerously) the problem as to whether the basis for imperialism in India was its net return as an economically profitable enterprise. While noting that particular individuals did gain by "the English connection with India," he observed that on the other side, there was " a very large offset" for "military and naval expenses. . . . Add to this the career of endless conquest and perpetual aggression in which the English are involved by the possession of India, and," Marx concluded, "it may well be doubted whether, on the whole, this dominion does not threaten to cost quite as much as it can ever be expected to come to."[148]

Why then did the British middle and upper class taxpayers go along with the imperialist enterprise? It gave a significance to their national existence, a more than economic justification to their work; it transformed history into poetry. This unexpected juncture in the revealed nature of man made Marx's historical materialism itself stumble. As Ronald Robinson and Jack Gallagher have written: "We must go deeper into the symbolism of the conscious calculations . . . of the policy-makers."[149] The most fortunate conjuncture was that where economic calculation coincided with the promptings of unconscious aspiration, as when John Stuart Mill was able to write with candor at the close of his *Principles of Political Economy:* "There needs to be no hesitation in affirming that Colonization, in the present state of the world, is the best affair of business, in which the capital of an old and wealthy country can engage."[150]

What, however, of the psychological character of those sometimes derided as "armchair imperialists," those whom we might call "the statesmen of imperialism" such as Disraeli, Joseph Chamberlain, Winston Churchill, Theodore Roosevelt? Not having left their homelands to dwell in the colonies (except briefly, for Churchill), their direct experience with backward races was meager. Moreover, as men often highly successful in their political careers at home, they were hardly candidates for the rubric of the Prospero complex that allegedly affects most the defeated and the failed. What then are the underlying traits of their imperialist motivation?

Disraeli, of course, stands as the pre-eminent model in the nineteenth century of the forthright, self-acknowledged imperialist prime minister. He cast upon imperialism the full glow of romantic colors, adorning it with the evocative imagery of Lord Byron, his favorite poet. In Disraeli's novel *Tancred,* an Arab Emir tells the hero: "Let the Queen of the English collect a great fleet and transfer the seat of her empire from London to Delhi . . . We will acknowledge the Empress of India as our suzerain . . . you see! The greatest empire that ever existed."[151] Disraeli took it as axiomatic that race was the decisive factor in history, "the key of history," he called it in *Endymion,* averring that "In the structure, the decay, and the development of the various families of man, the vicissitudes of history find their main solution—all is race."[152] This was much the same as Charles Darwin and Karl Marx occasionally said; all of them, to be sure, wrote before the sadistic lunacies of Adolf Hitler placed a pall of traumatic repression on mankind's ability to study the relevant facts. If one assumed that the races vary in their talents, then it followed, according to Disraeli, that all mankind would gain if that race evidently most advanced in justice and liberty held most of the powers of government. The British Empire, he declared in 1878, did not depend primarily on its fleets and armies; rather it rested on the fact "that in the Eastern nations there is a confidence in this country . . . they know that our Empire is an Empire of liberty, of truth, and of justice."[153]

Disraeli, however, recognized also that imperialism could take a destructive as well as a constructive form. Like Marx and Engels, he feared the unremitting threat to European freedom that emanated from the Russian Empire. Hence he was always concerned with preventing czarist expansionism from reaching the Mediterranean shores: "If the Russians had Constantinople, they could at any time march their Army through Syria to the mouth of the Nile, and then what would be the use of our holding Egypt? Not even the command of the sea could help us under such circumstances," he said in 1876.[154] His Liberal adversary Gladstone grumbled his suspicion "that Dizzy's crypto-Judaism" was the principle reason for his anti-Russian foreign policy.[155] But Marx and Engels, hardly pro-Jewish, shared Disraeli's views. Engels wrote in 1874: "Today official Russia is still the sanctuary and shield of the entire European reaction." And "the contribution of Karl Marx," he wrote in later years, was to emphasize repeatedly that "the Western European labor parties must of necessity wage an implacable war against Russian Czarism." No wonder that Stalin in 1934 suppressed Engels' still timely article, declaring, as he did so, that Engels had exaggerated the evil of Russian czarism.[156]

Imperialism and the extension of democracy, not its narrowing, were the dual essence of Disraeli's policy; he was the modern founder of democratic imperialism. Those who, like Lord Cromer, disliked him, judged Disraeli to be little better than an Oriental charlatan. Engels, on the other hand, identifying himself as having the same outlook as the working class, regarded Disraeli as among "the few members of the bourgeoisie who have shown themselves honorable exceptions"; for all the romanticism of Disraeli's circle, they had "the good intention, the courage to resist the existing state of things and prevalent prejudices"; Disraeli, wrote Engels, had secured the franchise for the working class in 1867 once they had proven their political capacity by, for instance, managing their own trade unions.[157] Disraeli, the Tory democratic imperialist, seemed somehow to have transcended the categories of historical materialism.

Above all, Disraeli acted as an imperialist on the historical truth that if a vacuum of international leadership arises, and if at that time the most ethical, civilized power fails to exert the needed leadership, then some less civilized government of people will seize the opportunity for aggrandizement by fulfilling that function. Rome and Carthage had thus contested for supremacy in the Mediterranean, and in the latter part of the nineteenth century Britain and Russia also were thus counterposed. No sadomasochist component in Disraeli's psychology moved him as an imperialist, though he was quite aware that imperialism, like every other political doctrine, might be twisted regressively to subserve such a purpose. His relations with his wife, his natural friendship and identification with the Jews from whom he was formally dissociated, his feeling toward the working class whom he enfranchised, were singularly free from neurotic or compulsive unconscious determinants. He abstained from joining Gladstone in the latter's "passionate opposition" to a divorce bill that aimed at making divorce available to ordinary men and women. Moreover, when John Stuart Mill moved in Parliament to confer suffrage on women, Disraeli was sympathetic, though he felt accurately enough that the issue was not yet on the political agenda.

Gladstone, the anti-imperialist, still spurned the idea of women's suffrage in 1889, regarding it as a "trespass upon the delicacy, purity, the refinement, the elevation of women's nature."[158] Gladstone's anti-imperialist ethic took only Britain to task among the European nations for her lapses from the highest moral standards. Disraeli, on the other hand, warning during the Sepoy Rebellion in 1857 "against meeting atrocities with atrocities," said that the worst thing was to follow the preachers of vengeance "as if we were to take our enemies for our model." Had a vengeful disposition lurked behind Disraeli's imperialism he probably would have turned upon the United States during its ordeal of civil war. Gladstone indeed heralded the Southern leaders for having made a nation, and the British government was preparing the ground for recognizing the Confederacy. Disraeli, however, resolved to maintain good will toward the United States, looked to its emerging from the war to exercise not only an "increasing influence" upon Europe, but to assume "those imperial characteristics . . . which seem to be the destiny of man."[159] But when Europe was cringing in 1878 before the victorious Russians, this old man of seventy-three was, as the Danish critic Georg Brandes wrote, "practically the only man in Europe . . . who had courage and firmness enough to bring Russia, intoxicated as she was with victory, to a stand."[160]

Similarly, among the small elite of the so-called "Liberal Imperialists," no Prospero complex seething in their repressed unconscious seems to have propelled their political decisions. The "Limps," as they were named—the younger generation of British Liberals who were cautiously, perhaps half-heartedly, imperialist—emerged during the years after 1886. Becoming known with the advent of the Boer War as "Liberal Imperialists," their leading personalities were such men as Herbert H. Asquith, Sir Edward Grey, and Richard Burdon Haldane, all eventually leaders in the Liberal Party. All were ambitious; all knew that political power would be theirs in due course. Their imperialist philosophy stemmed from the philosophical idealism of T. H. Green, with its ethic of duty to the social whole of humanity, or from Benjamin Jowett's Platonic mission, rather than from a quest for capitalist economic gain; their perspective converged with that of the Fabian socialist imperialist, Sidney Webb.

Bookish men, they lacked the imaginative venturesomeness, the energetic vigor of a Disraeli. It was as if Oxford idealism reduced the imperialist aim to the realm of appearance. In this sense they mark a turning point, a beginning in the decline of British imperialism. Although admiring Cecil Rhodes for his energy "in an abstract way," they could muster only little enthusiasm for his design for commercial expansion in Africa. Nor did they share the Disraelian vocation for resisting Russian encroachments in the Far East. Their attitude towards a policy of colonial economic development was tepid.[161] Desirous of an empire ruled by Platonic guardians with a high moral calling, they were shocked that Boer prisoners of war were congregated in prison camps in South Africa. Since their life's ethic found its texts in Green's *Lectures on Political Obligation*, Plato's *Phaedo*, or Aristotle's *Politics*, theirs was perhaps more specifically an Oxonian burden to bear than the white man's, but it is doubtful that this group of Britishers ever dreamt of the exotic women that presumably penetrated poor Prospero's sleep, as envisaged in the conjectures of "Left Psychoanalysis."

Though the features of the Prospero complex are misplaced in the portrayal of the central characters in British imperialism, the notion of the Prospero complex, in some form, remains a master tenet for the ideology of anti-imperialism. Allied to this doctrine, for instance, are the psychological concepts of Frantz Fanon that acquired a considerable vogue among Western intellectuals during the period of anti-imperialism. Fanon, a black psychiatrist living in Algeria, disassociated himself from that part of Mannoni's analysis which ascribed a "dependency complex" to native peoples.[162] But Fanon joined in alleging that brutality toward the native women lurked in the imperialist unconscious: "The European always dreams of a group of women, of a field of women, suggestive of the gynaceum, the harem-exotic themes deeply rooted in the unconscious." "Even in a normal European," he declared, "the act assumes a para-neurotic brutality and sadism. . . . In the dream, the woman-victim screams, struggles like a doe, and as she weakens and faints, is penetrated, martyrized, ripped apart."[163] The Negro, he says, opposed "the cult of the veil" to the "colonialist offensive." Colonial administrators thereupon allegedly retaliated by trying to strip the veil from women's faces; colonial aggressiveness "multiplied ten-fold each time a new face was uncovered;" it was "the rape of the colonizer."[164] For the "occupier" is a person "smarting from his failures" who, in overcoming the native women, humiliates their men."[165] But, on the other hand, "the veil protects, reassures, isolates," as Fanon presumably learned from the confessions and dreams of Algerian women; it struggles against the imperialist unveiler (this reforming Prospero), with its own "dialectic of the body and the world."[166] The veil is an anti-imperialist symbol in the lexicon of the Prospero complex.

Poor Prospero will fare badly whatever he does. In Algeria, the imperialist was condemned for trying to persuade women not to wear the veil. In the Pacific Islands, as in New Caledonia, on the other hand, the imperialist undertook to do the opposite; he persuaded the Melanesian and Polynesian women to cover their nakedness with shapeless garments, the "Mother Hubbard" dresses, dear to missionaries. Evidently, if he urges that the face, with all its communicative expressiveness be open to view and that the veil, symbol of female retreat, silence, and secondary status, be abandoned, the imperialist is condemned for rapine; on the other hand, if he urges that women's bodies be clothed and their sexuality withdrawn from public sight, he likewise stands condemned. Curiously, in all this literature, the anti-imperialist completely ignores the fact that the Soviet regime waged a far more extensive campaign among its Moslem population to persuade their women to relinquish their veils; their authorities also attempted to secure the "cooperation" of the central Asian men. Nonetheless, women unveiling themselves were subjected to insults, beatings, murder and violations, for "even native Communists often regarded an unveiled woman as fair game for their erotic lusts."[167] The theory of the Prospero complex, however, was contrived to make bourgeois Prosperos feel guilty, not Communist Prosperos.

That Melanesian women were frequent and prepared temptresses to American "occupiers" during World War II is statistically doubtful. In the islands of the South Pacific, the impressive fact was that the average American soldier showed a marked indifference, if not aversion, to "native" women, and usually longed to return to his own or sought the company of the small contingent of American, Australian, or New Zealand women in the auxiliary services. One finds it hard to credit Fanon's reports and generalizations concerning the dreams of "normal Europeans." But then even Freud was ready on the basis of the free associations of the only American Southerner he ever psychoanalyzed to venture sinister suggestions concerning the American national character. His one Southern analysand, himself a psychoanalyst, rather heatedly rebutted that Freud was misinterpreting his dream.[168]

The myth of the Prospero complex, however, exerts a strong influence on intellectuals whose consciences are, for quite other reasons, acutely suggestible to guilt-ignition. Thus Fanon rehearses, for example, the autobiography of a fellow-traveling psychiatric colleague who, upon his discovering his "bad conscience," repudiated his "belonging to the French nation."[169]

This etiology of dismembering one's self from one's society is one to which intellectuals are prone. The underlying ideological aim of such writers as Fanon is to undermine the confidence of the colonizers in their own cultural system while simultaneously affirming the superiority of the culture of the "colonized." The colonizers are to be imbued with guilt and stripped of their sense of vocation and pride in their achievement. The aim is to demonstrate the superiority of the undercivilized to the civilized, who are now presumably overcivilized, effete, degenerate. Their civilization must be shown to be bogus and purchased at the cost of a sexual repression that is the alleged source of their Negrophobia. Since white civilization allegedly destroyed the state of psychic innocence that once existed, its overturn will, it is argued, reinstate the pre-Manichaean equilibrium that once prevailed.

The doctrine that chromatophobia or Negrophobia arises from sexual repression is thus used to unbalance or undermine the philosophic self-confidence of developed societies while at the same time pressing forward the presumably superior norms of the undercivilized. What evidence, however, has been adduced that Negrophobia among white children is sexual in origin? A child hearing the story of Robinson Crusoe for the first time is indeed all attention at the mention of cannibals; there are men, black men, he learns, who eat other men. The purported phenom-enon excites the child's fear and imagination. The junglemen are canni-bals![170] Civilization for the child is defined primarily as a situation in which it stands in no danger of being eaten. The bestial is that which indeed reminds one of beasts who simply eat indiscriminately. Novelists from Defoe to Herman Melville have been strangely moved by this phe-nomenon; Melville, attracted by the simple beauty of the South Sea maidens, experienced the shattering realization that their society still feasted on human flesh.[171] Ralph Waldo Emerson confessed that for all his belief in a common Oversoul and his abolitionist convictions he had a "natural colorphobia," while the gentle Frenchman Alexis de Tocqueville found the physiognomy of the Negro "hideous."[172] No convincing evi-dence has been adduced that black features exercise, as the advocates of the Prospero complex maintain, a powerful sexual allure upon the over-whelming majority of whites. Adherents to the primitivist Caliban com-plex would consequently presumably reverse the grounds for guilt by having white persons condemn themselves for not having sexual desire for or relations with blacks; their reluctance to do so is then attributed to a sexual repression for which they should deservedly atone. A kind of aprioristic "psychoanalysis" is thus employed to propagate an ideology.

British imperialists were indeed much criticized for their having prac-ticed such a social separatism, their own way of life, and for having per-sisted in marrying British women, for intermarriages with women of the colonial peoples were relatively rare. At the other extreme, Portuguese traders in African villages behaved like complete anthropological rela-tivists; at the very outset they "went completely native, stripping off their clothes, tattooing their bodies, and speaking the local languages, and even joining in fetishistic rites." In India, they practiced an "unbridled sexual licence."[173] The Portuguese government evidently objected more to the resultant loss of revenue than to the racial intermixture. Yet British imperialism was far more progressive as far as the colonial people's welfare was concerned than the Portuguese, despite all the critical averrals concerning the relative sexual aloofness of Britain's imperialists. What Sir Andrew Cohen remembered after he left Uganda was "the graveyard outside Namirembe Cathedral in Kampala" with its "simple graves of many pioneers in missionary and government work, and of others who were stricken down as young men . . . The period was indeed a time of great pioneers, of great individualists who have left a lasting mark on these countries and who will not be forgotten by the African people."[174]

What then is the element of truth in the theory of the Prospero complex? It clearly belies the facts of the greater part of the history of modern Western imperialism. On the other hand, it does reflect the ideology which, beginning in the 1880s, was increasingly projected upon the whole imperialist movement and experience. An outpouring of writings by journalists, socialist critics and Marxists had their corrosive impact on the men themselves who undertook or would have undertaken imperialist careers. A man such as Cecil Rhodes could frankly consider himself a Darwinian,[175] though he never contemplated, as Darwin did, that "the lower races will have been eliminated by the higher civilized races throughout the world."[176] No later statesman would venture to call himself a Darwinian in today's Era of the Great Guilt. And virtually all modern theorists of imperialism have imbibed this admixture of guilt. The Prospero complex, thus wrote a chief advocate, Philip Mason, Director of the Institute of Race Relations in Great Britain, was "strong, until recently, among those who, like myself, crossed the seas to be leaders in colonial countries . . . I am one of the Prosperos."[177]

While self-castigation became a modal *a priori* emotive postulate for the Western intellectuals after World War I, on some rare occasions a scientist went for himself to study imperialism in practice and then demurred. The well-known zoologist and humanist, Julian Huxley, for instance, visited East Africa for four months in 1929 to study various aspects of native education. He reported that "the traveller in Africa . . . can simply feel proud of belonging to a nation which does a difficult job, demanding such unselfish devotion, honesty and hard work, and does it on the whole so well. Undoubtedly, our men have their defects compared with those of other Empires, such as the French or the Dutch. But these defects are perhaps mainly defects of intellectual attitude and limited outlook; in the routine of practical administration, our average of performance seems to stand the highest. If a contact with a bit of the British Colonial Empire has not yet made me a full-blooded devotee of *Kiplingismus,* it has certainly shown me the way to a spirit of Liberal Imperialism."[178] And even British India in his judgment had probably had "the most honest and self-sacrificing administration that any Empire has had to show."[179] Although Huxley later became the first director-general of the United Nations Educational, Scientific and Cultural Organization, such reports as his were little noticed in the age of anti-imperialism.[180]

A Caliban complex, generally speaking, is indeed the psychological formation peculiar to imperialist civilization as it evolves into its declining phase. It characterized St. Augustine and Salvian in the fifth century of the Roman Empire just as it does the theorists of anti-imperialism from Hobson to Mannoni and Philip Mason during the decline of Western empires. The last administrators of imperialism naturally imbibe from fellow intellectuals the fashionable guilt-consciousness; denigration of one's own people's achievements becomes a virtual rite of recitation at intellectual assemblies. Imparted in countless college classrooms of anthropology, sociology, and political science, students learn as an unchallengeable tenet that every culture is equally valid with every other, only the primitive ones more so, according to the neo-Marxist algebra. Such intellectual trends are the harmonic waves of undercurrents of emotion that, like the movement in the oceans, finally determine whether ships of state become ships of fools, with helmsmen navigating not by science but by ideology. During the nineteenth and twentieth centuries, the men of the Indian service "were chosen and trained on Plato's principles that Guardians should rule in the light of a vision of the Good and Beautiful,"[181] with help at critical points from Aristotle's *Ethics*.[182] The White Man's Burden became intolerably burdensome only when the anthologies of accusation compiled from Marx, Hobson, and Lenin were added to it.

C. America's Imperialist President: Theodore Roosevelt

Of all American presidents, Theodore Roosevelt most felt an imperialist vocation, which he applied resolutely and coherently in America's international decisions. True, he tried to avoid the word "imperialism," substituting instead the more neutral word "expansion." Indeed, he claimed during the electoral campaign of 1900: "There is not an imperialist in the country that I have yet met."[183] But this was a tactic of campaign linguistics, and in every respect Roosevelt held to an imperialist standpoint that was shared to varying degrees by a group of "intellectuals" with whom he was closely associated, including Henry Cabot Lodge, the first Ph.D. in the United States to devote himself to a political career, and Captain Alfred T. Mahan, the theorist of American sea power; the brothers Henry and Brooks Adams contributed their fears for the future of Western civilization. Roosevelt had won a historian's reputation with his three-volumed work *The Winning of the West*. Without benefit of German metaphysics, but perhaps unconsciously in the spirit of his Harvard teacher in philosophy, William James, Roosevelt declared:

Whether the whites won the land by treaty, by armed conquest, or, as was actually the case, by a mixture of both, mattered comparatively little so long as the land was won. It was all-important that it should be won, for the benefit of civilization, and in the interests of mankind. It is indeed a warped, perverse, and silly morality which would forbid a course of conquest that has turned whole continents into the seats of almighty and flourishing civilized nations. All men of sane and wholesome thought must dismiss with impatient contempt the plea that these continents should be reserved for the use of scattered savage tribes, whose life was but a few degrees less meaningless, squalid, and ferocious than that of the wild beasts with whom they held joint ownership. . . . Most fortunately, the hard, energetic, practical men who do the rough pioneer work of civilization in barbarous lands, are not prone to false sentimentality. . . . The most ultimately righteous of all wars is a war with savages, though it is apt to be also the most terrible and inhuman.[184]

A sociology that blended Darwinism with Lamarckianism was joined in Roosevelt's political theory with a Christian ethic.[185] Both were involved in his preoccupation with the question of how American civilization could avoid the decay and decline that had descended upon its Roman predecessor.[186] Like most Americans of his time, he numbered the Negro among the "inferior races,"[187] yet he incurred the wrath of many when he broke tradition by inviting the Negro educator, Booker T. Washington, to be his luncheon guest at the White House. He believed sincerely that every individual should be judged for his own qualities and admired talent, genius, artistic and scientific achievement wherever he found it.[188] Estimating racial achievements honestly, he admired the Japanese for their industry, discipline, and endurance,[189] and he thought the German kaiser was obsessed with "the Yellow Peril."[190] He endorsed in all consistency the Russian expansion into backward Turkestan and Manchuria as contributing to "the immeasurable benefit of civilization"; as a democrat, however, though he found much about the Russians that he admired, he added: "But I do not believe in the future of any race *while it is under a crushing despotism.*"[191]

Did a Prosperonian neurosis underlie Roosevelt's imperialist personality? His home life and relations with wife and children during his residence at the White House impressed friends and visitors as those "of warm-hearted people with great capacities of friendship." His love for his first wife was complete: "She was beautiful in face and form and lovelier still in spirit" he wrote a year after her death. He grew in the warmth of his second wife's affection and judgment; she was a childhood friend of his. And, in the words of a cool-headed critic, Henry F. Pringle, "everything considered, Roosevelt was the happiest President, with the possible exception of a distant kinsman . . . ever to dwell in the White House."[192]

A natural aristocrat, he still dealt with problems "with the directness of a North Dakotan cowboy."[193] Born to economic security, he nonetheless matured with a love for work, combining a devotion to detail with a flair for penetrating generalization. From childhood he had the historian's love for stories of great deeds done by heroic men, the Plutarchian theme, and began working as an undergraduate on what became the *Naval History of the War of 1812*. He had listened to his two favorite uncles, self-exiled to Britain, narrate their exploits as officers in the Confederate Navy and found them touched with nobility even in defeat. He felt acutely, when young, one gnawing insecurity. A weak child, asthmatic and nearsighted, he longed to have a body commensurate with the deeds to which he aspired; he had none of his elder brother's natural physical endowment. So he undertook to re-make his body. He exercised in the arts of combat; he boxed, wrestled, and fenced. He hiked and rode on plains, plateaus, and mountain paths. He sustained serious injury, and when he sought physical dangers he had to take the precautions of a myopic; he stowed a dozen pairs of glasses in his uniform and hat in the Cuban campaign, and several more in his saddle-bags; he did much the same when he went to Africa.[194]

His character emerged self-formed with a sense of balance that was physically grounded. His concern for his country's well-being was "deep-seated"; his strongest reaction would still be based on a "cautious middle-of-the-road approach to all questions."[195] When out of power, and ambitious for it, the play-actor in him would come forward, strutting with a Rough Rider's campaign hat at a Republican Convention or with the helmet of the big-game hunter on African safaris (that drew Mark Twain's mordant ridicule), and perhaps leading a needless charge in the environs of a Cuban hill. When he held, however, the responsibilities of power, wisdom replaced vanity. Such was the president who, reading in 1905 the poems of an unknown, impoverished author, Edwin Arlington Robinson, was moved by their sense of the deathless aspirations of transient men. Roosevelt wrote the poet at once a letter of appreciation; Robinson didn't have the clothes to accept an invitation to the White House. Roosevelt then contributed a review of the poet's work to a magazine, and secured the author a job with nominal duties in the Custom House of New York. He was the only president to review a book, albeit one of poems, while in the White House. Literary critics "resented the President's intrusion into their domains," and ridiculed his denominating Robinson, a "decidedly minor poet" in their estimates, as having a "touch of genius . . . just a little of the light that never was on land or sea." But Roosevelt's judgment proved the abiding one.[196] As William Henry Harbaugh wrote: "there was no modern president save TR who had such deep bonds with and unaffected interest in the nation's writers."[197]

Roosevelt indeed had grasped the essential basis of progressive imperialism—that the advancement of civilization, through a nation's achievement and leadership in science, culture, art, and a liberal respect for individual rights, superseded the shadowy claims of petty primitive tribal despotisms and warlords, feudal, pre-feudal, and post-feudal. He saw no reason why the project of a Panama canal, conducive to all the world's trade, should have to wait at the behest of a largely undercivilized collection of tribes in sparsely populated Colombia. Though he admired the fighting quality of the Boers in South Africa, he thought nonetheless, in 1899, that in their war with Britain "they are battling on the wrong side in the fight for civilization and will have to go under."[198] Withal, in a spirit of human sympathy for the defeated Boer theocrats, he forwarded contributions for their welfare raised by such sympathizers of Dutch ancestry as his cousin, the Harvard undergraduate, Franklin D. Roosevelt. His perception, however, failed when he persisted in classifying China, because of its military weakness, as a "backward people," and he became more preoccupied with teaching China a "lesson" than with halting the depredations of the Russian and German forces. He foresaw accurately enough, however, that "China will not menace Siberia until after undergoing some stupendous and undreamed-of internal revolution."[199] To his credit, in the face of an inflamed public and congressional opinion, Roosevelt tried to exempt visiting Chinese scholars and business men from the provisions of the Chinese Exclusion Act and to curb immigration inspectors from exercising bureaucratic cruelties against peasants and professors under the guise of a rigorous enforcement of law.

Cruelty, the humiliating of others, the contempt of humanity, were never part of Roosevelt's character. The values of civilization were his guides; frustrated resentments were not determiners of his decisions. He had dealt with his own deficiencies consciously and courageously, and they did not move him from an unconscious emplacement to degrade others. He admired his counterpart in Britain, the colonial secretary Joseph Chamberlain, who envisaged a joining of the United States and Great Britain into an Anglo-Saxon alliance. Both men while they were in office, as Howard K. Beale wrote, "worked for the common end . . . to build cooperatively a great English-speaking power in the world."[200] Probably such a preponderant world power would have prevented the outbreak of two world wars and long ago guaranteed the existence of an international order of peace. Instead, anti-imperialist governments and pacifist public opinion dictated an appeasement and collective self-immolating of military power, making possible the years of the Hitlerian hegemony.

Theodore Roosevelt's motives as a statesman have been denigrated. Even the diplomatic achievement that brought him the Nobel Peace Prize in 1906,[201] his tireless efforts that cajoled Russia and Japan into ending their war in 1905, have been depicted as a fortunate stroke. Roosevelt, it is said, got a compromise which suited the American interest through mutually weakening the two belligerents.[202] If that were the case, Roosevelt could have followed the example of Britain, which refused to cooperate at all in exerting its influence for peace; to Roosevelt's mind, Britain "wanted the war to continue until both Russia and Japan were exhausted."[203] Roosevelt staked his whole international prestige on a project that the foreign offices of Europe regarded as foolhardy; evidently none of them thought he would be successful.[204] He could have courted the widespread anti-Asian opinion in the United States by condemning the Japanese aggression; on the contrary, he worked for long hours with the Japanese, acquiring a reputation as "pro-Japanese";[205] he thought the Russians "under the present system" were "as untruthful, as unsincere, as arrogant" as human beings could be.[206] Almost in despair at times, when it seemed the negotiations might collapse, Roosevelt sought comfort and perspective in reading Gaston Maspero's newly translated *History of Egypt* and studied the negotiations between the Pharoah Ramses II and the Hittites. He hopefully concluded: "we are not so far behind the people who lived a few thousand years ago as I am sometimes tempted to think."[207]

And when the negotiations were over, both the Japanese and Russian diplomats paid tribute to the purity of Roosevelt's motive. The Russian envoy, Witte, wrote a friend that Roosevelt's charm was founded on the "elevation of his thoughts and that transparent philosophy which permeates his judgment." The Japanese envoy, Baron Kaneko, told Roosevelt: "Your name shall be remembered with the peace and prosperity of Asia." Indeed, it had been the president's personal appeal that had persuaded the emperor of Japan to drop his demand for a Russian indemnity.[208]

There are two types of economic motives that have affected history. We might call one variety the "rational economic" and the other, the "economic irrational." When a statesman chooses a policy aimed at advancing the material welfare of people generally, thereby making possible an advancement of civilization, a greater enjoyment of goods (in both the material and ethical senses), he works with an awareness of society's most ultimate long-term economic advantages. But there exists as well an "economic irrational." For instance, some Southern ideologists advocated slavery for its short-term profits, neglecting its tremendous social costs and rejecting altogether proposals to emancipate gradually, compensate for, repatriate or help the former slaves to colonize elsewhere, steps that might have prevented the Civil War which then proved the most costly and least economic of all the alternatives. In the case of the "economic irrational" strong unconscious factors of a sado-masochistic kind merge themselves with economic considerations. One meets this combination today among advocates of totalitarian communism. But the civilization of enlightenment, from Adam Smith, Benjamin Franklin, Voltaire, Diderot, and John Locke, has been based on achieving a rationally economic, political policy. The economic is then congruent with the highest, spiritual motives, with which indeed it is in symbiotic relation.

In this sense, Roosevelt at the Portsmouth Conference was pursuing a rationally economic imperialist policy for America. His and America's prestige rose throughout the world; nothing he had done "has appealed more strongly to human sympathies and understanding," wrote a bank president in New York. From Europe, the critical Senator Lodge wrote ungrudgingly: "We are the strongest moral force—also physical—now extant, and the peace of the world rests largely with us."[209] Roosevelt had indeed grasped the truth that a world peace would depend on the primacy of a nation that thus combined moral and physical power in a progressive, "imperialistic" primacy. And indeed, this was the brief period in American history where "not only conservative Republicans but Progressives were imperialists."[210]

For all his imperfections of character, this is why Theodore Roosevelt for a while seemed to the foremost progressive intellectuals to be the outstanding statesman of modern times. "He became for me," Walter Lippmann later recalled, "the image of a great leader and the prototype of Presidents. The impression is indelible." Roosevelt was the first president to realize with all its consquences that America had become a world power, "the first to prepare the country spiritually and physically for this inescapable destiny." Roosevelt knew too the portending dangers. "He knew the history of other nations. He knew the pathology of nations—the exhaustion of natural resources . . . the accumulation of wealth and the congestion of poverty, the concentration of power and the concentration of proletarian masses." Roosevelt knew that the time of ease was over, that justice, opportunity, and prosperity would be less "the free gift of Providence" and that America would have to brace itself for a new nationalism.[211] And ineluctably, the young Lippmann drew the consequence that the world would be faced by a choice of either the rule of the democratic, liberal empires or such as the Russian oligarchy. If democratic imperialism failed to prevail, "the world faces an indefinite vista of conquest and terrorism. . . . The weaker western civilization became, the stronger despotisms would be."[212]

Theodore Roosevelt and Walter Lippmann before Versailles and Yalta, before the collapsed treaties and the collapsed and collapsing League of Nations and United Nations, could still conceive of a world peace and world order founded on a coalition of several Western imperialist countries. Now, however, the British, French, and German imperialisms are historical by-gones. The United Nations has been transformed essentially into a forum dominated by undercivilized and underdeveloped societies in an intermittent coalition with the Soviet imperialism directed against the United States.[212] Perhaps a dualistic conflict slowly prepares itself of a kind utterly unlike those that have taken place since Rome and Carthage vied for the world's supremacy more than two millennia ago. Wars between proxenete forces in Central America, Africa, and the Middle and Far East are a first stage. The ultimate appeal to the world's peoples of the values of American civilization may, however, prove decisive. Unless envy triumphs, the cowboy is more trusted than the commissar.

American progressive intellectuals—Lippmann, Croly, Felix Frankfurter—valued Theodore Roosevelt's conceptions of the presidency as "an affirmative mechanism for society." Roosevelt's critics, on the other hand, have tried to associate his political philosophy with that of the Nazi Hitler. But as Felix Frankfurter said: Roosevelt's notion was "very different from this miserable thing called Fuehrer," for Roosevelt aimed to express the intellect and strength of the people, not to paralyze its intelligence and put it to sleep.[214] It was, in short, the distinction between progressive and regressive imperialism. Indeed, Roosevelt boldly originated the concept of the making of a new American race, as he told American historians they would record in the future the "formation of a new ethnic type in this melting-pot of the nations."

To Roosevelt, therefore, the Socratic midwife to the birth of the concept of the "melting pot", the Jewish playwright Israel Zangwill fittingly dedicated his play *The Melting Pot.*[215] The president, attending its opening in Washington on October 5, 1908, congratulated its author with his warm ebullience, shouting across the theatre: "That's a great play, Mr. Zangwill."[216] Hitler would have killed the author and burnt the play. How the concept of the melting pot can be adapted to meet the purposes of a "participatory imperialism" that might emerge under American aegis is one of the future's problems.

D. The Anti-Imperialist Psyche

To test the hypothesis that the imperialist character is affected by some distinctive disfigurement, complex, or neurosis, we can perform a crucial comparison. Let us set the imperialist character side by side with the anti-imperialist, and raise the following questions: Which showed more signs in his consciousness of racist animus, the anti-imperialist or the imperialist? Which used its movement as a vehicle for compensating for inadequacies in personality or qualification, the anti-imperialist or imperialist? Anything like a large inventory of names together with full biographical data is unavailable today, especially for the anti-imperialists. We may draw, however, from such works as Bernard Porter's *Critics of Empire* and A. J. P. Taylor's *The Trouble Makers,* a small group of names that were preeminent among the ideological anti-imperialists who were generally regarded among their contemporaries as having done most to convert British intellectuals and opinion to their standpoint: J. A. Hobson, E. D. Morel, and Leonard Woolf. Two leading British activist anti-imperialists, Roger Casement and T. E. Lawrence, whose roles were not that of literary ideologist so much as "man of action," are also of interest.

Hobson's seminal book *Imperialism* was certainly the most influential book published in the early twentieth century as far as the formation of opinion was concerned. Hobson evidently had strong racialist antipathies. His anti-Semitism toward the Jews in South Africa was often noted by his readers.[217] A critic observed that Hobson's chapter in *The War in South Africa* entitled "For Whom Are We Fighting" gave the answer: "The battle of the Jews." This was "an unworthy appeal to a discreditable prejudice," wrote the critic: "The whole chapter is intended to stimulate that most disgraceful passion. . . . The double measure of original sin with which they (the capitalists) are credited is explained by the supposition that they are dominated by Jews. . . . If this were a Jewish movement, it is at least strange that it should have the all but unanimous support of the Christian churches of South Africa."[218]

Through every edition of his classical *Imperialism,* to the "third entirely revised" edition of 1938, Hobson reiterated his view that the "men of a single and peculiar race" were chief constituents in "the central ganglion of international capitalism" and the indispensable actors in the outbreak of world war. Hobson shared with Adolf Hitler a conspiratorial view of the international role of Jews:

"United by the strongest bonds of organisation, always in closest and quickest touch with one another, situated in the very heart of the business capital of every State, controlled, so far as Europe is concerned, chiefly by men of a single and peculiar race, who have behind them many centuries of financial expertise, they are in a unique position to manipulate the policy of nations. No great quick direction of capital is possible save by their consent and through their agency."

Hobson invoked the melodramatic specter of the house of Rothschild as the underwriters of European war: "Does any one seriously suppose that a great war could be undertaken by any European State, or a great State loan subscribed, if the house of Rothschild and its connexions set their face against it?"[219]

Later historical scholarship has generally falsified the melodramatic role that Hobson projected upon Jewish bankers as the progenitors of imperialist policy and war. Gerson von Bleichröder, the foremost governmental banker during the Bismarck era, took a tepid view of the chancellor's imperialistic ventures in Samoa and Southwest Africa. As the historian Fritz Stern wrote: "There is no evidence whatever to suggest that Bleichröder at any time accepted any of the arguments, economic or ideological, for German colonialism."[220] He felt that these ventures were a money-losing business, and when he participated it was because Bismarck's government "expected him to"[221] and because, as a Jew, he evidently felt sensitive lest his patriotism be impugned. And when Hitler's Nazi regime brought war to Europe and the world, Bleichröder's grandchildren, despite pleas of military loyalty, were not exempted by Eichmann's office from the Nazi regulations; one granddaughter was deported to a Nazi camp in Riga, even though one brother was prepared to attest to Nazi sympathies.[222]

Hobson attributed an importance to Jewish bankers that was reminiscent of the popular anti-Semitic socialist propaganda that first flourished in Paris in 1848. But if they had had a fraction of such powers in 1939, Europe would not have taken its fateful course.

Apart from his animus against Jews, Hobson, for all his anti-imperialism, was no egalitarian; he believed the colonial primitive peoples were inferior in their native intelligence and thought that it would be the responsibility of some future international organization to arrange for their gradual elimination: "It might be necessary that similar measures [comparable to prohibiting bad parentage] should be enforced upon the larger scale by the mandates of organized humanity . . . A rational stirpiculture in the wide social interest might, however, require a repression of the spread of degenerate or unprogressive races." Hobson, however, stipulated that such a rational selection would be validated only if it were approved by an "international political organization."[223]

Curiously, Hobson's project for "a federation of civilized states" envisaged a behavior far more extreme than the actions of the political-economic imperialists that he deplored. To begin with, the proposed international organization, Hobson conceded, could never be democratic, for if it were, the world's colored majority might abrogate all the world's immigration laws, direct their peoples to European and American shores, and re-distribute the world's gross national product and income. "We cannot get the whole world to the level of civilization which will admit into the alliance," wrote Hobson.[224] Moreover, that colored bloc would certainly never vote for the extinction of any fellow member people. In short, for Hobson's "rational stirpiculture" to be practicable, the world would have to be controlled by the advanced, civilized minority.

What then is the underlying psychological impetus for Hobson's anti-imperialism? It seems to be the reaction-formation of a man with high ethical aspiration who yet feels within himself a strong repugnance to other races and peoples; feeling guilty about this repugnance, he sublates it within a "higher" ethical theory, according to which one's own nation, though respecting the diverse cultural-ethical patterns of the "lower races," will not try to civilize them. "Little England" will be little only physically, for Great England will have its literature, law and morals, its Shakespeare and Byron. Anti-imperialism can thus serve as an ideology for mitigating the guilt of the racial dislikes one feels; it grounds cultural isolationism in a doctrine of the apparent equality of all peoples, notwithstanding that some are deemed "degenerate or unprogressive."

Hobson was a loyal member of the Ethical Movement all his life. Shortly after he came to London in the late eighties, he joined the Ethical Society, and from 1879 on was a member of, then lecturer, for the South Place Ethical Society: "My close connection with this liberal platform, lasting continuously for thirty-six years, was of great help to me in clarifying my thought and enlarging my range of interests in matters of social conduct,"[225] wrote Hobson. Was there any sense of personal rejection on his part that might have prodded him, in counter-response, to taking a stance basically critical of his own civilization? Years later Hobson wrote that "the psychology of heresy is a subject that has not received the attention it deserves," that heresy is "not necessarily the free play of a reasonable mind" but rather the outcome of "a pugnacious self-assertion of superiority," and that "as ideas come out of the sub-conscious,"[226] he might have been affected by that cast of mind. Early in his academic life, in 1889, Hobson was denied permission by the London Extension Board to offer courses on political economy. Evidently the authorities disapproved of a book that Hobson had helped to write which maintained that over-saving was a cause of economic depression.[227] Displaced from the regular career of a lecturer in the Establishment, Hobson became instead its critic. Strangely, as we see, the very traits that (according to theorists of the Prospero complex) make for the imperialist psyche were exhibited by Hobson—the racial antipathies, the sense of superiority, and the failure to take the usual steps up to success in one's own society. Hobson, however, became an anti-imperialist, not an imperialist.

If Hobson was the intellectual mentor of the anti-imperialist movement, Edmund Dené Morel was its great organizer. "Morel has never had an equal as organizer and leader of a Dissenting movement," writes the historian, A. J. P. Taylor.[228] Secretary of the Congo Reform Association when it was organized in March 1904, Morel virtually mobilized the conscience of the European community to demand an end to the atrocities and slave system of Leopold II's Congo Free State. It was, writes Bernard Porter, "by means of Morel's indefatigable efforts to secure the support of influential men and organizations for his cause" that the Belgian Parliament was finally moved in 1909 to take responsibility directly for the Congo Free State.[229] "It is EDM versus Leopold all over again and the same *Root* policy under both Tyrants," wrote the ill-fated Roger Casement.[230]

The singular nobility of Morel's character evoked a rare tribute from the chief of the Belgian Workers' Party, Emile Vandervelde, the most respected of the second generation leaders of the Socialist International: "Among the men who I've known . . . few have to an equal degree inspired me with such sympathy and admiration for his marvelous qualities as a *fighting man,* the serene intrepidity with which he defied the worst attacks of the enemy, and—I must insist upon it—the loyalty and complete disinterestedness of his action exerted at first in his own country's colonies before he became involved with the misfortune of the black subjects of King Leopold."[231] Lenin tempered his snarling at "bourgeois" thinkers to acknowledge, in 1915, that Morel was "an exceptionally honest and courageous bourgeois who is not afraid to break with his own party," though, withal, "a bourgeois nevertheless."[232]

A distinctive doctrine arose called "Morelism." It combined an insistence on free trade, not monopoly, for the economic development of the colonial areas, with an indirect rule that safeguarded the native institutions and culture.[233] Morel did not have the socialist's abhorrence of commerce, the "cash nexus" (as Marxists, following Carlyle, called it) or the "acquisitive instinct" (in the ethicist idiom). For him "commerce" was "the greatest civilizing agent. The steps upward in the ethical development of the human race have been synonymous with the spread of commercial relations."[234] A later stage in his career, after the reform of the Belgian Congo was achieved, saw him the leading radical critic of Britain's foreign policy and its drift toward war with Germany. When war came nonetheless in 1914, Morel became secretary of the Union for Democratic Control, which shortly provided the chief agency for Britain's intellectuals opposing the World War: Bertrand Russell, Ramsay MacDonald, Charles Trevelyan, Norman Angell, and G. Lowes Dickinson, among others. Their pamphlets "exposing" the Entente's imperialist diplomacy sold widely. Always Morel was the animating spirit. As the society's historian wrote: "E. D. M. was the U.D.C., and the U.D.C. was E.D.M."[235]

Nonetheless, E. D. Morel, exemplar anti-imperialist, had all the traits that psychoanalytical critics have assigned to imperialists. His own racialism emerged blatantly in 1920 when French forces occupied the German Ruhr. An article by Morel on the front page of Labor's newspaper, the *Daily Herald,* bore the leads: "Black Scourge in Europe. Sexual Horror Let Loose By France on Rhine. Disappearance of Young German Girls." The leads reflected accurately the contents of Morel's article. France, wrote Morel, "is thrusting her black savages . . . into the heart of Germany." The "barely restrainable beastiality" of "primitive African barbarians," carriers of syphilis, was founded, in his view, on their distinctive racial physiology. They had committed rapes, "some of them of an atrocious character," because the Africans are "the most developed sexually of any" race, and "for well-known physiological reasons, the raping of a white woman by a negro is always accompanied by serious injury and not infrequently has fatal results."[236]Then Morel journeyed to Germany to study the facts at first hand. He reported on "the black menace" in a pamphlet entitled *The Horror on the Rhine.* The problem with the African soldiers, the Moroccan troops, was that their "sex impulse is a more instinctive impulse—more spontaneous, fiercer, less controllable impulse than among European peoples hedged in by the complicated paraphernalia of convention and laws." Consequently the black troops (in Morel's italicized words) *"must be satisfied upon the bodies of white women."*[237] The pamphlet, an "immediate success," was translated into several languages. Even the rationalistic Norman Angell, a close friend of Morel's, joined in the protest against the use of African troops, as did the famous leftist French novelists, Henri Barbusse and Romain Rolland, though the grounds they argued reached beyond the sexual: "The arming of the African negro," declared Angell, a Nobel Laureate for peace, "is the Servile State in its most sinister form." The French militarists, he charged, probably intend to employ these "Cannibals from the African forests" in a "war upon the Workers' Republic" (i.e., the Soviet Union).[238] Several respected persons and groups investigated Morel's charges and found them much exaggerated. The French social economist, Charles Gide, said Morel was affected with "outright Negrophobia."[239] Indeed, until his death in 1924, Morel kept speaking to audiences about the "black horror."[240] As Robert C. Reinders concludes: Morel and most of the British intellectual world regarded the African as an "inferior," though Morel actually never knew a single Negro except on a master-servant basis; his great campaign against the Congo atrocities had been conducted from Liverpool in the setting of a debate among the European intellectual class.[241]

Whatever the outcome of the scientific study of racial differences, the views of E. D. Morel, the chief of anti-imperialists, concerning Negro sexuality and intelligence coincided with those said to be the hallmark of the imperialist psyche, the Prospero complex. In addition, Morel was impelled by feelings both of guilt and discontent with his personal lot of the kind allegedly characteristic of the imperialist. A humble clerk during the 1890s in a Liverpool shipping firm much involved in the West African trade, Morel disliked (in his words) its "atmosphere of trickery and deceit, of shiftiness, of neglect: an atmosphere of foul and filthy talk, of gross ideals, and grosser methods." He longed for a higher vocation even as Clive, Rhodes, and Emin Pasha had. But he was vulnerable, as they were not, to a sense of guilt for the situation of the African black, and to the persuasion also of his friend, Mary Kingsley, that the European nations were inflicting their own technological and cultural values on tribal men who wanted to persist in their own way of life.[242] This was the white man's guilt for creating what Morel called "the black man's burden": "The hands of every European Power which has had dealings with him is stained deep with the blood of the African. For any such Power to approach the African problem on the morrow of the Great War otherwise than with a consciousness of past sins, would be to proclaim itself hypocrite in the eyes of the world."[243] When Morel went to prison for six months in 1917 on the charge of having sent anti-war pamphlets to the French novelist Romain Rolland who "au dessus de la mêlée" was trying to serve as the conscience of Europe, he could accept his punishment as both martyrdom and expiation. What it was in his personal background that made Morel so accessible to guilt is, of course, a matter of conjecture. Morel's own friends were perturbed that Morel, of half-French parentage and largely French upbringing, nevertheless accused France bitterly of being the architect of Europe's ruin, and to undo her damage wanted to help make a "golden bridge" between Britain and Germany.

Morel, often described as pro-German, was born in Paris, the son of a French official, Edmond Morel-de-Ville, and a Quaker Englishwoman.[244] He evidently repudiated his French father from the time he first criticized the firm in which he had been placed; these criticisms then evolved into criticisms of French diplomacy and the French recourse to "savagery" on the Rhine. In 1916, after the execution of his friend Roger Casement, Morel himself "began imagining plots against him on all sides." The reassurances of his lawyer and the former home secretary were of little avail, and Morel eventually required the care of a "nerve specialist."[245]

Not unlike some imperialists, "he was certainly unscrupulous in his means," writes A. J. P. Taylor, who regrettably adds, "perhaps also a French trait."[246] He had the feeling so usual among the practicing field imperialists, from Clive to Rhodes, that the London parliamentary statesmen were either corrupt or verbose weaklings. In 1917 Morel queried whether a debacle was in the offing since "such fifth rate men as Milner, Smith, Churchill, Carson, Henderson" were engaged in *"determining the destinies of a country";* and Churchill, especially, whom Morel delighted in defeating spectacularly in 1922 for the parliamentary seat at Dundee, he looked upon "as such a personal force for evil that I would take up the fight against him with a whole heart."[247] In short, the whole inventory of the traits ascribed to the imperialist can be found in the anti-imperialist Morel: the racial antipathy, the sense of personal inadequacy to be overcome, the "blocked mobility" in a conventional career, the rebellion against paternal authority, the messianism, and the unscrupulousness, conjoined with the conviction that historical right was on one's side.

The mantle of Hobson as the foremost theorist of anti-imperialism passed during World War I to the gentle, probing personality of Leonard Woolf. As secretary for more than twenty years of the Labor Party Advisory Committee on International and Imperial Questions, and chairman of the International Bureau of the Fabian Society, as the author of a series of thoughtful, critical books on imperialism, as literary editor of the *Nation,* and editor of the *Political Quarterly,* Woolf was an unrelenting, sophisticated critic of British imperialism and a pioneer advocate of some form of international government.[248]

His several volumes of autobiography enable us to understand more fully Leonard Woolf's character structure. What is most astonishing in Woolf's case is that his psychology fitted interchangeably into both the imperialist and anti-imperialist molds. For more than seven years, in his early manhood, Woolf worked as a civil servant in Ceylon in some of its most isolated areas. The imperialist system called out the best efforts and idealism of this young Jewish Cambridge graduate and admirer of G. E. Moore's *Principia Ethica.* "I rarely thought of anything else except the District and the people," wrote Woolf of himself. He was proud that he had "revolutionized" the district's salt industry; he was, in his words, "obsessed by my work." Nor did he regard his own devotion to his job as untypical of his fellow imperialist administrators. Woolf noted "the extraordinary absence of the use of force in everyday life and government. Ceylon, in 1906, was the very opposite of a 'police state.' There were very few people and outside Colombo and Kandy not a single soldier." Apart from "an interpreter, some police constables, and a few Tamils . . . I was single-handed."[249] His fellow imperialist administrators, wrote Woolf in his *Diaries,* were mostly men who strove to promote the well-being of the Ceylonese people, "in many ways astonishingly like characters in a Kipling story."[250] Was he driven to an imperialist career, as the theory of the Prospero complex would have it, by the desire for easy sexual conquest? "I had lived in Hambantota, a life of complete chastity except for one curious night," replies Woolf—hardly enough to constitute a Prosperonian;[251] he had on one occasion in Jaffna yielded to the advances of a young woman, it transpired, "of notorious reputation."[252]

Despite his anti-imperialism, Woolf's opinion of Ceylonese people and their culture was much the same as that held by his fellow imperialists. Woolf would not "sentimentalize or romanticize them." "They are . . . nearer than we are to primitive man," he wrote, "and there are many nasty things about primitive man." They had "the litheness and beauty of jungle animals," but the jungle, which Woolf made the grim protagonist of a novel *The Village in the Jungle,* was a place where man and his environment fought a bitter, hostile, endless battle, with man succumbing to hunger and fear.[253]

When he returned to London in 1911 for a year's leave, Woolf was still minded to return to his imperialist job. But he had fallen in love with Virginia Stephen. If she would not marry him, he thought, he had no ambition to rise to a colonial governorship. He proposed instead (in his words) to "immerse myself in a District like Hambantota for the remainder of my life," as others had done, "as a final withdrawal . . . married to a Sinhalese, I would make my District or Province the most efficient, the most prosperous place in the world."[254]

Virginia Stephen did marry him, and with no change whatsoever in his basic psychology, Woolf instead became a writer of anti-imperialist books. As an imperialist administrator he had always enjoyed his position and "the flattery of being . . . the father of the people," but he had also become "more and more ambivalent, politically schizophrenic, an anti-imperialist who enjoyed the fleshpots of imperialism."[255] "Nervous and uncomfortable" when he was inducted into "the Club . . . a symbol and centre of British imperialism," where "only the 'best people' and of course only white men were members,"[256] he never challenged the validity of the association, and his nervousness may well have been that of the shy young Jewish man; the Club's exclusivism was not greater than that of the Bloomsbury circle to which he returned.

Certainly Leonard Woolf could have had a career in the Home Civil Service after he passed the examinations, but feeling that he could not "face a lifetime in Somerset House," he "applied for Ceylon." All those intellectual associations at Trinity College and Cambridge that he prized, with Lytton Strachey, Maynard Keynes, and G. E. Moore, were interrupted for a life as "a very unconscious, innocent imperialist," as a cadet and assistant government agent traveling on jungle roads by bullock cart and resolving the disputes among Sinhalese men and women, Moslems and Buddhists.

Did some sense of personal inadequacy, of some deprivation, some rejection by society, the feeling of one denied a place commensurate with his talents, lead him toward an imperialist choice? Did he feel that only in a backward land could he possibly fulfill a vocation for power and leadership, a vocation equal and opposite to the powerlessness experienced at home?

Leonard Woolf himself belittled the influence on him of his Jewish birth and upbringing: "I have always felt in my bones and brain and heart English, and more narrowly a Londoner." Yet he also avowed that "nearly all Jews are both proud and ashamed of being Jews."[257] Added to that disequilibrating awareness was his family's actual experience of eleven years of poverty that followed his father's death when Leonard was just eleven. He went to Cambridge University as an outsider scholarship boy.

Evidently the Jewish theme preoccupied Leonard's youth and probably contributed to his choice of an imperialist career. The unusual novel he wrote within less than three years after his return from Ceylon, *The Wise Virgins,* reveals most directly Woolf's underlying emotions.[258] Repeatedly his Jewish painter-hero encounters during his courtship of Camilla Lawrence (Virginia Stephen) a dislike for Jews on the part of her friends and relatives: "There has never been a good Jew artist, and there never will be." "They're just like crabs or lobsters. They give me the creeps." "You were all right when you lived in Palestine before the dispersal . . . Since then . . . you've produced Mendelssohn and Barney Barnato." "[I]t's a characteristic of your race—they've intellect and not emotion." "I hate Jews." "I don't like Jews."[259] Woolf's mother objected bitterly to the scarcely concealed portrait of herself as a querulous, corpulent, unsympathetic, gracelessly aging Jewish woman.

But to his beloved Camilla, the hero Harry confided what being a

Jew means in modern times. "The only thing that a Jew is sentimental about is Judaism," but there it stops. "We're hard and grasping, we're out after definite things . . . which we think worthwhile . . . Money, money, of course. That's the first article of our creed, money, and out of money, power . . . We're always pouncing on them because they give power, power to do things, influence people . . . It's a sort of artistic feeling, a desire to create. To feel people moving under your hand or your brain, just as you want them to move! . . . You feel you're doing something, creating things, not being tossed and drifted through life with a few million other imbeciles."[260]

The "artistic feeling," a desire to create, bringing order and justice into people's lives where the savagery of the jungle hitherto prevailed— such were among the motives that made Woolf into an imperialistic administrator. Perhaps they answered in some way to the sense of inferiority he had by virtue of being a Jew. If so, the response was a rational one; working as a civil official in the Postal Service would no more have satisfied his artistic longing for creation on a social canvas than would have a stockbroker's chores and gambles, just as the gray streets of Paris would not have satisfied a Paul Gauguin longing for the diverse colors and entrancing light of Tahiti.

The same Leonard Woolf however, became within a few years the Labor Party's leading theorist of anti-imperialism. The young Platonist who dreamed of governing the most prosperous district in Ceylon and fulfilling the imperial vocation, now wrote in the coldest terms of that vocation as having been evoked by economic motives—markets, raw materials, and profits.[261] The "moral argument and ideas," he declared, were only a "halo round imperialism." Romantic adventurers and sentimental soldiers had satisfied their desires "for wandering, killing and conquering among the less fortunate and less civilized inhabitants of Asia and Africa," he charged, but his own role in Ceylon which fitted under none of these rubrics was blotted out.[262]

What is noteworthy, of course, is that the selfsame psyche with the same emotional traits, that subserved the making of an imperialist can, with a rotation of the social coordinates subserve instead the making of an anti-imperialist. In Britain, returned to the circle of critical intellectuals, literary experimentation and the ferment of social criticism, to the world of Shaw, Wells, and the new Labor Party, one's creative impulses were awakened to projects for world government; one's creative sense of justice, no longer contracted to the disputes among Sinhalese Buddhists and Moslems, the petty arguments over women's insults and land titles, reached to grand and daring schemes for the redistribution of the world's income, and the drawing of boundaries for new states. If Leonard Woolf, the imperialist administrator, had suffered from a Prospero complex, then by the same token, Leonard Woolf, the anti-imperialist critic, was hardly recovered. With one difference: where Leonard Woolf, the imperialist, spoke frankly about the repugnance he felt toward the primitive peoples, the anti-imperialist built up an ideological reaction-formation against such repugnancies. Since antipathies were repressed, all one's resentment was more likely to be rechanneled against one's own civilization and its guilt: "the economic system of Europe was imposed by force upon the subject peoples without regard to their social organization, their traditions, or their interests,"[263] wrote the re-fashioned Woolf.

A few months among fellow-intellectuals in England, and above all, his renewed intimacy with old associates among the Cambridge Apostles, contributed to Woolf's ideological shift. Affected with an arrogant homosexuality and a sardonic stance toward the bourgeois Benthamite, utilitarian society that knew not the indefinable good,[264] the Apostles bathed Woolf's psyche once more in Platonic intuition; the spirituality of the suffering Virginia, always poised precariously on the edge of insanity, was a final agent in transforming Leonard Woolf into an anti-imperialist. The most fundamental crucial event in our time, he then came to believe, "was the revolt in Asia and Africa against European imperialism and the liquidation of empires."[265] Yet, his abrupt metamorphosis into an anti-imperialist was not the outcome of his own imperialist experiences or the consequence of a conviction that he had been doing the devil's work in Ceylon.

Of that work he remained proud. Nevertheless, having taken up membership again in the intellectual class, he adopted as well their ideological standpoint, the rejection of bourgeois civilization, never quite asking himself whether that rejection involved the imperiling of advanced civilization itself. Though the Hogarth Press, that Leonard and Virginia Woolf founded, was the first publisher in Britain of most of Freud's books, it seems that Woolf, always ready to condemn the character of imperialists such as Lugard as selfish and sadistic,[266] forebore from analyzing the characters and motivations of the anti-imperialists. In a celebrated passage, Woolf declared: "Psychologically there is no difference between Captain Lugard and the people in past centuries who burnt and tortured men and women from the highest of religious motives."[267] Lugard, he said, afflicted as he was by "two of the greatest curses of mankind, muddle-headedness and sentimentality," was enabled thereby to deceive himself that he was acting "from noble motives." Subsequent history, however, was to demonstrate rather that the psychological isomorphism between the revolutionary, anti-imperialist intellectuals and the servants of the Inquisition was far more impressive.

Woolf's anti-imperialism grew, it must be observed, with the years of his marriage after 1912 with the later-famed novelist, Virgina Stephens. From its very beginning, the marriage tended to accentuate masochistic traits in Woolf. Virginia Stephens had told him quite frankly her doubts about marrying him: "Possibly, your being a Jew comes in also at this point. You seem so foreign. And then I am fearfully unstable." She informed him further: "As I told you brutally the other day, I feel no physical attraction in you"; when he kissed her, she added, "I feel no more than a rock."[268] Moreover, Woolf allowed himself to overlook the information, however lightly conveyed, that Virginia had already undergone periods of insanity and had attempted suicide once.[269] Her biographer notes that even if the full facts had been explained to Leonard Woolf, he "certainly would not have been deflected from his purpose of marrying Virginia." Their marriage on the physical side soon ended; Virginia Woolf resented "the quality of masculinity."[270] Virginia herself tried to mock at all sexuality, writing on their honeymoon: "Why do you think people make such a fuss about marriage & copulation?"[271] The pattern of illness and recurrent degrees of insanity persisted in Virginia's life; without whine or whimper, complaint or criticism, Leonard Woolf dedicated himself to caring for his wife. In the latter twenties she was involved in what she found to be a rewarding "Sapphist" intimacy that she commemorated in her autobiographical novel *Orlando*.[272]

To what extent may the political evolution of Leonard Woolf have been founded in his seeking a compensatory virile role in the emerging Labor criticism of the established order? Woolf projected his Jewishness upon the exploited peoples, who were more overtly contemned and despised;[273] their cause was his, and their exploiters were his. Was this involuted anti-imperialism a healthier response than the forthright entrepreneurial imperialism of Barney Barnato and Alfred Beit who were unattracted to an ideology at once messianic and masochistic such as Woolf's? Did the British Empire become a surrogate symbol for all those personal and social influences that converged in his sexual rejection by his wife?[274] Probably there is not a sufficient basis for answering these questions. Nevertheless, in terms of the crude criteria of sexual inadequacy and sexual failure that have been used by anti-imperialists to indict the imperialist personality as linked to a Prospero complex, it is noteworthy that the character of Leonard Woolf during his career as an anti-imperialist was precisely one delineated by such Prosperonian traits.

Apart from the literary anti-imperialist critics, there was the most tragic figure among the activist anti-imperialists, Sir Roger Casement. To the future novelist Joseph Conrad with whom, in 1890, he shared living quarters for three weeks in a station of the Belgian Congo Company, Casement appeared "a limpid personality" with a "touch of the conquistador" penetrating "an unspeakable wilderness" for months, and emerging with an undiminished gallantry.[275] Conrad regarded his meeting Casement "as a great pleasure," "a positive piece of luck," and found him "most intelligent and very sympathetic." And to Arthur Conan Doyle, the creator of Sherlock Holmes, Consul Roger Casement was "a man of the highest character, truthful, unselfish—who is deeply respected by all who know him."[276]

It was Casement who, as a British consul, wrote the reports that indicted King Leopold and his Congo Free State for the massive horrors of their rule before the aroused conscience of world opinion, and who was knighted by an admiring British government. But in 1916, in the middle of World War I, he was tried for high treason; he had sought to organize among Irish prisoners of war in Germany an Irish brigade for insurrection in Ireland against the British Empire. He was helped with German funds, equipment, and a submarine. It transpired that the personality that Conrad had regarded as "limpid" concealed depths of sordid involvement and duplicity. Casement's "secret diaries," which the British authorities allowed to circulate, told the story with a repulsive, even cynical detail. Conrad now found Casement a repellent person, a man "properly speaking, of no mind at all," not stupid, but "all emotion," with "not a trace" of greatness: "Only vanity. But in the Congo it was not visible yet."

"Only vanity"—such was Conrad's final summary of the underlying motivation of the most famed anti-imperialist, heroic, public personality of Britain at that time. Was then the posture of the conquistador and tribune of the voiceless, unheard oppressed perhaps the taut surface of the guilty homosexual who sought among the oppressed people compliant servants for his own deviant sexuality? Casement's diary narrated how he interlarded his homosexual usages with his investigative activities among the Putuwayo Indians in South America. Not, says a careful biographer, that he was so calculating as to have returned to that mission for its sexual opportunities: "But they may have provided the lure, which, even if he was not unaware, had put the idea into his mind."[277] Hiding from others as he coped with his guilt, and hiding from "a terrible disease," as he called what he saw as his affliction, he wrote in a poem:

> I sought by love alone to go
> Where God has writ an awful no
> Pride gave a guilty God to hell
> I have no pride—by love I fell.[278]

Like most literary anti-imperialists, he indulged his propensity for elevating primitive life above that of civilization. Traveling in America along the shores of Lake Champlain in July 1914, he addressed a silent exordium to the American Indians: "You have *life*—your white destroyers only possess *things*. That is the vital distinction . . . between the 'savage' and the civilized man. The savage is, the white man has. The one lives, and moves to be, the other toils and dies to have."[279] Yet Casement had himself seen the atrocities of primitive existence in Africa, intratribal as well as intertribal; he had tried, without success, to induce one local tribe not to put to death three slaves designated to provide company for their recently deceased chief. And notwithstanding his *a priori* primitivism, Casement held to a set of racial antipathies. For all his homosexual encounters, he hated any sort of racial mixture; he was disgusted by "hybrid" races; "something about the mixture of black with red, or of either with white, moved him to a fastidious distaste not always fastidiously expressed: 'Brazil and the Brazilians are vile . . . I can't bear them—mud-colored swine.'"[280] He had himself first come to Africa as a potential transport manager for the Congo Company. He had evidently been occupied with the procurement of ivory and its transport and served, too, for several months in 1888-89 with a surveying expedition for the Congo Railway Company.[281] He was rather reticent, as Conrad recalled, as to the "exact character" of his work, but it involved recruiting porters for the Company's caravans, as Conrad observed when he went with him on several "palavers" with the village chiefs.[282]

His anti-imperialism had had a slow psychological gestation. When the Anglo-Boer war broke out, Casement responded with a "fanatical devotion" to the British cause and undertook some dangerous assignments.[283] By 1907, however, he metamorphosed into an incipient Irish rebel; this knighted servant of the British Empire concurred with the Irish spokesman, Michael Davitt, that "the idea of being ruled by an Englishman is to me the chief agony of existence. They are a nation without faith, truth or conscience, enveloped in a panoplied Pharisaism and an incurable hypocrisy."[284]

Was Casement moved to hate Britain because its culture demanded the repression of his deviant sexual self?" Did his anti-imperialist stance serve to mitigate the guilt he felt for the contempt he harbored toward the backward persons who alleviated his sexual needs? The messianic martyr's role that Casement sought may well have been the obverse of his homosexuality. The boys of fourteen or fifteen who were his informants in the Congo and the Amazon knew the truth about the anti-imperialist that remained hidden even to the searching Joseph Conrad.

By contrast with Casement, the novelist Conrad could still preserve his faith in England as having in "her keeping the conscience of Europe." He had known at firsthand the workings of the repressive Russian imperialism, and he would not lightly throw aside the achievements of Western liberties. Therefore, while he condemned the Belgian chiefs in the Congo as "worse than the seven plagues of Egypt," he declined to become a primitivist ideologist. Rather, he felt that that the Belgian rulers had retrogressed toward the primitive, becoming like "African witch-men" who seemingly had temporarily "cast a spell upon the world of whites."[285] He insisted on trying to hold on to his sense of proportion and refused to tell Casement that while in the Congo he had ever seen or heard of cases of the severing of hands by Bangala tribesmen, who constituted the bulk of Leopold's Congo troops.[286]

Casement's vocation as an anti-imperialist was perhaps less the mandate of ethical intuition than the unremitting pressure of a cruel neurosis. Conrad, on the other hand, felt that the African native deserved respect not because he was primitive, but because he was human: "He shares with us the consciousness of the universe in which we live—no small burden."[287] But anti-imperialist Casement exalted the native consciously in the same measure that he denigrated him unconsciously.

The most romanticized of activist anti-imperialists among intellectuals and popular moviegoers alike is the ambiguous T. E. Lawrence. Zealous and efficient as the military representative for the British Empire among the Arabs during World War I, he had bought their loyalty in exchange for relatively large wage payments for each soldier. When the war ended, however, he felt that the promises he had made for post-war Arab independence were not being fulfilled. Thereupon he turned bitterly against the British Empire and wished to see its petrol royalties in Mesopotamia lost and its domain go the way of the Roman Empire's breakdown. "We pay too much for these things in honour and in innocent lives," he declared in his anti-imperialist mood.[288]

Lawrence himself was aware that a self-destructive ingredient permeated his anti-imperialist dedication: "I prostituted myself in Arab service," he wrote. "For an Englishman to put himself at the disposal of a red race is to sell himself to a brute, like Swift's Houhynyms [sic] . . . I've never told anyone before, and may not again because it isn't nice to open oneself out."[289] And in his masterpiece, *The Seven Pillars of Wisdom,* he wrote movingly: "Pray God that men reading the story will not, for love of the glamour of strangeness, go out to prostitute themselves and their talents in serving another race."[290]

Lawrence discerned that behind his anti-imperialist, Arab-costumed, public self was a harsh duplicity: he detested, disliked, and was contemptuous of the Arab people he was serving, and his anti-imperialist ideology was criss-crossed with masochistic lines. What indeed were his feelings concerning the Arab peoples? Of the Bedouins, he wrote: "The Bedu were odd people . . . They were absolute slaves of their appetite, with no stamina of mind . . . If forced into civilized life, they would have succumbed like any savage race to its diseases."[291] Of his Arab soldiers he noted that their housekeeping was mostly done by their Negro slaves, and as he watched the latter "tom-tom playing themselves to red madness each night . . . it hurt that they should possess exact counterparts of all our bodies."[292] It was hard for Lawrence to grant admission of these black auxiliaries to the human species. Although he was beside himself with fury when the French established their protectorate over Syria, Lawrence's own opinion of the Syrians was no endorsement of their capacity for self-government. The Syrian, he wrote, was an "ape-like people having much of the Japanese quickness, but shallow."[293] The Syrian people, in his view, were "impractical, and so lazy in mind as to be habitually superficial . . . From childhood they were lawless, obeying their father only from physical fear . . . [W]ith their superficiality and lawlessness went a passion for politics, a science fatally easy for the Syrian to smatter, but too difficult for him to master. They were discontented with what government they had . . . but few of them honestly thought out a working alternative."[294] As for the Saudi Arabians (as they are now called), they were, in Lawrence's judgment, a superstition-ridden people that had to be cajoled with the pretense that their chieftain [Hussein] was a war-leader: "Mecca was a hotbed of religion, quite impossible as the capital of any sort of state: the worst town in the Arab world. Yet for the war we had to pretend that he [Hussein] led."[295] As for the Turks whom they were fighting, they were no courageous foe either but a people enfeebled by their depravities. Nearly half the Turkish prisoners they examined were found to have "unnaturally acquired venereal disease." That was why they were the "least spirited soldiers in the world" and why the Turkish peasantry, that provided these conscript soldiers, had a declining birth rate; this was a people "dying of their military service."[296]

Again and again, Lawrence reminded himself that what kept his Arab army together were the high wages and subsidies he provided to the men and their chiefs; otherwise they could leave whenever they wished.[297] His own men he paid six pounds a month. "The money was clear income: this made the service enviable."[298] He regarded himself self-mockingly as "a little bare-footed silk skirted man" endowed, however, with the power "to hobble the enemy" by virtue of his "stores and arms and a fund of two hundred thousand sovereigns to convince and control his converts."[299] "It was our habit to sneer at Oriental soldiers' love of pay," remarked Lawrence. The Sharif Hussein of Hejaz was paying "two pounds a month for a man, four for a camel. Nothing else would have performed the miracle of keeping a tribal army in the field for five months on end." Often one gave money to great sheiks under the pretense of wage payments, "money that was a polite bribe for friendly countenance."[300] As late as 1920, Lawrence was still accounting for his payments to the abler son of Hussein, Feisal: "We paid Feisal money in March when he left England; we paid him more in Egypt; we may pay him more next month.[301] When the father Hussein was reluctant to renounce his own sovereignty over all Arabia, and remained obdurate even when more money and a yacht were added to the proposed subsidy, Lawrence wanted him to reimburse the whole last payment. They haggled over bribes and sovereignties.[302] Feisal could not understand the British imperialist temperament: "They hunger for desolate lands, to build them up"; Feisal preferred his backward nomadism and set himself against the imperialist: "Does the ore admire the flame which transforms it?"[303]

As the historian A. L. Rowse has documented, Lawrence's fusion of his own feelings with the cause of the Arab uprising for independence and the intensity with which he assumed an Arab self, identifying himself with their customs and speech, were founded evidently on his own homosexual relationship. *The Seven Pillars of Wisdom* was dedicated to the young Arab, Salim Ahmed Dahoum. A dedicatory poem "To S. A." conveyed the degree of Lawrence's homosexual attachment unmistakably. "The whole Arab epic," writes A. L. Rowse, "was Dahoum's monument." When questioned during the Versailles Peace Conference about the motives for his pro-Arabism, Lawrence replied: "Personal. I liked a particular Arab, and I thought that freedom for the race would be an acceptable present."[304]

Brought up in a strict Victorian setting, its rigor enhanced by a stern mother who felt herself sinful because of her own unmarried status, T. E. Lawrence was enveloped in the guilt of his own ways. He sought periodic flagellations to expiate his hidden evil. And he ignored all his own rational judgments of the capacity of the Arab peoples for democratic self-government. In the spirit of an ideologist, therefore, and as an anti-imperialist, he hailed Lenin in 1934: "Lenin was the greatest man—only man who had evolved a theory, carried it out, and consolidated."[305] Lawrence once called himself and his entourage "kindergarten soldiers."[306] Doubtless, having studied Freud with admiration, as one who had produced "a difference in all thinking henceforward,"[307] Lawrence probably also realized the strange regressive source of his anti-imperialist, Arab identification and ideology.

In short, what transpires from comparing the imperialist and the anti-imperialist psyches, is that, generally speaking, it is the anti-imperialist who is struggling to master some racial antipathy, or to diminish a resentment arising from lack of position or power, or to counteract some outright neurosis. Among the imperialists such as Lugard, Cromer, Rhodes, Barnato, Vogel, or Emin Pasha, we do not find such a pathetically sordid character as Roger Casement, twisting the embitteredness of his homosexual existence into a hatred for the Empire and an identification with the tribal primitives. Both imperialists and anti-imperialists agreed in regarding the blacks as primitive and backward, but in the case of the anti-imperialists, their expression, as with E. D. Morel, was apt to be more intemperate than that of the imperialists, who having negotiated realistically with peoples they believed inferior, were not impelled to construct defense-mechanisms against an alleged guilt. Both groups were equally ambitious, but the anti-imperialist ambition expressed itself mainly in some organization, book, report, or sometimes legislation directed against the existing social or political order in some respect. The imperialists were more rational and successful in resolving the personal rebuffs or rejections that may have prompted them to distant careers. They organized societies and founded industries that endure and that raised the levels of civilization and well-being. Their own personal lives had a pleasure of discovery and accomplishment not given to the anti-imperialists. For the latter, the end of the British and French Empires was the culminating achievement. Whether the vastly augmented massacres, corruption and exploitation that have marked the newly independent African and Asian countries and the rise of the regressive Soviet imperialism validate this achievement seems doubtful.

During past debates in the United States on imperialism, it has been frequently noted that most imperialists and anti-imperialists "shared identical assumptions about the superior intelligence and virtue of the Anglo-Saxons." Imperialists invoked such assumptions to justify taking up the "White Man's Burden"; anti-imperialists drew a contrary conclusion, pleading that other races not be brought under American rule lest the intellectual and moral standards of the American democracy be lowered.[308] Marxists have often said that racism is an ideological expression of imperialism; it would probably be at least as true that in modern times, racism has been the covert premise of an ideology of anti-imperialism.

The most well-known anti-imperialists have, moreover, been "intellectuals" in contrast to the imperialists. Even Emin Pasha would have rather called himself a scientist and would have separated himself from the socialist intellectuals. In his later years, J. A. Hobson, having read psychoanalytical literature, pondered on the psychological traits of the "intellectual." "Man," he observed, "is primarily a doer, not a thinker," and anyone who pursues a life of thought pays dearly "in terms of ultimate self-respect." Though in his consciousness the intellectual insists on "the dignity and importance of his intellectual function . . . underneath, in the hidden recesses of his mind, this sense of weakness and inferiority rankles."[309] According to Hobson's later self-insight, the propensity of intellectuals toward the anti-imperialist ideology arises from their inferiority complex; anti-imperialism is a way of trying to compensate, to assert their superiority over the imperialist doers whom they unconsciously envy. Hobson, in his later years, did basically revise his original economic interpretation of imperialism, making primary instead the craving for self-assertion, which could take many forms, one of which was economic, though "the play of other less 'materialistic' considerations supplies the main current of effort."[310] But it was the early Hobson whom Lenin read and virtually canonized for Marxist intellectuals. The later Hobson's emerging scientific wisdom was ideologically irrelevant.

Meanwhile, a new characteristic has definitely become dominant among contemprary anti-imperialists. The latter are frequently hostile to the white race and Western civilization, an attitude that Hobson, Morel, and Woolf would have repudiated. Contemporary anti-imperialists often demand some reparations on the part of Western civilizations for the technology and culture they have brought to peoples previously "unspoiled." They demand philosophically more than the acceptance of the moral equality of all human beings; they insist upon an *a priori* scientific postulate that all races are equal in intellectual and creative abilities—a postulate that the classical anti-imperialists, from Hobson to Woolf, actually rejected. The sense of guilt and the indictment of civilization, as we have seen, have grown manifold among contemporary Western anti-imperialists. Here we come once more upon the strange evolving trait of the Western intellectual class: it seems at times desirous of collaborating in its civilization's decline.

E. The Resurgence of African Tribal War and Massacre

The abrogation of imperialism brought a resurgence of tribal massacres in independent African states. Untramelled aggression exceeded the bounds imaginable by the most skeptical of Western anti-imperialists. Unforeseen, for instance, by Western observers was the series of mutual massacres that began in 1962 as Tutsi pastoral tribesmen and Hutu agricultural tribesmen killed each other—men, women, and children—in the regions of Rwanda and Burundi. Reprisal became genocide in 1970 when some "10,000 Hutu were slaughtered," with "the employed and the educated and the semi-educated" as "the special targets for revenge."[311] Killing one's opponents reduced their votes in a referendum.

A relative calm and mutual adjustment had prevailed so long as the provinces were under Belgian rule; an American anthropologist doing her field work in Rwanda in 1959-1960 wrote that she felt during her stay there "that the Belgian role in Rwanda was a mitigating, positive, and honorable one."[312] But later even a common Catholic tie could not restrain the developing tribal collective hatred and regression. The Vatican radio broadcast on February 10, 1964 noted that "since the genocide of the Jews by Hitler, the most terrible systematic genocide is taking place in the heart of Africa."[313] Then in Uganda, genocide was practiced by a malevolent autocrat as a "mass slaughter of hundreds of thousands of Ugandans" ensued, accompanied by the most revolting cruelties, with tribal, religious, and economic divergencies all compunded in mutual hatreds. The autocrat Idi Amin praised Hitler for setting an example in exterminating the Jews, as the Nazi culture, in a more primitive setting, was diffused in a curious symbiosis with Soviet Marxist ideas and the supporting funds of oil-rich Arab rulers.[314]

Especially traumatic for the hopes awakened by the end of British imperialism were the sanguinary events in West Africa. Nigeria, populous and rich in resources, with a fairly numerous section of intellectuals, had been the African colonial country where the hope seemed brightest for the flourishing of a parliamentary democracy when it became independent in 1960. But "by December 1965, Nigeria was on the brink of collapse."[315] The political parties, led by intellectuals, became a by-word for corruption; soldiers saw no necessity for taking orders from civilians, and tribal, ethnic, economic, and religious hatreds among the Hausa, Fulani, Yoruba, and Ibo, and a variety of smaller tribes became uncontrolled. Riots in the early summer of 1966 "quickly became a pogrom against Ibo sectors of northern cities," where about three thousand were killed. During September and October, 1966, in the northern Moslem Hausa-Fulani region, thirty thousand Ibos were killed. Their presence as traders, business men, and civil servants was resented; the Ibo, perceiving that they faced "a systematic extermination in the North" understandably lost confidence in the Nigerian polity.[316] There followed what one writer called "an exodus of Jewish proportions."[317] In the civil war that followed the secession of Biafra, massacres became the norm; when one town was abandoned and the federal troops entered, "the killing of Ibos began. It was done principally by the civilians, especially the Urhobos (a tough, warlike minority tribe) . . . [and] went on for three days . . . The massacres were completely indiscriminate, men, women and children were hacked to pieces." In another massacre, an Ibo-hating major "herded all the Ibo men and boys together [800 of them] and had them machine-gunned to death."[318] After two and a half years of warfare, came "Nigeria's Appomattox" on January 15, 1970; people were tired of the continuous bloodshed. Constant fear and lack of food had finally weakened the Ibo will to resist, despite the weapons they still held.[319] In Britain, the parliamentary political leaders, both Labor and Conservative, had supported the supplying of arms to the Nigerian government; back-benchers and lobbyists, on the other hand, especially those with Christian religious ties, were advocates of the Biafran cause. Western Europeans were much moved by humanitarian feelings, "notably in Scandinavia and Germany, the latter reacting strongly to the Biafran charge of genocide from subliminal feelings of guilt."[320]

Were tribal genocides, however, the fruits of the end of imperialism? A keen observer, John de St. Jorre, noted that through the Nigerian civil war a new, younger political elite concentrated its hold on power. "And as a class they showed a marked reluctance to risk their skins, their survival rate being close to an incredible hundred percent. Students, the future elites, on both sides of the line, but particularly in the Nigerian universities, were the greatest armchair warriors of all. I can find no record of a single student from the Western Universities of Ibadan and Ife rushing to join the colors though they were invariably fierce advocates of crushing the 'rebellion.'" One wondered whether this type of intellectual elite would find its natural haven in alignment with Soviet imperialism. The tropical African republics, on the other hand, that had formerly been under French rule, were largely spared atrocities and massacres because the new black rulers were able to summon French troops to maintain civil order when the republican regimes were in straits.[321]

V

THE END OF PROGRESSIVE IMPERIALISM

A. Race and the End of the Democratic Imperialism of the Pre-World War II Era

Apart from any feeling of guilt for the imperialist enterprise as a whole, the modern Western imperialist nations early concluded that they could never succeed in establishing the counterpart of the "participatory imperialism" that had characterized the Roman Empire. What do we mean by "participatory imperialism"? It is not the same as "democratic imperialism." The British government at the end of the nineteenth century was a democratically elected one, the highest example of a parliamentary democracy yet seen, and operating soon after the end of World War I with a universal franchise. A democratically elected home government, however, can rule an empire of colonies, protectorates, and provinces through an administration in which the subjects abroad may have little part in decisions of policy and appointment. An illiterate *indigène* from a French African or Pacific colony was not allowed to travel to France, and even an educated African could never aspire to be the premier of the French Republic.

On the other hand, the Roman imperialism was, at its height, a participatory one; any provincial citizen, a Gaul, a Spaniard, a Greek, might still possibly rise through the administration or military to become a consul or even an emperor. The Roman Empire never conducted universal imperial free elections; nor did the Roman plebs retain its say in the imperial choice. But it was a "participatory imperialism"; citizens of all peoples in the provinces could join and rise in the civil service and army. The free migration and circulation of peoples characterized a "participatory empire." The democratic imperialism of the United States, on the other hand, like that of Britain and France with respect to their colonies, was not freely open to migrants.

The age of capitalist imperialism was finally brought to an end in part because Britain, France, and the United States came to believe that, given the climate of guilt engendered by the anti-imperialists, an empire could not survive unless it consented to an egalitarian, self-denying immigration of races; this alternative, despite their guilt-consciousness, none would accept. Psychologically, therefore, they vetoed the undertaking of the kind of military-economic effort that the advancement of imperialism would have required. They were too guilty to maintain the old imperialism, but were repelled too by the notion of a racially commingled one.

The "age of imperialism" ended in part because racial masochism had its limits. The Englishman did not want to see England overrun with Hindu and African immigrants; the Frenchman did not want to see Senegalese, Malagasies, and Tonkinese peopling his avenues and boulevards; the American did not want to see Filipinos and West Indians populating his cities. British Laborites might sing hymns of universal brotherhood, but the Briton was prepared to stop singing these psalms when he realized that he was being asked to surrender his land or allow Asians and Africans to compete for his job. A British working class riding rejected a nominated Laborite foreign secretary, P. C. Gordon Walker, precisely because they disliked his racial egalitarianism.[1]

At the very beginning of the twentieth century James Bryce had perceived very clearly that a multiracial empire, committed to democracy, might be inherently unstable. The British Empire had an inner agent for cumulative disequilibrium which the Roman Empire had not known. "In the case of Rome there was a similarity of conditions which pointed to and ultimately effected a fusion of the peoples. In the case of England there is a dissimilarity which makes the fusion of her people with the peoples of India impossible,"[2] wrote Bryce. For the British in India, color formed "an unsurmountable barrier to intermarriage." "There was no severing line like this in the ancient world."[3] The Romans came into contact only marginally with black African tribes. "Nothing contributed more to the fusion of the races and nationalities that composed the Roman Empire than the absence of any physical and conspicuous distinctions between the races."[4] The British had ruled India, Bryce felt, "on principles of strict justice"; "a relatively small body of European civilians, supported by a relatively small armed force," had maintained peace and order. But there the analogy with the Roman Empire stopped, for the British could not go on to the fusion of races. The British, of course, had reason to fear the new Indian intellectual class they were calling into being—"European ideas have created a large class of educated and restless natives ill disposed to brook subjection to an alien race."[5] But the Romans, likewise creating a new intellectual class in Spain, in Gaul, in North Africa, nevertheless had little reason to fear them. For the intellectuals, all with careers open in the Roman service or the army, even the emperorship itself, had a common loyalty to the Empire.[6] Nobody, on the other hand, entertained the possibility that Britain could have an African or Hindu prime minister. That was why the Empire could not last. As A. P. Thornton wrote: "Imperialism included no melting-pot in its equipment."[7] Modern imperialism, unable to accept equality as a moral absolute, chose to be a transient order. Even when Disraeli had kindled the British imaginative conception of empire to its highest, the underlying reservation was articulated by his Liberal antagonist, William Ewart Gladstone, in 1878: "Especially it is inexpedient to acquire possessions which, like Cyprus, never can become truly British, because they have acquired indelibly an ethnical character of their own."[8] If such reservations were held with respect to the Greco-Turkish Cypriots, how much stronger were they felt for Burmese, Ugandans, Afghans, Fijians, and Zulus? The anti-imperialist "Little England" spirit might affirm with a highly moralistic vocabulary its refusal to exploit other races. More covert was the expression of its underlying psychological standpoint: though Englishmen could accommodate as fellow Britishers to their countrymen and descendants who had colonized Australia, New Zealand, and Canada, they felt a repugnance against thus receiving the colored races. The ideology of anti-imperialism itself could, as we have seen, be even more "racialist" than that of imperialism. England's leading anti-imperialist writer, J. A. Hobson, invoked Darwinian authority when he rejected any attempt to bring the colored races into a universal civilization with the white; such a notion, he declared, was "utterly at variance both with the 'theory of evolution' and with the facts of history . . . [D]eeply marked characters of historic race, physical and psychical . . . tend to express themselves firmly and constantly in widely divergent types of civilisation."[9]

This racialist reservation concerning the limit of empire reached deeply into the feelings of British labor, liberalism and radicalism. When Britain was aroused in 1865 by the cruelties committed under the Governor of Jamaica, Edward Eyre, the *Bee Hive,* the journal of London labor, declared that "the working classes of the United Kingdom have never subjected themselves to the charge of what is mockingly styled 'negro worship.'"[10] And Edward S. Beesly, the Comtist professor of classics who just the year before had given the opening founding address of the International Workingmen's Association, said: "I don't consider a black man a beautiful object . . . there can be no doubt that they belong to a lower type of the human race than we do, and I should not like to live in a country where they formed a considerable part of the population."[11] His friend Karl Marx had similar sentiments concerning the black race. And their views were shared by the middle and upper classes of Britain as well.[12]

Sixty years later in 1929, the English scientist Julian Huxley, encountering an unusually conscientious group of British officials in East Africa, noted the persistent barrier of race that excluded even educated blacks: "It is indeed remarkable to see how widespread (though by no means universal) and deep-rooted (though often unconscious) is the feeling of white men against the Europeanized, educated, or even progressive black. And the feeling is often strongest in those who have a whole-hearted liking for the unsophisticated native. . . . Europe cannot have it both ways," Huxley concluded.[13] If Europeans ruled in Africa by virtue of some "white superiority," Africans would try to learn their ideas and methods, and Europeans could not be hostile to their pupils' efforts. Yet it was also clear that the imperial mission faltered when it suggested a racial self-abnegation. Huxley still hoped that even if England declined as an industrial power, it could "yet remain great as the director of an Empire,"[14] because its men were endowed "with a gift for the administration of primitive peoples." If a racially unfused empire has its own source of instability, perhaps a novel type of imperialist structure remains to be fashioned by the world's political intelligence.

More recently, scholars have argued instead in the more congenial technological fashion that modern imperialism declined because it was incompatible with "modernization." Empires, according to the noted historians Ronald Robinson and Jack Gallagher, "fell when the processes of modernization threw up a fresh and more powerful wave of nationalism." Why, however, should "modernization" have produced a nationalist, separatist reaction? Romanization very rarely elicited a separatist reaction; why then did "modernization"? And the answer seems to lie in the limit of egalitarianism that had been reached. Because the African and Asian subjects alike knew that they would never be psychologically full citizens in a multiracially fusing empire, they necessarily responded as nationalists.[15]

True, the Portuguese Empire is often adduced as a demonstration of an empire founded on racial commingling.[16] The Portuguese imperialists are said to have found racial mixture natural to themselves because of their Catholic background, or because dark-skinned themselves, as the offspring of a Moorish intermixture, they looked at dark color as an index of nobility or intelligence.[17] Portuguese colonization, however, was a matter mostly of a few thousand young men who went womanless to distant continents. As C. R. Boxer, the Camões Professor of Portuguese at the University of London, writes: "It is unlikely that there were ever more than 10,000 able-bodied Portuguese men overseas in an empire which extended from South America to the Spice Islands, during the sixteenth century. The population of Portugal at this period probably oscillated at around a million, and a heavy annual emigration from the mother country was needed to fill the gaps caused by the wastage in the tropics. Relatively few female emigrants left Portugal during that century."[18] Although the Marquis of Pombal (1755-1777), prime minister in the later eighteenth century, tried (unsuccessfully) to end the color bar in the Portuguese Empire, he forebore from decreeing an equal status for the Negroes in West African colonies; he regarded them still as basically inferior though he did confer upon the Hindus of Goa a greater measure of religious liberties. Colored officers of Asian origins nonetheless were still unable to rise above a captain's rank, and colored Brazilian students remained unwelcome at the University of Coimbra.[19] In Brazil, during the eighteenth century, notes C. R. Boxer, "the free Negro and the dark-hued Mulatto had little or no hope of ascending the social scale, whatever their aptitudes and qualifications."[20] Where racial intermixture occurred extensively, it was in the dissolute, disorderly atmosphere of the newly-discovered gold and diamond mines of Brazil and in slave households where young adolescents were growing up "surrounded by half-naked colored women whom they could enjoy as they pleased."[21] Though the mulatto offspring experienced legal discrimination, Brazilians of all classes resented white Portuguese immigrants because the "more energetic" new-comers dominated the trade and commerce of the country.[22] By 1691, however, the Portuguese Brazilian empire had declined so much that it contributed to Portugal's unfavorable balance of trade. In 1689 a Jesuit had written expressively: "We shall shortly relapse into the savage status of the Indians, and become Brazilians instead of Portuguese."[23] Catastrophe was averted by the discovery of gold and diamonds. By the century's end, however, as the mines were depleted, a tired Portugal held on with little enthusiasm to its Brazilian imperial experiment in racial mixture.

B. The Unrealized Age of an American Imperialism: Prelude to Regression?

It took several centuries for the Roman Empire to be divested of its vocation for empire by religious cynicism. In a few contemporary decades, however, an infusion of guilt into the concept of imperialism has largely undermined such a vocation for leadership in the world's civilization on the part of the American and Western European peoples. Sumner Welles, the American under-secretary of state, undoubtedly spoke for an almost unanimous opinion when, during the first year of America's involvement in World War II, he declared in his famous Memorial Day address: "The age of imperialism is ended."[24] A growing and persistent ideological disaffection on the part of the intellectual class from about 1890 onward has led to an inhibiting self-doubt within American civilization. The United States, by all objective criteria, has probably been the most altruistic society that the world has known; in terms of the outlays in money, goods, food, services, expert knowledge, the lives of its citizens, the help it has rendered to oppressed persons, impoverished peoples, endangered invaded nations, or people persecuted for their religious or political beliefs, it has been without parallel in the history of mankind. Its people have welcomed Hungarian, Russian, Italian, and German revolutionists from 1848 onward; its government of 1861 led in a Civil War imbued with a moral fervor for the emancipation of black slaves; its Congress and public meetings condemned the pogroms at Kishinev in 1881; it characteristically transferred an indemnity from the Chinese government at the end of the Boxer Rebellion for use as a scholarship fund for Chinese students; it sent armies to fight on the European continent in wars in which it was not directly involved, following its belief that mankind's liberal democratic aspiration was being tested; it stood against a Japanese advance in the Far East although its economic interest in that region was peripheral and a Japanese hegemony in that region would have been a guarantee against postwar Communist supremacy. Peoples throughout the world, whatever their governments and regimes aver, regard America as an anomaly in world history, a nation that has elevated a spontaneous altruistic ethic into a considered national policy.

France, long influenced by a large section of Marxist intellectuals, has been reputed to be the most anti-American of Western European countries. Yet the public opinion polls in France have consistently indicated that America remains the foreign country they most esteem. In July 1939 on the eve of World War II, twenty-six percent chose the United States as the country they liked best as compared to seven percent for the Soviet Union. Then in 1947, a majority, fifty-one percent, felt that the Soviet Union would engage in a war of aggression, while only twenty percent felt that would be so in the case of the United States. In 1967, with all the writings and agitation against the American forces in Vietnam, and the considerable voting strength of the French Marxists, forty-seven percent of the people still signified that the United States was the country they felt most for as against twenty-five percent for the Soviet Union.[25]

Despite the widespread conviction of the sincerity and relative self-lessness of American policy, Americans themselves nurtured their self-doubt. A curious situation prevails: on the one hand, Americans and the world's peoples generally feel that the United States is the most altruistic nation; on the other hand, the advanced intellectuals, often regarded as the conscience of their respective societies (especially in the United States), denounce America as the most imperialistic, aggressive, power-arrogant country—everywhere, that is, with the strange exception of the highest intellectuals in the Soviet Union itself. Which brings us to the roles of doctrines of "imperialism" in the critique of Western civilization, as crucial in the latter case as the doctrine of the corrupt empire was for the Roman Christians.

Of all the words in the English language, the word "imperialism" has been translated to instill guilt in the members of Western civilization concerning their technology, their social system, and their position of leadership alike. Theories of imperialism, proposed by Marxist and neo-Marxist ideologists, have been covert emotive propositions for inducing a Western historical guilt. To do so, all of them are obliged to suppress evidence, and all have seen their chief predictions falsified. Most profess to believe that imperialism, the alleged "last stage in a moribund capitalism," will be followed by the birth of a new, higher civilization. "Imperialism," a word once bearing a connotation of pride, has been wrested from political reality and "masochized" with a variety of fantasies.

Especially after World War I, as Richard Koebner has narrated, one specific connotation appended to "imperialism" came to the forefront "on whose condemnatory use writers and orators of all the political world came to agree."[26] "Imperialism" became the favored common pejorative term of such diverse critics as Lenin, Hobson, and William Jennings Bryan, who weighed Western civilization in their Marxist, liberal, or Christian scales. Communist and Nazi ideologists alike took it as a slogan-word; if to the Leninist it signified the last stage of a condemned capitalism, to the Nazi it was the system of exploitation by an Anglo-Saxon and Jewish plutocracy. In the hands of the later ideologists of Arab, Asian and African countries, "imperialism" has become the vehicle for several convergent themes—the struggle against capitalism, the struggle against American prestige, the struggle against white civilization, the struggle against Jews, even the struggle against those outstanding in science and intellect.

Nineteenth-century liberals were the first to take the lead in a moral rejection of imperialism. Although the conservative prime minister, Benjamin Disraeli, embellished his vision of empire, of a *Pax Britannica,* with romantic imagery, his opponents, under the aegis of the Liberal leader, William Ewart Gladstone, tried to reverse the emotional coordinates to convert the word "imperialism" into "an anti-Disraeli slogan."[27] A Liberal publicist, Robert Lowe, led the way toward equating imperialism with power immorally used: "The triumph of Imperialism is most complete when power is most clearly manifested."[28] Disraeli noted presciently in 1863 that the "professors and rhetoricians" were inculcating hostility to the principle of empire; "prigs and pedants," he called them, but they had the potential for attaining an ascendancy in conscience.[29] Nevertheless, at the end of the nineteenth century, as late as 1898, there was still a high-tide in popular enthusiasm for imperialism. Britain, at that time, was identified as the mainstay of world imperialism. By the close of World War I, however, the United States, though scarcely in formal political terms an imperialist power, was regarded as the economic center of world imperialist resource.

It is doubtful that the critics of American imperialism hated it as much as they said. Even those who spoke the harshest words against the United States could not help regarding it as embodying an ethical spirit in politics more generous than the world had yet seen. Bertrand Russell, the famed English philosopher, had gone to prison for having, among other things, insulted American soldiers fighting on Britain's side. But in 1922 Russell acknowledged that he regarded America "as definitely better, in international affairs, than any other Great Power. The crimes of Versailles were crimes of the Old World, not of the New . . . America alone has stood for the independence and integrity of China. At Washington, America made a sincere effort to diminish the expense of naval armaments . . . America showed, after the war, a complete absence of that hunger for territory which distinguished all other victors. These are very great moral assets, and they make me, in common with most European radicals, feel that, if any one power is to be supreme in the world, it is fortunate for the world that America should be that one."[30]

America was indeed the one power in the world that after World War I, and especially World War II, had the military power and economic reserves to impose on the world a peaceful order and a devotion to the arts of civilization. Not since the emergence of Rome had the embattled, wounded nations of the world, with the pain of millions of dead, so longed for the guidance of what they regarded as a power that combined freedom and organization as no other had. The "pax Romana" would have found its successor in the "pax Americana."

What might, however, have been an age of American imperialism virtually failed at its beginnings not because of an "arrogance of power" but because the American ethic was simply ahead of anything that the world had seen in international politics. A blend of the Christian vocabulary with the Enlightenment values of Franklin, Jefferson, and Lincoln, and the pragmatic wisdom of James and Dewey, the American ethic expressed a belief in the goodness of men and in their basic decency, provided they could work and speak their minds. Its most popular cultural spokesmen were those such as Mark Twain, extolling the joys of a frontier boyhood that allowed no shams or hypocrisies, or Will Rogers, saying that he had never met a man he didn't like. They welcomed such writers as Sinclair Lewis who, while satirizing them for their hard work, unflagging optimism, and stumbling aspirations to culture, still shared the same virtues.

Because of the American ethic, Americans intervened generously to save the fledgling Bolshevik revolution at the time of its greatest peril in 1921-1922 when famine stalked Russia. Nothing like it indeed had ever been seen in the history of international relations; a country founded on liberalism and capitalism was prepared to rescue a regime that was committed to the violent overthrow of both.

Famine indeed has been a propelling agent in Russian history. The famine of 1891 had set in motion the sequence of events which culminated in the downfall of the Czarist political system.[31] The famine of the nineteen-twenties, however, far exceeded in its extent and intensity that of the earlier generation. As a young man Lenin had mocked at the do-gooding efforts of intellectuals on local relief committees; once more he was at first uncomprehending, hostile, and suspicious of the purported American good-will and capitalist humanitarianism. It rankled, moreover, that the American Relief was directed by the arch-capitalist Herbert Hoover. The possibility of a bourgeois, disinterested generosity contravened Lenin's textbooks on historical materialism and the capitalist system. When Hoover insisted that American personnel should be responsible for organizing the local relief committees and the selecting of the areas to be aided, Lenin forthwith demanded that he should be "slapped publicly before the whole world." Nonetheless, the plans of the American Relief Administration, under those conditions of mass starvation, prevailed; ideology yielded to biology. Indeed, a group of Soviet leaders arose who were "friends of the A.R.A.—Kamenev, Krassin, even Dzerzhinsky, the chief of the secret police.[32] Especially fortunate for the A.R.A. was the fact that Lev Kamenev was chosen by the Soviet government to act on its behalf with respect to relief questions. As H. H. Fisher recalled, "Kamenev was the friend at the Communist court to whom the leaders of the A.R.A. could turn when all else failed," a man "with a sense of proportion." To curb their own people's spontaneous thanks for the American food, Soviet ideologists had perforce to insinuate that the giving of food was the cloak for bourgeois subversive aims. Indeed, it was true that Herbert Hoover, both Quaker and secretary of commerce, occasionally allowed himself to hope that the demonstration of American altruism, transcending the divergencies of economic system, might encourage some liberal relaxation in the Soviet dictatorship. After all, as the League of Nations officials stated, this was the worst famine in modern times, defeated only because the American Relief mission at one time fed as many as ten million persons.[33] The Council of People's Commissars itself, at the final ceremony on July 18, 1923 that marked the end of the work, formally presented the Americans with its resolution: "Thanks to the enormous and entirely disinterested efforts of the A.R.A., millions of people of all ages were rescued from death, and whole cities and districts were saved from the horrible catastrophe that threatened them." In their name, the Council declared, it "considers it its duty, before the representatives of the entire world, to express its deepest gratitude to this organization, to its leader, Herbert Hoover," and to declare that the Soviet people "will never forget the help rendered to them through the A.R.A."[34] The famine, according to a Soviet statement, had struck "about 25 million" persons, of whom at least two million died before the ordeal subsided.[35]

In a country in which cannibalism in the country districts was becoming a frequent phenomenon,[36] the American Relief Administration during 1921-1923 fed more than twenty million starving persons; during one month alone, August, 1922, 4,173,339 children were fed.[37] Although America had been thrust into an economic depression, its people and its social service agencies from the American Friends Service to the Jewish Joint Distribution Committees and the Laura Spelman Rockefeller Memorial contributed large sums.[38] The Soviet contribution of gold rubles was but a small fraction of the American Relief outlay and was mainly used to help finance the purchase of seed grain. On the initiative, moreover, of President Harding and Herbert Hoover, Congress, in December 1921 authorized the use of the capital funds of the United States Grain Corporation to be used for the relief of the starving people of Russia.[39]

Furthermore, since Russia had become "a nation in rags and patches," and the manufacture of civilian clothing had almost ceased, the American Relief Administration distributed second-hand clothes, shoes, stockings, and woolen goods for children, and large quantities of materials to help people make clothes for themselves. As a large number of university professors had succumbed to starvation, disease, and suicide, so that "faculty meetings" consisted of "little more than mournful memorials," a special fund was provided for "the relief of intellectuals."[40] When one reads of the children of the Bolshevik Revolution, crouching listlessly in their "dirty garments," and resembling "in their starving lustreless eyes, the figures of animals rather than human beings,"[41] one is mindful that such were those who for sheer survival's sake later submitted to all the tyrannies of Soviet rule.

The American ethic remained a puzzle to the Soviet leaders. Would the Soviet leaders ever conceivably have rendered aid to a leading capitalist country without first having obtained major political concessions in return? From their Leninist standpoint, all ethics were the expressions of class interests, and there were no universal moral principles. Soviet Foreign Commissar Chicherin, acknowledging in January 1922 that America's action stood outside his categories, said: "America is a riddle." The Americans, according to the pro-Soviet correspondent for *The Nation* in 1923, Louis Fischer, had "very directly aided the present regime."[42] In October, 1921, Lenin wrote with an un-Marxist enthusiasm: "Hoover is really a *plus*," and "with Hoover we have something worthwhile."[43] Americans hoped the story would be told lovingly in Russian households for generations.[44] Perhaps it was, albeit quietly and privately. For within a few years Soviet textbooks were explaining that the American Relief Administration had been a counter-revolutionary plot hatched by the economic chieftains of the capitalist class.[45]

From the standpoint either of a realistic world politics, or a power politics, or of "Marxist dialectics," the American political ethic of feeding the enemy's citizens and thereby salvaging an enemy regime, simply made no sense; it was a political impossibility, the political equivalent of a perpetual motion machine. If the Bolsheviks, the self-declared foes of the American society, were in straits, it was politically foolhardy, from such standpoints, for the Americans to bail them out. The American ethic, for all its individualistic emphasis on self-reliance and its alleged bourgeois and Calvinst origins, took the tie of human responsibility seriously. If natural calamities descended upon a people through no fault of their own, then regardless of their race, religion, or social system, they deserved, in the American view, a helping hand. Perhaps a disorganized world, in which a totalitarian regime was consolidating itself, required a firmer hand to use American strength plainly to reinstate political freedom and economic progress. But American tradition provided little desire to prevail in alien settings, especially in the distant, backward Russian lands. American soldiers who had served briefly in Siberia, at the end of World War I reported that the Russian forces, both Bolshevik and anti-Bolshevik, behaved like savages reveling in massacres.[46]

Once again, after World War II, an American ethic of human co-responsibility ruled out the use of atomic bombs or any threat to use them, a strategy that might have promoted an American empire. Instead, an ethic of human fellowship merging with a self-punitive guilt threw aside the fruits of victory and helped transmute political power into a self-righteous impotence.

A simple thought-experiment, a *Gedankenexperiment,* easily performed, illumines the self-destructive vector in American post-war policy. Let us suppose that any Communist country such as the Soviet Union or Mao's China had possessed in 1945 or thereafter the monopoly of the atomic bomb, as America had for four years; what would it have done? It would have undoubtedly dictated its political will harshly, exhaustively, peremptorily, threateningly, and humiliatingly on the rest of the world. Though history happily spared us this crucial experiment, probably every Communist of every variety would agree as to the steps Joseph Stalin would have taken if circumstances had given him a monopoly of the atomic bomb. Directly Stalin would have dispatched an ultimatum to every one of the world's capitals, demanding capitulation to his directives lest he exact the direst penalty; not physical liquidation, as his ideologists previously called it, but a dialectically "higher" physical vaporization. Governments would have collapsed overnight as his agents of the secret police, taking control, would have commissioned pliant henchmen; if one recalcitrant Jan Masaryk, foreign minister in Czechoslovakia, was done to death during the Communist coup of 1948, like Premier Imre Nagy in Hungary in 1956, or tortured and deposed like Premier Dubcek in Czechoslovakia in 1968, countless thousands in Western Europe would have met such fates. Social and political systems would have been altered, for practical purposes, terminally and irreversibly as the liberal, democratic class would have been extirpated.

During this period the philosopher Bertrand Russell urged the United States to use its monopoly of atomic power as a timely lever for advancing the concord of nations. He called on America to act swiftly and to confront the Soviet Union with an ultimatum. Stalin, remaining shrewdly unmoved by the American pleas for the international control of the atomic bomb, reckoned accurately on the self-paralyzing power of the American idealistic ethic and its corps of uprighteous intellectuals and fellow travelers.[47] Russell rose in the House of Lords on April 30, 1947, to call for "an attempt to coerce the Russians, because I do not believe that they would unwillingly submit to inspection." He stated plainly that the Russians, in his view, were "completely mad and foolish" in their opposition to the American plan for internationalizing the atomic bomb, while the Americans, on the contrary, were acting with "a sense of responsibility" greater than that shown by his own countrymen.[48] The Labor government in Britain at this time utterly repudiated any notion of confronting Stalin with an ultimatum,[49] despite the fact that its leaders in 1945 were, as their prime minister later wrote, "acutely aware of the combination of Russian old-time and Communist modern imperialism which threatened the freedom of Europe." Indeed, Clement Attlee thought the Americans were rather naïvely hopeful about their relations with the Russians, "that the Americans had an insufficient appreciation of this danger," and that "the immense forces of Russia that threatened to give her complete power in Europe were held in check by this terrible weapon [the atomic bomb] in the hands of the West."[50]

Why then, was its power not invoked to end the Stalinist regime in the Soviet Union? Let us suppose that Britain and the United States had together declared publicly that Stalin's dictatorship, with its repression of human rights and liberal opposition, and its tactic of "take-over," constituted a perpetual menace to the peace and well-being of Europe. Let us suppose, moreover, that Britain and the United States had demanded that the Soviet regime convene the Constituent Assembly that it forcibly dissolved in 1918 and allow the first free, democratic elections since that time to take place in the Soviet Union, with full freedom of political speech and the freedom to organize opposition political parties. Lastly, let us suppose that this ultimatum had been broadcast to the Soviet people and the Soviet forces in central Europe. Would Joseph Stalin have been able to survive the open threat to his power? Or would not the suppressed liberal, democratic elements in the Soviet Union, taking heart that their cause was comprehended abroad, have reached out publicly to the Soviet people and the Communist party itself for the overthrow of Stalin? For so insecure did Stalin feel his hold on power during that post-war period, that he launched a series of purges and represssions which, if they did not reach the scale attained in the pre-war years, still functioned with camps, as Robert Conquest writes, that were from 1945 to 1953, "at first more deadly than ever," with few of the first year's batch surviving to the latter year.[51] An allied ultimatum, if it had been delivered during those years when Stalin was consolidating totalitarian dictatorship in Poland, Czechoslovakia, and Hungary and threatening the independence of Yugoslavia, might well have released the suppressed liberal, democratic longings in those countries as well as in the Soviet Union itself.

An incapacity to act, however, and the fear of the epithet "imperialist" tended to enervate Western conservative and liberal governments and their peoples.[52] Ten years later America itself virtually undermined the power of its allies in the Middle East, thereby promoting the disequilibrium in Western democratic industrial civilization and abetting the exploratory spread of the Soviet imperialism. It all began in July 1956, when Egypt, led by its President Nasser, seized the Suez Canal in a grandiose "anti-imperialist" action. The prime minister of Great Britain, Anthony Eden, pleaded with the president of the United States, Dwight D. Eisenhower, that the fate of the Western European nations was at stake. The ultimate issue, wrote Eden on September 6, 1956, was the menace of "united oil resources under the control of a united Arabia led by Egypt and under Russian influence. When that moment comes Nasser can deny oil to Western Europe and we here shall be at his mercy."[53] The other Arab countries, Eden warned, would finally be drawn toward the aim of humiliating advanced Western industrial civilization. "If Nasser says to them, 'I have successfully defied eighteen powerful nations including the United States . . . I have expropriated all Western property. Trust me and withhold oil from Western Europe. Within six months or a year, the continent of Europe will be on its knees before you,' will the Arabs not be prepared to follow the lead?" Eden reminded the American president of the grim consequences that had followed the appeasement of the Nazi Adolf Hitler, pursuing his design against European civilization; asking for America's benevolent neutrality, the British and French planned a joint military campaign to recover the Suez Canal.[54] When that invasion, however, took place the next month, the American president bluntly rescinded his previous intimation of benevolent neutrality. Reluctant to see the issue of "imperialism" raised in the midst of the ongoing presidential campaign, he declared that American public opinion would not condone the use of force. Whereupon the British and French forces were compelled to make an ignominious withdrawal; within a few years their virtually complete leave-taking from their colonies and protectorates in Africa and the Middle East was to be completed. Though the discovery of oil in the North Sea and the successful development of oceanic oil wells brought an unexpected aid to Britain, for the advanced Western nations and Japan, as a whole, the consequences of the control of the oil wells in the Middle East by the rulers of backward areas were soon to be apparent.

In its puzzled, searching self-doubt, America applied to itself and its allies a unilateral ethical standard that inevitably entailed a series of capitulations to Soviet and Middle Eastern nations that were themselves bound by no such ethic. A one-sided ethical standard in international politics can become the agency of self-destruction; it reinforces the weapons of those who have no scruples in using them to attack and discredit the values of civilization. Jews who many centuries ago would not bear arms on the Sabbath against the Romans were killed in inaction, and the Egyptian army did not scruple to attack the Israelis on Yom Kippur, 1973, simply because it was a sacred day for ethical reflection. Nor did Jewish non-violence deter the Nazis from their program of mass death. A collective sense of guilt becomes fashionable as one's own civilization is held to be corrupted by the evil it has wrought against the undercivilized. An emotional propensity in liberal democratic civilization to locate a sociological or theological original sin in one's self or society guides it in a regressive direction.

By October 1973, Anthony Eden's predictions were fulfilled. Emboldened by the American reversal in Vietnam, the Arab countries proceeded to threaten the stability of Western industrial civilization with their embargo on deliveries of oil; then, by raising its price through oligopolistic dictate, they imposed a tribute of "surplus value" that exceeded anything that capitalist imperialism had ventured. A tremendous disequilibrating strain, both economic and psychological, was superimposed on the world's prices. Only about fifteen thousand Saudi Arabians were employed in the oil industry, a small number compared to the country's half-million farmers and herdsmen. The extraction of oil is indeed a "capital-intensive" industry, that is, one where the investment funds are expended mostly on machinery and equipment rather than on wages and labor. These capital needs, as well as the managerial and technical skills and imagination, were provided mainly by the United States. But the oil revenues that Saudi Arabia extracted from the rest of the world rose immediately by several billions of dollars in 1973 and 1974 and to vaster sums in successive years. Two years later the World Bank estimated that by 1985 the oil exporting countries would have extracted for themselves from their oil revenues $1.2 trillion dollars.[55] Their estimate evidently proved too modest. The king of Saudi Arabia and his severalty of emirs and sheiks became the world's chief extractors of "surplus value" (in the Marxist sense). Saudi Arabia, as an organ of the British Marxist intellectuals noted lugubriously, "combines the most virulent tribal tyranny with the most advanced represssive techniques."[56] Thus, by grace of an indecisive Western civilization, numbed by a series of military defeats and withdrawals from North Africa to Asia and an overzealous "anti-Americanism" that flourished after the relatively lesser misdeeds and abuses known as "Watergate" were made known, a new form of backward state socialist spoliation, through tribute and oligopoplistic profit, was invented in the Middle East in 1973. Underlying that Western indecisiveness and failure of will were, of course, the several generations of cumulative criticism by Western intellectuals of "capitalism" and "imperialism." British socialist intellectuals, for instance, at great meetings of protest declared movingly in 1956 that the Suez invasion was the most shameful betrayal of all they stood for. In America President Eisenhower, a Republican, had somehow absorbed from the ideological clouds of a recent Marxist book a phrase about the dangers of the "military-industrial complex." The anti-imperialist mood encouraged readiness to condemn one's own social existence rather than to weigh dispassionately the probable consequences for the world's civilization of different alternatives.

The shattering impact of the Vietnamese defeat on the American people, and indeed, the Western nations generally, has been compared to that experienced when barbarian forces first overwhelmed Roman legions. In 378 A.D. at Adrianople a Roman army embattled on the Danube with an invading force of barbarian Goths was routed and destroyed. That defeat is generally regarded as a turning-point in the history of the empire. The faith of the Romans in their own invincibility was broken; henceforth barbarian tribal warriors too might expect to engage the Roman legions in battle with a reasonable prospect for victory. Roman leadership was falling into incompetent hands, Roman deserters were assisting the barbarians, and Roman towns were fearful.

The so-called Tet offensive in 1968 of the North Vietnamese Army was thus regarded by many articulate critics as the "Adrianople" of the United States. Not that it was a military defeat for the American and South Vietnamese forces. Indeed, as W. W. Rostow has written: "The Tet offensive was a military disaster for Hanoi."[57] The North Vietnamese Communist plan to inflict a military debacle upon the American troops at Khe Sanh, comparable to the catastrophe that the French knew at Dien Bien Phu in 1954, was frustrated. The civilian will of the American people, however, was weakened by the Tet offensive. Pham Van Dong, the North Vietnamese premier, had said late in 1962: "Americans do not like long, inconclusive wars and this is going to be a long, inconclusive war. Thus we are sure to win in the end."[58] Up until the Tet offensive, a plurality of the American people, often a decisive majority, had favored America's continued military effort in the Vietnam War. "In November 1966, for example, 73 percent believed that the United States should carry on at existing or higher levels of military activity, 18 percent believed troops should be withdrawn, 9 percent had no opinion." A year later, the figures still gave sixty-three percent as favoring the American involvement and thirty-one percent opposed. But the proportion of support became a minority after the Tet offensive: in June 1968, forty-nine percent of the American people wished their forces to begin withdrawal, whereas only forty-three percent still desired to continue or increase the American military effort.[59] The American will to stem the Communist advance was clearly diminished to that of a minority. True, the sense of defeat that Abraham Lincoln had felt in the summer of 1864 had been far greater, his support evidently far less, and the percentage of deserters in the Union Army was one-seventh of the enlistments.[60] But American intellectuals and newspapers in 1864 did not join in the kind of vociferous criticism that became the fashion in 1970.

The values on which the American nation was founded were challenged fundamentally. An ethos of self-hatred, or self-contempt, became the dominant mood in the latter years of the Vietnam War. The American soldier became an object of ridicule; the deserter, on the other hand, the draft dodger, and the public burner of his draft card became figures for admiration in newspapers. New Leftist and neo-Marxist intellectuals came to exercise a preponderant fashion-forming influence in magazines and literary reviews. The word "alienation," diffusing from the exhumed juve-nilia of Karl Marx to the tracts of an anti-liberal, refugee German Marx-ist who had been the "intellectual mentor" to a wartime Soviet espionage circle, became the querulous slogan of an assortment of disciples who toured the campuses of colleges and universities urging a general uprising against the American system, denouncing the Vietnam War, and advo-cating a variety of activities, from arson ("Burn, baby, burn,"), to escape through drugs and the terrorist explosion of bombs. No American soldiers had previously been asked to fight a war with such a consciousness that they were being made a mockery of at home.

The standard of judgment naturally brought to bear against the American troops projected the self-hatred of the most influential Ameri-can intellectuals. Hitherto, the judges of military ethics have always dis-tinguished between the cruelty or inhumanity which arises episodically in war under the stress of a breakdown of reason from that which arises from a calculated policy, coldly planned, commanded, and controlled by the highest authorities of the armed force. The behavior of the soldiers involved in the detestable "My Lai massacre" was generalized hyperbol-ically by American liberal and leftist intellectuals as representative of the deportment of all of the American army. Newspapers and television cameras brought to American homes an almost daily fare of first-hand views of the enemy dead and wounded, scenes of North Vietnamese captives maltreated by South Vietnamese, scenes of battles' devastation of families' homes, words of pending disaster for American forces in Saigon, in Khe Sanh. Television producers ran "easy cliché shots"; "very few newsmen were sufficiently experienced, interested, or informed to 'explain' the battle scene in its larger context";[61] newsmen who were personally fearful during some action like the Tet offensive projected their own "psychological effect" on the army.[62] The chief "commentator" on a vast television network, eloquently hostile to America's effort in the Vietnam War, was one whose own behavior under stress in World War II had, according to American airmen, not been above criticism.[63] Probably no war was ever waged with such a one-sided hostile reportage. No North Vietnamese newspapers or cameras covered the Hué massacre during the Tet offensive, which apart from its having been tenfold the magnitude of My Lai, was executed as part of a deliberate policy to obliterate South Vietnamese civilian leaders and their families; American reporters evinced only a peripheral interest in North Vietnamese cruelties.[64] No American television network made mention of the mass executions carried out by the North Vietnamese in Hué.[65] No North Vietnamese reporters, of course, brought news to the outer world as to how American prisoners were being tortured and mysteriously disappearing. "[A] contemporary media portrayal of events in Vietnam that was closer to reality would have made the Tet crisis less divisive, and would have resulted in the fundamental . . . issues of the war being less easily obscured," concludes Peter Braestrup in his comprehensive two volumes' study.[66]

Almost from the beginning of the war American intellectuals found an opportunity to indulge a riskless role as consciences, or super-egos, for the nation. The "antiwar ethos in New York appeared, by all counts, to help shape the choice of Vietnam-related stories for page one, although a widely shared journalistic predilection for 'disaster' stories may have shaped these choices [for *The New York Times*] more than anything else."[67] The South Vietnamese republic was criticized for not according more privileges to certain Buddhist groups, for not being fully democratic and representative of opposition groups, for not affording more complete freedom to its newspapers. Overlooked was the far more suppressed and subservient status of Buddhists in North Vietnam, the total extirpation through execution of groups opposed to the ruling Communist regime, and the complete absence of freedom of the press.[68] It seemed to be of no moment to the American intellectuals that they were, in the guise of a unilateral ethicism, advocating surrender to a totalitarian regime that was far more brutal and repressive than the government they freely criticized.

Accordingly, the conviction of the United States government itself steadily weakened. Having become through its cabinet secretaries and their advisors largely a government of intellectuals, it naturally wished to court favor with the intellectual class generally; it virtually granted them an unprecedented privilege of conducting propaganda on behalf of the Communists in North Vietnam. A stream of New Leftists, pacifists, Old Leftist intellectuals, and several famed women writers made pilgrimages to Hanoi as guests of the North Vietnamese Communists.[69] Feted and flattered as the genuine voice of the American people, they enjoyed swimming on the Vietnamese beaches and in turn warmly assured their grateful hosts of the growing efficacy of their propaganda in the United States on behalf of draft-dodging and desertion. These were no spokesmen for a hidden fifth column whom the North Vietnamese toasted but the verbalists for an Open Brigade of Literary Guerillas whose words perhaps contributed to the emotional climate in which the bombings of government and college buildings were accepted as relatively praiseworthy activity. Soon the neo-Leftists in America claimed that they were making it impossible for the president of the United States or any leading cabinet official to speak on any major American campus. The North Vietnamese rulers drew the appropriate conclusions: the American people were decadent and self-deprecating of their own society; clearly their government was a blundering Goliath who could be befuddled by ideological sling-shot.

A cult of civil disobedience, joined with civil disorder, for the first time became widespread among the intellectual class in the United States, as governmental authority deteriorated. In previous national crises, the newspapers had preserved of their own volition a certain caution for the national welfare and recognized that in time of war and national peril the additional sale of their copies might be a value secondary to the integrity of the nation's government. During the American Civil War, for example, the newspaper opposition to President Abraham Lincoln chose not to publish "secret papers," whereas during the Vietnam War, such publication, adorned with bravado and self-exhibitionism, was extolled as "investigative journalism." Thus in 1864, Horace Greeley, presidential aspirant and editor of the *New York Tribune,* told Abraham Lincoln that "nine-tenths of the whole American people, North and South, are anxious for peace—peace on almost any other terms." Greeley indeed wished to publish the papers concerning a secret meeting, in which he had taken part, with a Confederate mission; its purpose was to explore the possibility of a negotiated peace; those discussions came to naught because of Lincoln's intransigence. Lincoln himself at that time was nearly despairing of a Union victory. Though ready to accede to the publication of the papers, Lincoln wished "a few passages" to be omitted, explaining that they might "give too gloomy an aspect to our cause," beside suggesting that his administration was being influenced by "the carrying of elections as a motive of action." Both the *New York Tribune* and *The New York Times* in 1864 bowed to Lincoln's judgment and forebore publication of the secret pages.[70] Quite different was the behavior of *The New York Times* a little more than a hundred years later when, with much fanfare, it published the "Pentagon Papers," not because, as it conceded to the United States Supreme Court, they contained anything essentially new, but because the very publication of huge files of secret memoranda made light of the authority of a government that was trying to conduct a war.[71] The sense of responsibility shown by the opposition press in 1864 had metamorphosed into a stance of defiance in 1971.[72] Many American intellectuals were proud that they had chastened America in its "arrogance of power" from taking the imperialist direction. The postulate of the evil in "imperialism" was established as central to the ideology of the intellectuals, a postulate evidently no longer open to question. The alternative historical evolution of a powerful and dominant Soviet imperialism was curiously absent from the minds of even gifted novelists who in earlier troubled decades had been much concerned with the potential power of the Soviet totalitarian empire.

C. The Alternative of Soviet Totalitarian Imperialism

Slowly, toward the end of World War II in 1945, the idea began to take shape among both participants and observers that the war's most important consequence would be the emergence of two world-powers in opposition: one, the Soviet Union, aspiring consciously to a world hegemony; the other, the United States, reluctant by tradition to assume an imperial role but compelled to do so by Soviet thrusts in every continent.

The basic source of this Soviet imperialism could not be located within the coordinates of Marxist social geometry. The chief student and observer of the first stirrings of Soviet imperialism in the first decade of its history, Louis Fischer, notwithstanding his Marxist, pro-Soviet leanings, was finally driven to an altogether non-Marxist explanation for the workings of czarist imperialism. "The law which requires growth of every living thing made it incumbent on Czarism to register new conquests," he wrote. "Economic motives played a minor role in Russia's dream of Indian conquest."[73] Probably such a Bergsonian explanation will not satisfy those who are mindful that many organisms are parasitic and degenerative, having evolved toward a loss of function and structure. Nor does the Bergsonian aperçu illumine the all-important distinction between progressive and regressive imperialisms. Nevertheless, it is noteworthy that the scholar-correspondent who had worked personally with more of the Soviet technicians of foreign policy than any other American or Western European came to such a non-Marxist conclusion. For if czarist imperialism failed to fit into Lenin's formula that the mainspring of imperialism was the investment of the excessive, surplus capital derived from the exploitation of its working class, so likewise might the Soviet imperialism be the outcome of lines of causation foreign to Lenin's scheme.

The Soviet totalitarian system has evidently generated a non-terminating series of probes and seizures of power in foreign lands that are abetted by its aid, arms, and advice. The outstanding former foreign minister of the Soviet Union, Maxim Litvinov, at the risk of his life, warned the United States at the end of World War II of the perilous era that awaited it. Litvinov, a trusted co-worker of Lenin's for many years both before and after the revolution, and the guardian of the funds for the underground Bolshevik party, had in his long-time residence in England come to appreciate the ideals and values of Western civilization. His original ambition in life had been to be a librarian, and he married an English novelist, but this lover of books was transmuted nonetheless into a Bolshevik revolutionist. His diplomatic career as a foreign minister until 1939 had been one long effort to join the Soviet Union with the Western democratic nations to build a counter-force that could keep the Nazis and Fascists at bay. When he was dismissed from office in March 1939, the alternative direction toward a Nazi-Soviet pact and German war superseded any hope for collective security. In 1945, however, Litvinov, still an assistant minister at the Soviet Foreign Office, was an ineffectual witness to the handful of men shaping the new Soviet expansionist policy. Aware that his life was nearing its end, Litvinov dared repeatedly to admonish the United States that an implacable imperialist drive, of a menacing kind, was determining Soviet actions. Meeting one American journalist in June 1945, Litvinov asked pointedly: "Why did you Americans wait until right now to begin opposing us in the Balkans and Eastern Europe? You should have done this three years ago." For in 1941-1942, under the shock of Hitler's assault, when Stalin's regime felt itself precarious and dependent on American and Allied help, spiritual and physical, the opportunity for demanding political concessions from the confidence-shaken Stalin existed and was lost. Now, however, the motive for aggrandizement, in Litvinov's judgment, was dominant in Stalin's policy;[74] the Soviet striving for power far exceeded any needs for the security of the Soviet Union. It was not yet recognized that a regressive imperialism feels secure only to the degree that the world is rid of any possible rival.

A few months later, in November 1945, the American ambassador, Averell Harriman, chancing to meet Litvinov at a theater performance, asked him what the United States could do to satisfy the Soviet Union. Litvinov replied: "Nothing." As for himself, Litvinov felt he was powerless: "I believe I know what should be done but I am powerless." With the increased momentum of the totalitarian imperialist dynamic, any individual intervention seemed a venture in futility. Francis Bacon once wrote optimistically that knowledge is power; but the knowledge that is only of one's powerlessness does not alter the latter's character. A half-year later, on June 18, 1946, Litvinov confided to still another American newspaperman that only a condominium of the great powers might save the world, but that Moscow's appetite was now, however, probably insatiable. "If the West acceded to the current Soviet demands, it would be faced after a more or less short time with the next series of demands," said Litvinov. Two months later, Stalin dismissed Litvinov from his post. Litvinov, not yet silenced, told another journalist in September that Moscow was grabbing "all they could while the going was good."[75] The Soviet secret police later planned to murder Maxim Litvinov in a staged car collision, but according to Khrushchev, the plan failed because Stalin died and the police chief Beria was executed.[76]

Stalin was the explicit fashioner of the pattern of Soviet imperialism. In the first years of the Bolshevik revolution he had evoked Lenin's concern by the ruthlessness with which he acted to destroy the popular Menshevik republic in Georgia and to impress upon it a Soviet dictatorship. In 1940, Stalin completely shared Hitler's design for the carving up of what Hitler called "the British bankrupt state." When the Nazi ruler outlined his plan, Stalin's foreign minister, Molotov, replied "that he was in agreement with all that he had understood." Stalin had no quarrel with Hitler when the latter pointed out that "after the conquest of England the British Empire would be apportioned as a gigantic world-wide estate in bankruptcy of 40 million square kilometers." From this bankrupt state,

Hitler proposed for Russia gains more grandiose than its traditional long-ing for "access to the ice-free and really open ocean" and the control of the Straits to the Black Sea."[77] He blandished for the willing Stalin the prospect of a vast empire in Southeast Asia, "centered south of the ter-ritory of the Soviet Union in the direction of the Indian Ocean."[78] Stalin indeed claimed large slices of empire as the reward, as Foreign Minister Molotov told Hitler, for all that the Soviet Union had contributed to the Nazi military conquests in Europe ("the German-Russian agreement had not been without influence upon the great German victories.")[79] Hitler averred that if Germany and Russia stood together, "there was no power on earth which could oppose the two countries," and "their future suc-cesses would be the greater." Whereupon "Molotov voiced his agreement with the last conclusions of the Führer," and stressed the viewpoint "of Stalin in particular" that the relations of the two countries should be strengthened and activated.[80] Less than two weeks later, on November 26, 1940, having returned to Moscow, and having fully fortified himself with the considered authority of Stalin, Molotov formally notified the German ambassador that the Soviet Union was prepared to accept the draft of the Four-Power Pact with the Axis governments, provided that four stipula-tions for Soviet territorial gains or privilege were acknowledged; of the latter the principal one was "that the area south of Batum and Baku in the general direction of the Persian Gulf is recognized as the center of the aspirations of the Soviet Union."[81] Adolf Hitler at this juncture decided he had had enough of the Bolsheviks and preferred to be the world's undisputed imperialist master. He issued his orders on December 18, 1940, for Operation Barbarossa, "to crush Soviet Russia in a quick campaign."[82] In vain Stalin made public demonstrations of affection for the Nazis at a railway station in April 1941, throwing his arms around their ambassador and saying warmly to the German military attaché: "We will remain friends with you—in any event."[83]

Stalin did try at once when the war ended to realize part of the South Asian empire which Hitler had dangled before him as a reward for loyal coadjutorship. In August 1945 Stalin undertook to detach the province of Azerbaijan from Iran and to make it a Soviet satrapy; it was indeed "a first experiment in Soviet satellite tactics."[84] Under the guidance of occu-pying Soviet authorities and troops, an "Azerbaijan Committee for Na-tional Liberation" was organized, then metamorphosed into a "Demo-cratic Party" and joined by the pro-Soviet intellectuals of the Tudeh Party. Soon another puppet regime was proclaimed, the "Kurdish Peo-ple's Republic"; it appeared that the czarist dream for dominating Persia was to be achieved in a Soviet-controlled Iran. An armed coup (with So-viet support) was expected on the Persian New Year's Day, March 21, 1946; American observers saw Soviet tanks twenty-six miles from the cap-ital city, Teheran. Fruitlessly, the British and Americans protested that the

1942 Tripartite Treaty was being violated, that all three countries had promised to withdraw their forces within six months after the war's end. Stalin procrastinated cannily to test his quondam allies' will. But the United States still held the monopolistic power of the atomic bomb and steadfastly kept the Soviet violations of Iranian sovereignty on the agenda of the Security Council of the United Nations. Despite a dramatic walk-out by the Soviet ambassador, the Soviet regime finally agreed to withdraw its forces within six weeks, and although strikes were instigated at the oil wells of the Anglo-Iranian Oil Company, the Soviet forces withdrew from Azerbaijan by December, 1945, and the satrapic regime of Pishevari collapsed while he himself fled to the Soviet Union.

Ja'far Pishevari was an early representative of a new political type, the Soviet satrap, that the expansion of the Soviet Empire was to elevate and make well-known. A commissar of internal affairs in the short-lived Soviet republic of Gilan in 1920-1921, he then became an agent of the Communist International, surviving Stalin's purge through the good fortune of imprisonment in Iran. Released by amnesty in 1941, when the Soviet Union joined the war against Hitler, he published a left-wing Tudeh newspaper in November 1945 and led in seizing the government buildings in Tabriz with a force duly armed by the Russians. Curiously, shortly after his downfall he was reported to have been killed in a car accident near Baku. (This was a period when automobile accidents became a favorite means by which the Soviet secret police eliminated those whose existence, in its view, had become superfluous). Even when the Russians, however, withdrew from Azerbaijan, they endeavored to adhere to their principle of the irreversible increment; they secured an agreement that gave them a fifty-one percent share for 25 years in the ownership and revenues of the Azerbaijan oil company.[85]

Some years later Stalin confided to his daughter Svetlana Alliluyeva that if only Hitler had not turned upon him, together they could have ruled the world: "Even after the war was over, he was in the habit of repeating, 'Ech, together with the Germans we would have been invincible.'"[86]

To be sure, the successive chiefs of the Soviet regime have all averred that they were opposed to imperialism; each, however, has enlarged the domain of Soviet imperialism, both in theory and practice. Khrushchev declared that he was concerned only with the security of the Soviet Union, but his economic and military role in far-away Cuba added an extraordinary dimension to the rubric of Soviet security. As Khrushchev wrote: "For our part, we wanted Cuba to remain revolutionary and socialist, and we knew Cuba needed help in order to do so." To help the Cuban Communists maintain their dictatorial rule, it was necessary, according to Khrushchev "to install our missiles on the island, so as to confront the aggressive forces of the United States with a dilemma: if you invade Cuba, you'll have to face a nuclear missile attack against your own cities . . . We stationed our armed forces on Cuban soil for one purpose only: to maintain the independence of the Cuban people."[87]

But what had all this expansion to do with "Soviet security"? To maintain the "independence" of the Cuban Communist regime it was evidently essential to convert Cuba into a military and economic dependency of the Soviet Union and to extend the threat of nuclear missiles to the Caribbean and the American coastal cities. Soviet security was so insecure that it could no longer be satisfied with hegemony in Poland, Czechoslovakia, Eastern Hungary, and Bulgaria, but its controlling flag had to fly too in a Caribbean island stronghold.

Although Khrushchev was obliged to withdraw his missiles when President Kennedy proved ready to enforce a blockade of Cuba, the Soviet premier could well boast that he had won a notable victory; not only had he compelled the abrogation of the Monroe Doctrine, but he had also gotten the United States to promise to tolerate near its shores the existence of a Communist state in which Soviet political-economic influence would be paramount and which would be safeguarded by Soviet weaponry and Soviet "defensive" forces. It was a triumph, as Khrushchev virtually boasted, for Soviet imperialism. "For the first time in history, the Americans pledged publicly not to invade one of their neighbors and not to interfere in its internal affairs. This was a bitter pill for the U.S. to swallow. It was worse than that: the American imperialist beast was forced to swallow a hedgehog, quills and all. And that hedgehog is still in its stomach, undigested."[88]

Of course, the Cuban Communist regime has never allowed a free election during all the years of its quarter-century's control, despite its assurances when it seized power that elections would shortly be held. The generalization still holds that no Communist regime has ever allowed a free, democratic election since the Bolsheviks were defeated in the elections of 1917-1918 for the Constituent Assembly. Soviet hegemony in Communist satrapies is maintained through its control of the upper echelons of their Communist apparatuses.[89] Rome ruled many allied kingdoms through the control of their kings, and Britain and France used the tribal chiefs in Africa for indirect rule. The Soviet dominance of the party apparatus and secret police is the political mechanism for the extension and maintenance of Soviet empire.

The artisan of Khrushchev's fall in October 1964, Leonid Ilyich Brezhnev, added a new theorem to Soviet imperialist ideology. Known now as the "Brezhnev doctrine," it was promulgated September 26, 1968, shortly after the brief era of relative freedom in Czechoslovakia remembered as the "Prague Spring" had been ended harshly by an invasion of perhaps a half-million Soviet troops. As enunciated in *Pravda,* the "Brezhnev Doctrine" affirmed that the freedom of ruling Communist parties to determine their country's path of development was circumscribed: "any decision of theirs must damage neither the socialism in their own country, nor the worldwide workers' movement . . . This means that every Communist Party is responsible not only to its own people but also to all the socialist countries and to the entire Communist movement."[90]

To this theorem Brezhnev subjoined the corollary that the Soviet Union claimed the right to intervene whenever "socialism is imperilled" (voiced appropriately enough in November 1968 at the Congress of the restive Polish Communist Party). Thus Communist countries defined as loyal to the Communist Community possessed only a "qualified sovereignty." The Soviet Union alone was exempt from the limitation of sovereignty; its version of socialism was privileged, axiomatic, canonical, and binding on all other members of the socialist bloc of nations. Presumably the intervention of Polish, Czech, and Hungarian forces to restore socialism to the Soviet Union was only a meta-political possibility. Thus, in effect, the conception of a Soviet Communist imperialism was formulated in the terminology of Marxist doctrine.

Brezhnev's boldest imperialist venture came, however, late in December 1979, when he ordered the invasion of Afghanistan by Soviet forces. There was no effective pretext that the security of the Soviet Union was threatened by any unfriendly armed force in Afghanistan; Britain had departed from the Indian sub-continent several decades earlier and its age of Afghan Wars was as remote as Kipling's novels. No American, Indian, or even Pakistani force posed any discordant presence at the Afghan border. It sufficed, however, that a pro-Soviet president of Afghanistan had been assassinated by a Communist colleague and that the Marxist wing of the Afghan political-military elite felt its hold on power tenuous. An independent Asian country was transformed into a dependent satrapy.[91]

The tenure of Yuri Vladimirovich Andropov as general secretary of the Soviet Communist Party was brief. For fifteen years previously he had been head of the secret police. At his hands, the Soviet imperialist effort in the Americas probed for weak salients in the American defense. It found in the small island of Grenada a militant Marxist party ready to provide their Soviet protector with a new base. By October 1983, there were "nearly 900 Cuban, Libyan, Soviet, North Korean, East German and Bulgarian personnel . . . in Grenada to assist in the transformation of the island into a major military camp," and plans were being made for training Grenadian forces "chiefly in the Soviet Union."[92] The Soviet leaders cheerfully prepared to induct Grenada, led by the "New Jewel Movement," as it was called, as the newest jewel in the Soviet crown. When the chiefs of their respective general staffs met in Moscow on March 10, 1983, to consider the Grenadians' requests for military supplies, Marshal of the Soviet Union Nikolai V. Ogarkov declared magisterially:

"Over two decades ago, there was only Cuba in Latin America, today there are Nicaragua, Grenada, and a serious battle is going on in El Salvador."[93]

What, then, is the social source of the Soviet imperialist dynamic? It is not an imperialism born of an excess of "surplus value," or over-savings; the Soviet economy has not produced a plethora of profits that find no outlets for investment except abroad. If anything, the Soviet economy suffers from a shortage of capital funds that it could well use to expand and modernize its industrial base. Nor is Soviet imperialism a consumers' peoples imperialism in the way that Western imperialism was; it has nurtured no new waves of consumers' goods as bicycles, rubber tires, and home pianos constituted for British and American households of the nineteenth century.

Soviet imperialism, like the medieval Tartar variant, arises from the very poverty, drabness, and sense of inferiority that characterize its economy and social life as compared to that of Western Europe and America. The Tartar looking to the far southwest saw the flourishing towns of Arabia and Persia and heard of the rich rulers of the Romans and the Franks further to the west. He listened also to reports of the emperors in proud, comfortable China to the east; then he was filled with envy, bitterness, jealousy, and hatred for the aristocrats of civilization. Thus Soviet ideologists similarly experience resentment when they hear of the immeasurably greater creative achievement of Western capitalist society in the arts, sciences, and well-being of their citizens. They can no longer sound convincing to themselves as they repeat after seventy years their asseverations of the superiority of their socialist civilization to that of the capitalist. For the undeniable empirical fact is that millions of persons throughout the world long to emigrate to the Western capitalist lands and only some few eccentrics care to join the Soviet citizenry. More than a quarter of a million Jews managed, despite the severe legalistic constraints, to secure their departure from the Soviet Union during a decade in which the Soviet regime gingerly doled out a meager quota of visas. How many persons have of their own free will sought to immigrate to the Soviet Union even though no obstacles to their so doing are set by their Western European or American countries? Not only does the Soviet regime severely limit the chance of its citizens to travel, but when it does allow such journeys to some privileged artists and scientists it surrounds them with all sorts of safeguards against their defections, which nonetheless remain a regular by-product of such "cultural" exchanges. A disturbing anxiety persists for the Soviet regime that its citizens, especially its abler ones, look upon Soviet existence as partaking of the character of a colossal social penitentiary, where one's work and life lack the component of free choice that one would find in the West. International comparisons therefore are invidious to the Soviet rulers. Stalin sensed that the precarious stability of his regime was imbalanced by direct knowledge of the Western liberal alternative; therefore he virtually banned the travel of Soviet citizens to the West, tried to isolate its scientists and artists from the contaminating contact with their Western colleagues, and prohibited the entry of Western literature and films.

The Soviets effort to insulate their society from Western liberal civilization is, however, increasingly unsuccessful. From Western Europe, from such cities as Munich, come, for instance, the broadcasts of American and British radio stations, conveying accurate news, reading the forbidden writings of exiled Soviet dissident writers, and making available the news of the Soviet Union that the regime interdicts. So long as the Soviet citizenry, or any significant portion of it, is thus affected by Western "ideological" influences, the Soviet regime cannot help but feel insecure. It has always categorically insisted that "ideological coexistence" can have no place within Soviet borders. To eliminate the rival alternative to the Soviet ideology, its bourgeois loci of origin and diffusion must be extirpated; then Soviet imperialism can feel secure.

Indeed, unlike capitalist imperialism, the Soviet variety finds an inherent incompatibility in the presence of ideological competitors. During the nineteenth century British, French, Dutch, Portuguese, and Spanish modes of imperialism competed relatively peacefully side by side. But that kind of competitive coexistence is alien to the Soviet conception, for an alternative philosophy and way of life is regarded as a threatening class menace. No retreat can be made from that tenet because that would be to risk endangering the whole ideological basis for legitimizing the Soviet repressive state machine. The United States in the nineteenth century never seriously felt that its democracy was jeopardized by European political absolutisms. It preferred democracies, but felt sufficiently self-confident in its democratic way of life to dismiss the thought that a European absolutism might tempt its citizens. The Soviet regime, however, is anxiety-saturated, conscious that it has ruled for several generations through the agencies of dictatorial force, secret police, and ideological promises. An anxiety-saturated society diminishes its burden of anxiety if it can defeat, undermine, or eliminate its free competitor. Also, Soviet imperialism provides a much needed outlet for the accumulated aggressive tensions that are endemic in Soviet existence. The drab, dowdy lives with the long hours of waiting in queues for transport, for the purchase of food and clothes; the monotony and patronizing of the television news broadcasts, literature, and films; the organized pretense of meetings in factory and workplace; the tedious discourtesy that all expect from Soviet sales and bureaucratic personnel; the strain of always having to repress what one thinks and to utter instead what one knows is stupid but must be said; the cramped quarters in apartments shared by several often quarreling families; the repression of authentic religious philosophizing in favor of the stale official dialectical formulae so that "socialist humanism" becomes a secular inhumanism; the sports in which the mandate for Soviet triumph, by all means fair or foul, takes the joy from the game; the dominance of the local party organization that decides if and when you can ever travel for a vacation or attend a university—everywhere, and reaching into all society's interstices, social relations are compulsive and enmeshing and margins of freedom are vestigial. Moreover, Soviet socialism requires scapegoats, the safety-valves of planned economy.[94] One takes it out on the fellow worker, the customer, the medical or dental patient, the passenger, the pupil. The cumulated frustrations become all the more acute because one must repress one's natural inclination to criticize, to protest, and to resist.

Then comes the opportunity to alleviate these frustrations by participating in the collective, mass aggression of a warlike, imperialist campaign. Soviet soldiers were preeminent for the personal destruction that they wreaked on captured towns and townspeople. Stalin defended his troops' cruelty and rapine even when their objects were the women in allied Yugoslavia. When Milovan Djilas, a respected man high in Yugoslav councils, dared object, Stalin invoked the justifying authority on the human soul, Dostoevsky:

"Stalin interrupted: 'Yes, you have, of course, read Dostoevsky? Do you see what a complicated thing is man's soul, man's psyche? Well, then imagine a man who has fought from Stalingrad to Belgrade . . . How can a man react normally? And what is so awful in his having fun with a woman, after such horrors'"? Stalin boasted he had protected an Air Force major who killed a "chivalrous" engineer who tried to stop him from having "fun" with a woman; Stalin had instead decorated the Air Force rapist and murderer major.[95] Thus, the latter-day Raskolnikovs and Karamazovs, long repressed under their "barracks communism," as Karl Marx called it, vented their seething aggressive resentments upon helpless foreigners.

Soviet imperialism alleviates the enhanced frustrations of Soviet totalitarian societies. Precisely because there are no legal mechanisms for dissent or expressions of basic criticisms, and because the controls of the secret police and party officialdom through every petty level are so pervasive—precisely because maintaining the unsteady balance between the "real face" and the "official face" in everyday living is a perpetual strain with no escape from the formalized, unavowed hypocrisy—Soviet imperialism comes as a more engaging diversion.[96]

The comparative extent to which in a given society the conscious statements of people diverge from their unconscious feelings and ideas is a measure of the relative degree of repression in that society. That psychic divergence is, by all indications, more energized in Soviet society than in any other advanced industrial one in the world. Not a surplus of capital but an over-requirement of systemic repression impels the enthusiasm for Soviet expansionism.

In the long run, such Soviet imperialism must be directed against the advanced Western European centers; it cannot rest content with Afghanistans, Angolas, and Ethiopias, for the needling sense of the inferiority of Soviet culture and society engenders hatred and jealousy toward the West that can be assuaged only by conquest. Jealousy is most easily rationalized as a sense of injustice; even as the Tartars extracted tribute from the more advanced commercial and agricultural societies, so too the feeling grows that the Western capitalist nations owe a kind of ideological tribute to those who are "building socialism."

Curiously, at certain periods of history, it can happen that the more economically backward people may enjoy a military superiority over more advanced ones. The Tartar tribesmen enjoyed the advantage of a nomadic mobility; they could strike rapidly at European and Middle Eastern towns and, if they desired, raze them.[97] They could envelope and out-maneuver the heavy Chinese infantry. Thus, likewise, the Soviet totalitarian system confers on its forces advantages of rapid and secret decision that are lacking in a democratic society; it can, without evoking overt protest, allocate a far greater percentage of its gross national product to military outlays; it is not hamstrung by an opposition party that sometimes allows partisanship to tamper with the nation's capacity for military response. The drive of Soviet imperialism is easily reinforced by the sense of the tactical advantage that its system confers, at least for the short run, against its Western rivals. Such was one consideration that shaped the military thinking of Adolf Hitler and his National Socialists.

Soviet imperialism, moreover, can make common cause with all those currents in the world today that converge in what might be characterized as "the revolt of the undercivilized." Stalin was the prime mover of this revolt when, after World War II, he launched a massive assault against Western civilization, art, and science. The "Western" theories of relativity and quantum physics, its genetics, astronomy, and physiology were denounced as "bourgeois," as "undialectical," as "anti-materialist." The Bolshevik style in scientific theorizing, such as Lysenko's anti-genetic polemics, was held to be closer to the masses' way of thinking and hence closer to an understanding of the nature of reality.

Similarly, under Mao Tse-tung in Communist China the homely remedies of medieval folklore were extolled over Western medical technology and the intuition of the Cultural Revolutionary activist over the detached denizen of the laboratory and the library. Kwame Nkrumah in the Gold Coast mixed formal Marxist economic theory with the libations and revelations of primitivist ritual.[98] Fundamentalist theologies stir the souls of many Moslems in the Middle East resentful of the leadership of the advanced West. Though fundamentalist movements are now financed by the profits from oil sold mainly to Western industrial nations, these same fundamentalist movements revive seventh-century slogans to re-kindle their hatred for Western technology and all its works. A parasitic, "neo-proletarian" class thus arises in the Middle East that is "proletarian" in the original Roman sense that Marx employed when he wrote in 1877: "The Roman proletarians became, not wage-laborers but a *mob* of do-nothings"[99] and cited Sismondi approvingly: "The Roman proletarian lived almost entirely at the expense of society" unlike the factory workers of industrial society in the nineteenth century.[100] The "neo-proletarians," however, live like their emirs, imams, kings, and sheiks off the billions of dollars of profits extracted annually from the workingmen, engineers, technicians, scientists, seamen, and businessmen of the Western bourgeois world. Affected by the awareness of their parasitic, exploitative role and their presumable failure in not having contributed to modern science and technology, and envious of the Western "aristocrats" of labor and intellect, the "neo-proletarians" tend to revert to their traditionalist Moslem or tribal beliefs, to a fundamentalism that asserts the evil in Western morals and the basic falsehood of modern, Western science and values and the superiority of medieval or pre-medieval customs and ethics.

The undercivilized in diverse cultures thus converge in outlook; fundamentalist Moslems, Catholic liberation theologians, and African shamans feel a certain kinship with Soviet rigidities and the anti-Western animus. Mullah, friar, and commissar all repudiate the bourgeois world and its philosophy, and profess to speak for the dispossessed against the wealthy.

In the long run, however, Soviet imperialism, with its readiness to avail itself ruthlessly of all technology necessary to achieve its military and ideological hegemony, looks forward to using and subordinating the religious fundamentalists; its own controls on pure science would be more uninhibited were its political primacy unchallenged by any advancing Western democracies.

The developing Soviet empire still finds in the "mission of the advanced proletariat" an ideological underpinning far more effective than "the white man's burden" ever was for Western imperialists, for "the proletarian mission" combines Soviet imperialism with a revolutionary call to the Asian, African, and Latin American backward masses; it summons them to a great collective aggression against the overcivilized Western Europeans and Americans. Not even the French revolutionary and Napoleonic imperialism could wed so ingeniously an imperialist reality with a revolutionary, even regressive unconscious impulsion.

Lenin, in an interval of truth-speaking, had long ago in 1919 sharply told a Communist Party Congress: "Scratch many a Communist and you will find a Great Russian chauvinist."[101] Lenin was the first to translate Marxism into an assault on Western European civilization when he declared in 1923 that "the next military conflict" would be "between the counter-revolutionary imperialist West and the revolutionary and nationalist East, between the most civilized countries of the world and the orientally backward countries, which, however, account for the majority."[102] Before the Bolshevik revolution, Lenin, living in Western Europe, used to ridicule "Asian" traits, Asian backwardness, and Asian medievalness, and scold Russia for its Asian qualities. He spoke of Russia as "an absolutism impregnated with Asian barbarity," and declared: "In very many and very essential respects Russia is undoubtedly an Asian country, and, what is more, one of the wildest, most medieval, and shamefully backward of the countries."[103] After the revolution, he jubilated over the decline of European civilization: "No matter how the Spenglers . . . may lament it, this decline of the old Europe is but an episode in the history of the downfall of the world bourgeoisie, oversatiated by imperialist rapine and oppression of the majority of the world's population."[104] The law of history, in Lenin's view, condemned the world of "these civilized philistines" with their "parliamentary procedure" in which they acted "democratically"; that "old bourgeois and imperialist Europe, which was accustomed to look upon itself as the center of the universe, rotted and burst like a putrid ulcer."[105] For, in Lenin's view, the undercivilized were destined to triumph: "In the last analysis, the outcome of the struggle will be determined by the fact that Russia, India, China, etc. account for the overwhelming majority of the population of the globe.[106]

Despite all his attacks on "civilized" imperialism, however, Lenin vaguely foresaw the advent of a new variety of proletarian imperialism, although he insisted it would be a benevolent one. He wrote in the middle of World War I, emphasizing that Soviet socialism would not survive except in closest union with the backward peoples: "But does this mean that *we* proletarians wish to separate ourselves from the Egyptian workers and fellahs, from the Mongolian, Turkestan or Indian workers and peasants? Does it mean that *we* advise the laboring masses of the colonies to 'separate' from the class conscious European proletariat? Nothing of the kind . . . for otherwise socialism in Europe will not be secure."[107]

What, however, would Lenin do if a fundamentalist Moslem revivalist regime excluded a Soviet socialist people from access to its needed oil regions? What if various Asian and African peoples as professing antiimperialists did wish to *separate* themselves from a Russian socialist proletariat, even though it might thereby render the latter's economy less efficient? Lenin chose to trust in a pre-established socialist harmony, though it was clear that his premises authorized, if necessary, a socialist imperialism in the interests of the advanced proletariat.

Five years after the revolution, nonetheless, Lenin was dismayed that the apparatus of his party, led by Stalin, behaved in the fashion of the "typical Russian bureaucrat"; Stalin, according to Lenin, acted with "spite" against the "social nationalists," leaving the non-Russians without defense against "the Great Russian, the chauvinist, in substance a rascal and a lover of violence." Lenin admonished Stalin: "Spite as a rule is a very bad thing in politics," and he ridiculed the argument that "unity was needed in the apparatus."[108] He demanded that the "'freedom to withdraw from the union,'" indeed the right to secede from the Soviet Union, be a real one for the autonomous republics and that it not be obliterated as Stalin and Dzerzhinsky (the chief of the secret police) were doing: "The political responsibility for all this Great Russian nationalistic campaign must, of course, be laid on Stalin and Dzerzhinsky," wrote Lenin.[109] The "spite," however, that Lenin spoke of as a personal trait of Stalin's corresponded in large part to the spitefulness, the social hostility that pervaded the Soviet social order. A society of pseudo-comrades finds a defense against its own repressed mutual antagonisms in imperialist ventures that indulge a "Great Russian" use of force to whip other nations into line, to force submission to a Soviet imperialism.

Moreover, notwithstanding relatively "liberal" interludes, the Soviet totalitarian structure has a tendency to raise to its highest leadership personalities with paranoid characteristics. The latter are apt indeed to enact their inner tendencies externally in genocidal acts: an anti-Jewish genocide on the Hitlerian model; a massacre of some Asian ethnic group; or some nuclear bomb assault, as Mao once advised.

The Soviet leaders themselves concede, after the fact, that for about twenty years Stalin was prey to paranoid fears and suspicions that led him to exterminate not only almost the whole Bolshevik cadre that had made the revolution of 1917 but also whole strata of the peasantry, sections of engineers and technicians, and evidently the ablest military commanders. This era of "the cult of personality," according to Soviet excuses, was not the consequence of the Soviet social system but rather the accidental outcome of Stalin's paranoid personality. Could Stalin, however, a near-madman, have ruled his huge country and party unless his near-madness itself had corresponded to a popular psychological malady, or social "function"? In March 1963 Khrushchev told of the persecution mania that characterized Stalin from 1934 to 1954.[110] A similar totalitarian delusion later affected Mao Tse-tung, who not only believed in economic miracles such as the "Great Leap Forward," but sought to destroy the elder generation in the "Cultural Revolution," even as Stalin had; Mao was prepared to sacrifice hundreds of millions of his own people in a nuclear war (as Khrushchev twice told)[111] so long as it eradicated the American enemy. Totalitarian paranoia shows itself in such tenets as "the Bolshevik will can storm every fortress," even as it exalted Hitler with the conviction that his army, through its own will, could triumph over the Soviet forces at Stalingrad.

For the United States it is a matter of the highest concern that a high correlation exists between totalitarian systems and paranoid leadership, that they go so much hand in hand. For totalitarian leaders are predisposed to strike first, without warning, to bring down those whom they regard as enemies; they act without the compunctions that others have, without the scruples that preoccupy liberal, democratic, or constitutional governments. Only from 1945 to 1949, when the United States held a monopoly on the bomb, could it live in security from the paranoiacrat Stalin. Ever since 1949 that security has diminished steadily, so that in several categories of offensive weaponry the Soviet forces are now superior. Thus a regime more likely than others to have a paranoid leader, and holding a larger reserve in numbers and types of nuclear bombs, is also the most susceptible in its envious suspicion to the temptation of a decisive blow against the United States. By contrast, American policy—humanistic, optimistic, cherishing a belief in the goodness of all men—places its hopes in agreements that all men of good will would respect. The latter variety of humankind has not had a high frequency in the echelons of totalitarian leadership.

So long as the totalitarian system is not altered, the likelihood of the paramount role of secret police chiefs remains high. When the secret police is the single most powerful stratum of the ruling elite, those personality types most drawn to secrecy, deception, anonymity, and immunity to public control and responsibility, are most apt to become the society's dominant power. Andropov and Chernenko both held posts in the secret police, the former its highest place; the present incumbent, General Secretary Mikhail Gorbachev, it might be noted, was Andropov's protégé.

The hope that the Soviet ruling elite nonetheless is evolving into a rational technocratic one finds its principal support in the fact that, as many scholars have noted, a considerable number of members of the Politburo and the occupants of ministries are graduates of technical colleges and institutes. Therefore, it is argued, engineers are the ruling elite and a technocracy—calculating, rational economic—holds the places of Soviet power. The workings of the centrally planned economy, however, are such as to tend to elevate to leadership the disciplinarians and the monitors, for the planned economy limps inefficiently in every branch of industry except military manufacture, where the most powerful inducements are brought to bear.

The regime, from time to time, entertains thoughts of decentralized competition among autonomous enterprises; such a reform, however, would doubtless create a large number of unemployed, as the inefficient and redundant would be dismissed; then the Soviet Union would be confronted with the kind of unemployment that Yugoslavian competitive socialism has engendered. The virtue of the Soviet economy is that it maintains "full employment," even if much of it is concealed unemployment, a subsidy to maintain the inefficient and unskilled. The Soviet regime, furthermore, dares not allow large numbers of its workingmen to emigrate freely to jobs, temporary or permanent, among the Western European countries and to provide financial assistance to their Soviet families. Yugoslavia allows such emigration, but for the Soviet Union to do so would be to court defeat in the conflict with the United States and to undermine the primacy of the Soviet Communist Party. The specter of masses of unemployed confronting the party bureaucrats is a fearsome one to contemplate. To keep to their centrally planned economic system is the safest way to avoid the pitfalls of economic "adventurism" and to preserve the party bureaucrats with the strongest stake in social stability.

What psychological equivalent can the Soviet regime substitute for the mechanisms of competition that keep the search for efficiency among workingmen and managers vigorous within capitalist enterprises? Fear—that sharpens the sense of potential coercion—continuous anxiety, and a surveillance that prevents the laborer, clerk, or manager from being unobserved in some nook within the massive social system or escaping from the system in order to take things easily and allow his productivity to decline or to profit from corruption.

Economic crime is of two kinds. The first is simply the embezzling of profits or goods, or the acceptance of bribes, and the falsification of accounts. But the second has more clearly the embryonic features of capitalist enterprise: the family that virtually operates a private restaurant, or the carpenter who does repairs privately, or the private teacher of language or music, or the private hauler, or the private doctor or dentist. The tendency of the seeds of capitalism to take root and grow in the fertile inefficiencies of socialism must be watched and uprooted like weeds. The secret police are the sentries of the socialist system, for if the socialist system somehow contravenes the natural propensies of human nature to use freely one's own initiative and to express latent aggressive energies, the secret police must all the more vigilantly curb any incipient manifestations of these desires that have been intensified by the system's frustrations. The secret police is the primary agency of the Soviet communist system because the latter's economy is contra-human, lacking consonance with natural motivations; hence, non-economic, or extra-economic agencies of force and fear must counteract the system's defective economic incentives.

The operations of such a contra-human system are most effectively led by personalities that emulate many of Stalin's traits. His ruthlessness enforced discipline in an economic system which otherwise would have stumbled, lurched, and tottered even more; the lazy workingman faced fines that deprived him of food; the manager who made mistakes was possibly consigned to a labor camp. Those personalities most efficient in inflicting such cruelties are probably those more prone to enjoy extirpating ethnic minorities whom they regard as too critical or intelligent, such as the Jews, or too nomadic in their work habits, such as the Tartars or the gypsies. And such personalities are more prone to allow their own societies to find a sadistic satisfaction in such mass murders.

The Soviet social system was one, for instance, in which Stalin found it increasingly expedient and politically useful to activate his own strong anti-Semitic feelings, from the beginning of his career as a revolutionist until his last plot to execute a major operation of extermination against the Jewish people. His consistently expressed anti-Semitic feeling contributed to his rise to total power, for it provided a most popular outlet for the release of the Soviet "masses'" frustrated aggressions accumulating within the planned economy. One sees Stalin in 1907 at the London Congress of the Russian Social Democrats noting and recording the joke that since the majority of the Mensheviks, unlike the Bolsheviks, were Jews, "it wouldn't be a bad idea for us Bolsheviks to organize a pogrom in the Party."[112] One sees Trotsky at a loss during his intra-party struggle to combat Stalin's skillful use of anti-Semitism against him; [113] one sees the Soviet purges of the 30s achieving as one of their objectives the large-scale elimination of the Jews from the ranks of the leadership.[114] Never again would any Soviet leader say as Lenin had in 1917 that it was to "their merit" that the Jews had "provided a particularly high percentage . . . of leaders of the revolutionary movement" and of "representatives of internationalism compared with other nations."[115] One sees Stalin finally appearing in 1952 before the Politburo to present a demand, in indirect discourse, for the deportation and "liquidation" of the Jews. Pleading that many "hoodlum attacks" were taking place against "prominent Jews," and that there was danger of a "pogrom" against them Stalin proposed that "the best thing to do would be to relocate them, move them from Moscow and Leningrad to a safe place." Stalin further proposed that prominent Jews should be organized to petition for their own deportation; among those persuaded to respond was the violinist David Oistrakh. A pamphlet was then published by the secret police in 1953 urging the resettlement of the Jews away from the industrial regions. Meanwhile, in distant Birobidzhan, on the far Asian border, two barracks, each two kilometers long, were readied to receive the first shipments of deportees.[116] The so-called "doctors' plot" to poison Soviet leaders was then initiated to kindle the Russian people to an excited suspicion about the Jews. Like the "Grande Peur" during the French Revolution, when peasants were filled with fears that "the brigands are coming," so Russians went about fearing they were going to be poisoned by the Jews. Then Stalin died, and the whole plot was exposed as a hoax.

One may still hope that the totalitarian phase will prove to have been a transient one in Soviet history, and that rational men within the Soviet system finally will make the dominance of the irrational obsolete, and that the era of socialist sadism will be over. One clings to such a hope, and it is not historically improbable. A period of persistent economic failure, combined with Soviet defeats abroad, might be followed by a revival of political factions and free voting; the opening of a democratic discussion might be the prelude of a liberal reconstruction of the economy and the dismantling of the secret police.

On the other hand, the social selection exerted by the centrally planned economy is weighted toward a leadership by coercive personalities. The Khrushchev interlude was energized for a few years by psychological horror at the revelation of the crimes of Stalin and the Stalinists. Nevertheless totalitarian coercive imperatives were soon operating again; if Stalin's memory was briefly reviled, the Stalinists themselves were rarely brought to trial, and indeed usually retained their posts, despite their roles in having acted as concocters of falsehoods, denunciators, and torturers.[117] And soon the memory of Stalin himself was refurbished and restored to Soviet reverence. Why? Because the Soviet system itself seems to require the goad of an ominous figure. As the ousted liberal editor Aleksandr Tvardovsky wrote: those who "want to keep those methods and techniques in reserve" still held decisive posts.[118]

Stalinist methods are those that seem psychologically most conducive to the effective working of the Soviet planned economy. As the economist Alexander Gerschenkron has noted: "To a large extent, the economic irrationalities that exist in the Soviet economy are a consequence of, and inextricably connected with the mechanics of dictatorial rule. A high degree of autonomy granted to individual enterprises . . . would also deprive the dictatorship of one of its most important raisons d'être."[119] By comparison, the workings of the free market have, as Adam Smith said, the aspect of the workings of a gentle "invisible hand."

Never in the history of nations or social movements, furthermore, has a revolution been followed in its own homeland by so huge a literature testifying to the perversion and misdirection of human idealism into a system pervaded with an extreme amorality and indifference to human well-being and honor. The aftermaths of Cromwell's revolution, the American and French Revolutions, and Lincoln's Civil War knew no such outpourings of despair and disillusionment, the sense that humanity was blundering, perhaps irreparably, into the wrong road. Aleksandr Solzhenitsyn, Nadezhda Mandelstam, Petr Grigorenko, Andrei Sakharov, Pavel Litvinov, Andrei Sinyavski, Andrei Amalrik, Anatoly Marchenko, Anton Antonov-Ovseyenko, Alexander Dolgunov, Valery Chalidze, Lev Kopelev, were only some among the more world-known of those who spoke for the past sacrificial dead and, one hopes, for future liberated lives. It is a literature unparalleled in history of the ablest minds and most ethical spirits of a country raising their voices from within against their rulers' repression of human freedom and reiterating their stands from exile.

Nonetheless, faith in the Bolshevik revolution and the symbolic figure of Lenin remain strong among the middle and lower strata of Soviet intellectuals, and indeed among many in the West. The informative historian Roy A. Medvedev, despite his narration of cases of faith falsified, still avers his own continuing creed that "all of history, with its wars and revolutions, is the history of just such experiments," and that Lenin was right in saying that history wouldn't forgive the Bolsheviks if they delayed seizing power.[120] Underlying such statements is still a kind of belief in the quasi-divine character of the historical process, whose ways, like Job's God, need no justifying before humble men. But the Tartar wars that virtually destroyed the civilizations of the Khwarizmian Empire and Persia contributed no admirable experiment in human advancement; the Thirty Years' War that devastated the German states did not advance their moral level; and Hitler's experiment in destroying European Jewry may have destroyed the most extraordinary concentration of the highest human genetic endowment for which future history will probably pay dearly when it confronts its foreseeable and unforeseeable critical problems. Marx and Engels, for all their Hegelian glorifying of war and violence as the engines of history, had to acknowledge, in Engel's words, that "one single devastating war could depopulate a country for centuries and strip it of its whole civilization." Thus, when war ruined their irrigation systems, "whole stretches" were laid "waste and bare (Palmyra, Petra . . . Yemen, districts in Egypt, Persia and Hindustan.")[121]

Moreover, it has been a long and blatant misuse of the language of science that the Soviet regime has been described as having been conducting an "experiment." For if anything, the Soviet years have probably been the largest scale anti-experiment in history. For what is an experiment? It is an alteration of the given conditions, natural or social, in a certain specified way, and the careful and accurate recording of the consequences, together with a consideration of their bearing on the alternative hypotheses in question. If a medicine is tested on patients, the scientist is expected to record both negative and positive instances of response. What, however, if every scientist who reports negative instances were to be executed or imprisoned, his records destroyed, and he himself compelled to confess that he had misreported his observations intentionally? No scientist would regard such procedures as deserving of the name "experiment." Yet the most distinguished minds of our century—Freud, Dewey, Russell—have at different enthusiastic times called the Soviet system an "experiment." The totalitarian imperialist is hardly a philosopher of science or an experimentalist in social inquiry. Probably no modern society has gone to such lengths not to have accurate statistics concerning itself or to allow foreign observers to question its citizens without fear of reprisal as has the Soviet.

Finally, it is more than likely that history would have "forgiven" Lenin if he had not determined to advocate with all his powers a Bolshevik seizure of power. A coalition of socialist parties, including the democratic ones, or a Social Revolutionary parliamentary cabinet might have constituted the government after the latter's victory in the 1917-1918 elections; a civil war might have been obviated or been of lesser proportions; the famine of 1921-1922 the horrors of the collectivization period, the

Stalinist repressions, and above all, the rise of Naziism as a reaction to the fear of Bolshevism might have been spared Europe. Is it possible that the Bolshevik "experiment" initiated rather a mutation in what the great zoologist E. Ray Lankester called "degenerative evolution"?

D. The Grounds for an American Participatory Imperialism

More than a half-century after Charles and Mary Beard had ended *The Rise of American Civilization* with a paean to the dawn, not the dusk of the gods, their confidence seems to many to have been the glow of an untried hope. Signs have surely multiplied that a regressive phase of American civilization is not impossible. Might the summons, however, of novel crises themselves evoke a new, energetic, creative, and resourceful American leadership, a novel kind of imperialist movement? Or if the age of imperialism is not over, as Sumner Welles said it would be at the close of World War II, shall we witness the prelude to a Soviet imperialism whose consequence might be a decline of advanced civilization? Is the United Nations, founded as a forum for an emerging Parliament of Man, doomed in its present form by the conflict between Soviet imperialism and American democracy, as well as by the jealousy of numerous disimperialized Third World states toward the United States, and their underlying animus against Western civilization? When an American imperialism failed to emerge at the end of World War II, when its historical calling missed its time, was the regression of Western civilization countersigned?

Certainly, an American association of nations, or empire, if it were to arise, would try to invent a new and enlisting type of imperial structure. It probably would, in the first place, try to solve the conflict of the world's races by admitting into its governing and administrative elite those of all races and nationalities who had high abilities.[122] A conflict among national elites would be composed, as in the Roman Empire, by creating a world elite. The universalism of an American empire would be a moral and ethical one, with each individual equal in moral rights to every other; it would eschew *a priori* anthropological dogmas concerning the order of races with respect to the diverse types of ability. It would allow each culture to resolve its own problems and destiny in its own setting, provided that its solutions posed no threat to the lives of others, for every "cultural pluralism" has its limit, namely, that no culture which negates the voluntary existence of others can be regarded as meeting the minimal condition for a world unity. The landmark intuitions of human rights and equality, articulated in the natural rights metaphysics of the eighteenth century, would be re-cast consistent with the facts of developing genetic and human science. A rational approach toward elevating the moral and intellectual stature of all peoples would be the aim of a world participatory imperialism. In such a setting, it is likelier that a world population policy would emerge more nearly consistent with both the moral intuitions of mankind as well as the concerns of biologists for avoiding patterns of regression. The Athens of Socrates' time, the later Roman Empire, and the Spanish Empire of the sixteenth century did, in the view of such thinkers as Charles Darwin and J. B. S. Haldane, pay a heavy toll of decadence for their choices in sexual behavior.[123] An American association of nations would indeed exert its moral suasion to elevate the world's intelligence and potential progress.

The problems experienced by the United States today suggest by their own inner logic that they can be resolved only within the setting of an international association guided and guaranteed by American power, that is, by what we might call, if we surmount the hostile encrustations of the word, a novel American "imperialism." But the traumas of American experience in Vietnam, Central America, and the Middle East scarcely suggest the beginnings of such an American imperialist spirit. Let us, to begin with, therefore try to set forth those considerations that impel us toward an American imperialism, the growing need for such an evolution.

An international order can come about mainly in two ways: either through an agreement among the strongest nations, exerting their joint influence on others, or, the likelier alternative, through the dominant power of a single nation, that is, through imperialism. The philosopher Bertrand Russell, observing humanity at the end of World War I, thought the latter was indeed the alternative most practicable. Hopeful idealistic thinkers, on the other hand, have looked rather to the example of the American Constitution, a document that forged a unity among thirteen warring states. The League of Nations in their view was a pilot effort, followed by a slightly more effective United Nations; they cling to the faith that the internationalist experiment will yet succeed. The American Constitution, however, unified thirteen states that were virtualy racially homogeneous as far as their free citizens were concerned; the latter, moreover, largely shared a common culture and spoke the same language. The fear of a governmental emancipation of the black slaves, nonetheless, was enough to provoke a civil war, and rend the Constitution. The League of Nations broke apart in its fitful efforts to restrain the Nazi, Fascist, and Japanese imperial expansionist programs. The United Nations has proved itself utterly unable to restrain either Soviet expansionism in Czechoslovakia, Afghanistan and Poland, or Communist aggression and genocide in Vietnam and Cambodia, or terrorist operations and training by Libya and Cuba, or tribal genocides in Africa; two-thirds of its delegations, 102 of 157, demonstratively were absent when Israel on June 18, 1982, said it would wage war against a terrorist force that had terrorized itself and the host country of Lebanon.[124]

Why does the route of international collaboration fail? Why does the choice of alternatives tend to define itself as either the victory of an

American progressive imperialism or that of a Soviet regressive imperialism? Why does some mode of imperialist primacy appear to be the necessary condition in our time for the solving of our problems?

First: the equilibrium that currently exists between the United States and the Soviet Union is basically unstable. It is a "Carthaginian" equilibrium, as unstable as the ancient one between Rome and Carthage that required several wars to terminate. No change of regime in the Soviet Union can alter this situation unless it were to repudiate the Leninist-Brezhnevian ideology according to which the Soviet Union is the executor of an alleged historical law that decrees an evolving Communist world rule. The dictatorship of the Communist party cadres, and the legitimacy of the sacrifices it has demanded of its population, are linked intellectually to the ideology of the world-historic mission under Soviet supremacy. In the same fashion that every Communist party presumes itself finally destined to exercise leadership without domestic challenge in its own country, so too among the community of Communist nations history has allegedly assigned a similar role to the Soviet Union, the oldest, most experienced center of Lenin's doctrine. From the Soviet standpoint, so long as an American counter-power exists to give its independent support to a Yugoslavia or China in their deviations from the dogma of Soviet supremacy, the Soviet empire is obliged to make tactical concessions to a Tito, Mao, or Deng, even to a Lech Walesa. Their own empire and hegemony cannot be secure until the American counter-power is ended.

Second: the continuing Soviet-American disequilibrium makes the world's economy totter. To match Soviet weaponry, threats, "probings," "testings," and the strategic manipulation of the proxy forces of client, satellite, or satrapic regimes, the United States has been obliged to build a huge armament base altogether contrary to its own history and tradition. Such military budgets can be financed only through higher taxes or huge capital borrowings. The resources that might have been available for the growth of industry are diverted, measures of social welfare are imperiled, and monetary dislocations both domestic and abroad create burdens for a succession of industries—housing construction, automobile manufacture, the steel mills, and the banks. The capitalist economy then lacks the capital it needs to function. The Soviet economy is beset by an isomorphic set of critical problems only partially muted by the regime's direction of the newspapers and television. It used to be said a war-defense economy helps resolve the "contradictions" of capitalism; Keynes was often quoted to the effect that a construction program, even if it designed pyramids, helped the economy by maintaining full employment.[125] One wonders what the publicly financed construction of the pyramids did to Egyptian housing physically and to the private Egyptian housing industry. A macro-defense economy may, however, contribute to the decline of capitalism even as it did in Roman times.

Thirdly: as we have seen, as long as the Soviet imperialist dynamic persists the anxiety of a nuclear attack against the United States and possibly Western Europe will be ever-present. This danger is enhanced by two features of the Soviet political system; first, the absence of free political discussion, a chamber of debate, and an opposition press in the Soviet Union; and second, the amorality of Soviet political doctrine. A totalitarian political system exists only at the expense of the permanent state of anxiety of its neighbors; the latter become "anxiety societies." In a liberal democratic society such as the United States a preemptive strike against the Soviet Union is virtually out of the question. The debate from 1945 to 1949 on the ethics of the atomic bomb among editors, preachers and pacifists, captalists, clerks, women's organizations, students, and intellectuals made it unlikely that an American ultimatum would be sent to the Soviet Union during that period. The decisions of the Soviet leadership, however, are made in anonymity and secrecy. A lull in debate, even the deceitfully soothing quietness of a respite, would probably precede a sudden nuclear assault on the American cities and installations. Moreover, Soviet political doctrine defines the goodness of an act as the extent to which it assists in "proletarian" triumph, that is, the dominance of the Soviet Communist Party. For no group in the Soviet Union can publicly argue that the categorical imperative, or moral sense, or fellow-feeling for humanity, or religious intuition, transcends the criterion of partisan advantage; the Soviet Communists have no philosophy, only an ideology.

The United States will bear the primary responsibility for withstanding the Soviet power that engenders the "Age of Anxiety." Concomitant with that responsibility in the natural course of things would be the corresponding power—the devolvement upon the United States of the powers for arranging the planetary political existence: in short, an American imperialism.

Fourth: the situation of duopolistic American-Soviet enmity renders perpetual a series of proxy wars, initiated generally under conditions and terms dictated by the Soviet Union and aimed to promote its hegemony.[126] The use of Cuban forces in African Angola to suppress the party favorable to the West is an ongoing example; the equipping and training of the Syrian air force and a "Palestinian guerrilla" army for terrorist operations, bombings, raids, and bombardments in Israel, has been another; the North Vietnamese campaigns equipped and counseled by the Soviet Union, and similar services together with the dispatch of Cuban legionaries to undermine governments in Central American republics, all conformed to the strategic pattern of infiltration and conquest. "Proxy wars" remain a proliferant norm because the basic drive itself to war between the United States and the Soviet Union has perforce to remain frustrated. If the atomic bomb had not been invented, the aftermath of World War II would doubtless have seen a thrust by the Soviet forces aiming to reach the French shores of the Atlantic Ocean. A Soviet Western European empire, ruled through appropriate satrapic regimes such as Poland and Czechoslovakia are today, would have been founded; indeed the French Communist Party for several years anticipated a pending call to proxied power.[127] The fear of an American atomic bomb "delivered" upon the Kremlin alone preserved Western Europe from Soviet seizure. Now, however, the nuclear superiority of the United States is more doubtful and it has retreated from "brinkmanship" to avoid any outbreak of hostilities with the Soviet Union; even the last precept of the Monroe Doctrine has been allowed to wither into desuetude; despite the presumable victory in the "missile crisis" of 1962, the United States has permitted Soviet forces to be garrisoned in Cuba.

Thus, with the hostile feelings of the United States and the Soviet Union toward each other curbed in such an unprecedented fashion, the frustrated aggressive drives issue in surrogate ways. The proxy wars are a continuous provisional substitute for the major war whose prospect remains too awesome. Proxy wars, however, constitute a strain on nations' political nerves; tensions become exacerbated, and the possibility grows that some tensional situation, even a minor crisis, might enhance angers beyond the threshold of restraint. Can such a persistent situation of permanent crises be obviated without the dominant power of a responsible authority, a prevalent imperialism?

More than fifty years ago, as we have mentioned, the English philosopher Bertrand Russell wrote that "international anarchy" would not be resolved until "all the armed forces of the world are controlled by one world-wide authority," a measure which he expected "to be brought about through the world government of the United States."[128] The alternatives to American primacy are more sharply delineated today. Essentially, it is either "anarchy" or totalitarian rule. Such problems as those of population restraint, the suppression of terrorism, and the proliferation of atomic bombs among countries of the "Third World," can be resolved probably only through the advent of a dominant universal imperialism. In large areas of Asia, Africa, and Latin America the populations continue to grow at irresponsible rates that frequently negate any rises in national income. The unimpeded increases in population, especially in countries where the state sovereignties are indifferent to the problem, contribute to inter-tribal wars, massacres, and to emigrations, legal and illegal, to the advanced countries. Is the world to be a Malthusian one of warring populations?[129] The United Nations hardly seems a body that can resolve such problems as it becomes a forum for exacerbating the hostility between the advanced people and the backward ones. Will material aid for "development" become too burdensome if recipient countries refuse indefinitely to undertake measures to limit effectively their population growth? Meanwhile, almost all such countries find it nearly impossible to honor the debts they have so confidently contracted. Many such development loans have been made for political reasons rather than economic. Large projects, even if uneconomic, seemed a way of fending off the Soviet propagandist threat.

In the long run, a world policy will not be effective without the moral power and authority of a presiding world nation; the United States, by virtue of its moral and political inheritance, is the one country in which the greatest trust resides for the fair resolution of such questions. Certainly the Soviet Union, whose record for several genocidal actions against central Asian peoples during World War II has hardly earned the trust of nations.[130]

And what if, meanwhile, a proliferation of atomic bombs continues, and such weaponry finds its way into the hands of such partially civilized potentates as Colonel Qadaffi of Libya, or a Marshal Idi Amin of Uganda, or Khomeini of Iran, or an Emperor Bokassa of the central African Empire? Such rulers, obsessed by a hatred for science and civilization, would, as chieftains in the revolt of the undercivilized against the civilized, willingly connive at a massive, collective regression of mankind. Thus, so long as a conflict exists between the United States and the Soviet Union, an effective international authority is doubtless precluded; for the Soviet Communists, pursuing their "historic mission," do believe that they can use anti-civilizational movements to their own advantage as the raw material for "national liberation movements" and direct them against the United States. At any rate, the prospect of international terrorism reaching genocidal proportions through the use of atomic bombs—the possibility of suicidally minded, grandiose, fantasizing dictators availing themselves of bombs for threats, extortion, and blackmail against the civilized world—will probably persist unless an American organizing power becomes paramount.

Fifth: unless such an American-led association of nations emerges, the tendency of most of the world's backward peoples even when they call themselves "non-aligned" will be to engage in appeasing, flattering, and kow-towing to the Soviet Union.[131] Why is this? In their eyes, a practical wisdom dictates appeasing the Soviet Union; bound by no moral scruples, that regime will intervene with maximal military force whenever it sees an advantage. It is constrained neither by a Christian ethic nor a tradition of high-minded action; the commissar is feared, the "cowboy" is not; Brezhnev and his successors can be menacing, Carter and Reagan are good-natured and go to church. Schoolboys and teachers alike fear the class bully, not the class Boy Scout. Furthermore, the political regimes among the backward peoples are usually rickety, with a continual history of assassinations, palace revolutions and coups d'état. Beset by tribal hatreds, the animosities of religious sects, and the resentments of foreign, imported laborers in new industries, as in Kuwait, Libya and Saudi

Arabia,[132] their rulers, each always fearful of his country's unstable equilibrium, are acutely aware that the Soviet Union is the most expert power in the art of disequilibrating a regime, of enhancing every so-called "contradiction," until a "qualitative change," that is, a revolution, takes place. For the art of "dialectic" is essentially the Marxist sociotechnology for the intensifying of "revolutionary situations" (as Max Eastman long ago recognized).

Given the distinction between the political moralities of the cowboy and the commissar, the rulers of backward peoples regard it as expedient to appease the commissar by systematically opposing the United States in the United Nations, berating its civilization, and occasionally staging a vociferous demonstration in the Assembly Hall. They know that they thereby incur little risk, for America's policy is one of tolerance to "underdeveloped nations"; indeed, their opposition to America might even elicit from it increased material aid. As long as America, they reason, remains worried that they might enroll themselves as Soviet auxiliaries and add still another "people's republic" to the Soviet Empire, it will make every concession in aid, finance, materials, and technical advice that might conceivably retain for it some friendly relationship, even if minimal. To the Russians it is self-evident that all the Moslem furor against the American "Satan" is what Marx called "ideological nonsense." For if the Moslem zeal had been genuine, it would have turned powerfuly against the Soviet Union when the latter's forces occupied Moslem Afghanistan in December 1979. Everyone knows how Soviet Marxism has steadily reduced Moslem observances in central Asia. Nonetheless, the Syrian government, for all its Moslem militance, actually managed to defend the Soviet occupation.[133] The religious pretension seems at times to be what midwestern conjurors call "hoopla." The United Nations General Assembly never ventured to name the Soviet Union as an aggressor in Afghanistan, salving its conscience with an ambiguous formula for the departure of all "foreign" troops.

The Russians stand stolidly by. Their goal of domination remains fixed; they can afford to be patient with the political oscillations that in their view are moments in an evolution toward ultimate capitulation. The Soviet Union finds congenial the anti-American incantations that make the United States at times appear almost friendless, deprived of allies and adherents, and that evidently paralyze many Americans with a democratic self-doubt. Such is the outcome of the Third World principle of Soviet propitiation. Short of a positive American policy that, to defeat the strategy of Soviet expansionism, would construct the primacy of an American imperial association, it can scarcely be undone.

In the absence of an American imperialist policy, the curious travesty of a mirror-imperialism has arisen whereby several thousand Arab potentates, princes, and their retinues of princelings, sultans, and sheiks, generally not known for having done any useful labor in their lives, garner huge fortunes of many billions of dollars as payment for oil that Western technology and skill has educed from a desert sunk for several thousand years in a nomadic slumber. In the wake of America's military defeat in Vietnam and her moral bewilderment with Watergate, much relished by anti-imperialist elements for its confused diversion of American concerns, the backward Arab regimes succeeded in 1973 in extracting a manifold toll in the price of oil. A flow of Arab millionaire "business men" began to the United States; nobody knew in what sort of businesses they had made their fortunes; it transpired they were relatives of desert monarchs, or chosen children of the highly extended polygamous families, or former chiefs of services, intelligence and other. Quietly they bought American enterprises or deposited their funds in American banks. Occasionally, some comic episode would expose the character of these unparalleled extractors of "surplus value." One Saudi Arabian sheik, evicted together with his retinue of seventy-five aides from an opulent Hollywood hotel, had failed to present a valid check to pay for the bill for his fifty rooms on four floors; finally he met his bill for one and a half million dollars. Who was this Arab sheik? How had he secured his money? Nobody would say; he was known only for having "irked residents of Beverly Hills a few years ago by painting genitalia on nude statues that dotted the grounds of his estate."[134] Thus the Playboy of the Eastern World disported himself at the expense of the West.

From the oil revenues rendered as tribute by Western civilization to Middle Eastern lords of lands, the standard of living among several Arabic-speaking populations was elevated to parasitic proportions, so that emirates, conspicuous for neither industry nor innovation, as in Kuwait, enjoyed nearly the highest standard of living in the world. Such funds, too, financed the Palestinian guerilla forces and terrorists whose second generation grew to manhood with the psychology of professional gunmen. For a political decision had been taken not to absorb the entirety of the Palestinian expatriates into the citizenry of such oil-wealthy societies as Saudi Arabia, Libya, Iraq, and Algeria. Instead, Arab regimes decided that keeping unresolved the issue of the re-Arabization of Israel was a good political investment; it provided a channel to divert violent, rebellious emotions from the direction of Arab potentates toward the Jewish Israelis. Thus, the great wealth poured by the West into the East financed a kind of Arabic national socialism, a sharing of the spoils at the expense of the national character. The Middle East has meanwhile enjoyed abundant resources with which to subsidize instability and terrorism.

So long as the world's wealth flows disproportionately as an oil tribute to backward Arabic countries, the weapon of terrorism will be used by them at will against America and Western Europe. It is rarely used against the Soviet Union because the latter is feared. Was Western imperialism terminated prematurely in the Middle East? Are the terrorist indulgences of Iran, Libya, Syria, and Lebanese and Sudanese sects the inevitable penalty of the retreat of Britain and France during the post-World War II anti-imperial fervor? How much stability can be restored without the West's recapturing the oil revenues, that is, restoring imperialism? And would an evolution toward some resolution be possible, except under American leadership?

The Soviet Union's patronage of terrorism, the Arab variety included, directed against the aircraft, ships, and persons of the Western democracies, promotes a problem the latter find baffling. The Soviet Union sells arms to and morally supports all such operations except when very occasionally its own personnel chance to become victims. A good part of the huge Western payments to the Arab rulers thus find their way to Soviet coffers. Probably the Western countries would not have rendered such extortionate payments in the first place had not the Soviet Union been in the wings ready to reap political gains from Western armed conflict with the Arab regimes. America, France, and Italy refrain from actions against Libya lest the Arab potentate *in extremis* announce his affiliation with the Soviet bloc. The terrorist extravagances of Arab regimes are thus made possible by the persistent Soviet support of whatever embarrasses, diverts, or humiliates the Western democratic nations. With hindsight, it now seems, for instance, that when Italy in 1948 sought to retain a trusteeship over Libya, the consequences of an Italian imperialism might at least have spared the Western nations the terrorist base that a Colonel Qaddafi provided, and the contribution of the oil revenues to the Italian economy would have been spent for more civilized purposes.

Again, since it wished to avoid any suggestion of an imperialist policy, the United States during the decades after World War II has adhered to a defensive stance. The consequence was an accretion of defeats, small and large. Where Soviet intentions were frustrated was where foreign communist rulers with independent armed forces in favorable geographical locations perceived the long-run Soviet intent and broke with its apparatus. Disclaiming any intention of trying to intervene directly in areas occupied by the Soviet Union, the United States and its allies have never made an effort to send arms to the insurgents of adjacent Hungary, Czechoslovakia, or East Germany; the Western stand toward the Polish Solidarity movement remains that of a moral pacifism. In Vietnam, on the other hand, the Soviet Union had no qualms about providing resources necessary for repetitive invasions by the North Vietnamese during their Fifteen Years' War against the South Vietnamese and later the United States. In Central America they have acted similarly. In each case, the Soviet Union in effect chooses the place of battle, the time, and extent of commitment of resources; in every case, a propagandist campaign is conducted at the same time to isolate America diplomatically by encouraging Western allies, socialists, church groups, liberals, and intellectuals to call conferences and send delegations to meet with the revolutionists and discuss their grievances. The Soviet Communists have had since 1917 a rich experience in a not altogether unsuccessful management of Western intellectual opinion. Thus the United States is compelled to mount actions in regions and under conditions chosen by the Soviet Communists as most favorable to themselves. Can such purely defensive response eventuate in anything usually but defeat for the United States?[130]

The Russian mode of expansion, as its sympathetic expositor, Owen Lattimore, once stated, is founded on "the doctrine of the irreversible minimum." As Lattimore reviewed a series of international conflicts, some followed by Russian expansion, others not, he noted that even in those instances where the changes in the balance of power fell short of Russian aims, they "still represented some gain in Russia's favor, and a gain not likely to be reversed by foreseeable changes of fortune."[135] The Soviet increments of irreversible minima are integrated through their ideological equation into a presumably final, inevitable triumph; in every critical incident, the settlement involves something gained and added to the Soviet Empire. There are no minuses, only big pluses and smaller ones, in the Soviet political algebra.

The cardinal defections from the Soviet imperial design, those of Communist China under Mao Tse-tung and Deng Xiaoping, and Yugoslavia under Marshal Tito, achieved their political and economic independence. But would these national communistic states have come into existence had not the United States existed as a probable ally ready to send them aid in case of Soviet aggression? In 1948 Stalin dared not move against the Yugoslav "deserters" from the Cominform, for American arms and material aid were available to the Yugoslavs and America still held a monopoly on the atomic bomb. The Russians did indeed from time to time suggest they might bomb the Chinese nuclear installations; the fear, however, that the United States might finally gather the fruits of a Soviet-Chinese war restrained them; the prospect, too, of Chinese armies in the Long March tradition maintaining resistance with the help of American supplies delivered on the Pacific coast, was unpleasant. Therefore, for the nonce the Soviet rulers wait, probing instead America's "soft underbelly" (in Churchill's phrase) in Central America, the Middle East, Southeast Asia, and tropical Africa, while enjoying the blessing of world church bodies that believe they pursue a "higher ethic" by assisting victories for the Soviet Leninists and Moslem fundamentalists, unsecret sharers in hatred for the liberal Western civilization. American critics of American civilization ratified the "historical inevitability" manifested through "the revolutionary instincts of the masses" in the executions conducted by Khomeini's followers as they seized power in Iran. Willy-nilly, as America awaits with self-restraint the maturation of events that might unify the national will, Soviet confidence has grown in its role as guide to the "democratic" colonial revolutions and "national liberation movements"; the outcome—the irreversible increments of Soviet imperialism. Perhaps the British built their empire as Seeley said, "almost in our own despite," in between intervals of absent-mindedness.[136] The Soviet rulers are not absent-minded.

The Soviet rulers indeed look forward to an era when, with America defeated, the leverage for the defection of national states and Communist parties will have vanished. The Soviet Empire might then exert a virtual sovereignty over large parts of several continents. The world's peoples have consciously and unconsciously left the responsibility for leadership decision and risk to the United States. The Polish Solidarity labor movement, persecuted and imprisoned by a martial dictatorship directed by the Soviet Union, looks primarily to the United States for support. Soviet dissidents, the Soviet democratic movement from Sakharov to Solzhenitsyn, remain appalled that America allows itself to be swayed by hostile critics into accepting defeat in countries from Vietnam to Central America; it is a measure of their recognition that the world's freedom is linked to an American imperial power.

Nonetheless, it is clear that much in the American character and society resists this role.[137] If and when cumulative crises finally compel the United States to try to assume both the power and responsibility, the regressive impact of the consecutive Soviet reactions may be difficult to reverse.

Meanwhile, whenever the world's peoples are at loggerheads with each other, and they can speak for themselves, they turn spontaneously to the United States as the arbiter of justice. Whether it involves a war in the Falkland Islands between Britain and Argentine militarists, or a Palestinian terrorist force in straits seeking to withdraw, or the people of Israel surrounded by vindictive neighbors, all recognize that the world's one fair-minded great power is the United States. And correspondingly, all nations tend to blame the United States for their difficulties, whether social, economic, military, or moral. In short, the world assigns the responsibility for its well-being to America, but it hesitates to acknowledge the commensurate exercise of power that is required. When the world's peoples drop their indoctrinated, propagandist postures, America remains the chief morally responsible power to whom they turn.

Strangely, too, the most potent cultural force for the rise of an American imperialism is the wonderful simplicity in grammar, the rich factuality and common sense of the American English language. Long ago Macaulay, in February 1835, foresaw that English would emerge as the future world language.[138] And indeed, in the parliaments of India and African republics, English has emerged as the unifying speech. Even in the Soviet Union, visiting Asian technological missions use English to speak to their Soviet hosts.[139] If the Babel-like profusion of languages, according to myth, once contributed to confusion and war, the American language, unquestionably an easier one to learn than the Russian and far more adapted to industrial needs, helps diffuse American values and what has been called "the American spirit."

The makers of the American nation, such men of diverse political philosophy as John Adams and Benjamin Franklin, had a conception of an imperial republic that would lead the world's nations into the making of polities such as its own; Providence itself, they felt, would use America for the "illumination" and "emancipation" of all mankind.[140] Adams, in accepting the ideal of the perfectibility of man as set forth by Priestley, Condorcet, Diderot and Godwin, made the American republic its executor throughout the world: "Our pure, virtuous, public-spirited federative republic will last forever, govern the globe, and introduce the perfection of man," he wrote to his old friend Thomas Jefferson on November 15, 1813.[141] "It would seem," said an obscure professor, Woodrow Wilson, in 1902, as he was being inaugurated as president of Princeton University, that in the "new age" that was before us, "we must lead the world."[142] To Franklin D. Roosevelt, more than four years before he was elected to the presidency, it seemed clear that the originators of the Constitution had carefully considered all the conceivable modes of government "in the hope that what the United States finally adopted might serve as a pattern for all mankind."[143] He felt that the United States must take up again the responsibility for world leadership.

As he flew across oceans and continents to consult with Allied leaders, Roosevelt got hurried glimpses of backward peoples under imperialist rule living on the edge of survival. In British Gambia he was shocked by the natives' poverty and, according to his son, Elliott, expostulated: "Fifty cents a *day* . . . Dirt. Disease . . . Life expectancy—you'd never guess what it is. Twenty-six years . . . Their cattle live longer!"[144] In all that time's uncertainty, he observed of the Moroccans, that "taking it by and large, they trust the Americans the most."[145] And the trusteeships that he envisaged would have rested primarily on trust in the Americans as the most selfless and altruistic power in the world. In that sense he envisaged the emergence of an Imperial Republic. But Roosevelt, perhaps wisely, kept his distance from any scheme suggesting annexation, aggrandizement, or above all "imperialism."[146] The underlying conviction, however, shared by most men at that time though often only vaguely, and repressed by the political vocabulary, was precisely that stability and progress would be assured only with the rise of such an American imperial republic.

NOTES

Chapter I — Imperialism

1. Hitler told Prime Minister Neville Chamberlain in 1938 that the Nazi ideology precluded any attempt on Germany's part to establish an empire. According to Adam Ulam, this deceptive statement still expressed a profound truth: "Every durable empire has been based, in principle at least, on toleration of racial and national differences." (Adam Ulam, *Stalin: The Man and His Era* [New York, 1973], p. 551. Regressive imperialisms, such as the Mongol and Spanish, have, however, accommodated themselves to an ideology of racial hierarchy.

2. J. J. Saunders, *The History of the Mongol Conquests* (New York, 1971), p. 56.

3. Ibid., p. 65. Cf. Luc Kwanten, *Imperial Nomads: A History of Central Asia* (Philadelphia, 1979), pp. 119, 129. Kwanten proposes the interesting theory that the steppe nomads wanted to control the sedentary states who provided them with a market for horses and who sold them agricultural and luxury products (p. 112). But why then exterminate so much of one's market? As George Vernadsky said: "The sudden outburst of aggressive energy among the Mongols in the early thirteenth century remains a psychological riddle." (Vernadsky, *The Mongols in Russia* [New Haven, 1953], p. 5). Cited in Kwanten, p. 10.

4. Saunders, *Mongol Conquests*, p. 56. The destructive character of Timour's imperialism was described by his contemporary, Ibn Khaldun, and vividly set forth in Edward Gibbon's *The History of the Decline and Fall of the Roman Empire*, ed. J. B. Bury (London, 1902), 7: 70. Walter J. Fischel, *Ibn Khaldun and Tamerlane* (Berkeley, 1952), p. 46.

5. Saunders, *Mongol Conquests*, p. 67. See also B. Ya. Vladimirtsov, *The Life of Chingis-Khan*, trans. D. S. Mirsky (Boston, 1930), pp. 88, 167.

6. Saunders, *Mongol Conquests*, p. 69.

7. Eileen Power, "The Opening of the Land Routes to Cathay," in Arthur Percival Newton, *Travel and Travellers of the Middle Ages* (n.d., n.p.), p. 144. Also cf. Kwanten, *Imperial Nomads*, p. 149.

8. Ralph Fox, *Genghis Khan* (New York, 1936), p. 226.

9. Ibid., p. 155.

10. Power, "Land Routes to Cathay," p. 136.

11. Salvador de Madariaga, *Hernan Cortés, Conqueror of Mexico* (Chicago, 1955), pp. 112, 138, 201, 292, 238.

12. J. H. Parry, "The New World," *The New Cambridge Modern History*, ed. G. R. Elton (Cambridge, 1968), 2: 564.

13. J. H. Parry, "Colonial Development and International Rivalries Outside Europe," *The New Cambridge Modern History*, ed. R. B. Wernham (Cambridge, 1971), 3: 512-513.

14. J. H. Parry, "The New World, 1521-1580," *The New Cambridge Modern History*, ed. G. R. Elton (Cambridge, 1968), 2: 580.

15. Parry, "The New World," pp. 582-583.

16. Sherburne Friend Cook and Leslie Byrd Simpson, *The Population of Central America in the Sixteenth Century*, Ibero-Americana, no. 31 (Berkeley, 1948).

Also, Sherburne Friend Cook and Woodrow Borah, *The Indian Population of Central Mexico, 1531-1610,* Ibero-Americana, no. 44 (Berkeley, 1960).

17. J. H. Parry, "The New World," p. 589.

18. Woodrow Borah, "Latin America 1610-60," *The New Cambridge Modern History,* ed. J. P. Cooper (Cambridge, 1971), 4: 717.

19. Cited in Roland Dennis Hussey and J. S. Bromley, "The Spanish Empire under Foreign Pressures," *The New Cambridge Modern History* (Cambridge, 1971), 6: 344, 345.

20. Ibid., p. 345.

21. Ibid., p. 349.

22. Ibid., p. 345.

23. Victor Hugo, *Ruy Blas,* III, ii.

24. V. G. Kiernan, "Marx, Engels, and the Indian Mutiny," *Homage to Karl Marx,* ed. P. C. Joshi (New Delhi, 1969), p. 144.

25. Abram L. Harris, "John Stuart Mill: Servant of the East India Company," *The Canadian Journal of Economics and Political Science* (May, 1964), 30: 185-202.

26. C. Lestock Reid, *Commerce and Conquest: The Story of the Honorable East India Company* (London, 1947), p. 244. Harris, "Mill: Servant of the East India Company," p. 189.

27. J. A. Hobson, *Imperialism: A Study,* 3rd ed. (London, 1938), pp. 282, 366-367.

28. Rosa Luxemburg, *The Accumulation of Capital,* trans. Agnes Schwarzchild (London, 1951), p. 416. With a slightly different metaphor, the leading Fabian critic of imperialism wrote: "The part played by Europe in the world during the last hundred years has been that of a political octopus." (Leonard Woolf, *Empire and Commerce in Africa: A Study in Economic Imperialism* [London, 1920; rpt. 1968] p. 221).

29. Luxemburg, *Accumulation of Capital,* p. 446.

30. Ibid., p. 446.

31. Ibid., p. 466-467.

32. Rosa Luxemburg, *The Accumulation of Capital—an Anti-Critique,* trans. Rudolf Wichmann (New York, 1972), p. 147.

33. V. I. Lenin, *Imperialism: The Highest Stage of Capitalism* (New York, 1939, p. 82.

34. V. I. Lenin, *Imperialism and the Split in Socialism* (Moscow, 1954), pp. 7-8.

Chapter II – Understanding Progressive Imperialism

1. William Scott Ferguson, *Greek Imperialism* (Boston, 1913), p. 62. "He [Alexander] bade them all consider as their fatherland the whole inhabited earth . . . as akin to them all good men, and as foreigners only the wicked; they should not distinguish between Grecian and foreigner." (*Plutarch's Moralia,* trans. Frank Cole Babbitt [Cambridge, Mass., 1936], p. 329).

2. W. W. Tarn, *Alexander the Great, Vol. I, Narrative* (Cambridge, 1948), pp. 145-147. *Quintus Curtius,* trans. John C. Rolfe (Cambridge, Mass., 1946), 2: 497; 1: 77. As Ernest Barker points out, Zeno began to teach in Athens in 301 B.C., more than twenty years after Alexander's acts were "fully fledged" in 324 B.C. The idea of the *cosmopolis,* the world-state, to supersede the *polis,* the city-state, was born in those acts. Cf. Ernest Barker, *From Alexander to Constantine* (Oxford, 1956), p. 7.

3. Tingfu F. Tsiang, *Labor and Empire: A Study of the Reaction of British Labor, Mainly as Represented in Parliament, to British Imperialism Since 1880* (New York, 1923), p. 218. "[T]he bulk of working-class opinion," notes Henry Pelling, may have shared the expansionist optimism of the first months of the South African war," but he believes that they veered away as economic gains failed to materialize. He gives little weight, however, to various items of evidence ranging from music hall song to the victories of imperialists in working class constituencies. (Henry Pelling, *Popular Politics and Society in Late Victorian Britain* [London, 1968], pp. 99-100).

4. Tenney Frank, *Roman Imperialism* (New York, 1914), p. 253.

5. Ibid., p. 257.

6. Ibid., p. 250-251.

7. Henry C. Boren, *The Gracchi* (New York, 1968), p. 35.

8. Plutarch, *The Lives of the Noble Grecians and Romans,* trans. John Dryden, rev. Arthur Hugh Clough, rpt. (New York, 1932), p. 1006.

9. D. R. Dudley, "Blossius of Cumae," *The Journal of Roman Studies,* vol. 31 (1942), p. 98.

10. Joshua Prawer, *The Crusaders' Kingdom: European Colonialism in the Middle Ages* (New York, 1972), pp. 5, 467-472. Steven Runciman, *A History of the Crusades,* 3 vols. (Cambridge, 1962), 1: 92. Cf. Jonathan Riley-Smith, *What Were the Crusades?* (London, 1977), pp. 62-65.

11. Ibn Khaldun, the Tunisian statesman-sociologist of the fourteenth century, was contemptuous of the Arabs, as "of all peoples, the least versed in the crafts," because they were "deeply rooted in nomadism, far removed from sedentary society." He regarded them as a people given to pillage, as "accustomed to rob other people; for they get their wealth at the point of their spear and set no limit to their depredations." Hence, when the Arabs conquered a country, according to Ibn Khaldun, "they soon put an end to all established rules safeguarding property, and by so doing ruin civilization." Nevertheless, Ibn Khaldun conceded, their adopting the religion of Islam did alter the Arabs' character; it made them fit to rule by imposing moral restraints on their habits and uniting them. But when they began to reject religion they lost their calling of statesmanship and respect for authority, "returned to their wilderness," and reverted to "their original barbarism." (*An Arab Philosophy of History; selections from the Prolegomena of Ibn Khaldun of Tunis,* trans. and arr. Charles Issawi [London, 1950], pp. 56, 59).

12. To Rosa Luxemburg it was simply an axiom that "International Socialism" would bring "free independent nations with equal rights." She advanced no grounds beyond a Kantian conviction that "To the Socialist, no nation is free whose national existence is based upon the enslavement of another people." (*The Crisis in the German Social-Democracy,* rpt. [New York, 1969], p. 95).

13. "The truth was that in 1970 there was in Central Europe a Soviet Empire. This Empire was bitterly hated by all the subject peoples, including most members of communist parties . . . The Soviet policy had all the unpleasant features of old-style imperialism, but it was much worse . . . the most aggressive empire that had ever existed in the heart of Europe." (Hugh Seton-Watson, *The New Imperialism,* new ed. [London, 1971], pp. 99-100).

14. *The New York Times,* February 7, 1966.

15. Leon Trotsky, "Again and Once More Again on the Nature of the U.S.S.R.," *The New International,* vol. 6 (Feb. 1940), p. 14.

16. Joseph A. Schumpeter, "The Sociology of Imperialisms," *Imperialism and Social Classes,* trans. Heinz Norden (New York, 1951), pp. 84, 90.

17. Ibid., p. 85.

18. Ibid., p. 94.

19. William E. Leuchtenburg, "Progressivism and Imperialism: The Progressive Movement and American Foreign Policy, 1898-1916," *The Mississippi Valley Historical Review: A Journal of American History*, vol. 6 (1952), p. 503.

20. When General Napoleon Bonaparte embarked in 1798 with his army for the conquest of Egypt, Frenchmen were sincere and honest in believing that "their Revolution had a real *mission civilisatrice* to perform, and that French *lumières* would happily replace the anarchic misery brought about by the rule of the twenty-three Beys." (A. B. Rodger, *The War of the Second Coalition 1798 to 1801* [Oxford, 1964], p. 18). Cf. Pieter Geyl, *Napoleon: For and Against*, trans. Olive Renier (New Haven, 1949), p. 170.

21. Leuchtenburg, "Progressivism and Imperialism," pp. 487-488.

22. Fred H. Harrington, "The Anti-Imperialist Movement in the United States," *The Mississippi Valley Historical Review*, vol. 22 (1935), pp. 219, 230.

23. Herbert Croly, *The Promise of American Life* (New York, 1909), p. 169.

24. "[T]he rise of an expansionist philosophy in the United States owed little to economic influences." (Julius W. Pratt, *Expansionists of 1898: the Acquisition of Hawaii and the Spanish Islands* [Baltimore, 1936], p. 22).

25. Ibid., p. 351.

26. Ibid., p. 316.

27. Richard C. Brown, *Social Attitudes of American Generals, 1898-1940* (New York, 1979), pp. 330, 368, 373, 365, 369.

28. Ernest Schneider, *Joseph Schumpeter: Life and Work of a Great Social Scientist*, trans. W. E. Kuhn (Lincoln: University of Nebraska, 1975), pp. 1-2.

29. Walter Bagehot in his influential *Physics and Politics* (New York, 1873), p. 218, had already written of "some mysterious atavism—some strange recurrence of a primitive past" that always threatened to destroy the slight improvements that the preceding generation had made.

30. Eduard Bernstein, *Evolutionary Socialism: A Criticism and Affirmation*, trans. Edith C. Harvey (New York, 1961), pp. 146-149. Bernstein, though of Jewish descent, even regarded Zionism as a "tribal atavism." See Roger Fletcher, *Revisionism and Empire: Socialist Imperialism in Germany 1897-1914* (London, 1984), p. 148. In his latter years, however, in the aftermath of World War I, Bernstein became more sympathetic to the project for a Jewish Palestine.

31. As Schumpeter wrote: "The old idea of a subconscious personality . . . was . . . made operational with unsurpassed effectiveness by Freud. Again I cannot . . . do more than point to the vast possibilities of application to sociology—political sociology especially—and economics that seem to me to loom in the future: a Freudian sociology of politics (including economic politics) may some day surpass in importance any other application of Freudianism." Likewise, he thought that there was a "potential fertility for the social sciences" in the ideas of those pupils of Freud, "notably of Alfred Adler," who had departed from Freud's system. (Joseph Schumpeter, *History of Economic Analysis*, ed. Elizabeth Boody Schumpeter [New York, 1954], pp. 798-799).

32. Howard B. White, "Bacon's Imperialism," *The American Political Science Review*, vol. 53 (1958), p. 489. Also see Howard B. White, *Peace Among the Willows: The Political Philosophy of Francis Bacon* (The Hague, 1968), p. 81.

33. Francis Bacon, "Of Plantations," *Francis Bacon's Essays*, Everyman's Library (New York, 1968), p. 104.

34. Bacon, "Of the True Greatness of Kingdoms and Estates," *Francis Bacon's Essays*, Everyman's Library (New York, 1968), p. 92.

35. Ibid., p. 96.

36. Francis Bacon, "Of Empire," *Francis Bacon's Essays*, Everyman's Library (New York, 1968), p. 60.

37. Bacon, "Of the True Greatness of Kingdoms and Estates," pp. 90-91.

38. Maurice Cranston, *John Locke: a biography* (London, 1957), pp. 107, 110, 119-120, 422-423.

39. A. A. Luce and T. E. Jessop, eds., *The Works of George Berkeley, Bishop of Cloyne*, vol. 7 (London, 1955), pp. 369-370.

40. A. A. Luce, *The Life of George Berkeley, Bishop of Cloyne* (London, 1949), pp. 97, 99, 110, 138.

41. Ernest Campbell Mossner, *The Life of David Hume*, 2nd ed. (Oxford, 1890), pp. 202, 553-554.

42. Y. Laissus, "Gaspard Monge et l'expédition de'Egypte (1798-1799)," *Revue de Synthèse*, vol. 81 (1960), pp. 309-336. John Herivel, *Joseph Fourier: The Man and the Physicist* (Oxford, 1973), p. 99. A. B. Rodger, *The War of the Second Coalition 1798 to 1801* (Oxford, 1964), p. 18. Also cf. Harold C. Deutsch, *The Genesis of Napoleonic Imperialism* (Cambridge, Mass., 1938), pp. xx, xxi.

43. In the latter part of the eighteenth century, under the inspiration of Sir Joseph Banks, Royal advisor at Kew Gardens, "It was natural that exiled medical men, stationed in places far removed . . . should become ardent Botanists. It is more significant still that persons of all classes of life who were condemned to wander in foreign lands and seas, were aroused to habits of observation and to take a share in the work of adding to the sum of human knowledge." (Edward Smith, *The Life of Sir Joseph Banks, President of the Royal Society* [London, 1911], p. 95).

44. Francis Darwin, et. al., eds., *More Letters of Charles Darwin* (London, 1903), 1: 70

45. John H. Kautsky, "J. A. Schumpeter and Karl Kautsky: Parallel Theories of Imperialism," *Midwest Journal of Political Science*, vol. 5 (1961), p. 118.

46. Thomas F. Power, Jr., *Jules Ferry and the Renaissance of French Imperialism* (New York, 1944), p. 5. A. P. Thornton, *Doctrines of Imperialism* (New York, 1965), p. 182. Curiously, English positivists, unlike their French colleagues, were opposed to imperialism. Thus, the English positivists were "generally hostile to Britain's role in India," and against "war and empire in Africa, Asia, or anywhere else." When British public opinion was elevating General Gordon as a martyr in the Sudan, English positivists said "the cause of civilization is not served by launching amongst Savages a sort of Pentateuch knight-errant," (Martha S. Vogeler, *Frederic Harrison: The Vocation of a Positivist* [Oxford, 1984], pp. 136, 191).

47. Power, *Jules Ferry*, pp. 46, 70-71, 129, 162, 182, 185, 198. Henri Brunschwig, *French Colonialism, 1871-1914; Myths and Realities*, trans. W. G. Brown (New York, 1966), pp. 76-77, 96.

48. Agnes Murphy, *The Ideology of French Imperialism, 1871-1881* (New York, 1968), pp. 108-109.

49. Sarah Gertrude Millin, *Cecil Rhodes* (New York, 1933), p. 40.

50. K. Marx and F. Engels, *On Colonialism* (Moscow, n.d.), pp. 306-307.

51. Harold R. Weinstein, *Jean Jaurès: A Study of Patriotism in the French Socialist Movement* (New York: 1963; rpt. 1973), pp. 143, 147, 144.

52. Marcel Liebman, *Les Socialistes belges 1895-1914: La Révolte et l'organisation* (Brussels, 1979), p. 224. Of Vandervelde, Sir Arthur Conan Doyle wrote: "What M. Labori was to Dreyfus, M. Vandervelde has been to the Congo, save that it is a whole nation who are his clients." (Sir Arthur Conan Doyle, *The Crime of the Congo* [New York, 1909], p. 93).

53. David Landes, "Some Thoughts on the Nature of Economic Imperialism," *Journal of Economic History*, vol. 21 (Dec. 1961), p. 510.

54. Ibid., p. 510.

55. Gilbert Murray, "Satanism and the World Order," *Tradition and Progress* (Boston, 1922), pp. 205-206.

56. Cited in Irving Babbitt, *Democracy in Leadership* (Boston, 1924), p. 17, from the introductory note by Henri Bergson in E. Seillère, *Balzac at la morale romantique.* Also see Henri Bergson, *Écrits et Parôles,* ed. R. M. Mossè-Bastide (Paris, 1959), 3: 492-494.

57. Ronald Hyam, *Elgin and Churchill at the Colonial Office 1905-1908: The Watershed of the Empire-Commonwealth* (New York, 1968), pp. 503-505.

58. Grace Hudley Beardsley, *The Negro in Greek and Roman Civilization: A Study of the Ethiopian Type* (Baltimore, 1929), p. 119. R. G. Collingwood, the Oxford philosopher-archeologist, noted: "It is this that makes the Roman Empire a different thing from all modern empires. The empires of modern times are rent by a racial cleavage between a governing race and a governed, which are too far apart to unite into a single whole." (Collingwood, *Roman Britain,* new ed. [London, 1959], p. 8). See the more complex survey in Frank M. Snowden, Jr., *Before Color Prejudice: The Ancient View of Blacks* (Cambridge, Mass., 1983), p. 100. Snowden notes: "The color black, for the Greeks and Romans . . . evoked a negative, and white a positive image."

59. *The Revolutionary Movement in the Colonies: Theses Adopted by the Sixth World Congress of the Communist International* (New York, 1929, rpt. 1933), pp. 12-13.

60. Multatuli, *Max Havelaar,* trans. Roy Edwards (Leyden and London, 1967), p. 129. Cited in Peter King, *Multatuli* (New York, 1972), p. 28.

61. Alfred Russel Wallace, *The Malay Archipelago,* 10th ed. (London, 1890), pp. 73-75.

62. Warren S. Thompson, *Population and Peace in the Pacific* (Chicago, 1946), pp. 253, 255.

63. Paul M. Sweezy, *Monopoly Capitalism* (New York, 1972), p. 18. "Capitalist development theory is unable to perceive underdevelopment . . . as a consequence and part of the process of the world expansion of capitalism." (Theotonio Dos Santos, "The Structure of Dependence," *The American Economic Review,* vol. 60 [May 1970], p. 231). According to the dependency standpoint not only do the dependent countries lose control over their own resources, but the "technical and cultural capacity as well as the moral and physical health of their people" are limited. While the advancement of technology is retarded, manpower is "superexploited." (Dos Santos, p. 231).

64. Barry Commoner, "Science and the Sense of Humanity," *The Humanist,* 30, No. 6 (Nov.-Dec. 1970), p. 12.

65. Ibid., p. 13.

66. *The Revolutionary Movement in the Colonies,* pp. 13-14.

67. R. Palme Dutt, *The Problem of India* (New York, 1953), p. 44. "Imperialism has retarded the economic development of India. Before British rule . . . [t]he products of Indian industry were more than a match for European products. It is *since* British rule that India has been reduced to an extreme backward level in the world scale." India's industry, according to Dutt, was much destroyed, relegating it "to the role of an agricultural appendage of imperialism." (p. 71).

68. Andre Gunder Frank, *On Capitalist Underdevelopment* (Bombay, 1975), p. 25.

69. Andre Gunder Frank, in James Cockcroft, Andre Gunder Frank, and Dale L. Johnson, *Dependence and Underdevelopment: Latin America's Political Economy* (New York, 1972), p. 20.

70. V. I. Lenin, *Imperialism and the Split in Socialism* (Moscow, 1954), pp. 12, 13, 22. Marx himself recognized that capitalist imperialism was impelled by its own search for profit to keep on developing the industries of "underdeveloped" countries. Thus he wrote in 1853: "The more the industrial interest became dependent on the Indian market, the more it felt the necessity of creating fresh productive powers in

India . . . You cannot continue to inundate a country with your manufactures, unless you enable it to give you some produce in return." What happened, according to Marx, was that the Indians themselves obstructed the British efforts to "industrialize" their company: "they [the British] found that in all attempts to apply capital to India they met with impediments and chicanery on the part of the Indian authorities." (Karl Marx, "The East India Company—Its History and Results," in Marx and Engels, *The First Indian War of Independence 1857-1859* [Moscow, n.d.], p. 30).

71. Cecil Roth, *The Sassoon Dynasty* (London, 1941), pp. 75, 99, 101, 226.

72. Rhoads Murphy, *The Outsider: The Western Experience in India and China* (Ann Arbor, 1977), p. 85. David Owen, *British Opium Policy in India and China* (New Haven, 1934). Sherry Abel, "Sassoon," *The Universal Jewish Encyclopedia* (New York, 1943), 9: 373-379. Walter J. Fischel, "Sassoon," *Encyclopaedia Judaica* (Jerusalem, 1971), 14: 896-901.

73. William Foster, *The East India House: Its History and Associations* (London, 1924), pp. 219, 214.

74. Eric Stokes, *The English Utilitarians and India* (Oxford, 1959), p. 48.

75. Foster, *The Great India House,* pp. 208, 222-223.

76. John Stuart Mill, *Memorandum of the Improvements in the Administration of India during the Last Thirty Years and the Petition of the East India Company to Parliament* (London, 1858), pp. 52-54.

77. Ibid., pp. 54-55.

78. Ibid., p. 69.

79. Ibid., p. 29.

80. Ibid., p. 29. "All authorities agree," wrote Vera Anstey (*The Economic Development of India,* 4th ed. [London, 1952], p. 38) that a "great increase" in the Indian population took place between the beginning of the nineteenth century and the first census in 1872.

81. Mill, *Memorandum of Improvements,* p. 85. Cotton had provided the usual clothing in India as early as 445 B.C. See Buchanan, *The Development of Capitalistic Enterprise in India,* p. 194.

82. Mill, *Memorandum of Improvements,* pp. 20-21.

83. Ibid., p. 113.

84. Geroid Tanquary Robinson, *Rural Russia Under the Old Regime* (New York, 1932; rpt. 1949), p. 78. Richard Pipes, *Russia under the Old Regime* (New York, 1974), p. 19.

85. Mill, *Memorandum of Improvements,* p. 27.

86. Ibid., p. 26.

87. Ibid., pp. 90-92.

88. Ibid., pp. 31, 48, 49.

89. Ibid., p. 78.

90. Ibid., p. 94.

91. James Mill, *The History of British India,* 2nd ed., 6 vols. (London, 1820), 6: 17-18.

92. Anstey, *Development of India,* pp. 40-42.

93. Roger Fletcher, "A Revisionist Looks at Imperialism: Eduard Bernstein's Critique of Imperialism and Kolonialpolitik, 1900-1914," *Central European History,* vol. 12 (1979), p. 270. Roger Fletcher, *Revisionism and Empire: Socialist Imperialism in Germany 1897-1914* (London, 1984), pp. 154-159.

94. Edward Kardelj, "The Crisis of Capitalism and the Imperative of Socialism," trans. K. Udovichi, *Socialist Thought and Practice,* vol. 17 (Oct. 1977), p. 19.

95. Michael Harrington, cited in Walter Galenson, "Note from an Innocent Abroad," *New America,* vol. 15 (Feb. 1978), p. 9.

96. Tony Smith, "The Underdevelopment of Development Literature: The Case of Dependency Theory," *World Politics,* vol. 31 (1979), p. 249.

97. C. F. Remer, *Foreign Investments in China* (New York, 1933), pp. 239, 241.

98. Ibid., pp. 333, 335.

99. Harold Schiffrin, "Sun Yat-Sen's Early Land Policy: The Origin and Meaning of 'Equalization of Land Rights'," *Journal of Asian Studies,* vol. 16 (August 1957), pp. 549-564. Harold Schiffrin and Pow-Key Sohn, "Henry George on Two Continents: A Comparative Study in the Diffusion of Ideas," *Comparative Studies in Society and History,* vol. 2 (1959), pp. 85-108. Maurice William, *The Social Interpretation of History: A Refutation of the Marxian Economic Interpretation of History* (Brooklyn, 1920).

100. Karl Marx and Frederick Engels, *Selected Correspondence* (Moscow, 1956), p. 134. Marx wrote in 1858: "The difficult question for us is this: on the Continent the revolution is imminent and will also immediately assume a socialist character. Is it not bound to be crushed in this little corner, considering that in a far greater territory [China] the movement of bourgeois society is still on the ascendant?"

101. Andre Gunder Frank, "Development of Underdevelopment or Underdevelopment of Development in China," *The Development of Underdevelopment in China: A Symposium,* ed. Philip C. C. Huang (White Plains, 1980), p. 93.

102. Peter Ward Fay, *The Opium War, 1840-1842: Barbarians in the Celestial Empire in the Early Part of the Nineteenth Century and the War by Which They Forced Her Gates Ajar* (Chapel Hill, 1975), p. 12.

103. Ibid., p. 203. John Morley, *The Life of William Ewart Gladstone* (New York, 1904), 1: 226-227.

104. Fay, *The Opium War,* p. 129.

105. The backwardness of "Oriental" Middle Eastern societies is also largely attributed to imperialist exploitation. "Capitalism intensifies and conserves pre-capitalist modes of production," writes Bryan S. Turner, *Marx and the End of Orientalism* (London, 1978), p. 81.

106. "The general mobilization of all able-bodied men at the time of the French Revolution would hardly have been feasible without a notable expansion of industrial output, combined with a growing desire to put the work of scientists and engineers to the most efficient practical use." John U. Nef, *War and Human Progress: An Essay on the Rise of Industrial Civilization* (Cambridge, Mass., 1950), p. 318. For the destructive impact of war, see also pp. 65-66, 226, 412, 173, 105.

107. Dexter Perkins, *A History of the Monroe Doctrine,* p. 135. Curiously, in 1864 President Lincoln had allowed an offer to be made to the president of the Confederacy that the Southern armies should, under an armistice, proceed to Mexico to join forces with the Mexican Republicans under Juarez. Jefferson Davis rather liked the idea, but it disappeared in the last hectic months of the Civil War. (Ibid., p. 128).

108. Ibid., p. 129.

109. The Canadian version of the "dependista" mentality is likewise less based on the "branch plant" character of its economy than on the fact that Canadian sovereignty owes its existence to the military protection afforded by the United States against the Soviet neighbor. As a resident in Canada for a decade, it seemed to me that its most unusual phenomenon was the amount of intellectual energy expended in this prosperous society by its nationalist, socialist ideologists to instill a sense of "dependency" resentment against the United States. Naturally, they were joined in the endeavor by a brigade of anti-American Americans, many of them deserters or draft dodgers.

110. Dexter Perkins, *A History of the Monroe Doctrine,* rev. ed. (Boston, 1955), pp. 394-395.

111. Ibid., p. 198.

112. Ibid., p. 27.

113. Ibid., p. 384.

114. "Diplomatic Protection of Foreign Investments Abroad," *Foreign Policy*

Association Information Service, vol. 3, no. 3 (April 13, 1927), p. 37.

115. Charles A. Beard and Mary R. Beard, *The Rise of American Civilization,* new ed. (New York, 1934); 1:436.

116. Ernest R. May, *The Making of the Monroe Doctrine* (Cambridge, Mass., 1975), p. 27.

117. See the unusual collection of documents in Thomas Harrison Reynolds, *As Our Neighbors See Us: Readings in the Relations of the United States and Latin America 1820-1940* (1940), pp. 81-83, p. 170 ff., pp. 101-102. J. F. Rippy, "Literary Yankee-phobia in Hispanic America," *Journal of International Relations,* vol. 12 (1922), pp. 350-371, 524-538. An American equivalent in self-excoriation is Edward Weisband, *The Ideology of American Foreign Policy: A Paradigm of Lockian Liberalism* (Beverly Hills, 1973), p. 22 ff.

118. Perkins, *Monroe Doctrine,* p. 387.

119. J. Rippy, *British Investments in Latin America, 1822-1949: A Case Study in the Operations of Private Enterprise in Retarded Regions* (Minneapolis, 1959), p. 10.

120. Ibid., p. 172.

121. Leland Hamilton Jenks, *The Migration of British Capital to 1875* (New York, 1938), p. 169. After the Napoleonic Wars, British capital investment in the United States seriously began. "The crisis of 1825 and particularly that of 1837 and that of 1847 were, insofar as the City [London] was involved, caused by the defaulting of certain of the United States and of certain South American countries or by the collapse of great mining and plantation enterprises." In 1913, the British owned $3.3 billion in American securities; by 1929, this had dropped to $1.56 billion. (M. Palyi, "Foreign Investment," *Encyclopedia of the Social Sciences,* vol. 6 [New York, 1931], pp. 367, 373).

122. Sir George Paish, "Great Britain's Capital Investments in Individual Colonial and Foreign Countries," *Journal of the Royal Statistical Society,* vol. 74, pt. 2 (1911), pp. 167-187.

123. Dorothy R. Adler, *British Investments in American Railways, 1834-1898,* ed. Muriel E. Hidy (Charlottesville, 1970), pp. 192-193.

124. Ibid., p. 198.

125. Ibid., p. 191.

126. Lenin, *Imperialism: The Highest Stage of Capitalism,* p. 13. Lenin, *Imperialism and the Split in Socialism,* p. 25. Karl Marx and Frederick Engels, *Correspondence 1846-1895,* trans. Dona Torr (New York, 1935), pp. 399. Karl Marx and Frederick Engels, *On Britain,* (Moscow, 1953), pp. 28-29.

127. H. G. Wells, *The War in the Air* (London, 1907), pp. 34, 42.

128. Hesketh Pearson, *G. B. S., A Full Length Portrait* (New York, 1942), p. 127.

129. Harvey Goldberg, *Life of Jean Jaurès* (Madison, 1962), pp. 217, 226.

130. Sir Arthur Conan Doyle, "The Adventure of the Solitary Cyclist," *The Return of Sherlock Holmes* (New York, 1905), p. 94.

131. D. C. Field, "Mechanical Road-Vehicles," *A History of Technology,* eds. Charles Singer, E. J. Holmeyard, A. R. Hall, and Trevor L. Williams (Oxford, 1958), 5: 414-415.

132. Robert P. Scott, *Cycling Art, Energy, and Locomotion* (Philadelphia, 1889), pp. 140-143.

133. Howard and Ralph Wolf, *Rubber: A Story of Glory and Greed* (New York, 1936), pp. 405, 407, 408, 22, 123, 296, 298, 289. Carl W. Mitman, "Charles Goodyear," *Dictionary of American Biography* (New York, 1932), 4: 413-415. Bernhard Waldemar Kaempffert, ed., *A Popular History of American Invention* (New York, 1924), 1: 163-170.

134. Wolf, *Rubber,* p. 405.

135. W. L. Sumner, *The Pianoforte*, rev. ed. (London, 1971), p. 39. Cited in Scipione Maffei, *Giornale dei Letterati d'Ialia* (1711).

136. William B. White, *Theory and Practice of Piano Construction* (New York, 1906; rpt. 1975), p. 21. At the Great Exhibition in Philadelphia in 1876, "the first-class American pianos exhibited excelled the best instruments of European makes in every respect." Also, they were able to withstand the climatic changes in America better than those imported from Europe. (Sumner, *The Pianoforte*, p. 65. Daniel Spillane, *History of the American Pianoforte: Its Technical Development, and the Trade* [New York 1890; rpt. 1969], p. 260).

137. "The beautiful keys made by Herrnburger Brooks [that came to be "the oldest established action makers in the world" with "their products now in demand by the piano makers of many countries for their finest instruments"] were a "delight both to the fingers and eyes. Ivory is still the material *par excellence* for covering the natural keys: it takes a high polish, is durable and possesses an exquisite velvety quality to the touch of sensitive fingers." (Sumner, *The Pianoforte*, pp. 83, 133). Around 1900 in the East Side of New York "a new and virulent epidemic, known as 'Piano Mania'" swept through the poorest tenements. ("Darwinism," *Alliance Review*, vol. 1 [1901], p. 65).

138. American firms began manufacturing piano keys in the 1850s. Many firms vanished, but one, for instance, Comstock, Cheney and Company in Connecticut, acquired "a large circle of customers in Boston and New York" and employed a large number of workingmen. (Spillane, *History of the Pianoforte*, p. 327).

139. Charles Wilson, *The History of Unilever: A Study in Economic Growth and Social Change* (London, 1954), 1:9.

140. Ibid., p. 10.

141. Sir Alan Burns, *History of Nigeria*, 8th ed. (London, 1972), pp. 69, 297, 299.

142. Reginald Reynolds, *Beards* (New York, 1949; 1976), p. 284.

143. Wilson, *History of Unilever*, 1:38. All the tropical products from palm oil to chocolate inspired corresponding modes of advertising in Britain. As their appeal was consciously economic and utilitarian, it was not "ideological" in the Marxist sense that involves "unconscious" processes. Cf. John M. MacKenzie, *Propaganda and Empire, the Manipulation of British Public Opinion, 1880-1960* (Manchester, 1984), pp. 22, 26.

144. Charles Schuyler Castner, *One of a Kind: Milton Snavely Hershey 1857-1945* (Hershey, Pennsylvania, 1983), p. 149 ff. Samuel F. Hinkle, "Chocolate," *The Encyclopedia Americana*, International ed. (Danbury, Conn., 1983), 6: 621.

145. The British government in the Gold Coast encouraged cacao cultivation by independent farmers. (The cacao tree was not native to Africa and was first introduced to the Gold Coast in 1879 by a native blacksmith). "It has thus come about that the greatest cocoa output in the world is produced by free native farmers, working on their own account." (Iolo A. Williams, *The Firm of Cadbury 1831-1931* [London, 1931], p. 147).

146. Williams, *Cadbury*, pp. 6, 13, 178. Cf. Polly Hill, *The Migrant Cocoa-Farmers of Southern Ghana: A Study in Rural Capitalism* (Cambridge, 1963), pp. 15-17. Sara S. Berry, *Cocoa, Custom and Socio-Economic Change in Rural Western Nigeria* (Oxford, 1975), pp. 215-216.

147. Andre Gunder Frank, in Cockcroft, et al., *Dependence and Underdevelopment*, p. 9.

148. Morris D. Morris, "Towards a Reinterpretation of Nineteenth-Century Indian Economic History," *Indian Economic and Social History Review*, vol. 5 (March, 1968), pp. 6-7. Cited in Tony Smith, "The Case of Dependency Theory," p. 255.

149. "By the end of the twelfth century it was already clear . . . that the Muslims

would soon be out of the race." (George Sarton, *The Life of Science: Essays in the History of Civilization* [Bloomington, 1948; 1960], p. 157).

150. Vera Anstey, *The Economic Development of India,* 4th ed. (London, 1952), p. 209.

151. Ibid., pp. 260, 261.

152. Sunil Kumar Sen, *The House of Tata (1839-1939)* (Calcutta, 1975), p. 7. Also cf. Daniel Houston Buchanan, *The Development of Capitalistic Enterprise in India* (New York, 1934), pp. 143-145.

153. Buchanan, *Capitalistic Enterprise in India,* pp. 17, 147-148.

154. Ibid., p. 1.

155. Verrier Elwin, *The Story of Tata Steel* (Bombay, 1958), p. 16.

156. Sen, *Tata,* pp. 9, 22. B. Sh. Saklatvala and K. Khosla, *Jamsetji Tata* (New Delhi, 1970), p. 12.

157. Sen, *Tata,* p. 18.

158. Ibid., p. 24.

159. Anstey, *Development of India,* p. 262.

160. Ibid., pp. 131-132. Daniel Thorner, *Investment in Empire: British Railways and Steam Shipping Enterprise in India 1825-1849* (Philadelphia, 1950), p. 12.

161. Sen, *Tata,* p. 29.

162. Ibid., p. 33.

163. Elwin, *The Story of Tata Steel,* p. 36.

164. Ibid., p. 23.

165. Ibid., p. 17.

166. Dadabhai Naoroji, *The Manners and Customs of the Parsees* (n.p., 1862), *Tracts,* vol. 156. Cited in Sen, *Tata,* p. 159.

167. Elwin, *The Story of Tata Steel,* p. 14. Sen, *Tata,* p. 21. Saklatvala and Khosla, *Jamsetji Tata,* p. 4.

168. Elwin, *The Story of Tata Steel,* p. 121.

169. Panchanan Saha, *Shapurji Saklatvala: A Short Biography* (New Delhi, 1970), pp. 4, 6, 11.

170. Anthony Sampson, *The Seven Sisters: The Great Oil Companies and the World They Shaped* (New York, 1975; 1976), pp. 275, 344.

171. Oriana Fallaci, "A Sheik Who Hates to Gamble," *The New York Times Magazine,* September 14, 1975, p. 18.

172. *The New York Times,* January 10, 1986.

173. Melvin Richter, *The Politics of Conscience: T. H. Green and His Age* (London, 1964), p. 52. John MacCunn, *Six Radical Thinkers: Bentham, J. S. Mill, Cobden, Carlyle, Mazzini, T. H. Green* (London, 1910), pp. 255-256. L. H. Gann and Peter Duignan, *The Rulers of British Africa 1870-1914* (Stanford, 1978), p. 198.

174. Eric Stokes, *The English Utilitarians and India* (Oxford, 1959), p. 45. Bruce Tiebout McCully, *English Education and the Origins of Indian Nationalism* (New York, 1940), pp. 20, 35, 59, 195-196, 232, 229-230, 224-223, 283, 24. Also cf. George Otto Trevelyan, *The Life and Letters of Lord Macaulay* (London, 1876), 1: 342, 345.

175. Granville Eastwood, *Harold Laski* (London 1977), p. 92. "Next to Great Britain and the United States, nowhere is Laski's memory more revered than in India. Very many hundreds of young men and women from that country came under his influence at the London School of Economics." The similar experience and revolutionary formation of Kwame Nkrumah, the first prime minister of Ghana, and the influence of American and English ideas on him (as well as his later undoing) are well-analyzed in Henry L. Bretton, *The Rise and Fall of Kwame Nkrumah: A Study of Personal Rule in Africa* (New York, 1966), pp. 22-28.

176. *Toward Freedom: The Autobiography of Jawaharlal Nehru* (New York, 1941), p. 233.

177. David Brion Davis, *The Problem of Slavery in Western Cultures* (Ithaca, N.Y., 1966) p. 118. Cited in Eric Williams, *From Columbus to Castro: The History of the Caribbean, 1492-1969* (London, 1970), p. 205. Richard Baxter, the most influential Puritan minister of the seventeenth century, denounced those who caught "poor Negroes" as among "the common enemies of mankind," while those who bought them, and used them "as beasts, for their mere commodity," were "fitter to be called incarnate devils than Christians."

178. John Locke, *Two Treatises of Government*, ed. Peter Laslett, 2nd ed. (Cambridge, 1967), pp. 302-303. Locke attempted a "half-hearted defense of slavery," notes R. I. Aaron in *John Locke*, 2nd ed. (Oxford, 1955), p. 276.

179. Margery Perham, *Lugard: The Years of Adventure, 1858-1898* (London, 1956), pp. 79-80.

180. Rev. William Monk, ed., *Dr. Livingstone's Cambridge Lectures* (Cambridge, 1858), pp. 1, 21.

181. George Seaver, *David Livingstone: His Life and Letters* (New York, 1957), pp. 60, 141, 389, 350, 476.

182. Ibid., p. 183.

183. Ibid., p. 186.

184. Ibid., p. 69.

185. Ibid., pp. 470-471, 186.

186. Ibid., p. 21.

187. Ibid., pp. 79-81.

188. Ibid., p. 291.

189. Edward Clegg, *Race and Politics: Partnership in the Federation of Rhodesia and Nyasaland* (London, 1960), p. 33.

190. George Delf, *Jomo Kenyatta* (New York, 1961), pp. 60-61. Ronald Segal, *African Profiles* (Baltimore, 1962), pp. 198-211, 154, 160, 170, 94, 89. Colin Legum, *Congo Disaster* (Baltimore, 1961), pp. 49-95.

191. I once observed the agitation, organization, and strikes by the Indochinese coolies in New Caledonia that finally led in 1945 to the end of the coolie labor system (indentured labor enforced through corporal punishment). There was an unwitting cooperation between the colony's sole "Communist," Mme. Tunica, and Father Zimmerman, the priest-missionary to the coolies. See Lewis S. Feuer, "End of Coolie Labor in New Caledonia," *Far Eastern Survey,* vol. 15 (1946), pp. 264-267. Also cf. Virginia Thompson and Richard Adloff, *The French Pacific Islands: French Polynesia and New Caledonia* (Berkeley, 1971), p. 451. Ms. Thompson tells the story of how the Indochinese coolies appealed to the American command to intervene with the French authorities to end the coolie labor system. (She predates that appeal, however, by one year). She correctly infers that its reference to Abraham Lincoln shows that the document "could hardly have originated with the illiterate coolies whose names were appended to it," though she erroneously attributes its origin to Mme. Tunica. I composed the first draft of the document; it was much revised and translated into "excellent French" by Mme. Tunica. I suggested such an appeal to the American command for two essential reasons—to curb the French mining managers' customary recourse to physical punishments and to bring American moral pressure against the continuance of forced indentured labor. A copy of the appeal was sent at the same time to a distinguished lawyer in the colony, Maître G. Bourdinat, proud scion of a Paris Communard exile.

192. Bankole Timothy, *Kwame Nkrumah: His Rise to Power* (London, 1955), p. 172. In 1951, as the anti-imperialist movement was growing rapidly, schoolteachers were, next to chiefs, the largest single group in the Legislative Assembly of 1951. (David E. Apter, *The Gold Coast in Transition* [Princeton, 1955] pp. 223-236, 295-296). Kwame Nkrumah, *Ghana: The Autobiography of Kwame Nkrumah* (New York, 1957), p. 52.

193. Such a subject as primitive economics, writes Malinowski, is "of value to those who wish to develop the resources of tropical countries, employ indigenous labor and trade with natives." The study of primitive law should likewise yield "the guiding principles of Colonial legislation and administration." (Bronislaw Malinowski, *Crime and Custom in Savage Society* [New York, 1926], pp. 1-2).

194. Lincoln University in Pennsylvania was the alma mater to a generation of African revolutionary intellectuals who became their countries' anti-imperialist leaders. (Maureen Daly, "African School Tie," *New York Times Magazine*, April 28, 1957, p. 20).

195. Kwame Nkrumah, *Africa Must Unite*, new ed. (New York, 1970), p. xiii. Dennis Austin and Robin Luckham, eds., *Politicians and Soldiers in Ghana 1966-1972* (London, 1975), pp. 13, 15, 26. Philip Foster and Aristide R. Zolberg, *Ghana and the Ivory Coast: Perspectives on Modernization* (Chicago, 1970), pp. 120-122.

196. Henry L. Bretton, *The Rise and Fall of Kwame Nkrumah*, p. 148.

197. Ibid., p. 80.

198. W. H. Taylor, "Missionary Education in Africa Reconsidered: the Presbyterian Educational Impact in Eastern Nigeria," *African Affairs*, vol. 83 (1984), pp. 202, 194, 205.

199. Henri Brunschwig, "The Decolonization of French Black Africa," *The Transfer of Power in Africa: Decolonization 1940-1960*, Prosser Gifford and William Roger Louis, eds. (New Haven, 1982), pp. 223-224.

200. Léopold Sedar Senghor, *African Socialism*, trans. Mercer Cook (New York, 1959), pp. 27-32. Ullis Beier, "In Search of an African Personality," *The Twentieth Century*, vol. 165 (April, 1959), p. 347. Albert Thibaudet, *La République des Professeurs* (Paris, 1927). Also cf. S. Okechukwu Mezu, *The Poetry of Léopold Sedar Senghor* (Cranbury, N.J., 1973), pp. 7-8.

Chapter III - A Case Study: The Jews Under the Varieties of Imperialism

1. Isaac Bloch, "Alexander the Great," *The Jewish Encyclopedia* (New York, 1906), 1: 341.

2. Cf. Norman Bentwich, *Hellenism* (Philadelphia, 1917), pp. 31, 29, 187. Avigdor Tcherikover, *Hellenistic Civilization and the Jews*, trans. S. Applebaum (Philadelphia, 1959), p. 142. Max Radin, *The Jews Among the Greeks and Romans* (Philadelphia, 1915), p. 368. W. E. D. Oesterley, *The Jews and Judaism During the Greek Period* (1941; rpt. Port Washington, 1970), pp. 16-17. Donald W. Engels, *Alexander the Great and the Logistics of the Macedonian Army* (Berkeley, 1978), p. 56. Alexander's imperialism has been sharply criticized by recent scholars; the anti-imperialist philosophy that prevailed after World War II as the British, French, and Dutch empires were being dismantled may have influenced this adverse judgment. Nonetheless, the impressive fact remains that the legends and traditions of the Jews depict Alexander in the most favorable terms, as one mindful of the customs and welfare of the conquered people and as one who evoked their loyalties. Each of these stories is chiefly fiction, yet the statistical fact of the unanimously favorable judgment of Alexander remains highly significant as evidence, especially when one remembers that other emperors scarcely fared so well. (Cf. Simon Dubnow, *History of the Jews from the Beginning to Early Christianity*, trans. Moshe Spiegel, rev. ed. [South Brunswick, N.J., 1967], 1: 457-458. Ralph Marcus, "Alexander the Great and the Jews," in Josephus, *Jewish Antiquities, Appendix C* [Cambridge, Mass., 1937], 6: 512 ff. Israel J. Kazis, ed., *The Book of the Gests of Alexander of Macedon* [Cambridge,

Mass., 1962], p. 4 ff. E. Badian, *Studies in Greek and Roman History* [Oxford, 1964], p. 192 ff.) The Stoic philosophy of the world-state may well have been conceived by Phoenician-Jewish intellectuals inspired by the brief Alexandrian imperialist interlude. As the Phoenician towns lost their political sovereignty, their citizens frequently became converts to Judaism: "A vanishing world factor, the Phoenician, disappeared within the new world factor, the Diaspora Jew." (Salo Wittmayer Baron, *A Social and Religious History of the Jews,* 2nd ed. [New York, 1952], 1: 176). I might add that the philosophy of the Phoenician founder of Stoicism, Zeno of Citium, appears to have been identical with that of the young Elihu at the close of the *Book of Job.*

3. "A Treatise Against Flaccus," *The Works of Philo Judaeus,* (London, 1855), vol. 4, sec. 7, p. 70.

4. Dora Askowith, *The Toleration of the Jews Under Julius Caesar and Augustus* (New York, 1915), cited from Josephus, *Jewish Antiquities.* Bentwich, *Hellenism,* p. 33.

5. "A Treatise on the Virtues and Office of Ambassadors," *The Works of Philo Judaeus,* vol. 4, p. 134.

6. Ibid., pp. 131-132. Suetonius, *The Lives of the Twelve Caesars,* ed. Joseph Gavorse (New York, 1931), p. 48.

7. Askowith, *Toleration of the Jews,* pp. 205, 10, 119.

8. Ibid., pp. 201-202, 205.

9. A. N. Sherwin-White, *Racial Prejudice in Imperial Rome* (Cambridge, 1967), p. 96. "By the end of the fourth century the Jews had attained to great prominence and to the highest classes of citizenship." (Harry Friedenwald, "Jewish Physicians in Italy," *Publications of the American Jewish Historical Society,* no. 28 [1922], p. 136).

10. Cicero and Tacitus both regarded Judaism as a superstition; Tacitus was puzzled that Jews clung to it so tenaciously. Horace thought Jews swallowed a lot of nonsense, a view shared by the rhetorician Quintilian. Dio Cassius, Plutarch, Apuleius, and Strabo all scorned the allegedly superstitious Jews. Cicero, Juvenal, Plutarch, and the skeptic Sextus Empiricus derided the Jews' prohibition against eating swinish food. Especially irrational did the Jews' refusal to fight on the Sabbath appear to the Roman thinkers, for the Jews had allegedly lost Jerusalem to Pompey because he had chosen to attack on the Sabbath when they refused to bear arms. To Dio Cassius, Strabo, and Plutarch, this seemed a stupidity born of fanaticism. Seneca, Tacitus, and Juvenal all felt the institution of the Sabbath made for sloth, but scarcely, as some aver, because they saw in the Sabbath a threat to their aristocratic rule of a slave society. Slave systems in South and North America have co-existed with the observance of the Sabbath. (Cf. N. W. Goldstein, "Cultivated Pagans and Ancient Anti-Semitism," *The Journal of Religion,* vol. 19 [1939], pp. 346-364).

11. Sherwin-White, *Racial Prejudice,* pp. 92-93.

12. Cecil Roth, "Are the Jews Unassimilable?", *Jewish Social Studies,* vol. 3 (1941), pp. 5-7, rpt. in *Personalities and Events in Jewish History* (Philadelphia, 1953).

13. S. G. F. Brandon, *Jesus and the Zealots: A Study of the Political Factor in Primitive Christianity* (Manchester, England, 1967), pp. 31-34, 48-49.

14. Solomon Katz, *The Jews in the Visigothic and Frankish Kingdoms of Spain and Gaul* (Cambridge, Mass., 1937), p. 118. Radin, *Jews Among Greeks and Romans,* p. 371. Clyde Pharr, et al., eds., *The Theodosian Code and Novels and the Sirmondian Constitutions* (Princeton, 1952), p. 467*ff.*

15. L. Rabinowitz, *Jewish Merchant Adventurers: A Study of the Radanites* (London 1948), p. 36. Irving A. Agus, *Urban Civilization in Pre-Crusade Europe,* (Leiden, 1968), 1: 12-13. *The Itinerary of Rabbi Benjamin of Tudela,* trans. A. Asher (New York, 1927), pp. 36, 37, 38, 47, 55.

16. Baron, *History of the Jews*, p. 313. Rabinowitz, *Merchant Adventurers*, p. 37.

17. Katz, *The Jews in Spain and Gaul*, p. 22.

18. Ibid., p. 21.

19. Ibid., p. 116.

20. Rabinowitz, *Merchant Adventurers*, p. 39.

21. Henri Pirenne, *Mohammed and Charlemagne*, trans. Bernard Miall (New York, 1939), p. 174.

22. Rabinowitz, *Merchant Adventurers*, pp. 9-10.

23. Katz, *The Jews in Spain and Gaul*, p. 133.

24. Cecil Roth, *The House of Nasi: The Duke of Naxos* (New York, 1948), p. 42.

25. Roger Bigelow Merriman, *Suleiman the Magnificent 1520-1566* (Cambridge, Mass., 1944), p. 178. Albert Howe Lybyer, *The Government of the Ottoman Empire in the time of Suleiman the Magnificent* (Cambridge, Mass., 1913), p. 85.

26. Cecil Roth, *The House of Nasi: Doña Gracia* (Philadelphia, 1948; rpt. New York, 1969), pp. 88-90. Also cf. Israel M. Goldman, *The Life and Times of Rabbi David Ibn Abi Zimra* (New York, 1970), p. 191.

27. Roth, *Doña Gracia, pp. 90-91*. Goldman, *Rabbi Zimra*, pp. 145-151.

28. Cited in Roth, *Doña Gracia*, pp. 96-97.

29. Marc D. Angel, *The Jews of Rhodes: The History of a Sephardic Community* (New York, 1978), pp. 41-42.

30. Roth, *Doña Gracia*, p. 112.

31. Ibid., p. 156.

32. Cecil Roth, *The Duke of Naxos*, p. 161.

33. J. P. Mahaffy, *Descartes* (Edinburgh, 1881), pp. 50-51. Also see Elizabeth S. Haldane, *Descartes: His Life and Times* (London, 1905), pp. 115-116.

34. Cecil Roth, *A Life of Menasseh ben Israel: Rabbi, Printer, and Diplomat* (Philadelphia, 1945), p. 225 ff.

35. Lucien Wolf, ed., *Menasseh ben Israel's Mission to Oliver Cromwell* (London, 1901). p. 88. E. H. Lindo, trans., *The Conciliator of R. Menasseh ben Israel: A Reconcilement of the Apparent Contradictions in Holy Scriptures* (London, 1842). Cecil Roth, *A Life of Menasseh ben Israel* (Philadelphia, 1934). Albert M. Hyamson, *A History of the Jews in England*, 2nd ed. (London, 1928), p. 147. Lewis S. Feuer, *Spinoza and the Rise of Liberalism* (Boston, 1958), pp. 6, 259-261.

36. M. Kayserling, "Isaac Aboab: The First Jewish Author in America," *Publications of the American Jewish Historical Society*, no. 5 (1897), p. 128.

37. Samuel Oppenheim, "Early History of the Jews in New York: 1654-1665," *Publications of the American Jewish Historical Society*, no. 18 (1909), p. 8.

38. R. H. M. Elwes, trans., *The Chief Works of Benedict de Spinoza*, rev. ed. (London, 1919), vol. 1, *Tractatus Theologico-Politicus*, p. 264.

39. John de Witt, *Political Maxims of the State of Holland*, trans. from the Dutch (London, 1743), pp. 44, 49.

40. Cecil Roth, *A Life of Menasseh ben Israel*, p. 231.

41. Ibid., pp. 238-244.

42. Ibid., p. 256.

43. Ibid., pp. 258-261.

44. J. H. Parry and P. M. Sherlock, *A Short History of the West Indies*, 3rd ed. (London, 1971), p. 58.

45. S. A. G. Taylor, *The Western Design: An Account of Cromwell's Expedition to the Caribbean*, 2nd ed. (London, 1969), pp. ix, x.

46. Gedalia Yogev, *Diamonds and Coral: Anglo-Dutch Jews and Eighteenth-Century Trade* (Leicester, 1978), p. 60.

47. N. Darnell Davis, "Notes on the History of Jews in Barbadoes," *Publications of the American Jewish Historical Society*, no. 18 (1909), p. 129. The Jews

contributed far beyond their proportion in numbers or wealth to the support of the dispensary for the poor. (p. 146).

48. Jacob A. P. M. Andrade, *A Record of the Jews in Jamaica from the English Conquest to the Present Time* (Kingston, Jamaica, 1941), pp. 5-14. Henry E. Kagan, "Jamaica," *The Universal Jewish Encyclopedia* (New York, 1948), 6: 35.

49. Parry and Sherlock, *West Indies*, pp. 87-88.

50. Yogev, *Diamonds and Coral*, p. 61.

51. Ibid., pp. 69, 71-72.

52. Ibid., p. 70.

53. Ibid., p. 72.

54. Cecil Roth, *The History of the Jews of Italy* (Philadelphia, 1946), p. 440. Cecil Roth, "Military Service," *Encyclopaedia Judaica* (Jerusalem, 1971), 11: 1559.

55. Roth, *Jews of Italy,* p. 446. "In every Italian city which the French Army entered, the ghetto gates were removed, hacked to pieces and burned, the shameful badges thrown away, and the symbols of freedom—Trees of Liberty—planted by the delivered Jews . . . For the first time in the history of the Italian Jewry, the commander of a victorious army appeared not as an oppressor but as a liberator of the Jewish people." (Franz Kobler, *Napoleon and the Jews* [New York, 1976], p. 18). For all of Napoleon's divagations in policy and tactical "betrayal" of Venetia to Austria, the "Cisalpine Republic," the first Napoleonic state in Europe, was "the starting point of something more long-lived than the Napoleonic Empire—the Italian *risorgimento.*" (George Macaulay Trevelyan, *Manin and the Venetian Revolution of 1848* [London, 1923], pp. 15-16, pp. 28-29).

56. Kobler, *Napoleon and the Jews*, p. 35.

57. Ibid., p. 183. Cf. Georges Lefèbvre, *Napoleon: From Tilsit to Waterloo, 1807-1815,* trans. J. E. Anderson (New York, 1969), pp. 187, 226.

58. Antonio Dominguez Ortiz, *The Golden Age of Spain, 1516-1679,* trans. James Casey (New York, 1971), p. 280.

58. Ibid., pp. 228-289.

60. Roger Bigelow Merriman, *The Rise of the Spanish Empire in the Old World and in the New* (New York, 1918), 4: 676.

61. Ibid., pp. 677-678.

62. Henry Kamen, *The Spanish Inquisition* (New York, 1965), pp. 139-140. Cf. Roger Bigelow Merriman, *The Rise of the Spanish Empire,* 1: 200-201.

63. Ortiz, *Golden Age,* p. 225.

64. Kamen, *Spanish Inquisition,* p. 102.

65. Cecil Roth, *The Spanish Inquisition* (1937; New York, 1964), p. 250.

66. Ibid., p. 88.

67. Ibid., p. 86.

68. Ortiz, *Golden Age,* p. 216. Kamen, *Spanish Inquisition,* pp. 76, 99. Cf. William H. Prescott, *History of the Reign of Philip the Second, King of Spain* (Philadelphia, 1869), 3: 435.

69. Jaime Vicena Vives, *Approaches to the History of Spain,* trans. Joan Connelly Ullman (Berkeley, 1967), p. 98.

70. Ortiz, *Golden Age,* pp. 139-140, 49-51, 31-32, 305, 332.

71. Salvador de Madariaga, *The Fall of the Spanish American Empire* (London, 1947), p. 245 ff.

72. C. H. Haring, *The Spanish Empire in America* (New York, 1947; rpt. 1963), p. 5.

73. Ibid., p. 15.

74. Ibid., p. 258.

75. Ibid., p. 70. "The Crown . . . grown accustomed to employing absolutist formulae in the government of the Indies . . . the important institutions there, judicial, ecclesiastical, economic and local, became converted into one vast centralized civil service, designed to endorse arbitrary legislation." (J. H. Parry, *The Spanish Theory of Empire in the Sixteenth Century* [Cambridge, 1940], p. 72). The political philosopher Francisco de Vitoria was an isolated voice in his call for an empire based on commerce rather than conquest. (Parry, *The Spanish Theory of Empire*, p. 24).

76. Haring, *Spanish Empire*, p. 31.

77. Ibid., p. 31.

78. Ibid., p. 187.

79. Ibid., p. 189-190.

80. Seymour B. Liebman, *The Inquisitors and the Jews in the New World* (Coral Gables, 1974), pp. 19-20.

81. Judith Laikin Elkin, *Jews of the Latin American Republics* (Chapel Hill, 1980), pp. 11-12. Martin A. Cohen, "Peru: Colonial Period," *Encyclopaedia Judaica* (Jerusalem, 1971). 13: 322. Liebman, *The Inquisitors*, p. 191.

82. Elkin, *Latin American Republics*, pp. 8, 11.

83. Ibid., p. 215.

84. Haring, *Spanish Empire*, pp. 41, 257.

85. Ibid., pp. 66, 203, 205.

86. Ibid., p. 294.

87. Ibid., p. 241.

88. Ibid., p. 242.

89. Ibid., p. 251.

90. J. A. Hobson, *The War in South Africa: Its Causes and Effects* (London, 1900), p. 11. James Bryce, *Impressions of South Africa*, 3rd ed. (1897; New York, 1900), p. 319. M. J. Bonn, *Wandering Scholar* (New York, 1948), p. 119.

91. Hobson, *The War in South Africa*, pp. 11-13. J. A. Hobson, *Confessions of an Economic Heretic* (London, 1938), pp. 25-26, 38-42. H. N. Brailsford, *The Life-Work of J. A. Hobson* (London, 1948), pp. 6-8. H. M. Hyndman, the Marxist chief of the Social Democratic Federation, similarly denounced the South African War as "the Jews' war . . . an abominable war on behalf of the German-Jew mineowners and other international interlopers." He gave such offence by his assault on "'the Jewish International'" that a motion of censure was introduced at a party conference in August, 1900. (Chushichi Tsuzuki, *H. M. Hyndman and British Socialism* [London, 1961], p. 128).

92. Gustav Saron and Louis Hotz, eds., *The Jews in South Africa: A History* (Cape Town, 1955), p. 357. Cecil Headlam, "The Failure of Confederation, 1871-1881," *The Cambridge History of the British Empire* (Cambridge, 1936), 8: 450.

93. Sarah Gertrude Millin, *Cecil Rhodes* (New York, 1933), p. 17.

94. Saron and Hotz, eds., *The Jews in South Africa*, p. 352.

95. Ibid., p. 356.

96. Ibid., pp. 147, 335, 353, 354.

97. Ibid., pp. 354, 341.

98. Ibid., p. 145.

99. Ibid., pp. 356, 362, 359.

100. Ibid., pp. 367, 431, 343.

101. According to Sarah Gertrude Millin, of the score of men who "made extremely large fortunes" in Kimberley, there were more than half of them Jews." (*Cecil Rhodes* [New York, 1932], p. 21).

102. Saron and Hotz, *The Jews in South Africa*, pp. 192-195.

103. Stanley Jackson, *The Great Barnato* (London, 1970), p. 40. Millin, *Cecil Rhodes*, pp. 36-37.

104. Jackson, *Barnato,* pp. 72, 25, 18, 10, 19, 43.

105. Ibid., pp. 44, 35, 57, 223.

106. Ibid., pp. 210-212.

107. Ibid., p. 38.

108. Sir David Harris, *Pioneer, Soldier and Politician, Summarised Memoirs of Colonel Sir David Harris* (London, 1931), pp. 96, 100 ff., 193 ff. Jackson, *Barnato,* p. 224.

109. George Seymour Fort, *Alfred Beit: A Study of the Man and His Work* (London, 1932), p. 22. Also Lionel Phillips, *Some Reminiscences* (London, 1924), pp. 26-27, 34-35, 71, 141-144, 164-165, 207-209. Maryna Fraser and Alan Jeeves, eds., *All That Glittered: Selected Correspondence of Lionel Phillips, 1890-1924* (Cape Town, 1977), p. 14.

110. Fort, *Alfred Beit,* p. 14.

111. Ibid., p. 163.

112. Ibid., p. 54.

113. Ibid., p. 90.

114. Ibid., p. 92.

115. Ibid., p. 58.

116. Fraser and Jeeves, eds., *All That Glittered,* Foreword.

117. Eric Rosenthal, *Gold! Gold! Gold! The Johannesburg Gold Rush* (New York, 1970), p. 63.

118. Ibid., p. 79.

119. Ibid., p. 354.

120. Ibid., pp. 302-303. Cf. William M. Gibson, "Mark Twain and Howells: Anti-Imperialists," *The New England Quarterly,* vol. 20 (1947), p. 436, 440 ff. Mark Twain, *Following the Equator: A Journey Around the World* (Hartford, 1898), p. 654 ff., p. 168. As his later pessimist mood deepened, Mark Twain came to share the anti-imperialist ethos dominant among American writers.

121. Rosenthal, *Gold!,* p. 117.

122. Ibid., p. 115.

123. Ibid., p. 29.

124. Theodor Gregory, *Ernest Oppenheimer and the Economic Development of Southern Africa* (Cape Town, 1962), p. 15.

125. The South African miners' strike in 1922 was inspired by an amalgam of Marxism, anti-Semitism, and the determination to maintain the color bar. The workers distributed a satirical pamphlet that featured a song "Haggenheimer the Jew," set to a musical comedy tune. Directed against the anti-hero, the Jewish capitalist, it was a composite portrait of the "Randlords" who rose from the diggings to knighthoods and then became celebrated patrons of the arts—Beit, Barnato, Joel, Sir Lionel Phillips, Sir Julius Wernher, Sir Joseph Robinson and, of more recent vintage, Sir Ernest Oppenheimer. (Cf. Anthony Hocking, *Oppenheimer and Son,* [New York, 1973], pp. 99-101).

126. W. P. R., "Sir Julius Vogel," *The Dictionary of National Biography* (Oxford, 1921-1922), Supplement, 22:1374.

127. For a glimpse of the handful of Jews in Melbourne in 1848, see Cecil Roth, ed., *Anglo-Jewish Letters 1158-1917* (London, 1938), pp. 297-300.

128. Raewyn Dalziel, *Sir Julius Vogel* (Wellington, 1968), p. 23.

129. Keith Sinclair, *A History of New Zealand* (Harmondsworth, 1959), pp. 150-151.

130. Ibid., pp. 154, 210.

131. R. M. Burdon, *The Life and Times of Sir Julius Vogel* (Christchurch, 1948), pp. 10, 15, 9, 210, 227.

132. Ibid., p. 183.

133. Ibid., p. 113.

134. Ibid, p. 143.

135. Roth, *The Sassoon Dynasty,* p. 207.

136. Siegfried Sassoon, *Siegfried's Journey (1916-1920)* (New York, 1944), pp. 180, 223, 202. D. Felicitas Corrigan, *Siegfried Sassoon: Poet's Pilgrimmage* (London, 1973), pp. 19, 39. Michael Thorpe, *Siegfried Sassoon: A Critical Study* (London, 1963), p. 163.

137. Chaim Bermant, *The Cousinhood: The Anglo-Jewish Gentry* (London, 1971), pp. 287, 291, 294, 307, 364.

138. P. F. Clarke, *Lancashire and the New Liberalism* (Cambridge, 1971), p. 259. Randolph S. Churchill, *Winston S. Churchill, Vol. II. 1901-1914. Young Statesman* (Boston, 1967), pp. 80-84. Also see Martin Gilbert, *Winston S. Churchill, Vol. V. 1922-1939, The Prophet of Truth* (Boston, 1977), pp. 1069-1072. Martin Gilbert, *Churchill's Political Philosophy* (Oxford, 1981), pp. 14-15, 37-39.

139. George Schweitzer, *Emin Pasha: His Life and Work,* 2 vols., Introduction by R. W. Felkin (1898; rpt. New York, 1969), 1: v.

140. Schweitzer, *Emin Pasha,* 1:21-22.

141. Ibid., p. 29, 39. G. Schweinfurth, et al., *Emin Pasha in Central Africa, Being a Collection of His Letters and Journals,* trans., Mrs. R. W. Felkin (London, 1888), p. xii.

142. Schweitzer, *Emin Pasha,* 1:115-116. A. J. A. Symons, *H. M. Stanley* (New York, 1933), p. 82.

143. Schweinfurth, *Emin Pasha in Central Africa,* p. xvi.

144. Schweitzer, *Emin Pasha,* 1:117-118, 256.

145. Schweinfurth, *Emin Pasha in Central Africa,* p. 437.

146. Symons, *H. M. Stanley,* pp. 94-95, 100.

147. "I should be independent like the Rajah of Sarawak, and that it should be possible for me to govern my country in the same way as Rajah Brooke does." (Schweitzer, *Emin Pasha,* 1:xxxii. Iain R. Smith, *The Emin Pasha Relief Expedition, 1886-1890* [Oxford, 1972], p. 145).

148. Schweinfurth, *Emin Pasha in Central Africa,* p. 509.

149. Schweitzer, *Emin Pasha,* 2:14. Smith, *Relief Expedition,* p. 227.

150. Henry M. Stanley, *In Darkest Africa, or the Quest, Rescue and Retreat of Emin, Governor of Equatoria* (New York, 1890), 2:241. Stanley's expedition for the relief of Emin Pasha inspired posters for meat products as well as a children's board game in England. (John MacKenzie, *Propaganda and Empire: The Manipulation of British Public Opinion, 1880-1960* [Manchester, 1984], p. 28, 26).

151. Smith, *Relief Expedition,* p. 243.

152. Schweitzer, *Emin Pasha,* 2: 293-297.

153. Ibid., 2: 301, 82, 130, 39. A. J. Mounteney-Jephson, *Emin Pasha and the Rebellion at the Equator: A Story of Nine Months' Experience in the Last of the Soudan Provinces,* 3rd ed. (1980; rpt. New York, 1969), pp. 61, 204-205, 477. Smith, *Relief Expedition,* pp. 151, 289.

154. Schweitzer, 2: 307.

155. Mounteney-Jephson, *The Rebellion at the Equator,* p. 32.

156. Schweitzer, *Emin Pasha,* 2: 310-311.

157. Ibid., p. 308.

158. Schweinfurth, *Emin Pasha in Central Africa,* p. xxiii. Emin "had arrived penniless" in Equatoria, "and he was never to grow rich. His generosity, his inability to hold on to money became a joke in the city." He had a "natural gentleness and kindness" and gaiety. "He did his own housework and shopped in the market-

place." (Cf. Olivia Manning, *The Remarkable Expedition: The Story of Stanley's Rescue of Emin Pasha from Equatorial Africa* [London, 1947], p. 25).

159. Schweitzer, *Emin Pasha*, 2: 39, 130.

160. Ibid., p. 38.

161. Ibid., 1: 3.

162. Ibid., pp. 132, 137.

163. Stanhope White, *Lost Empire on the Nile: H. M. Stanley, Emin Pasha, and the Imperialists* (London, 1969), p. 142.

164. Schweitzer, *Emin Pasha*, 1: 5.

165. Ibid., p. 5.

166. Mounteney-Jephson, *The Rebellion at the Equator*, p. 476.

167. Smith, *Relief Expedition*, p. 34.

168. Schweitzer, *Emin Pasha*, 2: 29-31.

169. Ibid., pp. 132, 137.

170. Stanley, in his public lectures in England, is said to have raised "curious suspicions" that Emin was a Jew, with the given name Isaak recorded in the register of the Jewish congregation. See Manning, *The Remarkable Expedition*, pp. 256-257 and Smith, *Relief Expedition*, p. 13. Mr. Smith in his fine work states that Emin's family "may have been Jewish in origin." There can really be little doubt of it. His cousin, Rabbi Samuel Wolfenstein, emigrated from Breslau to America where his son, Dr. Leo Wolfenstein of Cleveland, Ohio, and his grandchildren, the psychologist Martha Wolfenstein, the mathematician Samuel Wolfenstein, and the physicist, Lincoln Wolfenstein, heard the story of their kinsman, Eduard Schnitzer. Also cf. Frederick T. Haneman, "Emin Pasha," *The Jewish Encyclopedia* (New York, 1903), 5: 152-153.

171. Harry Friedenwald, "The Medical Pioneers in the East Indies," *The Jews and Medicine: Essays* (Baltimore, 1944), 2: 439.

172. "Sir Matthew Nathan," *The Dictionary of Scientific Biography, 1931-1940* (London, 1949), pp. 645-646.

173. R. E. Wraith, *Guggisberg* (London, 1967), p. 13.

174. Ibid., p. 100.

175. Ibid., pp. 47-48.

176. Ibid., p. 116.

177. Ibid., pp. 79, 114-115.

178. Ibid., pp. 108-109.

179. Ibid., pp. 141-142.

180. Ibid., pp. 148, 222.

181. Ibid., p. 158.

182. Ibid., p. 159.

183. Ibid., pp. 292, 73, 50.

184. "Elinor Glyn's name [wrote the producer Samuel Goldwyn] is synonymous with the discovery of sex appeal for the cinema." (Antony Glyn, *Elinor Glyn: A Biography* [New York, 1955], p. 277).

185. Wraith, *Guggisberg*, p. 23.

186. Ibid., p. 250.

187. Ibid., p. 251.

188. Ibid., p. 5.

189. Ibid., p. 271.

190. Cited in Geoffrey Serle, *John Monash: A Biography* (Melbourne, 1982), p. 377.

191. Viscount Montgomery of Alamein, *A History of Warfare* (New York, 1983), p. 484.

192. Serle, *John Monash*, p. 386.

193. Serle, *John Monash,* p. 380. "Sir John Monash," *Encyclopaedia Judaica* (Jerusalem, 1971), 12: 237-238.

194. "Caught Amid Extremes: Sir Roy Welensky," *The New York Times,* March 24, 1959, p. 16.

195. "Sir Roy Welensky," *Encyclopaedia Judaica* (Jerusalem, 1971), 16: 442.

196. Lord Blake, "Foreword," in J. R. T. Wood, *The Welensky Papers: A History of the Federation of Rhodesia and Nyassaland* (Durban, 1983), p. 23.

197. Ibid., p. 23.

198. Clegg, *Race and Politics,* p. 99.

199. Ibid., p. 125.

200. *The New York Times,* March 24, 1959, p. 16.

201. Lord Blake, "Foreword," p. 24.

202. Lord Alport, *The Sudden Assignment* (London, 1965), p. 223.

203. Ibid., p. 230.

204. R. D. Pearce, *The Turning Point in Africa: British Colonial Policy 1938-48* (London, 1982), pp. 97-98, 94, 195, 201, 181-182, 207.

205. Bermant, *The Cousinhood,* p. 192. A British officer and friend for seven years of the later infamous Idi Amin writes of "the Governor, Andrew Cohen: Politically, he was an intellectual left-winger, shy to the point of often being withdrawn, and always hideously uncomfortable in the sartorial regalia of his office . . . He was a visionary, who dedicated his work to a united and free Uganda." (Iain Grahame, *Amin and Uganda: A Personal Memoir* [London, 1980], p. 53).

206. Bermant, *The Cousinhood,* p. 194.

207. Sir Andrew Cohen, *British Policy in Changing Africa* (London, 1959), p. 76.

208. Count Harry Kessler, *Walther Rathenau: His Life and Work,* trans. W. D. Robson-Scott and Lawrence Hyde (New York, 1930), pp. 130-131.

209. L. H. Gann and Peter Duignan, *The Rulers of German Africa 1884-1914* (Stanford, 1917), p. 53.

210. Joachim O. Ronall, "Dernburg," *Encyclopaedia Judaica* (Jerusalem, 1971), 5: 1554.

211. Gann and Duignan, *Rulers of German Africa,* p. 182-184, 228.

212. Ibid., pp. 123-124.

213. Ibid., pp. 178, 180-182.

214. Ibid., pp. 185-186.

215. Ibid., p. 183.

216. C. Abramsky, *War, Revolution and the Jewish Dilemma* (London, 1975), p. 11.

217. Isaiah Friedman, *Germany, Turkey, and Zionism 1897-1918* (Oxford, 1977), p. 417.

218. Ibid., p. 234.

219. Stephen M. Poppel, *Zionism in Germany: The Shaping of a Jewish Identity* (Philadelphia, 1977), p. 79.

220. Friedman, *Germany, Turkey, and Zionism,* pp. 352-353.

221. Ibid., p. 368.

222. Ibid., p. 368.

223. Ibid., pp. 370-371.

224. Jehuda Reinharz, *Fatherland or Promised Land: The Dilemma of the German Jew, 1893-1914* (Ann Arbor, 1975), p. 223.

225. Ibid., p. 233. Hans Morgenthau, *The Tragedy of German-Jewish Liberalism,* Leo Baeck Memorial Lecture, no. 4 (New York, 1961), p. 7.

226. Bernard Wasserstein, *Britain and the Jews of Europe, 1939-1945* (Oxford, 1979), p. 14. Also see Barnet Litvinoff, ed., *The Letters and Papers of Chaim Weizmann* (New Brunswick, 1979), vol. 18-Series A, pp. 270-271, 279, 321. N. A. Rose, *The Gentle Zionists: A Study in Anglo-Zionist Diplomacy* (London, 1979), pp. 4-5, 224.

227. Isaiah Berlin, *Personal Impressions,* ed. Henry Hardy (London, 1980), p. 52.

228. Wasserstein, *Britain and the Jews of Europe,* p. 56.

229. Ibid., p. 57.

230. Ibid., p. 14. Rose, *The Gentle Zionists,* p. 128.

231. Ibid., p. 284.

232. Ibid., p. 275.

233. Ibid., pp. 278-279. It is noteworthy that although the Jews in the Soviet Union were regarded as a nationality, they were not allowed by Stalin or his successor to be constituted into Jewish divisions or regiments. (See Dov Levin, "Vulf Vilensky: A Soviet War Hero," *Soviet Jewish Affairs,* vol. 14 [1984], p. 25, 28-29). When Stalin met with the Polish representatives in December 1941, to plan the reconstruction of the Polish Army from the ranks of the Polish prisoners and exiles, he wanted no Jews in the new force. As the record of the meeting discloses, Stalin said: "The Jews are miserable soldiers . . . yes, the Jews are bad soldiers," while Polish generals Sikorski and Anders hastened to agree. (Wladyslaw Anders, *Mémoires 1939-1946,* H. J. Rzewuska, trans., [Paris, 1948], pp. 132-133).

235. Chaim Weizmann to Lady Violet Bonham-Carter, 13 March 1949 in Barnet Litvinoff, ed., *The Letters and Papers of Chaim Weizmann* (Jerusalem, 1980), vol. 23-Series A, p. 263. Also see Norman Rose, *Lewis Namier and Zionism* (Oxford, 1980), p. 123.

236. Wasserstein, *Britain and the Jews of Europe,* p. 31.

237. Martin Gilbert, *Winston S. Churchill* (London, 1976), 5: 681, 998.

238. Ibid., p. 281.

239. Wasserstein, *Britain and the Jews of Europe,* pp. 281-282.

240. Ibid., p. 353.

241. Mark DeWolfe Howe, *Holmes-Pollock Letters, The Correspondence of Mr. Justice Holmes and Sir Frederick Pollock, 1874-1932* (Cambridge, Mass., 1941) 2: 192.

242. Wasserstein, *Britain and the Jews of Europe,* pp. 354-355. As to the American failure to aid the beleaguered and death-consigned Jews, see David S. Wyman, *The Abandonment of the Jews: America and the Holocaust 1941-1945* (New York, 1984), pp. 100, 307, 331 ff. Henry L. Feingold, *The Politics of Rescue: The Roosevelt Administration and the Holocaust, 1938-1945* (Rutgers, 1970), p. 301.

Chapter IV - The Imperialist Spirit and the Anti-Imperial Mind

1. Eric Halladay, "Henry Morton Stanley: The Opening Up of the Congo Basin" in Robert I. Rotberg, ed., *Africa and Its Explorers: Motives, Methods and Impact* (Cambridge, 1970), p. 247 ff.

2. Cf. Robin Maugham, *The Slaves of Timbuktu* (New York, 1961), p. 217.

3. In the third century "large contingents of Negro slaves" were employed in what is now Iraq; a major slave revolt took place. S. D. Goitein, *Jews and Arabs, Their Contacts Through the Ages,* 3rd rev. ed. (New York, 1974), pp. 100-102.

4. Fawn M. Brodie, *The Devil Drives: A Life of Sir Richard Burton* (New York, 1967), pp. 286, 145. The enslavement of African blacks by Moslem traders was practiced from the Middle Ages on. Cf. Melvin M. Knight, "Medieval Slavery," *Encyclopedia of the Social Sciences,* vol. 14 (New York, 1934), p. 79. "About one out of ten" survived the eunuchoid operation performed prior to embarking on the trans-Sahara caravan. (Cf. George Schweitzer, *Emin Pasha: His Life and Work* [Westminster, 1898; rpt. New York, 1969], 1: 113, 115, 256).

5. The observations of Gustav Nachtigal, a German physician who traveled through the African interior between 1869 and 1874 gave much evidence for the widespread and deep-rooted existence of slavery in many parts of Africa as well as its especial use by Moslem traders. The estate of Lamino, of the court of Bornu in 1871, had several thousand slaves, while ordinary people might normally own one or two slaves. Even "a penurious scholar might hope to own a handful of slaves." Slavery in each country Nachtigal visited was a "highly important institution," and in some area slaves constituted a majority of the population. Moslem law gave to slave-raiding among non-Moslems some characteristics of a religious war. According to Allen G. B. Fisher and Humphrey J. Fisher, to explain why scholars have failed to study these workings of an "independent African" slave trade while they have concentrated on the Atlantic trade would take one into "the realms of psychology." (Allen G. B. Fisher and Humphrey J. Fisher, *Slavery and Muslim Society in Africa* [London, 1970], pp. 2, 3, 11, 12, 17).

6. Bernard Lewis, *Race and Color in Islam* (New York, 1971), p. 103.

7. The "predatory revolution," it has been suggested, began when food-gathering prehistoric men made the transition to becoming the hunters of mammalian herds. From this standpoint, predatory imperialism was at first the behavior of men toward animal herds; the next stage would have been its extension to human herds. (Cf. Lewis R. Binford and Sally R. Binford, "The Predatory Revolution: A Consideration of the Evidence for a New Subsistence Level," *American Anthropologist,* vol. 68 [1966], pp. 509-510). The domestication of animals and the pastoral economy, however, approximate the imperialist model much more closely, but are hardly describable as composed of predators related to their prey.

8. Gunnar Myrdal, *Economic Theory and Under-Developed Regions* (London, 1957), p. 19 ff. Sometimes interventions are possible that, by making for spiraling upward movements, break the "vicious circle" in which a social system may find itself.

9. Alfred J. Lotka, *Elements of Mathematical Biology* (New York, 1924), pp. 281-293.

10. Philip Mayer, *Townsmen or Tribesmen: Conservatism and the Process of Urbanization in a South African City,* 2nd ed. (New York, 1971), pp. 2-4. Leonard Plotnicov, *Strangers to the City: Urban Man in Jos, Nigeria* (Pittsburgh, 1967). Monica Wilson and Archie Mafeje, *Langa: A Study of Social Groups in an African Township* (New York, 1963), pp. 173-181. Peter C. W. Gutkind, ed., *The Passing of Tribal Man in Africa* (Leiden, 1970), pp. 3-5.

11. Cockcroft, et al., *Dependence and Underdevelopment,* p. 310.

12. Cf. Thomas Hodgkin, "Some African and Third World Theories of Imperialism," in Roger Owen and Bob Sutcliffe, eds., *Studies in the Theory of Imperialism* (London, 1972), pp. 109-113.

13. S. Bourguin, "Foreword," in John Selby, *Shaka's Heirs* (London, 1971), p. 7. Selby, *Shaka's Heirs,* pp. 47, 64, 77. The desolation which Shaka's "revolution" spread brought many communities to cannibalism. "Between one and two million people perished in the revolution." A contemproary African admirer nonetheless writes: "Behind the cannibal he saw a human being whose potential could be developed by subjecting him to the right discipline." (Jordan K. Ngubane, "Shaka's

Social, Political and Military Ideas," in Donald Burness, *Shaka, King of the Zulus, in African Literature* [Washington, D.C., 1976] pp. 147, 152, 160).

14. D. H. Reader, *Zulu Tribe in Transition: The Makharya of Southern Natal* (Manchester, 1966), pp. 5, 10.

15. C. T. Bennis, *The Warrior People: Zulu Origins, Customs, and Witchcraft* (London, 1975), p. 73. Cited from George M'Call Theal, *South Africa* (New York, 1902), p. 287.

16. The literature on the attractions of "African socialism" has a long lineage. Cf. Dudley Kidd, *Kafir Socialism and the Dawn of Individualism* (1908: rpt. New York: Negro Universities Press, 1969). "Socialistic ideals affect almost every conception of the Kafirs." (p. vi.) "[T]he most extraordinarily well-developed spirit of altruism and *camaraderie* . . . is very rarely equalled amongst Western nations." (p. xi).

17. Clegg, *Race and Politics*, pp. 18, 21, 31.

18. P. T. Bauer, *Dissent on Development, Studies and Debates in Developmental Economics* (Cambridge, Mass., 1972), p. 175 ff. Cf. Edward W. Said, *Orientalism* (New York, 1978), pp. 322, 327, 317.

19. P. T. Bauer, "Western Guilt and Third World Poverty," in *Equality, The Third World, and Economic Delusions* (Cambridge, Mass., 1981), p. 84. The World Council of Churches gave grants through the 1970s to such groups committed to terrorism and violence as Frelimo in Mozambique and the MPLA in Angola, both advocates of Marxist dictatorships, as well as the Patriotic Front in Rhodesia. (*The Toronto Sun*, June 21, 1979). Bauer, *Dissent on Development*, p. 146 ff., p. 181.

20. Cited in Bauer, "Western Guilt," p. 6.

21. Catherine Ann Cline, *E. D. Morel 1873-1924: The Strategies of Protest* (Belfast, 1980), p. 46.

22. Bernard Semmel, *Democracy versus Empire: The Jamaican Riots of 1865 and the Governor Eyre Controversy* (New York, 1969), p. 74.

23. Edmund D. Morel, *King Leopold's Rule in Africa* (London, 1904; rpt. Westport, 1970), p. xii.

24. Edmund D. Morel, *History of the Congo Reform Movement*, eds. William Roger Louis and Jean Stengers (Oxford, 1968), p. 243.

25. Edmund D. Morel, *Great Britain and the Congo: The Pillage of the Congo Basin* (1909; rpt. New York, 1969), p. 121.

26. E. D. Morel, *Red Rubber*, introduction by Sir Harry H. Johnston (1906; rpt. New York, 1969), pp. xi, xiii, xiv, xvii. Sir Harry Johnston, *The History of a Slave* (London, 1889). "Enslavement by conquest had been a well-establshed institution in African societies for a very long time. When the captured slave was not integrated by adoption . . . he remained at the mercy of the victor and could be killed, sometimes eaten . . . or else he could be sold. The last possibility depended on the existence of an outside market." (J. Suret-Canale and Boubacar Berry, "The Western Atlantic Coast to 1800," in J. F. A. Ajayi and Michael Crowder, eds., *History of West Africa*, 2nd ed.[New York, 1976], 1: 460.

27. E. D. Morel, *The Black Man's Burden* (Manchester, 1920), pp. xi, 4-5.

28. Brian Inglis, *Roger Casement* (London, 1973), pp. 63-65, 296, 383-385.

29. William Roger Louis in Morel, *History of the Congo Reform Movement*, p. 215.

30. Ibid., pp. 213-215, 217-218.

31. Ibid., p. 167.

32. Susanne Howe, *Novels of Empire* (New York, 1949), pp. 87, 94.

33. H. N. Brailsford, *The Life-Work of J. A. Hobson* (Oxford, 1948), pp. 6-8.

34. V. G. Kiernan, *Marxism and Imperialism* (London, 1974), pp. 234-235.

35. Karl Marx, *Notes on Indian History (664-1858)* (Moscow, n.d.), p. 148.

Cited in Kiernan, *Marxism and Imperialism,* p. 224. Marx and Engels, *Basic Writings on Politics and Philosophy,* ed. Lewis S. Feuer (New York, 1959), pp. 450-451.

36. V. I. Lenin, *The National-Liberation Movement in the East,* trans. M. Levin (Moscow, 1957), pp. 269, 297, 227. J. P. Nettl, *Rosa Luxemburg* (London, 1966), 2: 579, 592-595.

37. Nettl, *Rosa Luxemburg,* abridged ed. (London, 1969), p. 517.

38. D. K. Fieldhouse, "Imperialism: An Historiographical Revision," *The Economic History Review,* 2nd series, vol. 14 (1961), pp. 207-208.

39. Ibid., pp. 207-209. With respect to French imperialism, Melvin M. Knight had long since noted: "The French colonies as a whole have imported more than they exported since 1900—in their trade with other countries, France included." *(Morocco as a French Economic Venture, a Study of Open Door Imperialism* [New York, 1937], p. 189). According to the authoritative analysis of Harry D. White, during the period from 1880 to 1913 "French Colonial ventures necessitated a net overflow of money for Colonial Administration, public works and for military expenditures." As far as foreign investment was concerned, the percentage return to the French was less than to the British. The largest part of it was in bonds which dropped in return from 5 percent in 1880-1886 to less than 4 percent twelve years later, then recovering. During the period from 1880 to 1913, France invested abroad annually sums varying from one hundred to two thousand million francs. One billion francs, for instance, went to China, but even China, given its undeveloped state, bought less than 200 million francs of French goods. The annual capital export as a whole was about equal to the total revenue receipts, which means that French capitalist enterprise was extracting no "surplus value" from its foreign investment, although a gain was secured through cheaper prices paid by the French consumers for such commodities as rubber and coffee, drawn from colonial countries. One-fourth of France's foreign holdings were Russian; these became worthless with the Bolshevik revolution. Lastly, the industrial stagnation in France and its halting technological advances were probably due to the fact that surplus capital was directed abroad rather than to home investment. (Harry D. White, *The French International Accounts 1880-1913* [Cambridge, Mass., 1933], pp. 81, 95, 110, 130, 145, 151, 289, 296-298). As far as Indo-China (including what is now called Vietnam) was concerned, France evidently did not reap an economic advantage.The chief student of their economic interrelations before World War II concluded that though "as a result of French activity the average standard of living of the Indo-Chinese has risen in fifty years," the value of colonization for France must not be measured in purely financial terms. (Charles Robequain, *The Economic Development of French Indo-China,* trans. Isabel A. Ward [New York, 1944], pp. 344, 348).

40. Fieldhouse, "Imperialism," pp. 208, 209.

41. Claude G. Bowers, *Beveridge and the Progressive Era* (Boston, 1932), pp. 121-122, 134, 250 ff. John Braeman, *Albert J. Beveridge: American Nationalist* (Chicago, 1971), pp. 67, 113-115.

42. Julius W. Pratt, *America's Colonial Experiment* (New York, 1951), pp. 200-202.

43. O. Mannoni, *Prospero and Caliban: The Psychology of Colonization,* trans. Pamela Powesland, 2nd ed. (New York, 1964), pp. 103-104. Philip Mason, *Prospero's Magic: Some Thoughts on Class and Race* (London, 1922). The "Prospero Complex," according to another author, is still shown by the resentment white people allegedly feel that the African Negroes have not been more thankful for the whites' decolonization. (Christine Bolt, *Victorian Attitudes to Race* [London, 1971], p. 222). Also see Octave Mannoni, "Psychoanalysis and the Decolonization of Mankind," in Jonathan Miller, ed., *Freud: The Man, His World, His Influence* (London, 1972), pp. 86-95. Another author, Thomas J. O'Donnell, writes: "Though little known, the

best book on the subtleties of colonialism and imperialism is Dominique O. Mannoni's *Prospero and Caliban."* (Stephen E. Tabachnick, ed., *The T. E. Lawrence Puzzle* [Athens, Georgia, 1984], p. 95). Also see Philip Mason, *Patterns of Dominance* (London, 1970), pp. 12, 19, 88-89. Mannoni's book, under its original title *Psychologie de la Colonisation* has been characterized as "the most original and widely discussed analysis" of the supposed political immaturity of the colonial peoples. It was evidently written, according to Paul Sorum, "in collaboration with France's leading psychoanalytic theorist, Jacques Lacan." (Paul Clay Sorum, *Intellectuals and Decolonization in France* [Chapel Hill, 1977] p. 80). Mannoni wrote in 1966 that he "would still say essentially the same things, but in a very different way." (O. Mannoni, "The Decolonization of Myself," *Race,* vol. 7 [1966], p. 327).

44. Miguel Cervantes in "Celoso extremeno," *Novelas ejemplares,* cited in C. R. Boxer, *Race Relations in the Portuguese Colonial Empire: 1415-1825* (Oxford, 1963), p. 86.

45. The theory of the "Prospero Complex" is also held by Philip Mason, *Prospero's Magic: Some Thoughts on Class and Race* (London, 1962), p. 87. The "Prospero Complex" was, he writes, "strong, until recently among those who, like myself, crossed the seas to be leaders in colonial countries, where we could resort to magic. By the colonial magic, I mean the bluff which for about a century made it possible for a handful of people from the competitive cultures to rule far greater numbers from the static cultures." The British, however, he felt, "usually produced a better kind of Prospero for the colonies than the French system." However, on his premises, since the British were far more sexually repressed they should have exhibited more sublimational aggressive economic exploitation.

46. Mannoni, *Prospero and Caliban,* p. 98.

47. Ibid., p. 199.

48. Helene Deutsch, "Lord Jim and Depression", *Neuroses and Character Types: Clinical Psychoanalytic Studies* (New York, 1965), p. 356.

49. Mannoni, *Prospero and Caliban,* pp. 104-105. Mannoni's book is described as "this Freudian account of the motive and product of imperialism." (Thornton, *Doctrines of Imperialism,* p. 196). According to a neo-Leftist writer, Lord Jim has the psychology of a "Peace Corps volunteer," while *Heart of Darkness* is "about the decay of European civilization." (Cf. Jonah Raskin, *The Mythology of Imperialism* [New York, 1971], pp. 151, 164). Rather, though, *Heart of Darkness* is Conrad's portrayal of what happens when a European allows himself to regress to the African tribal ways of cannibalism and cruelty; moral depravity comes when the vocation for civilization is abandoned. Leftist writers, defending the tribal ethic, declare that primitive cannibalism recognized the concrete humanity of the subject. Small comfort to the subject who was going to be turned into an object of consumption, i.e., alienated and eaten. Conrad himself defended the British Empire as devoted to the idea of liberty, "which can only be found under the English flag all over the world." (Cf. Frances B. Singh, "The Colonialistic Bias of *Heart of Darkness,"* Conradiana, vol. 10 [1978], no. 1, pp. 46, 51).

50. The most thorough study of Conrad's personality that has been done shows convincingly how little his character had in common with the personalities of the outstanding Western imperialists. Conrad's major protagonists, like himself, were always engaged in "self-injuring behavior," even as he "courted these very calamities which he ostensibly dreaded." Such characters as Lord Jim, Heyst, and Tom Lingard, when faced by an external threat of annihilation, "display a posture of passivity and a stance of inertia which strongly suggest some secret complicity with their supposed enemies." (Cf. Bernard C. Meyer, *Joseph Conrad: A Psychoanalytic Biography* [Princeton, 1967], p. 334). This dominant strain of masochist self-destruction from which Conrad sought an escape in a "therapy of action"—his flight to the sea to

escape what he called "the intolerable reality of things," "my own obscure Odyssey"—could hardly describe a Rhodes, Barnato, or Julius Vogel; they were not seekers of obscurity in the sea. (Meyer, *A Psychoanalytic Biography,* pp. 33-34, 211). Nor in their relations with women were they characterized by the Conradian pattern of "a weak and passive man . . . pierced by the shafts of an all-powerful androgynous woman." (Ibid., p. 47).

51. Jerry Allen, *The Sea Years of Joseph Conrad* (New York, 1964), pp. 145-147, 120 ff.

52. Ibid., p. 147. A variant account by Norman Sherry notes, nonetheless, that "Williams did not spend years attempting to run away from his past as Jim did." (Norman Sherry, *Conrad's Eastern World* [Cambridge, 1966], p. 80).

53. Allen, *The Sea Years of Joseph Conrad,* p. 228.

54. Ibid., p. 196.

55. Joseph Conrad, *The Rescue* (New York, 1920), p. 3. Allen, *The Sea Years of Joseph Conrad,* p. 200.

56. Robert Payne, *The White Rajahs of Sarawak* (New York, 1960), p. 5.

57. Steven Runciman, *The White Rajahs: A History of Sarawak from 1841 to 1946* (Cambridge, 1960), p. 50.

58. Robert Pringle, *Rajahs and Rebels: the Ibans of Sarawak Under Brooke Rule, 1841-1941* (Ithaca, 1970), p. 2.

59. Payne, *The White Rajahs,* p. 20.

60. Ibid., p. 25.

61. Runciman, *A History of Sarawak,* p. 57.

62. Ibid., p. 58. Payne, *The White Rajahs,* p. 98.

63. Runciman, *A History of Sarawak,* p. 68. Payne, *The White Rajahs,* pp. 55-56.

64. Alfred Russel Wallace, *My Life: A Record of Events and Opinions* (New York, 1905), 1: 345-346. James Marchant, *Alfred Russel Wallace: Letters and Reminiscences* (New York, 1916), pp. 48-49. Alfred Russel Wallace, *The Malay Archipelago* (1869; rpt. London, 1890), pp. 69-73. Norman Sherry, *Conrad's Eastern World,* pp. 141-147. Florence Clemens, "Conrad's Favorite Bedside Book," *The South Atlantic Quarterly,* vol. 33 (1939), pp. 305-313.

65. Payne, *The White Rajahs,* p. 99.

66. Runciman, *A History of Sarawak,* p. 97.

67. Ibid., pp. 96, 267.

68. Cf. Martin Green, *Dreams of Adventure, Deeds of Empire* (New York, 1927), pp. 342-343.

69. George Woodcock, *The Crystal Spirit: A Study of George Orwell* (New York, 1966), p. 273.

70. George Orwell, *Burmese Days* (new ed. 1934; New York, 1950), pp. 68-69. As the hero Flory puts it: "The British Empire is simply a device for giving trade monopolies to the English—or rather to gangs of Jews and Scotchmen." Astutely, Orwell depicts the anti-imperialist mood as anti-Semitic and xenophobic. (Ibid., p. 40).

71. U Nu, *The People Win Through* (New York, 1957), pp. 18-19. Richard Butwell, *U Nu of Burma* (Stanford, 1963), pp. 19, 22.

72. U Nu, *Burma Under the Japanese,* trans. J. S. Furnivall (London, 1954), pp. xxix, 29, 10, 85, 71. *The New York Times,* January 12, 1953.

73. George Orwell, "England Your England," in *Inside the Whale and Other Essays* (Harmondsworth, 1962), p. 84.

74. Sonia Orwell and Ian Angus, eds., *The Collected Essays, Journalism and Letters of George Orwell,* 4 vols. (Harmondsworth, 1970), 4:139, 142.

75. Philip Woodruff, *The Men Who Ruled India: The Founders* (rpt. New York, 1964), p. 128.

76. Hans Kohn, *Nationalism and Imperialism in the Hither East* (London, 1932), p. 62. cited in A. P. Thornton, *Doctrines of Imperialism*, p. 154.

77. Cited in George Woodcock, *Who Killed the British Empire? An Inquest* (New York, 1974), pp. 258-259.

78. Lewis Mumford, in a discerning essay "The Uprising of Caliban" (1954), wrote: "I propose to personify the demoralizing force of modern barbarism by the figure of Caliban. . . . for Caliban, read the id, the primitive underworld self, and for Prospero, the superego." (Lewis Mumford, *Interpretations and Forecasts: 1922-1972* [New York, 1973], pp. 334-335).

79. Frederick Engels, "Persia and China," (May 27, 1857), in Marx and Engels, *On Colonialism*, p. 115.

80. Marx, "The Indian Revolt," (September 4, 1857), *On Colonialism*, pp. 130, 132. Also, on the "civilization-mongering British government," see Marx, "The Opium Trade," (September 25, 1858), *On Colonialism*, p. 191.

81. Mannoni, *Prospero and Caliban*, p. 98. We might observe that Luis de Camões, the great epic poet of Portuguese imperialism and the voyages of Vasco da Gama, in his youth brimmed with so much excess energy that he was called the "Swashbuckler". Though he was compromised at home in various violences and disgraced, and had lived through a tragedy-laden childhood, there are still no signs that a Prosperonian guilt motivated him. (Aubrey F. G. Bell, *Luis de Camões* [Oxford, 1923], pp. 70-71).

82. John Strachey, *The End of Empire*, (London, 1959: rpt. New York, 1960), p. 23.

83. Bertrand Russell, *Why Men Fight* (New York, 1917), p. 231.

84. J. A. Hobson, *The War in South Africa: Its Causes and Effects* (London, 1900), p. 13.

85. Keith Feiling, *Warren Hastings* (Hamden, 1967), p. 11.

86. Philip Woodruff, *The Men Who Ruled India: The Guardians* (London, 1954; rpt. 1963), p. 17. The largest British army ever assembled in India, that which put down the Sepoy Rebellion of 1857, numbered 120,000 men, of which only 38,000 were Europeans. A regressive empire could not have rested on so small a force. (Gayl D. Ness and William Stahl, "Western Imperialist Armies in Asia," *Comparative Studies in Society and History*, vol. 19 [1977], p. 20).

87. Stuart Cloete, *Against These Three, a Biography of Paul Kruger, Cecil Rhodes, and Lobengula, Last King of the Matabele* (Boston, 1945), p. 185. Dan Colvin, *The Life of Jameson* (London, 1922), 1: 13, 64.

88. Mark Bence-Jones, *Clive of India* (London, 1974), pp. 2-6.

89. Feiling, *Warren Hastings*, p. 9.

90. Woodruff, *The Men Who Ruled India: The Founders*, p. 122.

91. Millin, *Cecil Rhodes*, pp. 130-131, 381. Also see Luther Munford, "Rhodes Scholars: No Longer All White," *The American Oxonian*, vol. 59 (1972), pp. 1-4. Rhodes, as a parson's son, was representative of a large class that experienced the imperialist calling. The sons of parsons were later the most numerous group among the recruits to the British colonial service in Africa. Thus, twenty percent of the men who joined the East African service between 1895 and 1918 were parsons' sons, while in the Sudan thirty-three percent were in this category. Oxford, the university pre-eminent for sending graduates to the colonial service, was still much under the influence of the philosopher Thomas H. Green. He inspired Oxonians with an idealist philosophy of devotion to the common good, to the whole in which their own selves would be realized. (See Gann and Duignan, *The Rulers of British Africa 1870-1914*, pp. 198-200).

92. Millin, *Cecil Rhodes,* pp. 169-170, 247.

93. Anthony Hocking, *Oppenheimer and Son* (New York, 1973), p. 28.

94. Feiling, *Warren Hastings,* pp. 11, 61, 235-236, 322. To look at the later trial of Hastings with a sociological perspective it is well to bear in mind the conclusion of P. J. Marshall: "Of the Europeans who entered the Company's service in the eighteenth century, a large proportion died in India, others went bankrupt, and others struggled for many years to make enough money to enable them to return home with an 'independence.' Yet some men did succeed in amassing great wealth and became the 'Nabobs' of popular legend." (P. J. Marshall, "The Personal Fortune of Warren Hastings," *The Economic History Review,* 2nd series, vol. 17 [1964], p. 299). Hastings, with a fortune of £75,000, was not among the latter. But he had violated the act that prohibited the accepting of presents. (Ibid., p. 295). He lost a "sizeable" fortune through "generosity, carelessness, and extravagance." (Ibid., p. 299).

95. Bence-Jones, *Clive of India,* pp. 261, 302, 71, 247-249, 261, 28, 157, 11.

96. John Rosselli, *Lord William Bentinck: The Making of a Liberal Imperialist 1774-1839* (London, 1974), pp. 84, 209, 220, 275, 276, 210, 211.

97. Ibid., pp. 56, 59, 272.

98. Hobson, *The War in South Africa: Its Causes and Effects,* pp. 12, 61.

99. Millin, *Cecil Rhodes,* p. 20. Also, Cloete, *Against These Three,* pp. 85-86.

100. Cloete, *Against These Three,* p. 201.

101. Millin, *Cecil Rhodes,* pp. 159-160. Cloete, *Against These Three,* pp. 91, 434.

102. Millin, *Cecil Rhodes,* p. 248.

103. Alan Paton, *Cry, The Beloved Country: A Story of Comfort in Desolation* (New York, 1950), p. 168.

104. Gregory, *Ernest Oppenheimer and the Economic Development of Southern Africa,* p. 304.

105. Ibid., pp. 470, 480. In 1957 Harry F. Oppenheimer succeeded his father, Sir Ernest, as chairman of the Anglo-American Corporation. He retired on June 1, 1982 at the age of seventy-three years. He had been "the main backer" of the liberal opposition, the Progressive Federal Party, and the reforms he advocated in labor relations were "now become widely accepted." (*The New York Times,* June 22, 1982).

106. Franklin and Mary Wickwire, *Cornwallis: The Imperial Years* (Chapel Hill, 1980), p. 28.

107. Ibid., pp. 111-113.

108. Herbert Alick Stark, *Hostages to India, or The Life Story of the Anglo-Indian Race* (Calcutta, 1936), pp. 15, 20. V. R. Gaikwad, *The Anglo-Indians: A Study in the Problems and Processes Involved in Emotional and Cultural Integration* (Bombay, 1967), p. 16. H. S. Bhatia, ed., *European Women in India: Their Life and Adventures* (New Delhi, 1979), p. 92.

109. Frank Anthony, *Britain's Betrayal in India: The Story of the Anglo-Indian Community* (Bombay, 1969).

110. Stark, *Hostages,* p. 25. Bhatia, *European Women,* p. 47.

111. Stark, *Hostages,* p. 91.

112. Bhatia, *European Women,* p. 94.

113. Stark, *Hostages,* p. 125.

114. Anthony, *Britain's Betrayal,* p. viii.

115. Bhatia, *European Women,* p. 47. Stark, *Hostages,* pp. 91-95, 54.

116. Anthony, *Britain's Betrayal,* pp. 15-16.

117. Woodruff, *The Men Who Ruled India: The Founders,* p. 232.

118. Woodruff, *The Men Who Ruled India: The Guardians,* pp. 174, 129.

119. Ibid., pp. 353, 234.

120. Ibid., pp. 286, 289. See especially the evidence presented by the unimpeachable Thomas R. Malthus concerning the work of the young officials of the East India Company in British India. (T. R. Malthus, *Statements Respecting the East-India Company* [London, 1817] in *The Pamphlets of Thomas Robert Malthus* [New York, 1970] pp. 237, 243-246). Also see H. Morse Stephens, *An Account of the East India College at Haileybury (1806-1857)* in A. Lawrence Lowell, *Colonial Civil Service* (New York, 1900), p. 291 ff.

121. John William Kaye, *The Administration of the East India Company: A History of Indian Progress* (London, 1853), p. 661.

122. Woodruff, *The Men Who Ruled India: The Guardians*, p. 349.

123. Stanley Jackson, *Rufus Isaacs, First Marquess of Reading* (London, 1936), p. 241.

124. Gann and Duignan, *The Rulers of British Africa 1870-1914*, p. 240.

125. Ibid., pp. 241-242.

126. Sydney Olivier, "An Empire Builder," *The Contemporary Review*, vol. 87 (Jan.-June 1905), pp. 699-702. William James found "a moral and metaphysical profundity" in its "parable." (Sydney Olivier, *Letters and Selected Writings*, ed. Margaret Olivier [New York, 1948], p. 127).

127. Bernard Shaw, "Some Impressions," in Sydney Olivier, *Letters and Selected Writings*, p. 13. Also see Lord Olivier, *White Capital and Coloured Labor* (London, 1929), pp. 26-27.

128. "Perhaps the most effective factor [in the recruitment of labor] has been the operation of economic incentives . . . They [some observers] have noted that in certain areas 'the shopkeeper probably provides a far greater incentive than the taxgatherer' . . . Young men are bored by the limitations of village life and seek work to satisfy their desire for adventure and independence," and prefer "what they can get with their money over leisure and the products of village communism." (Lord Hailey, *An African Survey: A Study of Problems Arising in Africa South of the Sahara* [London, 1938], pp. 648-649. Also see pp. 604-605, 694, 1659).

129. Margery Perham, *Lugard: The Years of Adventure 1858-1898* (London, 1956), p. 59.

130. Ibid., pp. 58, 61.

131. Ibid., p. 65.

132. Ibid., p. 71.

133. John Flint, "Frederick Lugard: The Making of an Autocrat, (1858-1943)," in L. H. Gann and Peter Duignan, eds., *African Proconsuls: European Governors in Africa* (New York, 1978), p. 299.

134. Ibid., p. 306.

135. Ibid., p. 291. George Padmore, *Africa: Britain's Third Empire* (London, 1949; rpt. New York, 1969), p. 50. The Fabian of Bloomsbury, Leonard Woolf, wrote that Lugard was "employed at twenty-one in shooting Afghans in the Afghan War, at twenty-seven Africans in the Sudanese campaign, and at twenty-eight Burmese in the Burma campaign." Leonard Woolf, *Empire and Commerce in Africa; a study in economic imperialism* (London, 1920; rpt. 1968), p. 273. Richard Wright and Azinna Nwafor, in George Padmore, *Pan-Africanism or Communism* (New York, 1971), pp. xxi, xxv.

136. Gann and Duignan, *African Proconsuls*, pp. 15, 16.

137. The comprehensive account of Lugard's life by his friend, the scholarly, judicious Hailey, sympathetically omits all mention of the episode. Cf. Hailey, "Frederick John Dealtry Lugard," *The Dictionary of National Biography, 1941-1950* (London, 1959), p. 533.

138. Perham, *Lugard*, p. 67.

139. Ibid., p. 600.

140. Hailey, "Lugard," *Dictionary of National Biography*, p. 536.

141. Flint, *The Making of an Autocrat*, p. 205.

142. Perham, *Lugard*, p. 572.

143. Ibid., p. 570.

144. Flint, *The Making of an Autocrat*, p. 310.

145. Sir Andrew Cohen, *British Policy in Changing Africa* (London, 1959), pp. 12-13.

146. Millin, *Cecil Rhodes*, p. 61. Cloete, *Against These Three*, pp. 270, 273.

147. Earl of Cromer, "Lord Curzon's Imperialism," *Political and Literary Essays: Third Series* (London, 1916), p. 10.

148. Karl Marx, "British Incomes in India," (Sept. 21, 1857) in Marx and Engels, *On Colonialism*, pp. 143-144.

149. Ronald Robinson and John Gallagher, with Alice Denny, *Africa and the Victorians; the Climax of Imperialism* (New York, 1961), p. 25. George Shepperson notes that "historians have not devoted enough energy to explaining why" the rationalization for imperialism so often took an economic form. See William Roger Louis, ed., *The Robinson and Gallagher Controversy* (New York, 1976), p. 165.

150. John Stuart Mill, *Principles of Political Economy with Some of Their Applications to Social Philosophy*, ed. W. J. Ashley (London, 1971), pp. 9, 71.

151. Benjamin Disraeli, *The Works of Benjamin Disraeli*, vol. 16, *Tancred or The New Crusade*, 20 vols. (New York, 1904), part 2, p. 122.

152. Benjamin Disraeli, *Lord George Bentinck: A Political Biography* (London, 1852; new ed. 1905), p. 215. *Wit and Wisdom of Benjamin Disraeli, Earl of Beaconsfield* (New York, 1881), p. 288.

153. *Wit and Wisdom*, pp. 112-113.

154. C. C. Eldridge, *England's Mission: The Imperial Idea in the Age of Gladstone and Disraeli 1868-1880* (London, 1973), pp. 217-228.

155. Cecil Roth, *Benjamin Disraeli, Earl of Beaconsfield* (New York, 1952), p. 142.

156. Karl Marx and Frederick Engels, *The Russian Menace to Europe*, eds. Paul W. Blackstock and Bert F. Hoselitz (Glencoe, Illinois, 1952), pp. 242-243, 25.

157. Marx and Engels, *On Britain* (Moscow, 1953), pp. 328, 476, 526.

158. Philip Mangus, *Gladstone: A Biography* (London, 1954), p. 383.

159. William Flavelle Monypenny and George Earle Buckle, *The Life of Benjamin Disraeli, Earl of Beaconsfield*, 6 vols. (New York, 1913-1920), vol. 4 (1916), pp. 332, 333-334. Robert Blake, *Disraeli* (New York, 1967), p. 377.

160. Georg Brandes, *Lord Beaconsfield*, trans. Mrs. George Sturge (New York, 1880), pp. 235-236.

161. H. C. G. Matthew, *The Liberal Imperialists: The Ideas and Politics of a Post-Gladstonian Elite* (Oxford, 1973), pp. 154-155, 160, 293-294. Richard Burdon Haldane, *An Autobiography* (New York, 1929), pp. 8, 229. Frederick Maurice, *Haldane 1856-1915* (London, 1937), p. 34. Stephen Koss, *Asquith* (London, 1976), pp. 6, 81. J. A. Spender and Cyril Asquith, *Life of Herbert Henry Asquith, Lord Oxford and Asquith*, 2 vols. (London, 1932) 1:37.

162. Frantz Fanon, *A Dying Colonialism*, trans. Haakon Chevalier (New York, 1967), p. 64.

163. Ibid., p. 46.

164. Ibid., p. 42.

165. Ibid., pp. 39, 41.

166. Ibid., p. 59.

167. Fannina W. Halle, *Women in the Soviet East*, trans. Margaret M. Green (London, 1938), p. 175. The Mother Hubbard dress in which missionaries attired native women was described by Mary Kingsley as helping produce "the well-known

torpidity of the mission-trained girl" by making her look "very like a tub." (Catherine Barnes Stevenson, *Victorian Women Travel Writers in Africa* [Boston, 1982], p. 133.

168. Abram Kardiner, *My Analysis with Freud: Reminiscences* (New York, 1977), p. 76.

169. Fanon, *Colonialism,* p. 175.

170. "The threat of being devoured," notes the psychoanalyst Bettelheim, "is the central theme" of classical fairy tales, one of those "basic psychological constellations which occur in every person's development," that "can lead to the most diverse fates and personalities." (Bruno Bettelheim, *The Uses of Enchantment: The Meaning and Importance of Fairy Tales* [New York, 1976], p. 169).

171. Herman Melville, *Typee: A Peep at Polynesian Life,* (New York, 1846), chapter 31. Charles Roberts Anderson, *Melville in the South Seas* (New York, 1939), pp. 109-110.

172. Thomas Wentworth Higginson, *Cheerful Yesterdays* (Boston, 1899), p. 174. Alexis de Tocqueville, *Democracy in America,* ed. Phillips Bradley, trans. Henry Reeve (New York, 1945), 1:372.

173. C. R. Boxer, *Race Relations and the Portuguese Colonial Empire: 1415-1825* (Oxford, 1963), pp. 9, 60-61, 65.

174. Sir Andrew Cohen, *British Policy in Changing Africa* (London, 1959), p. 15.

175. Millin, *Cecil Rhodes,* p. 256.

176. Ibid., p. 256. *Autobiography of Charles Darwin,* ed. Sir Francis Darwin (London, 1929), p. 154.

177. Mason, *Prospero's Magic,* p. 87.

178. Julian Huxley, *Africa View* (New York, 1931), p. 125.

179. Ibid., p. 461.

180. Julian Huxley, *Memories,* 2 vols. (Harmondsworth, England, 1972), 1: 171-172, 187-188. *Memories* (New York, 1973), 2: 13 ff.

181. Woodruff, *The Men Who Ruled India: The Guardians,* p. 15.

182. Royal Institute of International Affairs, *The Colonial Problem: A Report by a Study Group of Members* (London, 1937), p. 109: "There is discernible in colonial policy an element of the Aristotelian theory that some men are born for the superior occupation . . . and that others are born with . . . minds fitted for the humbler kinds of toil."

183. Howard K. Beale, *Theodore Roosevelt and the Rise of America to World Power* (Baltimore, 1956), p. 68.

184. Theodore Roosevelt, *The Winning of the West* (New York, 1894), 3:44-45.

185. Cf. Thomas G. Dyer, *Theodore Roosevelt and the Idea of Race* (Baton Rouge, 1980), p. 37 ff.

186. Roosevelt, pursuing such study, even while president, took the time to read Ferrero's *Greatness and Decline of Rome* in the original Italian. Oscar S. Straus, *Under Four Administrations from Cleveland to Taft* (Boston, 1922), p. 177. Also see Dyer, *Roosevelt and the Idea of Race,* p. 37.

187. Roosevelt, *The Winning of the West,* p. 28.

188. Beale, *Roosevelt and the Rise of America,* p. 31.

189. Ibid., p. 265 ff, p. 30.

190. Ibid., p. 436.

191. Ibid., p. 263.

192. Henry F. Pringle, *Theodore Roosevelt: A Biography* (New York, 1956), pp. 36-37, 328.

193. Beale, *Roosevelt and the Rise of America,* p. 13.

194. Pringle, *Roosevelt: A Biography,* pp. 129, 359.

195. Beale, *Roosevelt and the Rise of America,* p. 453.

196. Emery Neff, *Edwin Arlington Robinson* (New York, 1948), p. 141 ff.

197. William Henry Harbaugh, *The Life and Times of Theodore Roosevelt*, rev. ed. (New York, 1963), p. 434.

198. Beale, *Roosevelt and the Rise of America*, pp. 333, 100.

199. Ibid., pp. 241, 182.

200. Ibid., p. 152.

201. Pringle, *Roosevelt: A Biography*, p. 196.

202. Charles A. Beard and Mary R. Beard, *The Rise of American Civilization* (New York, 1927), 2: 497.

203. Beale, *Roosevelt and the Rise of America*, p. 305.

204. Ibid., p. 305.

205. Ibid., pp. 309-310.

206. Ibid., p. 310.

207. Ibid., p. 304. G. Maspero, *History of Egypt, Chaldea, Syria, Babylonia, and Assyria*, ed. A. H. Sayre, trans. M. L. McClure, 9 vols. (London, 1903).

208. Beale, *Roosevelt and the Rise of America*, pp. 294, 306-307.

209. Ibid., pp. 307-308.

210. Ibid., p. 461.

211. Walter Lippmann, *Public Persons*, ed. Gilbert A. Harrison (New York, 1976), pp. 126-127.

212. Walter Lippmann, *The Stakes of Democracy* (New York, 1915), pp. 219-220.

213. An undercivilized society is one in which there is a relatively widespread animosity toward and repression of individual free thought and speech, in which science is lacking, or is actively opposed, in which the productivity of labor and inventiveness in technology lag behind, and the arts remain at a low level of expressive capacity, while a large variety of non-logical beliefs influence one's actions in everyday life.

214. Harlan B. Phillips, ed., *Felix Frankfurter Reminisces* (New York, 1962), p. 112. David W. Levy, *Herbert Croly of the New Republic: The Life and Thought of an American Progressive* (Princeton, 1985), p. 124.

215. Dyer, *Roosevelt and the Idea of Race*, p. 131.

216. Maurice Wohlgelernter, *Israel Zangwill* (New York, 1964), pp. 176-177. Zangwill's dedication of *The Melting Pot* read: "To Theodore Roosevelt In Respectful Recognition Of His Strenuous Struggle Against the Forces That Threaten To Shipwreck The Great Republic Which Carries Mankind And Its Fortunes, This Play Is, By His Kind Permission, Cordially Dedicated." (Israel Zangwill, *The Melting Pot*, rev. ed. [New York, 1914]. Philip Gleason, "The Melting Pot: Symbol of Fusion or Confusion?," *American Quarterly*, vol. 16 (1964), p. 24 ff).

217. Hobson's view was shared by some labor leaders. John Burns, who was a cabinet minister in 1914, said in 1900 that "the South African Jews have . . . no bowels of compassion," and that they, "the persecuted of all time" had "gained a cash ascendancy." Another assailed the "cosmopolitan Jews" with neither country nor patriotism. (Henry Pelling, *Popular Politics and Society in Late Victorian Britain*, 2nd ed. [London, 1979], p. 84).

218. J. Guiness Rogers, "The Churches and the War," *The Contemporary Review*, vol. 77 (1900), pp. 616-617. Also cf. Peter Clarke, *Liberals and Social Democrats* (Cambridge, 1978), p. 92. "Some of his [Hobson's] despatches admittedly contain certain passages searching for evidence of Jewish connexions."

219. Hobson, *Imperialism: A Study*, 3rd ed. (London, 1938), pp. 56-57.

220. Fritz Stern, *Gold and Iron: Bismarck, Bleichröder, and the Building of the German Empire* (New York, 1977), p. 417.

221. Ibid., p. 416.

222. Ibid., p. 548.

223. Hobson, *Imperialism,* pp. 190-191.

224. Ibid., p. 193.

225. Hobson, *Confessions of an Economic Heretic* (London, 1938), p. 57.

226. Ibid., p. 90-91.

227. Ibid., p. 30.

228. A. J. P. Taylor, *The Trouble-Makers: Dissent Over Foreign Policy 1792-1939* (London, 1969), p. 121.

229. Bernard Porter, *Critics of Empire: British Radical Attitudes to Colonialism in Africa 1895-1914* (London, 1968), p. 271.

230. Ibid., p. 271.

231. Emile Vandervelde, *Souvenirs d'un Militant Socialiste* (Paris, 1939), p. 75.

232. V. I. Lenin, "English Pacifism and English Dislike of Theory," *Collected Works,* vol. 18, *The Imperialist War* (New York, 1930), p. 164.

233. Ibid., p. 261.

234. Cited in Porter, *Critics of Empire,* p. 258.

235. Taylor, *The Trouble-Makers,* p. 121.

236. *Daily Herald,* April 9, 1920. Cited in Robert C. Reinders, "Racialism on the Left: E. D. Morel and the 'Black Horror on the Rhine'," *International Review of Social History,* vol. 13 (1968), Part I, p. 1.

237. Cited in Reinders, "Racialism on the Left," pp. 4-5.

238. Ibid., pp. 11-12, from Norman Angell, *Fruits of Victory* (London, 1921), pp. 325, 410. Also cf. Albert Marrin, *Sir Norman Angell* (Boston, 1979), pp. 193-194.

239. Reinders, "Racialism on the Left," p. 19.

240. Ibid., p. 21.

241. Ibid., p. 27.

242. Stevenson, *Victorian Women Travel Writers,* p. 133.

243. E. D. Morel, *The Black Man's Burden* (London, 1920), p. 22.

244. F. Seymour Cocks, *E. D. Morel: The Man and His Work* (London, 1920), p. 15 ff. Kingsley Martin, "Edmund Dené Morel," *Encyclopedia of the Social Sciences,* vol. 11 (New York, 1933), pp. 9-10.

245. Catherine Ann Cline, *E. D. Morel 1973-1924: The Strategies of Protest* (Belfast, 1980), pp. 110-111.

246. Taylor, *The Trouble-Makers,* p. 109.

247. Ibid., p. 109.

248. Leonard Woolf, *Beginning Again: An Autobiography of the Years 1911-1918* (London, 1964), pp. 226-227.

249. Leonard Woolf, *Growing: An Autobiography of the Years 1904-1911* (London, 1964; New York, 1975), pp. 247, 180, 185, 178, 92-93.

250. Duncan Wilson, *Leonard Woolf: A Political Biography* (New York, 1978), p. 40. Woolf, *Growing,* p. 46.

251. Wolf, *Growing,* p. 154.

252. Ibid., pp. 67-68.

253. Woolf, *Growing,* pp. 54, 212. Leonard Woolf, *The Village in the Jungle* (New York, 1926; rpt. Delhi, 1975), pp. 28, 17.

254. Woolf, *Growing,* p. 247.

255. Ibid., pp. 158-159.

256. Ibid., p. 135.

257. Leonard Woolf, *Sowing* (London, 1960), pp. 13, 196, 38.

258. Leonard Woolf, *The Wise Virgins* (London, 1914; rpt. New York, 1979), introduction by Ian Parsons, p. xiii. Duncan Wilson, *Leonard Woolf,* p. 11.

259. Woolf, *The Wise Virgins,* pp. 98-99, 93-94, 30.

260. Ibid., pp. 111-112.

261. Leonard Woolf, *Economic Imperialism* (London, 1930), p. 42.

262. Ibid., pp. 17, 19.

263. Leonard Woolf, *Imperialism and Civilization* (New York, 1928), pp. 47, 91.

264. "At no time in the history of the world has there existed a society of human beings dominated by such a universal economic passion as ours is. It is the passion of buying cheap and selling dear." (Leonard Woolf, *Empire and Commerce in Africa: A Study in Economic Imperialism* [London, 1920], p. 36).

265. Leonard Woolf, *Downhill All the Way, An Autobiography of the Years 1919-1939* (New York, 1967), p. 235.

266. Woolf, *Empire and Commerce,* p. 291.

267. Woolf, however, did note the "streak of aggressive cruelty" in Wittgenstein's nature. (Leonard Woolf, *The Journey Not the Arrival Matters: An Autobiography of the Years 1939-1969* [New York, 1969], p. 48).

268. Quentin Bell, *Virginia Woolf: A Biography* (London, 1972), 1: 185. Virginia Woolf wrote in 1930: "How I hated marrying a Jew—how I hated their nasal voices, and their oriental jewelry, and their noses . . . what a snob I was." (Cited in Selma S. Meyerowitz, *Leonard Woolf* [Boston, 1982], p. 15).

269. Bell, *Virginia Woolf,* 2: 18.

270. Ibid., p. 6.

271. Ibid., pp. 116-117, 132.

272. Ibid., p. 15.

273. Meyerowitz, *Leonard Woolf,* p. 57.

274. Victoria Sackville-West, Virginia Woolf's friend, wrote of her: "She has never lived with anyone except Leonard, which was a terrible failure, and was abandoned quite often." (Nigel Nicolson, *Portrait of a Marriage* [1973; rpt. London, 1974], p. 212).

275. Frederick R. Karl, *Joseph Conrad: The Three Lives* (New York, 1979), p. 288. Brian Inglis, *Roger Casement* (London, 1973), pp. 31-32.

276. A. Conan Doyle, *The Crime of the Congo* (New York, 1909), p. 57.

277. Inglis, *Roger Casement,* pp. 194, 179.

278. Ibid., pp. 382-383. "[H]e regarded homosexuality as an affliction; for the individual unfortunate, and for the community unhealthy." (Inglis, *Roger Casement,* p. 384. Also, B. L. Reid, *The Lives of Roger Casement* [New Haven, 1976], p. 38).

279. Inglis, *Roger Casement,* p. 263.

280. Reid, *Lives of Roger Casement,* pp. 81-82.

281. Ibid., pp. 9-11.

282. Karl, *Joseph Conrad:* p. 289.

283. Roger Sawyer, *Casement: The Flawed Hero* (London, 1984), p. 34.

284. Inglis, *Roger Casement,* p. 151.

285. Karl, *Joseph Conrad,* pp. 553-554.

286. Ibid., p. 553.

287. Ibid., pp. 553-554.

288. Stephen E. Tabachnick, ed., *The T. E. Lawrence Puzzle* (Athens, Georgia, 1984), pp. 231-232, 120-121.

289. Philip Knightley and Colin Simpson, *The Secret Lives of Lawrence of Arabia* (New York 1970), pp. 178-179.

290. T. E. Lawrence, *The Seven Pillars of Wisdom: a Triumph* (London, 1935), p. 31.

291. T. E. Lawrence, *Revolt in the Desert* (New York, 1927), p. 62.

292. Ibid., p. 57.

293. Lawrence, *Seven Pillars,* p. 47.

294. Ibid., p. 335.

295. *T. E. Lawrence to His Biographers, Robert Graves and Liddell Hart* (New York, 1963), p. 51.

296. Lawrence, *Seven Pillars*, p. 56.

297. Ibid., p. 339.

298. Lawrence, *Revolt in the Desert*, p. 196.

299. Ibid., p. 122.

300. Lawrence, *Seven Pillars*, pp. 103, 214.

301. Aaron Klieman, "Lawrence as Bureaucrat," in S. E. Tabachnick, *The T. E. Lawrence Puzzle*, p. 262.

302. Ibid., p. 255.

303. Lawrence, *Seven Pillars*, p. 100.

304. A. L. Rowse, *Homosexuals in History: A Study of Ambivalence in Society, Literature and the Arts* (New York, 1903), p. 258.

305. *T. E. Lawrence to His Biographers*, p. 211.

306. Lawrence, *Seven Pillars*, p. 195.

307. *T. E. Lawrence to His Biographers*, p. 211.

308. Nelson M. Blake, "Foreword," in Rubin Francis Weston, *Racism in U.S. Imperialism, The Influence of Racial Assumptions on American Foreign Policy, 1893-1946*, 2nd ed. (Columbia, S. C., 1973), p. x.

309. J. A. Hobson, *Free-Thought in the Social Sciences* (New York, 1926), p. 54.

310. Ibid., pp. 206-207.

311. Leo Kuper, *Genocide: Its Political Use in the Twentieth Century* (New York, 1982), p. 63.

312. Helen Codere, "Field Work in Rwanda 1959-1960," in Peggy Golde, *Women in the Field: Anthropological Experiences* (Chicago, 1970), p. 162.

313. Ian and Jane Linden, *Church and Revolution in Rwanda* (Manchester, England, 1977), p. 283.

314. Semakula Kiwanuka, *Amin and the Tragedy of Uganda* (Munich and London, 1979), pp. 196-197, 164.

315. John M. Ostheimer, *Nigerian Politics* (New York, 1973), p. 56.

316. Ibid., pp. 62-65. John de St. Jorre, *The Nigerian Civil War* (London, 1972), p. 373.

317. de St. Jorre, *Nigerian Civil War*, p. 110.

318. Ibid., pp. 164-165.

319. Ibid., pp. 407-408.

320. Ibid., p. 358. A. H. M. Kirk-Greene, *Crisis and Conflict in Nigeria: A Documentary Sourcebook 1966-1970* (London, 1971), 2: 135, 46-47.

321. de St. Jorre, *Nigerian Civil War*, p. 374. Robert Legvold, *Soviet Policy in West Africa* (Cambridge, Mass., 1970), p. 285 ff., pp. 325-330. Anton Bebler, *Military Rule in Africa: Dahomey, Ghana, Sierra Leone, and Mali* (New York, 1973), p. 133.

Chapter V - The End of Progressive Imperialism

1. Cf. Sheila Patterson, *Immigration and Race Relations in Britain, 1960-1967* (London, 1969), pp. 19, 128.

2. James Bryce, *Studies in History and Jurisprudence*, 2 vols. (New York, 1901), 1: 53.

3. Ibid., p. 54.

4. Ibid., p. 55.

5. Ibid., p. 70. Four years after India won its political independence, a book appeared by an Indian, an "untouchable," Nirad C. Chaudhuri, *The Autobiography of an Unknown Indian* (London, 1951). Its dedication summed up the greatness and necessary end of British imperialism: "To the memory of the British Empire in India

which conferred subjecthood on us but withheld citizenship: to which yet every one of us threw out the challenge: 'Civis Britannicus Sum' because all that was good and living within us was made, shaped, and quickened by the same British rule.'" (p. v) The British could grant subjecthood and all its benefits, but the racial fusion that was the corollary of citizenship was something that no race in modern times has ever willingly undertaken. That was why the British Empire had to end. The Fabian socialists Bernard Shaw and Sidney Webb, in their memorable pamphlet in 1901, *Fabianism and the Empire,* endorsed the conjunction of socialism and imperialism as making for a higher civilization and efficiency. But their fellow Fabian, Graham Wallas, observed that they overlooked the surd barrier of race, that the European nations, founding empires, were "gathering round them bodies of dependent peoples, in many cases greatly outnumbering themselves, but without either political rights or the prospect of assimilation by intermarriage." A world ethic, such as the Romans had, was, under such conditions, impossible, unless the Western societies chose to elevate what they regarded as a masochist principle into the basis for their political philosophy. (Martin J. Wiener, *Between Two Worlds: The Political Thought of Graham Wallas* [Oxford, 1971], p. 106).

6. Bryce, *Studies,* p. 36.

7. Thornton, *Doctrines of Imperialism,* p. 181.

8. W. E. Gladstone, "England's Mission," *The Nineteenth Century,* vol. 4 (1878), pp. 560-584. Cited in C. C. Eldridge, *England's Mission: The Imperial Idea in the Age of Gladstone and Disraeli 1868-1880* (London, 1973), p. 227.

9. J. A. Hobson, *The Social Problem: Life and Work* (New York, 1902), p. 275. Cited in Bernard Porter, *Critics of Empire: British Radical Attitudes to Colonialism in Africa 1895-1914* (London, 1968), p. 181.

10. Christine Bolt, *Victorian Attitudes to Race* (London, 1971), p. 83.

11. Royden Harrison, *Before the Socialists: Studies in Labor and Politics, 1861-1881* (London, 1965), p. 85.

12. Karl Marx and Frederick Engels, *Historisch-Kritische Gesamtausgabe,* ed. D. Ryazanov, (Berlin, 1930), 2: 354-356, 360-363. Cited in Lewis S. Feuer, *Marx and the Intellectuals* (New York, 1969), p. 2. "By the 1860s . . . the upper and middle classes of the English people, especially the latter, had come to believe that Negroes were innately inferior beings who consequently did not rate equal consideration with themselves." (Bolt, *Victorian Attitudes,* p. 105).

13. Julian Huxley, *African View* (New York, 1931), pp. 458-459.

14. Ibid., p. 465.

15. Before the anti-imperialist fashion began to spread in 1905, recalls the Indian writer Nirad C. Chaudhuri in *Clive of India: A Political and Psychological Essay* (London, 1965), p. 11, although "educated and thoughtful Indians" were emotionally anti-British, "intellectually not one of them denied that British rule had rescued India from anarchy and brought peace and prosperity to the Indian people."

16. The Portuguese discovery of the routes to East Africa and India in Vasco da Gama's voyage of 1497-1499 was a "calamitous disaster" for the Arab trading posts and hegemony in East Africa. Thus, "the great age of Muslim culture . . . was brought to a rude and abrupt close." (R. B. Serjeant, *The Portuguese of the South Arabian Coast* [Oxford, 1963], p. 11).

17. Gilbert Freyre, *Brazil: An Interpretation* (New York, 1945), pp. 19-21.

18. C. R. Boxer, *Four Centuries of Portuguese Expansion, 1415-1825: A Succinct Survey* (Johannesburg, 1961), p. 20.

19. Ibid., pp. 82-84. C. R. Boxer, *Race Relations in the Portuguese Colonial Empire 1415-1825* (Oxford, 1963), p. 84.

20. Boxer, *Race Relations,* pp. 120-121.

21. Boxer, *Four Centuries,* pp. 75-77, 84.

22. Ibid., p. 88.

23. Ibid., p. 73.

24. William Roger Louis, *Imperialism at Bay 1941-1945: The United States and the Decolonization of the British Empire* (Oxford, 1977), p. 155.

25. George H. Gallup, ed., *The Gallup International Public Opinion Polls* (France, 1939, 1944-1975; New York, 1976), 1: 2, 68, 110. In 1947, when the future of France seemed uncertain, and the power of the French Communist Party had polarized French society, forty-nine percent of the polled felt that the Soviet Union was "the one nation which seeks to dominate the world" as compared to forty-two percent for the United States. Meanwhile, an overwhelming majority felt that the Soviet Union had taken the lead in offensive armaments; as early as 1961, sixty-eight percent felt the Soviet Union led in long-range ballistic missiles and rockets as compared to only eight percent for the United States. (Ibid., p. 95, 110, 298).

26. Richard Koebner and Helmut Dan Schmidt, *Imperialism: The Story and Significance of a Political Word, 1840-1960* (Cambridge, 1964), p. 278.

27. Ibid., pp. 134, 137.

28. Ibid., p. 149.

29. Ibid., p. 47.

30. Bertrand Russell, "Hopes and Fears as Regards America," *The New Republic*, vol. 30 (March 15, 1922), p. 70. Barry Feinberg and Ronald Kasrils, eds., *Bertrand Russell's America: His Transatlantic Travels and Writings* (London, 1973; New York, 1974), vol. 1, p. 221.

31. "The famine [of 1891] was the beginning of the end for Imperial Russia. From 1891 on, the Tsar's government faced a crescendo of criticisms which would culminate first in the revolution of 1905 and then the total collapse of 1917 . . . The occurrence of a major famine in Russia seemed to indicate that the Empire was falling still further behind the advanced and prosperous countries of the West." (Richard G. Robbins, Jr., *Famine in Russia 1891-1942* [New York, 1975], p. 176).

32. Benjamin M. Weissman, *Herbert Hoover and Famine Relief to Soviet Russia* (Stanford, 1974), pp. 54, 154. Also cf. Harold Henry Fisher, *The Famine in Soviet Russia, 1919-1923, The Operations of the American Relief Administration* (New York, 1927), pp. 51-53, 73-74. Also cf. Louis Fischer, *The Soviets in World Affairs: A History of Relations Between the Soviet Union and the Rest of the World,* 2 vols. (London, 1930), 1: 175. Khrushchev was the only later Soviet statesman to acknowledge "the aid extended to Soviet people after the Civil War, during the terrible famine of 1921-1922, when ARA, the American Relief Administration, was set up to aid the starving population." The committee, he added, "was headed by Herbert Hoover . . . and we thank you well." Shortly afterwards, he sent missiles to Cuba. (*Khrushchev in America, full texts of the speeches made by N.S. Khrushchev on his tour of the United States, September 15-27, 1959* [New York, 1960], p. 111).

33. Weissman, *Herbert Hoover and Famine Relief,* p. 199.

34. Ibid., p. 177. Fisher, *The Famine in Soviet Russia,* pp. 399-400.

35. Frank M. Surface and Raymond L. Bland, *American Food in the World War and Reconstruction Period; Operations of the Organization Under the Direction of Herbert Hoover, 1914-1924* (Stanford, 1931), p. 244. Frank Alfred Golder and Lincoln Hutchinson, *On the Trail of the Famine* (Stanford, 1927), p. 18.

36. Herbert Hoover, *An American Epic: Famine in Forty-Five Nations: The Battle on the Front Line* (Chicago, 1961), 3: 439-440, 443.

37. Surface and Bland, *American Food,* p. 247.

38. Ibid., pp. 246-247, 255.

39. Ibid., p. 245. Hoover, *An American Epic,* p. 448.

40. Hoover, *An American Epic,* pp. 464-465. Surface and Bland, *American Food,* p. 250.

41. Hoover, *An American Epic,* p. 438.

42. Weissman, *Herbert Hoover and Famine Relief*, pp. 129, 201.

43. Ibid., p. 123. "Hoover," it was reliably reported, "had great faith in the Slavs and felt Russia and America had a big common future." (Louis Fischer, *Men and Politics: Europe Between the Two World Wars* [New York, 1941; rpt. 1946], p. 148).

44. Weissman, *Famine Relief*, p. 183.

45. Ibid., p. 186.

46. The cruelties of the anti-Bolsheviks were recounted by the commanding general of American troops in Siberia in William S. Graves, *America's Siberian Adventure 1918-1920* (New York, 1931), pp. 245-246. Cf. George Stewart, *The White Armies of Russia* (New York, 1933), p. 250.

47. Walter Bedell Smith, *My Three Years in Moscow* (New York, 1950), pp. 54, 221, 224, 315.

48. *The Parliamentary Debates (Hansard)*, 5th series, vol. 147, House of Lords (London, 1947), pp. 274-275. Also cf. Kingsley Martin, *Editor* (London, 1968), pp. 195-196. What the United States might have done to the Soviet Union, but decided not to, was set forth in a famous magazine issue to which such writers as Arthur Koestler, Edward R. Murrow, Allan Nevins, and the labor leader Walter Reuther, contributed. "Preview to the War We Do Not Want," *Collier's*, vol. 128, no. 17 (October 27, 1951), pp. 4-129.

49. As late as the Korean War, Prime Minister Attlee required and received personal assurances that no use of the atomic bomb was contemplated. (Harry S. Truman, *Memoirs, Vol. Two, Years of Trial and Hope* [New York, 1956], p. 410).

50. C. R. Attlee, *As It Happened* (New York, 1954), pp. 205-226.

51. Robert Conquest, *The Great Terror: Stalin's Purge of the Thirties* (New York, 1968), p. 494. Zbigniew K. Brzezinski, *The Permanent Purge: Politics in Soviet Totalitarianism* (Cambridge, Mass., 1956), p. 149. Several persons in the Soviet Union who had been sentenced to the labor camps during the post World War II period told me, however, that in their opinion the purges at that time were more severe and widespread, though less publicized, than those in 1936-1938. These conversations took place when I was an exchange professor in the Soviet Union for the spring semester of 1963.

52. *The Memoirs of Anthony Eden: Full Circle* (Boston, 1960), p. 520.

53. Thus, the call for "a liberation from globalism . . . the self-appointed responsibilities of a world policeman and the crumbling alliances that inflate our national egos." (Ronald Steel, *Pax Americana* [New York, 1967], pp. 352-353).

54. When the Egyptian nationalization of the Canal took place, the leader of the British Labor Party, Hugh Gaitskell, also compared Nasser to Hitler, saying there were "circumstances in which we might be compelled to use force, in self-defence or as part of some collective measures." He hedged his discourse, however, with the nullifying reservation that the approval of the United Nations be secured. Thus, when the British and French governments did undertake action, he could join in the widespread denunciation of their "imperialist aggression." (Cf. Leon D. Epstein, *British Politics in the Suez Crisis* [Urbana, Illinois, 1964], p. 66).

55. Anthony Sampson, *The Seven Sisters: the great oil companies and the world they shaped* (New York, 1979), Paperback ed., p. 358. Oil revenues in Saudi Arabia for the year 1981 were expected by Western economists to rise to $123.5 billion dollars; "earnings" for 1980 had stood at $103 billion dollars. (*The New York Times*, March 2, 1981).

56. Fred Halliday, "Saudi Arabia: Bonanza and Repression," *New Left Review*, no. 80 (July-August 1973), p. 20.

57. W. W. Rostow, *The Diffusion of Power: An Essay in Recent History* (New York, 1972), p. 464. "While the Tet offensive in early 1968 had achieved for Hanoi a traumatic psychological victory within the United States, it was a military disaster

for its promoters within South Vietnam." (Sir Robert Thompson, *Peace Is Not At Hand* [London, 1974], p. 62).

58. Rostow, *The Diffusion of Power*, p. 435.

59. Ibid., p. 483.

60. Ella Lonn, *Desertion During the Civil War* (New York, 1928), p. 226.

61. Peter Braestrup, *Big Story: How the American Press and Television Reported and Interpreted the Crisis of Tet 1968 in Vietnam and Washington* (Boulder, 1977), 1: 138, 139, 337-338.

62. Ibid., pp. 126, 334-335.

63. Eric Sevareid, *Not So Wild a Dream* (New York, 1946), pp. 254-255, 300.

64. Braestrup, *Big Story*, pp. 221, 231.

65. Ibid., p. 283.

66. Ibid., p. 671.

67. Ibid., p. 49. Among the "stringer" reporters, "several were draft-dodgers." (p. 29).

68. Doan Van Toai, "A Lament for Vietnam," *The New York Times Magazine*, March 29, 1981, p. 64 ff.

69. The visits to Hanoi began in 1965 and continued. There were also meetings between New Leftists and "Our Friends in Vietnam," and a "full-scale, sit-down, dress-up conference between New Left and NLF/North Vietnamese delegates" in Czechoslovakia in September 1967. (Andrew Kopkind, "The Sixties and the Movement," *Ramparts*, vol. 11 [February 1973], p. 32).

70. Robert S. Harper, *Lincoln and the Press* (New York, 1951), pp. 311-313.

71. Cf. Lewis S. Feuer, "Why Not a Commentary on Sevareid?", *National Review*, vol. 27 (August 15, 1975), p. 876.

72. As Sir Robert Thompson observed, however: "The whole design [of the American strategy] was defensive. There was no question at any time of equipping the South Vietnamese Army with weapons which might have enabled it to attack North Vietnamese supply routes and rear bases." (*Peace is Not at Hand*, p. 63.) Thompson had directed the successful actions in Malaya after World War II against the Communist guerrilla forces.

73. Fischer, *The Soviets in World Affairs*, p. 420.

74. Vojtech Mastny, "The Cassandra in the Foreign Commissariat: Maxim Litvinov and the Cold War," *Foreign Affairs*, vol. 54 (January 1976), p. 373.

75. Ibid., pp. 372-374.

76. *Khrushchev Remembers*, trans. Strobe Talbott (Boston, 1970), p. 262.

77. Documents of German Foreign Policy, Series D, vol. 11: *The War Years 1940-1941*, pp. 558, 561.

78. Ibid., p. 565.

79. Ibid., p. 552.

80. Ibid., p. 554.

81. Raymond James Sontag and James Stuart Beddie, eds., *Nazi-Soviet Relations 1939-1941: Documents from the Archives of the German Foreign Office*, Department of State, Washington, D.C., 1948, p. 259.

82. Ibid., p. 260.

83. Ibid., p. 324.

84. Peter Avery, *Modern Iran* (New York, 1965), p. 386.

85. George Lenczowski, *Russia and the West in Iran, 1918-1948; a Study in Big-Power Rivalry* (Ithaca, 1949), pp. 300, 289. Lenczowski, *The Middle East in World Affairs*, 4th ed. (Ithaca, 1980), p. 182ff. Avery, *Modern Iran*, p. 388, 398.

86. Svetlana Alliluyeva, *Only One Year*, trans. Paul Chavchavadze (New York, 1969), p. 392. Lev Kopelev, the much admired Soviet dissident, wrote in 1967: "Today it is generally known and has been proved that Stalin attempted to turn the 1939-41 nonaggression pact with Germany into a treaty of friendship, that, in official

documents and speeches, he called the enemies of Hitler imperialist aggressors and that he in fact forbade all antifascist propaganda." (Stephen F. Cohen, ed., *An End to Silence: Uncensored Opinion in the Soviet Union from Roy Medvedev's Underground Magazine "Political Diary,"* trans. George Saunders [New York, 1982], p. 54).

87. *Khrushchev Remembers: The Last Testament,* ed. Strobe Talbott (Boston, 1974), pp. 510-511.

88. Ibid., p. 512.

89. The Persian Empire was the first to be administered through a system of satrapies. There were about twenty satrapies, or provinces, each of which was ruled by a satrap, who enjoyed a large measure of autonomy and wielded the military and civil authority virtually as a king. However, the satrap was always watched and informed upon by spies and could be called to account and even deposed by the emperor. (J. H. Iliffe, "Persia and the Ancient World," in A. J. Arberry, ed., *The Legacy of Persia* [Oxford, 1953], pp. 8-9. Ehsan Yarshater, ed., "Introduction," *The Cambridge History of Iran,* vol. 3 (pt. 1) [Cambridge, 1983], pp. lxxiii, xxiii).

90. John Dornberg, *Brezhnev: The Masks of Power* (New York, 1974), p. 229.

91. Zhores Medvedev, *Andropov* (Oxford, 1983), pp. 168-169.

92. Paul Seabury and Walter A. McDougall, eds., *The Grenada Papers* (San Francisco, 1984), p. 17.

93. Ibid., p. 190.

94. An unusual Soviet Communist editor, who was expelled from "the Party" because of his frank analysis, wrote in the late 1960s: "In general, Stalinism represents (to some extent) the powerless worker's longing to settle the score for his day–to–day humiliations with the help of some harsh justice from the top. Impotence seeks a higher power to avenge itself." (L. Okunev [Len Karpensky], "Words Are Also Deeds," in Stephen F. Cohen, ed., *An End to Silence: Uncensored Opinion in the Soviet Union from Roy Medvedev's Underground Magazine "Political Diary",* trans. George Saunders (New York, 1982), p. 308).

95. Milovan Djilas, *Conversations with Stalin,* trans. Michael B. Petrovich (New York, 1962), pp. 110-111, 95.

96. A. M. Nekrich, "June 22, 1941", trans. Vladimir Petrov in Vladimir Petrov, *"June 22, 1941": Soviet Historians and the German Invasion* (Columbia, S.C., 1968), p. 113.

97. Field Marshal Viscount Montgomery of Alamein, *A History of Warfare* (New York, 1983), pp. 370-372.

98. In the wake of the Chinese "cultural revolution" similar "cultural revolutions" for "Africanization" and "authenticity" swept such countries as Chad, Zaire, Kenya, Ethiopia, and Uganda. Pre-colonial tribal rites were restored, and the vogue was anti-intellectual and anti-scientific. In Ethiopia, the Falashas, presumed to be Jews, were suspect for having introduced such technical skills as ironworking and plough-making in their role as blacksmiths. (Adda B. Bozeman, *Conflict in Africa* [Princeton, 1976], pp. 65, 278).

99. Karl Marx and Frederick Engels, *Correspondence 1846-1895,* trans. Dona Torr (New York, 1934), pp. 354-355.

100. Karl Marx, *Capital: A Critique of Political Economy,* ed. Frederick Engels, trans. Samuel Moore and Edward Aveling (Chicago, 1906), p. 652.

101. Merle Fainsod, *How Russia Is Ruled,* rev. ed. (Cambridge, Mass., 1963), pp. 361-362.

102. V. I. Lenin, *The National-Liberation Movement in the East,* trans. M. Levin (Moscow, 1957), p. 315.

103. Ibid., pp. 38, 42.

104. Ibid., p. 297.

105. Ibid., pp. 296-297.

106. Ibid., p. 315.

107. V. I. Lenin, "A Caricature of Marxism and Imperialist Economism," *Collected Works,* trans. M. S. Levin, Joe Fineberg, et al. (Moscow and London, 1960), vol. 23 (August 1916-March 1917), pp. 66-67.

108. Ibid., pp. 307-308.

109. Ibid., pp. 307, 311.

110. Roy A. Medvedev and Zhores A. Medvedev, *Khrushchev: The Years in Power,* trans. Andrew R. Durkin (New York, 1976), p. 148.

111. *Khrushchev Remembers,* p. 470. *Khrushchev Remembers: The Last Testament,* trans. Strobe Talbott (Boston, 1974), p. 255.

112. J. V. Stalin, *The London Congress of the Russian Social-Democratic Labour Party (Notes of a Delegate)* (Moscow, 1955), p. 13.

113. Leon Trotsky, "Thermidor and Anti-Semitism," *The New International,* vol. 7, no. 5 (May 1941), pp. 92-93.

114. Roy A. Medvedev, *On Stalin and Stalinism,* trans. Ellen de Kadt (Oxford, 1979), p. 159.

115. V. I. Lenin, *The Revolution of 1905* (New York, 1934), p. 55.

116. Anton Antonov-Ovseyenko, *The Time of Stalin: Portrait of a Tyranny,* trans. George Saunders (New York, 1981), pp. 290-291. Medvedev, *On Stalin and Stalinism,* p. 159.

117. See, for instance, supporting evidence in Stephen Cohen's *An End to Silence,* pp. 118, 124-132, 158-159.

118. Ibid., p. 169.

119. Alexander Gerschenkron, *Continuity in History and Other Essays* (Cambridge, Mass., 1968), p. 488.

120. Roy A. Medvedev, *The October Revolution,* trans. George Saunders (New York, 1979), p. 185.

121. Marx and Engels, *Correspondence 1846-1895,* p. 67.

122. The sociologist Franklin Henry Giddings long ago observed that a "democratic empire" had proved itself possible in Britain and America and, like de Tocqueville, he foresaw the future conflict between the alternatives of an English-speaking dominant empire or a Russian one. (Franklin Henry Giddings, *Democracy and Empire* [New York, 1900], pp. v. 3).

123. Lewis S. Feuer, "The Sociobiological Theory of Jewish Intellectual Achievement: A Sociological Critique," in *Ethnicity, Identity, and History: Essays in Memory of Werner J. Cahnman,* eds. Joseph B. Maier and Chaim I. Waxman (New Brunswick, 1983), pp. 93-123.

124. *The New York Times,* June 19, 1982.

125. John Maynard Keynes, *The General Theory of Employment, Interest and Money* (New York, 1936), pp. 131, 220.

126. It is strange to recall that a group composed mainly of distinguished academic personalities who advised President Roosevelt and the State Department on foreign policy in 1943 found it "reasonable to assume that Russia might remain co-operative after the war." (Louis, *Imperialism at Bay,* p. 74).

127. R. W. Johnson, *The Long March of the French Left* (New York, 1981), pp. 34-36.

128. Bertrand Russell, *Living Philosophies* (New York, 1931; rpt. 1941), pp. 18-19.

129. *The New York Times,* July 19, 1982.

130. Aleksandr M. Nekrich, *The Punished Peoples: The Deportation and Fate of Soviet Minorities at the End of the Second World War,* trans. George Saunders (New York, 1978). Robert Conquest, *The Nation Killers: The Soviet Deportation of Nationalities* (New York, 1970).

131. Walter Laqueur, *The Political Psychology of Appeasement: Finlandization and Other Unpopular Essays* (New Brunswick, New Jersey, 1980), p. 138.

132. "Saudi Arabia is an immigrants' country par excellence. The indigenous population probably numbers no more than 5 million as against 1.5 to 2.0 million foreigners. About half of these are Yemenis; the rest are Egyptians, Sudanese, Palestinians, Syrians, Lebanese . . . Yemenis do most of the heavy unskilled labor." In Kuwait, sixty percent of the population are immigrants. (Peter Duignan and L. H. Gann, *The Middle East and North Africa: The Challenge to Western Security* [Stanford, 1981], pp. 97, 91).

133. *1981 Britannica Book of the Year* (Chicago, 1981), p. 644.

134. *The New York Times,* July 13, 1982.

135. Owen Lattimore, *Nationalism and Revolution in Mongolia* (New York, 1955), p. 44.

136. Sir J. R. Seeley, *The Expansion of England* (London, 1883; rpt. 1936), p. 16.

137. Louis, *Imperialism at Bay,* p. 154.

138. George Otto Trevelyan, *The Life and Letters of Lord Macaulay* (London, 1876), 1: 401.

139. In 1963, in Moscow, I encountered a group of Indonesian engineers who were doing their "on the job" training in Soviet projects. When I asked in what language they communicated, they told me smilingly that naturally it was in English.

140. See Albert K. Weinberg, *Manifest Destiny: A Study of Nationalist Expansionism in American History* (Baltimore, 1935), p. 17.

141. *The Writings of Thomas Jefferson,* ed. H. A. Washington, 9 vols. (New York, 1859), 6: 258.

142. Ray Stannard Baker, *Woodrow Wilson: Life and Letters,* vol. 4, *President, 1912-1914,* 8 vols. (New York, 1931), p. 85.

143. Franklin D. Roosevelt, "Our Foreign Policy: A Democratic View," *Foreign Affairs,* vol. 6 (1928), p. 573.

144. Elliott Roosevelt, *As He Saw It* (New York, 1946), p. 75.

145. Elliott Roosevelt, ed., *F. D. R.: His Personal Letters, 1928-1945,* 1st ed. (New York, 1950), 2: 1493.

146. Roosevelt "immediately recognized the catchword 'imperialism' as a politically disastrous issue." (Louis, *Imperialism at Bay,* p. 354).

NAME INDEX

Aboab, Isaac da Fonseca, 64
Abramsky, C., 98
Acheson, Mary, 126
Adams, Brooks, 142
Adams, Henry, 142
Adams, John Quincy, 38, 215
Adler, Alfred, 19, 133, 219n.31
Agus, Irving, 60
Albu, George, 75, 80
Albu, Leopold, 80
Alexander the Great, 1, 21, 217-218n.2, 228n.2; influence on Judaic development, 57-58; racial equality ideal, 13, 217n.1
Alliluyeva, Svetlana, 189
Amalrik, Andrei, 202
Amin, Idi, 132, 166, 209, 236n.205
Andropov, Yuri Vladimirovich, 191, 199
Andros, Edmund, 21
Angell, Norman, 152, 153
Anstey, Vera, 46
Antonov-Ovseyenko, Anton, 202
Apuleius, 229n.10
Arendt, Hannah, 97
Aristotle, 13, 21, 121; influential writings, 138, 142
Asquith, Herbert H., 137
Attlee, Clement. 179, 254n.49
Augustine, Saint, 142
Aurelius, Marcus, 124
Avicenna, 89

Babcock, Alpheus, 43
Bacon, Francis, 20, 187
Baden-Powell, Robert, 129
Bagehot, Walter, 219n.29
Bain, Alexander, 30
Banks, Sir Joseph, 220n.43
Baranow, Samuel, 76
Barbusse, Henri, 153
Baring, Sir Evelyn: *see* Cromer, Lord
Barker, Ernest, 217n.2
Barnato, Barney, 71, 115, 122, 124, 156, 159; gold mining, 75, 76, 80, 233n.125; as Jewish imperialist in South Africa, 76-78, 97; psychological motives for im-

perialism of, 83-84, 123, 164, 242n.50
Bates, Henry Walter, 22, 87
Bauer, Otto, 19
Bauer, P. T., 107-108
Baumann, Isaac, 75
Baxter, Richard, 227n.177
Beale, Howard K., 145
Beard, Charles A., 111, 204
Beard, Mary, 204
Bebel, August, 88
Beesly, Edward S., 170
Beit, Alfred, 78, 122, 124; gold mining, 75, 79, 80, 233n.125; as a Jew, 71, 115; personality of, 76, 83-84, 123, 126, 159
Benjamin of Tudela, 60
Bentham, Jeremy, 50
Bentinck, Lord William, 125-126
Bentwich, Norman, 58
Bergson, Henri, 25
Berkeley, George, 20, 21
Berlin, Isaiah, 100
Bernstein, Eduard, 19, 33, 219n.30
Berthollet, Claude Louis, 22
Bettelheim, Bruno, 247n.170
Beveridge, Albert J., 113
Bevin, Ernest, 103
Bismark, Chancellor Otto von, 149
Blossius, 14
Bokassa, Jean-Bedel, 132, 209
Bonaparte, Napoleon: *see* Napoleon I
Boxer, C. R., 171-172
Bozeman, Ada, 256n.98
Brandes, Georg, 137
Braestrup, Peter, 183-184
Brezhnev, Leonid Ilyich, 190-191, 209
Brodie, Fawn M., 238n.4
Brooke, James, 117-118, 120, 234n.147
Bromley, J. S., 8-9
Brown, Richard Carl, 18-19
Broz, Josip: *see* Tito, Marshal
Bryan, William Jennings, 17, 174
Bryce, James, 74, 169
Buber, Martin, 99
Burke, Edmund, 109, 124, 125
Burns, John, 248n.217
Burton, Richard, 104